SALMON,
TROUT
& CHARR
OF THE WORLD

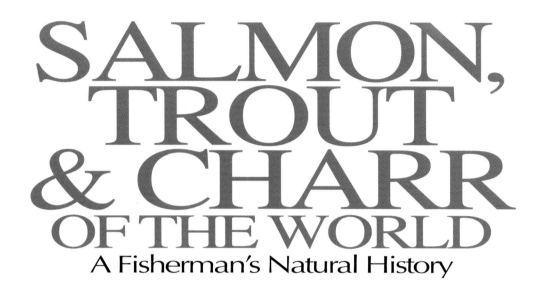

SALMON, TROUT & CHARR OF THE WORLD
A Fisherman's Natural History

RUPERT WATSON

SWAN·HILL
PRESS

Copyright © 1999 Rupert Watson

First published in the UK in 1999
by Swan Hill Press, an imprint of Airlife Publishing Ltd

British Library Cataloguing-in-Publication Data
A catalogue record for this book
is available from the British Library

ISBN 1 85310 888 X

Typeset by Rowland Phototypesetting Limited,
Bury St Edmunds, Suffolk
Printed in Hong Kong

Swan Hill Press
An imprint of Airlife Publishing Ltd
101 Longden Road, Shrewsbury, SY3 9EB, England
E-mail: airlife@airlifebooks.com

Contents

Acknowledgements

The subjects of this book live in the cooler regions of the northern hemisphere, and, unsurprisingly, the people that work with them are similarly distributed. They all love the fish they study, and, without exception, opened the doors of their homes and offices, as well as of their stores of knowledge, with huge generosity of time and spirit.

Pacific salmon are probably more studied at the University in Seattle than anywhere else in the world. My introduction to the corridors of the University's School of Fisheries came from Ray Hilborn, who is a professor there, and, with Ulrike, welcomed me to Seattle on my first visit to that vibrant city. Through him I soon met Andrew Hendry, who has been a fount of help and encouragement ever since; having read and revised my text, he provided me with illustrations and references, and introduced me to many of his colleagues. I owe him more thanks than I could ever hope to convey in this brief acknowledgement. Also in Seattle, Jeff Silverstein answered my questions on masu salmon, Greg Mackey read the chapters on rainbow and cutthroat trout, and Greg Ruggerone provided me with some splendid photographs.

Chris Harvey of the University of Wisconsin reviewed my chapters on brook and lake charr, and in Britain Elly Baroudy and Ron Greer read the one on Arctic charr. Peter Hutchinson of the North Atlantic Salmon Conservation Organisation (NASCO) in Edinburgh went through the chapter on Atlantic salmon, as well as helping me find illustrations and answering countless queries with unfailing grace. Kate Klippensteen was a wonderful source of information on salmon in Japan, and also introduced me to the work of a particularly fine photographer, Kazutoshi Hiyeda. Ben Scott Knight was particularly helpful in finding photographs and information on masu in Taiwan.

Photographing fish in their native northern rivers is no work for the faint-hearted, and attracts committed individuals with a particular passion for the creatures they pursue, as well as an enthusiasm for sharing the results of their work that goes far beyond the boundaries of commerce. It has been a delight to deal with Richard Grost in Oregon, Natalie Fobes in Seattle, Greg Syverson in Alaska and Gilbert van Ryckevorsel in Nova Scotia. Many other people, including my brother Julian, have either lent me photographs or taken them specifically for the book and I thank you all for your efforts. All the line drawings were done by Karen Laurence, whose imagination was only given the free rein it really deserved when it came to designing the headers and tailers of each chapter.

I know that those who work in libraries are expected to help visiting readers and researchers, but I still remain astounded by the extent to which every library I visited seemed staffed by people prepared to put themselves far further out than common courtesy demanded. To those who work in the libraries of the Natural History Museum in South Kensington, the Freshwater Biological Association at Windemere, the School of Fisheries in Washington, the cities of Vancouver and Anchorage, and the University of British Columbia, thank you for those extra thoughts and talks that so often helped elevate research from drudgery to delight. Thank you too to Malcolm Elliott in Windermere, and to the biologists at Icicle Seafoods, at the fish hatcheries at Priest Rapid, Issaquah,

Elmendorf, Nitinat River, Metolius River and elsewhere in the Pacific Northwest, as well as at the Alaskan Department of Fish and Game, who all gave time and assistance with that rare gift that suggested they had nothing else to do all day but talk to me.

In the course of my travels, I imposed upon friends and strangers alike, who all offered me the most generous hospitality and support. I would particularly like to thank Sue Tribolini and Mike Clutter in Seattle, Patrick and Ann Gilbert-Hopkins in Vancouver, Gay Alkoff on Salt Spring Island, Val Burris in Oregon and Paul and Joyce Palmer in Anchorage, all of whom welcomed me into their homes with warmth and kindness that I hope one day to reciprocate. As I wrote this book, Mary Ann welcomed me into her life with warmth and love that I am able to reciprocate unreservedly.

Caitlin Fraser typed the bibliography time and time again, and Tom Heaton read all the chapters; as a BBC editor he brought a tautness to my writing which it often sorely lacked. To him, and to all those people who live and work with the fish that I only write about, I can only say thank you again, and if mistakes, whether of fact or grammar, still linger on, they are mine and not yours.

Introduction

The modern map of the natural range of salmon, trout and charr is potent testimony not only to their questing urge to seek out new territories, but also to their powers of survival. Their world is often a wild and distant one, where even Nature struggles to help them into remote mountain valleys or above plunging waterfalls. Lack of spawning grounds may prevent them breeding in otherwise ideal environments, or frozen streams bar their way up from the sea. Where life is easier, in more hospitable parts of the northern hemisphere, mankind has all too often turned what were once fish-filled waters into poisoned, lifeless wastes. Yet in cool, clean lakes and rivers all through Asia, America and Europe, the subjects of this book are still swimming through their lives, just as they have done since their ancestors began following the ebbing tides of melting ice inexorably northwards.

I have found no single word, scientific or otherwise, for salmon, trout and charr as a group of fish, although I think it is true to say that they are all informally grouped in the minds of many sport fishermen as 'game fish'. It is my choice to gather them together as subjects of a book. A taxonomically neater arrangement might have been to include huchen and Siberian lenok, which, by most reckonings, together with salmon, trout, charr, and the strange Adriatic genus of *Salmothymus*, make up the sub-family Salmoninae. The decision to exclude these mysterious fish may seem illogical and, I must admit, stems largely from their mystery, which makes information on them very hard to find.

Authors are allowed a degree of licence in the composition of their works, and in mine I have indulged myself by focusing on those features of these fish's lives which particularly fascinate me. I am especially intrigued by the extraordinary two-year life-cycles of pink salmon and the fish's inexplicable success in the Great Lakes. Equally intriguing is the success of sea-going chinook in New Zealand, the phenomenal spread of rainbow trout around the world and the sea lampreys' devastation of the lake charr in the Great Lakes. Why have brook charr retreated so quickly in the face of exotic introductions into their native waters, yet been so adept at displacing indigenous salmonids further west, and why have neither brook charr nor rainbow trout really established themselves in Britain?

Being all so closely related, the subjects of this book often have much in common with one another in the way they live their lives. Where this is so, I have tried not to describe such overlaps more than once. This is the main reason for not having separate chapters on each Pacific salmon, but rather having one chapter focusing on what distinguishes them from each other, and two on those aspects of their lives which are common to them all. In many other instances a description of one fish's habits is equally applicable to those of its closest relatives. So, for example, much of what I have written about rainbow trout beyond their native range applies equally to brown trout, and there is more about fresh-water feeding in the chapter on brown trout than in any other. Commercial and subsistence fishing is discussed in some detail in the chapter on Pacific salmon and man, but not in the one on rainbow trout, even though steelhead are just as likely to be caught in nets set for salmon. Moreover, one fish often touches the life of another in some way, whether as competitor, predator or prey. The disastrous impact of introduced lake charr on the cutthroat trout of Yellowstone Lake could be mentioned equally appropriately in the chapter on either of them, and the same could be said of a comparison between young brown trout and Atlantic salmon, or the dependence of ferox brown trout on Arctic charr.

In writing this book, I have attempted to flesh out the sharp-edged skeleton of science, and so bring some of the more technical aspects of the lives of these wonderful fish within reach of the lay reader. This can be a dangerous approach. It risks merely zigzagging from the Scylla of straight science to the Charybdis of anthropomorphism, but I hope that in the greater part of this book I have managed to chart a course down that all-too-narrow channel of good natural history writing in between.

I am also aware that one of the difficulties in trying to use a mid-Atlantic vocabulary, understandable to readers in both America and Europe, is that one actually ends up confusing everyone on both sides of the ocean. Terminology tends to vary – 'redd' may mean a single nest, or a group of nests excavated by one fish, or the whole area of spawning gravel; 'parr' is often a brief stage in a European salmonid's life, but seldom in an American one's; 'still waters' are lakes and reservoirs in Britain, but not in America, where I am often told that lake or reservoir water is never still. All I can say is that I have done all I can to keep confusion to a minimum, and that to help do so, I have also provided both metric and non-metric measurements of weights, volumes and distances.

The systems for describing a fish's age also differ, both from one side of the Atlantic to the other, and within continents. When does a salmonid's life begin – when the fertilised egg settles into the gravel, when the alevin bursts out of its shell, or when the little fish swims up towards the surface to begin feeding for itself? Suffice it to say that the system I have used in this book ages fish by winters since hatching, separating the fresh-water and marine stages of their lives with a decimal point. So a chinook salmon which has spent two winters in the Yukon River and four at sea, returns to spawn in the autumn (or fall!) as a 2.4 fish.

No less confusing can be the taxonomic subdivisions below the species level. A species may be subdivided into subspecies or merely into identifiable races, which are less distinct from each other than subspecies. There are no fixed rules governing whether or not a race in fact merits the distinction of a subspecies. Deciding whether fish like the different trout in Lough Melvin should be elevated to specific status is often equally subjective. A 'population' is basically a group of potentially interbreeding individuals which may constitute a race, a subspecies or even a species. 'Stock' is a more abstract term and usually describes several populations, more often in the context of human management.

As I wrote this book, I never ceased to be astounded by how recent was the end of the last Ice Age – not more than 15,000 years ago, a mere twinkling in cosmic history. I make no apology for mentioning repeatedly how the earth looked before the great thaw began, with its Bering land bridge, south-stretching ice fields and dramatically lower sea levels. Equally astounding is the change wrought to the earth's face by the ravages of the melting ice, and the fact that very few populations of salmon, trout or charr have been where they are for more than 12,000 years.

Britain lags far behind America in awareness of its salmonid heritage. Apart from one or two notable research projects, such as those focusing on the trout in Lough Melvin or the Arctic charr in Windermere or Loch Rannoch, the genetic diversity within each so-called species remains largely ignored. It is almost as if, having reverted to the post-Victorian principles of grouping, rather than splitting, species, ichthyologists felt they were then excused any further genetic research into the salmon, trout and charr in the British Isles. Whatever the taxonomic status of individual populations, or the current thinking with regard to what is and is not a species, there is no excuse for ignoring the huge variety within each species, which often rests in lakes beside roads, not in waters a distant day's march from the nearest habitation. Very much more remains to be discovered while this variety still exists, and before it has been irrevocably adulterated by exotic genes. This is especially so of Arctic charr, most populations of which, despite occasional imports of foreign stock by fish farmers, still remain relatively pristine. In very few rivers do Atlantic salmon remain unaffected by the genes of hatchery escapees, and only the most remote Scottish trout lochs have survived the nineteenth century efforts of anglers or Highland lairds to improve on Nature with pony-loads of fry.

As yet there is certainly no danger in Britain of the wood of the species becoming obscured by the sum of its trees, but I still feel urged to sound a soft note of warning. During my travels through America, I was repeatedly struck by the time, effort and money deemed worth expending on conserving isolated fragments of a species. Of course a species is the sum of its parts, be these described as subspecies, races, stocks or populations, and of course some of these parts may be well on their way down the evolutionary road to true specific status. However, there seems a need to draw a line below which conservation is a luxury, not an ecological or moral necessity, and I would draw that line very much nearer the species level than it is presently drawn in much of America. If this means Snake River chinook are doomed because they cannot look after themselves, then so be it. May a lesson be learnt, the price of cheap electricity duly recognised, and the huge amounts of resources which presently sustain these salmon diverted to reversing the fortunes of some other creature with a more viable future in a less modified environment than today's Columbia River.

I still love fishing, although I am increasingly ill at ease with the idea of catching large bags of trout. None the less, I like to eat trout, and am quite unashamed at the thought of keeping the fish I catch, unless of course my doing so may prejudice the wellbeing of their population. Man's dentition is clear evidence of his present design as an omnivore. In the repeated attempts to elevate *Homo sapiens* above the realms of Nature, of which, so far as I can see, he is so obviously part, the natural link between man as predator and fish as prey has become obfuscated by a great fog of piscatorial political correctness. This demands that most fish be returned to the water, usually so someone else can again inflict upon them the pain and trauma of being caught. That gaining pleasure at the expense of another creature's pain is, by any definition, cruelty seems to be conveniently omitted from the equation.

In my youth, I used to visit cousins on the Isle of Mull, off the west coast of Scotland. About two hours' walk from their farmhouse was a cluster of small lochs, close to the edge of magnificent cliffs, which dropped 300 m (1,000 ft) sheer down into the sea. None of the lochs had any permanent inflows, and so brown trout had never been able to breed in them. Most of the lochs lay in smooth granite hollows, but one clearly tapped a different geological vein from all the others. Round its edges grew marigolds and other aquatic plants, and further out, tall stems protruded above the water's surface. This was the 'reedy loch', and, so my cousin told me casually one evening, was rumoured once to have been stocked with brook charr – the mythical 'fontinalis' – although so far as he knew, no one had fished it for decades.

I can still remember the tramp over the moor. It was one of those days that Edward Grey describes with such exquisite sensitivity, although then I had yet to read his *Fly Fishing*:

> Often after walking a mile or two on the way to the river, at a brisk pace, there comes upon one a feeling of 'fitness', of being made of nothing but health and strength so perfect, that life can have no other end but to enjoy them. It is as though till that moment one had breathed

with only a part of one's lungs, and as though now for the first time the whole lungs were filling with air. The pure act of breathing at such times seems glorious. People talk of being a child of Nature, and moments such as these are the times when it is possible to feel so; to know the full joy of animal life – to desire nothing beyond.

There are times when I have stood still for joy of it all, on my way across the wild freedom of a Highland moor, and felt the wind, and looked upon the mountains and water and light and sky, till I felt conscious only of the strength of a mighty current of life, which swept away all consciousness of self, and made me a part of all I beheld.

When I reached the cliffs, and peered gingerly over the edge, a golden eagle launched itself from a ledge below, showing the pale rump of its immaturity, which for a moment had me thinking it was a sea eagle. How many people had seen a golden eagle backed by the grey, faraway sea? Further on I turned inland from the cliffs, towards the lochs, and on the first one a solitary red-throated diver seemed to be feeding. What, I wondered, did it find to eat? Were there at least sticklebacks in those seemingly barren pools?

At the reedy loch I sat down to make up a cast, tying a Grouse and Claret onto the tail and, I think, a Peter Ross on the dropper. Then, leaving my bag on a tussock, I started fishing. The ring of vegetation forced me to wade far out, almost up to my waist, before I was able to reach a gap between the reed tops, which still kept snagging my flies as I retrieved them. For a good hour I fished, perhaps more, landing my flies into whatever patches of open water I could find. Nothing broke the gentle ripple, dragonflies hummed around the surface, and it seemed only too apparent that if brook charr had ever nibbled insect larvae off these stalks, they had long since ceased to do so. Then the fish took.

It was probably only on for half a minute, but that was time for enough thoughts to fill a book. Growing in size by the second, it tore off through the reeds, tugging the tip of my seven feet of cane – my first fishing rod – down towards the water. There was then a moment's stillness during which I remembered I had left my net where I started fishing. Then the fish set off again, this time in an arc across me, and of course the dropper caught on one of the stems and the cast broke. With the tail fly went that supreme moment of my dreams, when I walked into the kitchen, late for supper, and laid a three pound brook charr on the table, confounding local fishing lore, astounding my cousins and securing my entry in fishing annals and record books throughout the country. Oh the gulf between the fish in the bag and the story of the one which might have got there, but never did.

I seldom revisit scenes of lost fish in the hope of rescuing triumph from disaster, and I never went back to the reedy loch. For me the wildness and the wonder of these salmon, trout and charr live on in the memory of that one creature, helped, it is true, by my never having even seen it.

This book is not about fishing at all. It is about the fish, their lives and how they come to be where and what they are. The mass migrations of thousands of breeding sockeye offer some of the most dramatic spectacles in the natural world, but it is the powers that enable them to navigate round the ocean, far out of human sight, and to find their way back to the stretch of river where their lives began, that are truly astonishing. In the tundra lakes of northern Canada, lake charr are living unseen lives in almost total darkness for more than sixty years, and even closer to the North Pole, far from human habitation, Arctic charr are searching out newly unfrozen streams – waterways to inland homes they have never been able to reach before. I want more people to part the surface of the water, not just fishermen, but anyone who seeks to fit other pieces into the great ecological jigsaw of life. I hope this book will encourage them to do so.

1
The fish – What, Where and Why?

Fifteen thousand years ago, most of the lakes and rivers where salmon, trout and charr live today were frozen solid. Ice fields covered nearly all of what is now Canada and the Great Lakes, and permafrost underlay the great swath of tundra stretching through northern Asia. All of Scandinavia was iced over, as were Ireland and Britain north of a line stretching from the Thames estuary to the Severn. Below that line, tundra merged England with France across a non-existent English Channel. With so much water tied up in ice, the world's sea levels were up to 90 m (300 ft) lower than they are today, and a broad bridge of land linked Alaska and Siberia. An edge of permanent sea ice joined Canada to Britain, via the southern tip of Greenland; and Iceland too was frozen over.

Neither ice-covered country nor tundra could sustain the ancestors of present-day fresh-water fish, and so they ranged far south of where the temperature allows them now. Then, the climate in Mexico may have been like British Columbia's today, and conditions in the Mediterranean resembled those in the modern Baltic Sea. Scattered areas of fresh or brackish water held out against the surrounding ice, providing refuges for those cold-water species of fish able to breed in them or in seasonal inflowing rivers. A huge lake probably covered the southern end of the North Sea, and others on the edge of the tundra, like Great Salt Lake in America and the Black and Caspian Seas, provided even more ideal environments for fresh-water fish.

Fifteen thousand years ago, the last Ice Age was at its coldest and ice spread as far south as it had ever done in Pleistocene times. Then one day, the tide turned imperceptibly, and the earth began to warm again. The frontiers of ice started to recede, sea levels rose, and retreating glaciers and huge floods of meltwater carved valleys out of the countryside and created waterways to the sea. Salmon, which had been pushed relentlessly southwards for thousands of years by the invading cold, found their world expanding once more, and began edging their way up the continental coastlines, colonising one stream after another. Inland, away from the sea, trout and charr moved on rivers of melting ice into huge glacial basins and over watersheds, like those along the tangle of mountain ranges in the south-western United States, that today seem quite impossible for fish ever to have crossed. The earth was revealing its face again with, as geology marches, extraordinary speed, and in little more than 5,000 years freshwater fish had reached most of the waters which nurture them today.

This great ichthyological diaspora still goes on, even though its course is far easier to trace by telescoping times past than reading the signs of the present. Cold has always delineated the northern boundaries for all salmon, trout and charr, and continues to do so, just as warmth confines them within the southern edges of their range. While cutthroat trout in the deserts of Utah and Nevada are now being forced to adapt to life in the aquatic remnants of the Bonneville and Lahontan Basins at an evolutionary gallop or die, far to the north salmon and charr are still probing new frontiers round the Arctic Ocean's shores.

The different species of salmon, trout and charr were shaped much more by the evolutionary pressures of earlier climatic and topographical upheavals than those of the last Ice Age. Never the less, if these fish are left where they are for long enough, new forms will gradually emerge which may one day merit the status of their own species. Time moves too slowly for us to know whether the earth is still thawing, and whether sea levels are continuing to rise by nearly 40 cm (16 in) every century. And is the globe warming artificially, or are the currents of the earth's climate still too powerful for mankind to influence? One thing is certain and that is that neither climate nor evolution stand still – the one is largely the product of the other – and as surely as winter follows summer, the tide of ice will one day turn and start to head south again, pushing all life before it. When it does, the inexorable spread of fish northwards, which has continued since the end of the last Ice Age, will be reversed; much of the biodiversity in temperate latitudes will be destroyed, and evolution halted in its tracks. Sockeye will then no longer swim the rivers of Kamchatka, Arctic charr will be frozen out of all their Scandinavian strongholds, and the fossils of tomorrow will be left for posterity in the mud of the Yukon delta or the peaty headwaters of the River Tweed.

The Kobuk River in Alaska, north of the Arctic Circle – one of the last rivers to unfreeze at the end of the Ice Age and now home to chum salmon, Arctic charr and several species of whitefish including sheefish.
(Author)

This book is about the salmon, trout and charr of today, suspended on their evolutionary pathway at the end of the twentieth century. In scientific terms, these are all those species of fish, maybe twelve, maybe twenty, depending on what makes a species, within the genera *Salmo*, *Oncorhynchus* and *Salvelinus*. They, along with fish from other genera, all belong in the Salmonidae family, united by form, physiology, behaviour and habitat preferences – which also crucially and intriguingly distinguish them. They are all fish of the northern hemisphere and can all survive in both fresh and sea water, although some of them make so little use of this ability that evolution may ultimately deny them it. Their young are hatched in gravel nests, or in cracks and crevices between slabs of rock or larger stones. They are all born with their own in-built food supply, which gives them several crucial weeks to ready themselves for life in the open water before they swim up to begin feeding for themselves. Fleshy little adipose fins adorn their backs, although these are less distinctive family badges than they are often made out to be; several catfish, piranhas, tigerfish and a whole range of other species from the tropics of Africa and South America have them too.

To spread knowledge and information about the earth's creatures, whether tribally or globally, they need to be named. Once enough have names these tend to be grouped together according to perceived similarities. But, like beauty, 'similarity' is subjective. Primitive societies arranged their natural world according to their own perceptions of the plants and animals within it, and even today some might still divide snakes into poisonous or non-poisonous ones, and plants into edible or inedible. Until the enlightened thinking of the Renaissance finally filtered into the sciences, the Western world retained a similarly naive approach – typified in an early entomological treatise which split insects into 'those bestowed by the Creator as a pestilence upon mankind . . . and for the benefit of mankind'.

Well over 2,000 years ago Aristotle's great mind had focused on the problem of classifying animals, and, millennia ahead of his time, arranged them 'according to their modes of life, their activities, their habits and the parts of their bodies'. He also sowed the seeds of the idea of 'the Great Chain of Being'. This organised the natural world in a chain, or ladder, of increasing perfection, from the plants through simple animals to man at the top. With no thought that species ever altered, the idea was equally easily embraced by science as by religion, which saw in the chain the whole unchanging panoply of God's creation.

Much of the surge of scientific interest in the sixteenth century was inspired by great voyages of trade and exploration. Ships returned laden with exotic commodities and merchandise, and also with descriptions, or even specimens, of extraordinary animals which all needed names. Notwithstanding their antiquity, Aristotle's thoughts were also only then filtering up to northern Europe, and early lists of plants and animals reflected his belief that they should be united by perceived similarities of form or behaviour.

This ancient legacy had altered very little by the time it reached the great Swedish naturalist Carl Linnaeus, who continued to rely upon Aristotle's criteria for the development of his binomial system to inventory the creations of God. The natural world had, he believed, remained unchanged since Creation, and although in later life Linnaeus began to acknowledge that 'it is possible for new species to come into existence in the plant kingdom' the system's design gave no thought to ancestry. All the world's plants and animals were arrayed before Linnaeus's eyes just as God had made them, each quite distinct from the other, and he took up his task of grouping and cataloguing them. Today, taxonomy is as much concerned with uniting as dividing, but, for all its imperfections,

Linnaeus's system of nomenclature has still to be bettered.

The binomial system itself is relatively neat and simple. Every plant or animal has two names, a generic noun, like *Oncorhynchus*, describing the kind of creature it is, and the adjective, *mykiss*, which precisely identifies the species within the kind. There is usually a price for simplicity and in this case it is the system's inability to cope with the whole range of creatures that are already edging beyond the boundaries of their own species, either into those of another or even into taxonomically uncharted territory of their own. Probably no other family of animals – certainly no other family of fish – is so unsatisfactorily compartmentalised by the binomial system, as the Salmonidae. The system requires rigid demarcation lines between species by which the continual flow of evolutionary change refuses to be confined. To some extent, the addition of an informal, more subjective, subspecies tag, like *O. m. kamloops*, allows for the further subdivision of a species, yet it also only serves to emphasise its indivisibility; and below the subspecies level are races and stocks, often precisely identifiable even to the naked eye, but seemingly quite unnameable.

Within each of the binomial parameters of, for example, *Salmo trutta*, *Oncorhynchus mykiss* and *Salvelinus alpinus*, are whole continuums of populations of slightly different fish, merging seamlessly into one another, which science will probably never succeed in describing with Linnaeus's or any other simple system. Perhaps the present trend towards grouping species together, rather than splitting them, is an admission of this, as well as an unconscious acknowledgement that the slippery eel of true taxonomy is actually ungraspable.

At the heart of the great taxonomic web of life are the kingdoms which spread out through the arterial network of phylum, class, order, family and genus, to the tiny capillaries at its ends. These categories may be subdivided or 'super-grouped' to reflect relationships still more accurately, although often with a lack of scientific consensus which therefore tends to negate the very accuracy it is meant to achieve. The subjects of this book provide a supreme example. They are universally accepted as all being members of the Salmonidae family, but there is no happy agreement as to what else belongs in the family, nor as to how whatever else does should be further subdivided. The closest best known relatives of the salmon, trout and charr are grayling and whitefish, which sometimes rest neatly in their own families, Thymallidae and Coregonidae respectively. This leaves the Salmonidae family to gather up the salmon, trout and charr in *Salmo*, *Oncorhynchus* and *Salvelinus*, as well as including *Hucho* and several other lesser-known genera of fringe fish. More often, though, whitefish and grayling also find themselves in Salmonidae, which thus becomes so cluttered that it needs splitting into sub-families – Thymallinae, Coregoninae and Salmoninae – and that is how they are grouped in this book.

Because ancestry is the critical criterion of taxonomy, scientific names usually say far more about the relations of an animal than about the animal itself. *Salmo trutta* and *Salmo salar* are physically similar enough to share a genus and therefore a relatively recent common ancestor. However, taken in isolation, and even with a knowledge of Latin, neither the generic name *Salmo* nor species name *trutta* is any help in describing a brown trout. The name *Oncorhynchus* reveals no more than that all its species have hooked jaws, not even that they are fish! Taxonomy often seems obsessed with relationships, and continually squanders the opportunity to use the name of a species to convey information about it.

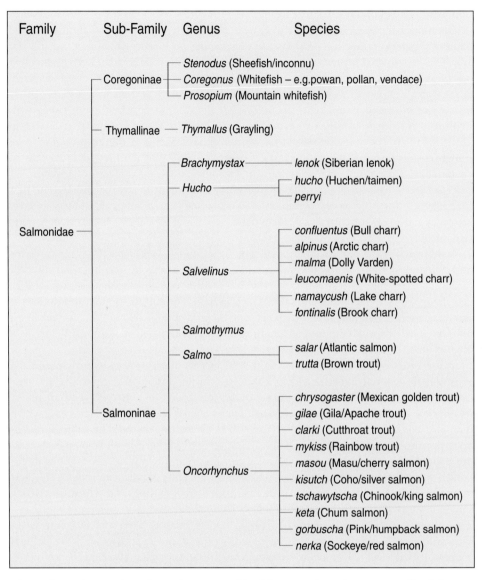

Family	Sub-Family	Genus	Species

Coregoninae
- *Stenodus* (Sheefish/inconnu)
- *Coregonus* (Whitefish – e.g.powan, pollan, vendace)
- *Prosopium* (Mountain whitefish)

Thymallinae — *Thymallus* (Grayling)

Brachymystax ——— lenok (Siberian lenok)

Hucho ———
- hucho (Huchen/taimen)
- perryi

Salvelinus ———
- confluentus (Bull charr)
- alpinus (Arctic charr)
- malma (Dolly Varden)
- leucomaenis (White-spotted charr)
- namaycush (Lake charr)
- fontinalis (Brook charr)

Salmothymus

Salmo ———
- salar (Atlantic salmon)
- trutta (Brown trout)

Oncorhynchus ———
- chrysogaster (Mexican golden trout)
- gilae (Gila/Apache trout)
- clarki (Cutthroat trout)
- mykiss (Rainbow trout)
- masou (Masu/cherry salmon)
- kisutch (Coho/silver salmon)
- tschawytscha (Chinook/king salmon)
- keta (Chum salmon)
- gorbuscha (Pink/humpback salmon)
- nerka (Sockeye/red salmon)

Salmonidae — (Salmoninae)

A Salmonidae family tree showing the principal species referred to in this book.

Sometimes the species adopts the name of its 'discoverer' – who was usually doing no more than reveal to Europe what had long been known elsewhere. Cutthroat trout still carry the name *Oncorhynchus clarki* after William Clark. Both he and Meriweather Lewis were painstaking recorders of all they saw and experienced in their exploration of the Louisiana Purchase, and their achievements are not to be belittled. However, *clarki* is no help to anyone trying to identify or imagine a cutthroat trout, and the fish is far better described by its colloquial English name, which focuses straight onto the distinctive orange slashes under the fish's chin. Rainbow trout are also ideally described as such, and *mykiss* adds nothing to the hooked jaw of *Oncorhynchus* except the ethnic association of the original Kamchatka name, which sockeye, as *O. nerka*, also follow.

That the best way of describing a creature is by name is self-evident, and the greatest attribute of the Linnaean system is now its universal adoption, which avoids at least some of the confusion resulting from over-reliance on colloquial names. Salmon, trout and charr are often collected up together, somewhat imprecisely, under the umbrella of 'game fish' – an expression which uneasily attempts to combine elements of science and sport. Biologically, spotting patterns, less distinctive scales and soft-rayed dorsal fins can all help to set them apart from other members of their family, while together their so-called sporting qualities elevate them in the eyes of fishermen far above all other fresh-water fish.

'Salmon, trout and charr' is a perfectly adequate, if somewhat cumbersome, description of a well recognised group of fish, but using common names for its component parts can be particularly confusing. There are both salmon and trout in both the *Salmo* and *Oncorhynchus* genera. Brook and lake charr are usually misdescribed as brook and lake trout, and in tropical oceans there are fish passing under local names of sea trout, Cape salmon, salmon bass or rock salmon, which bear no resemblance to conventional trout or salmon at all. What in Chile and Argentina are known as sea salmon are actually sand perch.

The Linnaean system provides an international standard which avoids these contradictions, and the names of many species have remained unchanged since the publication of the tenth and definitive edition of *Systema Naturae* in 1758. The system may even be as good as will ever be devised, yet the taxonomy of some species seems cursed with continual confusion, and brown trout are just one of these (see Chapter 4). There is nothing fundamentally wrong with *Salmo trutta* as a name, but the seemingly unresolvable question is how far the name should stretch. When is a brown trout not a brown trout?

The limits of a genus can be likened to the borders of a country. These borders are now, by the end of the twentieth century, fairly well defined. There is no argument about what is part of Sweden or Switzerland, although the colonial borders still separating African states are less secure, and disputes occasionally end with territory being shifted from one state to another. The edges of most genera are also relatively well established, even though species may still sometimes move between them, and rainbow trout and its close relatives were recently captured from *Salmo* by *Oncorhynchus*.

Within a country, regional or provincial boundaries are more transient, and are often redrawn for administrative, electoral or economic reasons; land that was once part of one region is moved into another, or taken from one or more regions to create a new one altogether. So it is with species. The borders of the genus usually enclose all its species with reasonable certainty, but within that enclosure, the boundaries of the species are frequently being realigned. Should all the fish in *Salmo* that are not *salar* fall within the boundaries of *trutta*, or should some of those marbled trout from Yugoslavia or plankton-sievers from Lough Melvin take a chunk out of *trutta* territory and occupy the regions of their own species? Do Mexican golden trout merit their complete independence from rainbow trout, or should they be part of a sort of federation within the rainbow region?

When Carl Linnaeus set to work, he relied on the more obvious physical characteristics of a creature to help classify it, aided where possible by knowledge of its habits. Judged by these criteria, silvery sea-going trout and small red-spotted fresh-water trout could never share a species, as they do today; so he named the Swedish river trout *Salmo trutta*, sea trout *Salmo eriox* and the brook trout of smaller Scandinavian streams *Salmo fario*. Linnaeus described over 10,000 different species, and much of his formidable work literally stood up to examination under the microscopes that allowed his successors to see what he never could. However, microanalysis often tended to merge into overanalysis, and relying on minute, usually internal, differences these successors soon became obsessed with splitting species on the slightest pretext. And of course while they looked for what was different, they often lost sight of what was the same.

Critical to the ascription of a fish to a particular species was its colour. This was obviously important, but blindly relying on it denied the possibility of any environmental influence on a fish's pigmentation. '*Nimium ne crede colore*' say the ichthyologists – attach minimal importance to colour. Trout are sometimes almost chameleon-like in their ability to blend into their environment. The golden hues of the bull trout help conceal it against the estuary sand, and the silvering of smolts which prepares them for life at sea is no indicator of species, merely of a stage in their existence. Diet also influences colour, and nibbling carotene-rich shrimps and snails round the shallows, as gillaroo do, may give them red spots and more vivid skins. A fish's colours also often change dramatically as spawning time approaches. Rainbow trout turn intense pink on their flanks and gill covers, silver sockeye become brilliant crimson, while Arctic and brook charr take on brilliant reds, yellows and oranges – transformations which all make the non-breeding fish almost unrecognisable as belonging to the same species. Fish also change with age: thus young Atlantic salmon smolts were long considered a different species (*Salmo salmulus*) from the adults which they eventually became, as were the spawned-out kelts (*Salmo argentus*).

Theoretically, counting what are known as 'meristic characteristics' was an even more reliable method of separating populations of similar looking fish. With naive enthusiasm, Victorian researchers counted scales, the soft spines in fins (fin rays), gill rakers, vertebrae and the worm-like appendages of the stomach (pyloric caeca), whose function is still uncertain. Variations from whatever the norm was thought to be were hailed as proof of new races, subspecies and even species – which might bear the name of him who had wielded the scalpel. The tentacles of the caeca, in particular, were counted and recounted in the hope of gathering evidence that a particular population of trout was distinct enough from all others for this to be reflected in a new name. The smaller the sample, the easier it usually was to make a case for such distinction, and there is no doubt that average numbers of meristic characteristics often differ between populations. However, among larger samples the range is usually too wide to make these characteristics any real use as tools of identification. The average number of vertebrae in one population of brown trout may be fifty-eight and in another sixty, but individuals in both may have fifty-eight, fifty-nine or sixty.

Many of the differences in meristic counts no longer appear to confer any functional advantage. Having either 130 or 150 scales along its lateral line, or ten or twelve rays in its anal fin, are not perceived as adaptations to help fit a trout for its particular environment, but could well help to trace its descent. Other meristic counts may, over the course of thousands of generations, have been influenced by natural selection, and any similarities between different populations are thus no indication of common ancestry, merely examples of parallel evolution.

Gill rakers are bony projections of a trout's gill arches and act as plankton filters, like a whale's baleen. Their numbers tend to vary, even within a species, according to the extent to which fish rely for their food on animal plankton, which itself often depends on whether they have evolved to live in lakes or rivers. Brown trout are not great plankton eaters and have on average fifteen gill rakers, but deep blue sonaghen, which live in the open waters of Lough Melvin, use seventeen much longer ones to help them strain out planktonic water fleas. Although some cutthroat trout have as few as fifteen too, those left

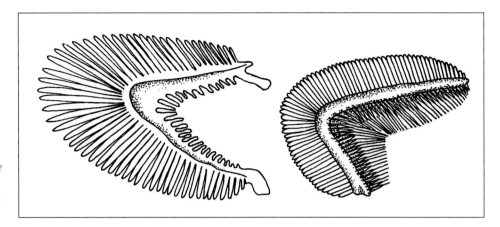

Typical gill rakers (on the inside of the arch) from, left, a charr, and right, a whitefish.

in the Nevada streams, which once drained into Ice Age Lake Lahontan, still evince their lake-living ancestry with as many as twenty-eight. That Arctic charr are, as a species, particularly dependent on free-floating food is quite apparent from their gill raker count of between nineteen and thirty-two, while some species of whitefish, like the vendace, are even more committed plankton eaters and have over forty.

For all their shortcomings as reliable aids to identification, these meristic counts are still some use in identifying similar looking species. The recently described bull charr may often be distinguished from Dolly Varden charr by the shape of its head and the arrangement of its cranium bones, as well perhaps by its more piscivorous, bottom-dwelling habits. However, counting certain meristic anatomical features can also help, at least to decide when a fish is not a bull charr. In particular, bull charr have fourteen to nineteen gill rakers and Dolly Varden eleven to twenty-six; bull charr's vertebrae counts vary from sixty-two to sixty-seven, while Dolly Varden have anything from fifty-seven to seventy. Numbers of anal and dorsal fin rays do not differ sufficiently to aid identification, nor do scale counts, which are too variable to be of much help, but this is exactly what one would expect of fish which may be so closely related that they are hardly species distance apart.

Scale counts can also help separate more distant relatives if identification is not otherwise easy, and avoid any need for dissection. At sea, coho and pink salmon look quite alike, but having between 121 and 148 scales along their lateral line gives coho a rougher feel to their skin than pinks, which have between 147 and 205. Scale counts from the lateral line to the adipose fin are also often the most reliable way of distinguishing sea-going brown trout (between thirteen and sixteen) from Atlantic salmon (nearly always less than thirteen but more than ten).

Today, the evidence provided by biochemistry is far more important than any other in classifying fish and determining relationships between them, and was crucial to the decision to move rainbow and cutthroat trout out of *Salmo* into *Oncorhynchus*. The most fundamental biochemical testimony is provided by counts of chromosomes and the knowledge of how many have one arm or two. Chromosome numbers can vary within a species: brown trout have seventy-eight to eighty-two, Atlantic salmon fifty-four to sixty-four and rainbow trout fifty-eight to sixty-four, tempting taxonomists to try and connect fish with similar counts, even though doing so can produce confusing and contradictory conclusions.

Much more helpful evidence than chromosomes can provide comes from analysing the

DNA of which genes are composed, either directly or by electrophoretic testing of proteins. Direct analysis is not far removed from genetic fingerprinting techniques, but focuses on the mitochondrial DNA; this is passed down the female line and because it evolves faster than ordinary (nuclear) DNA is of much more use in trying to establish evolutionary pathways. Protein analysis is cheaper, quicker and requires less technical expertise, but is also less satisfactory in that the proteins are two steps away from the crucial DNA. DNA controls the composition of proteins through amino acids, and therefore breaking down the proteins should theoretically produce a reasonably clear picture of the DNA itself. Although this picture is often sketchy, the technique has proved particularly helpful in determining relationships between fish from different areas, as well as the genetic proximity of one species to another. It has shown, for example, that masu salmon are genetically closer than any other Pacific salmon to cutthroat and rainbow trout; also that ferox brown trout in Lough Melvin are more closely related to ferox from charr-filled lochs in Scotland than to the other forms of brown trout with which they share their Irish home.

When Linnaeus began cataloguing God's creations, he classified them all according to their observed characteristics. Almost exactly a hundred years later, in 1859, Charles Darwin dropped the great boulder of *The Origin of Species by Means of Natural Selection* into the pool of natural history. Taxonomy in particular was, almost overnight, turned on its head and given a further dimension to its studies. Classifying and grouping the Earth's plants and animals remained its true purpose, but now it had to look back over its shoulder, at common ancestry as well as common form and behaviour. No longer was the natural world seen as frozen immutable since Creation. Suddenly it had a history, and if the animals of today were the product of millions of years of yesterday, then tracing their evolutionary trail was the surest way of determining the relationships between them.

Now one single criterion overrules all others in drawing a family tree – ancestry. Closely related species are like one another because they are closely related – and so the closer the relatives the tighter the group. This approach has removed much of the subjectivity from taxonomy, which was once as much an art as a science. Very often, invoking the additional evidence of ancestry does not alter conclusions reached using Linnaean principles of observation, and it speaks loudly for the efficacy of the binomial system that it has survived to name the creations both of God and of evolution. None the less, the task of tracing a species' ancestry continues to rely heavily on speculation, and still no rules regulate how different one animal needs to be from another before becoming its own species.

Today's web of life on earth has salmon, trout and charr grouped together in the Salmonidae family. Relationships based on observed similarities (phenetic relationships) are still crucial to the creation of any family tree. Ultimately, however, it is shaped by ancestral closeness (phylogenetic relationships), and the only certain evidence of this comes from tracing family histories back down through the Earth's earlier ages – Pleistocene, Pliocene, Miocene, Oligocene and Eocene, and even deeper. Such evidence is usually sketchy and far fuller of gaps than substance; all the same, it is possible to recreate an evolutionary road of sorts, which ends with salmon, trout and charr in the taxonomic slots they now occupy. This entails working out what characteristics unite them with, and what separate them from, their relatives. To some extent geographic distance may reflect genetic distance, and so it is also important to try and understand how fish come to live where they do today.

'Bony, teleost fishes' is how salmonids (members of the Salmonidae family) are typically — and tautologically because 'teleost' means 'bony' – described. They are comparatively little changed from the earliest fossil records, although these are actually of very little help in tracing the family's history because of the huge gaps between the first fossils and the next ones in time. This is frustratingly typical of fossil records, prompting the thought of evolution progressing in bursts after long settled periods of equilibrium, rather than in a stately slow march.

The current fossil father of salmon, trout and charr is probably *Eosalmo driftwoodensis* from British Columbia, which lived about fifty million years ago. Its adipose fin was already a tiny boneless appendage, which probably had no more practical use then than now, so raising the question why it has not yet disappeared from the backs of its descendants. Its anal fin was much larger than any of the others on its body, and twice the size of a modern trout's or salmon's. It looked quite like its present-day successors and was already far removed from whitefish or grayling – suggesting that somewhere deeper in the Earth's history may be other skeletons, twice as old and not very different. Yet for all its slender, salmon-like shape, there seems no doubt that when it swam the huge lake covering the mud where its bones were laid, it did so with no competition from any other species of salmon, trout or charr.

The first fossil evidence of a split in the family line only appears fifteen million years ago – thirty-five million years after *E. driftwoodensis* died. These are Pliocene fossils, also from western North America, which show that by then the family had already diverged several times. Somewhere, fossils are lying unfound which will help fill in this huge gap in the family history, but it is still clear that fifteen million years ago a charr was already well on the way to becoming a charr, and the Atlantic trout and salmon had probably also already branched off the trunk of the family tree.

Until more fossils are unearthed, any evolutionary history of the Salmonidae family must draw more on imagination and intelligent speculation than on hard information. Timing the appearance of the different branches accurately, with the knowledge available today, is almost impossible, although establishing the order of their appearance is less difficult. Perhaps the first bud on the Salmonidae branch started to shoot 100 million years ago, when Laurasia and Gondwanaland had already begun to fragment into the recognisable shapes of modern continents and the Atlantic Ocean was about the size the Mediterranean is now. This was probably the start of the whitefish lineage, which some reconstructions show as having begun too long ago for whitefish to be included in the Salmonidae family – as they are in this book – and thus deserving of their own, Coregonidae.

Whitefish still cling to their vestigial adipose fin and tolerance of salt water, although this is superfluous to whitefish in the lakes, lochs and loughs of the British Isles. There, they are little known, herring-like creatures, small-headed and scaly and quite similar to grayling, but with no spots at all and not nearly such distinctive dorsal fins. They are usually still-water spawners, and scattering their eggs and milt over gravel shoals on lake beds allows them to breed in the winter when, in more northerly latitudes, rivers and streams may be frozen solid. Their classification is a taxonomist's nightmare, made even more so by the different colloquial names given to the same species, as well as by the hybridisation between so-called species, usually after introductions of exotic fish by man.

In Britain, whitefish are rare enough to be protected – ichthyological curios which are in fact often plentiful in the ever-decreasing number of lakes where they occur. Powan turn up in Lochs Lomond and Eck in Scotland, Ullswater and Haweswater in the Lake

District (as 'schelly' after their large scales) and in Lake Bala in North Wales; there, until recently they were considered a separate species with the vernacular name 'gwyniad', derived from their silvery whiteness. Vendace still survive in Bassenthwaite and Derwentwater in the Lake District, but probably nowhere else in Britain. Pollan are now considered to be the same fish as Arctic cisco and are found, quite illogically, only in scattered loughs throughout Ireland, far away from the nearest populations, which are in eastern Europe.

Islands are always harder for fresh-water fish to reach, and whitefish only found their way unaided to a few British still-water outposts as the ice melted at the end of the last Ice Age, eventually breaking the land link between England and France. Yet in continental Eurasia and America, they are so widespread that threats to the many different species come more from commercial overharvesting than environmental degradation. Arctic cisco are highly valued as food fish by Alaskan and Canadian Indians, as well as by the fishermen of Lake Baikal, where, as 'omul', they were so heavily exploited that fishing had to be suspended. More vendace are caught in Finland than any other fish except perch and pike, and as 'Siberian cisco' they are also netted commercially further east.

A sheefish, before being returned to the Kobuk River in Alaska.
(Author)

Whitefish are generally plankton feeders, filtering tiny free-floating animals through far more gill rakers than any of their relatives. Not surprisingly they grow much more slowly and are smaller than trout and charr, often competing with charr before these are large enough to prey on other fish. A few whitefish become piscivorous, and lake whitefish certainly never reach the 10 kg (22 lb) or more that they do in the Great Lakes without turning to a diet of forage fish. The greatest piscivores are the sheefish – named '*poisson inconnu*' by French settlers in Canada and still sometimes called 'inconnu'. They live for twenty years or more, reach weights of over 25 kg (55 lb) and were once popular as dog and human food with the Inuit and Inupiat Eskimos, who ensnared migrating fish in nets or fished for them through the ice with hooks of bone or ivory. They are also found in Siberian and other Asian rivers, but gather most of their size in estuaries before running upstream to spawn – in the Yukon River as far as 1,500 km (930 miles). They are alone in their genus and are distinguished both by their size and by a distinctively protruding lower jaw. This clearly separates sheefish from those other whitefish whose upper jaws project further than their lower, allowing them to augment their normal diets of plankton with food sucked off the lake bottom – often including their own eggs.

Like other salmonids, towards the northern end of their range whitefish tend to be much more inclined to migrate. No whitefish in Britain ever goes to sea, nor, incidentally, does any Arctic charr, but around the shores of the Arctic Ocean *Coregonus* whitefish are great travellers. As well as the sheefish, there is a third genus, *Prosopium*, whose species are, on the whole, much less migratory. They are often broadly termed 'mountain whitefish', although this name is more properly given to one particular species, *P. williamsoni*; these are common in lakes and larger rivers on both sides of the Rocky Mountains, which they may share with either bull charr or Pacific trout.

The next ancestral green bud to appear on the Salmonidae family tree was to start the grayling branch. All grayling belong to the same genus and are distinct enough also to occupy at least their own sub-family, Thymallinae; indeed, like whitefish, they are often given their own family, Thymallidae. The combination of large distinctive scales, great sail-like dorsal fins supported by both spiny and soft rays, and early summer spawning, sets them apart from whitefish and from salmon, trout and charr; none the less, the adipose fin and preference for cool well-oxygenated streams and gravelly spawning grounds is enough to ensure that they are never far away on any family tree.

While grayling occasionally reach an estuary, they are ill at ease in the sea, and never colonised Ireland, Iceland or Greenland – lending support to the arguments in favour of the family's fresh-water origins (see Chapter 2). There is only one species of grayling in Europe. This Linnaeus named *Thymallus thymallus*, but the genus has spread far on the currents of fresh water, and now comprises probably six species in all, dispersed throughout much of Europe, North America and Asia – including Siberia, Mongolia and Lake Baikal. Some of the distinctive gaps in their distribution map, like the Hudson Bay drainage, are intriguing, as is the existence of several populations around the Adriatic coast, each of which is quite disconnected from its neighbours.

In between the grayling and what might be called the true salmon, trout and charr, is a sort of taxonomic no-man's-land, where several species of fish swim whose classification is as uncertain as much else about them. Little is known about the Siberian lenok, not least because its home rivers are difficult for researchers to reach, and until recently its life had been obscured from the eyes of Western ichthyologists by a political iron curtain. Several strange salmonids live in some of the rivers emptying into the Adriatic Sea, suggesting that the forces driving evolution were far more powerful there than anywhere else in the Mediterranean. One such fish, once thought to create a taxonomic link between trout and grayling, lives in some of the rivers of the eastern Adriatic coast – and also has its own genus, *Salmothymus*. There may even be more than one species of *Salmothymus* in these rivers, and in Lake Ohrid, on the borders of Albania and Macedonia, is a small smelt-like fish whose primitive skeleton suggests it should leave *Salmothymus* for *Acantholingua*, all of whose other members are now extinct.

More familiar, but no less intriguing, are the huchen and taimen, which, being relatively common throughout the Asian continent and even parts of eastern Europe, have been well researched and occupy a less contentious place on the family tree. Huchen were known to Linnaeus, who christened them *Salmo hucho*, grouping them with Atlantic salmon on the basis of obvious similarities of shape, size and colour. That great Victorian species splitter of the British Museum, Dr Albert Gunther, was the first to accord them their own genus, *Hucho*, and this classification, unlike most of his others, still endures today. Some would even say that huchen and lenok are deserving of their own sub-family, Huchoninae, but at least it is quite clear what fish fall within the *Hucho* border, even if the species boundaries within it are forever shifting. The shortage of English names adds to the confusion, and colloquially, the names 'huchen' and 'taimen' are used to describe fish which are both generally thought to be subspecies of *H. hucho*. The true huchen are confined to the Danube basin – usually to tributaries rather than to the main stream itself – and have found their way up into what are now Austria and Hungary. Taimen are much more common and occur in most of the great Asian river systems draining the continent northwards into the Arctic Ocean.

A much more distinct line divides *H. hucho* from *H. perryi* than huchen from taimen. *H. perryi* look and behave like their own fish, and live in a few streams on the western Pacific coast; crucially, they also go to sea, which immediately sets them apart from their congeners, as do their spotted tails and dorsal fins. They roam around the shores of the Sea of Japan, coming up to spawn and spend the winter in the rivers of Japan and the Russian mainland north of Vladivostok. Their richer marine diet helps them to a larger average, but not maximum, size than the fresh-water species, although record fish still exceed 60 kg (130 lb).

Most taimen are caught commercially, so giant fish are less likely to be reported. Even if they are, their capture may never be trumpeted beyond the borders of Siberia or Mongolia. One of the few reliable records is of a fish caught in 1943 from a tributary of the Khatanga River in northern Yakutsk, which weighed 105 kg (230 lb). Because taimen tend to live in larger rivers than their Danube-dwelling kin, they may grow bigger, although average-sized fish of both subspecies weigh between 5 and 10 kg (11 and 22 lb). Danube huchen can also grow huge without ever going to sea, and once occasionally topped 50 kg (110 lb); now a fish half that size would be remarkable. Like sturgeon and lake charr, huchen and taimen take many years to reach these great sizes, even on their diets of other fresh-water fish, and so are perilously vulnerable to overfishing. They are not selective feeders and the extensive range of the taimen's recorded prey is evidence both of its widespread distribution and varied habitat. Salmon, whitefish and grayling are food for the taimen of cold rocky lakes and rivers, while those in more sluggish waters live off whatever members of the carp family (Cyprinidae) they can find.

'Show me your teeth and I will tell you what you are,' the early French taxonomist Georges Cuvier is supposed to have challenged. It is unlikely he had the Salmonidae in mind at the time, but there is no group of animals to which his words could be better applied. More specifically, it is the teeth on the vomer bone, running down the roof of a fish's mouth, that are one of the truest indicators of species relationships, and the lack of these teeth neatly groups *Hucho* closer to *Salvelinus*, the charrs, than to any other genus. This is supported by the simple presumption that their mutual ancestor lost its vomerine teeth before the branch of the family tree forked into huchen and charr.

Salvelinus is as complicated as any other genus in its family. Generally though, there is little doubting its parameters, and the only fish perhaps resting uneasily on its borders is a charr from north-eastern Russia, which may be deserving of its own genus (see Chapter 5). Lake charr and brook charr are two of the easiest subjects of this book to classify, and there is no suggestion that they should be split, amalgamated or dealt with in any other way than they are.

Lake charr are confined to North American lakes, and are less tolerant of salt water than any other salmon, trout or charr, from which they are also distinguished by their strong inclination to spawn in still waters. Being so attached to their ancestral breeding

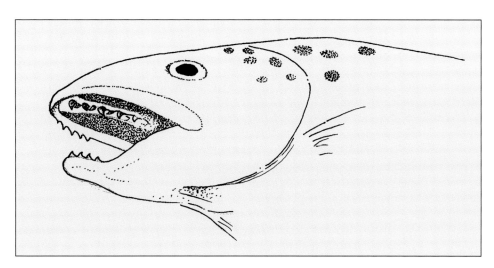

The vomer bone on the roof of a brown trout's mouth.

grounds, they easily evolved into quite distinct races, which often shared the same lake. Much of this diversity found a home in the American Great Lakes, but most of that has now disappeared, rasped away by the suckers of sea lampreys. Of course lake charr from the icy depths of Great Bear Lake in the Northwest Territories have very different genetic profiles from those in the more mellow waters of Maine or Vermont, but only different enough to trouble the conservationists, not the taxonomists. Both lake and brook charr are usually misdescribed as 'trout'. This may be confusing today, but was wholly reasonable when early European settlers needed a name for fish so closely resembling the brown trout with which many of them had once been familiar. Brook charr are also confined to North America – the north-east of the continent – and despite undoubted racial differences, they too pose few problems of subspecific classification, whether born in New Brunswick, New York or Nova Scotia.

That the taxonomy of the remaining charrs is tortuously complex should be no surprise, considering that natural populations are spread throughout much of Europe and Scandinavia, in most of the flowing fresh waters inside the Arctic Circle, round the Pacific rim from Washington to Japan, and far into the Asian heartland. To some extent it is enough to say that they are all Arctic charr-like, and they are all treated in a single chapter in this book; but some of the differences between them are more than subtle. Dolly Varden were first distinguished from true Arctic charr in 1792 and have remained a true species apart ever since. *S. confluentus*, the bull charr of the north-western USA and British Columbia, only achieved specific status in 1978, after due recognition of the importance of the broader head and larger, fish-swallowing mouth by which it is now distinguished.

Over on the other side of the Pacific Ocean, charr classification is further complicated by the lack of common language, insufficient research and the sheer remoteness of much of the country. Dolly Varden are common all the way down the coast, but in Japan and on the Russian mainland there is a small charr with particularly pale markings, colloquially called white-spotted charr and usually given the name *S. leucomaenis*. Further north, on the Kamchatka Peninsula, live other strange relations named stone charr, which some researchers allot to their own species, *S. albus*, and others regard as a race of the white-spotted fish. As always, what seems most important is that there are charr in Kamchatka, and that they are similar to *leucomaenis*; splitting or grouping them is largely of academic interest only. More scientifically fundamental is the discovery of odd relict populations of charr in remote waters, which may have long been known to the local inhabitants for what they are, but when compared to other charr for the first time, are found to be utterly distinct. Distant Russian lakes throw up continual surprises – strange charr with particularly long fins or small mouths – which will need much more investigation before their position on or near the *Salvelinus* branch becomes clearer.

The same teeth which the mutual charr/huchen ancestor lost after it left the trunk of the family tree remained on the vomer bones of the other fish as they divided again into those of the Atlantic and Pacific basins – *Salmo* and *Oncorhynchus*. Diversification always follows geographical separation, and after the free exchange of genes between the fish of one ocean and the other was finally prevented by some meteorological upheaval or cataclysmic rearrangement of the planet's land masses, the Atlantic and Pacific fish each set off on their own evolutionary pathways. Speculating on how this split may have occurred means mentally recreating not only a much warmer world but also a very different map of its oceans and land masses.

Brown trout are essentially European fish; they have made landfall no further afield than Iceland. This suggests that the *Salmo* family is of European origin, and that it was from the eastern Atlantic that salmon spread out to colonise the coast of North America, rather than *vice versa*. Both Pacific and Atlantic salmon are intolerant of very cold water, and round much of the Arctic coastline of Asia and North America the only migratory salmonids are Arctic charr and sometimes whitefish. In a warmer, older world these northern waters might easily have sustained the common ancestor of *Salmo* and *Oncorhynchus*, and it seems likely that a dramatic, long-term cooling of the planet effectively created a barrier of freezing sea along the northern shores of Asia, which ever since then has prevented fish in the Pacific and Atlantic basins from interbreeding. Evidence from sequencing genes to determine how long ago *Salmo* and *Oncorhynchus* shared a gene pool suggests the two genera separated about twenty million years ago, and this would have coincided with the start of the Miocene age, which ushered in a much colder era.

There are other scenarios, both complementary and contradictory, which could have influenced the divergence of the salmonids. It is also suggested that the thermal barrier came down between populations of the common ancestor along the north coast of North America rather than Asia, but the 'Europeanness' of the *Salmo* genus indicates otherwise. Then could the Bering land bridge have influenced the emergence of genera or species in the family? It has risen out above the sea many times, always when the earth was at its coldest and ice sheets hoarded vast amounts of water, and only began to disappear around 15,000 years ago. The bridge was actually up to 1,600 km (1,000 miles) wide and would have created a quite impenetrable barrier between the Arctic and Pacific Oceans. However, it is unlikely ever to have isolated different populations of the same fish from each other, because whenever it emerged all fresh waters to the north would have been frozen solid.

Potentially much more significant in the generic split between *Salmo* and *Oncorhynchus* might have been the changing shape of the great northern land mass which once stretched from what is now North America through Greenland to Eurasia. When this started breaking up into the identifiable outlines of today, it may first have cracked between Eurasia and Greenland, so allowing an easier flow of fish into the embryonic Atlantic from the Eurasian side of the Arctic Ocean than the American. And then is it significant that as little as three million years ago the sea flowed freely over the Panama land bridge between North and South America? Probably not, because it is likely to have been too warm for salmon, trout or charr so far south, and by then they were already very like the fish they are today.

The influence of geography on the split of *Salmo* into *salar* and *trutta* is far less obvious, because the two share streams all the way down the eastern Atlantic shores. Perhaps during an earlier era, great barriers of rock and ice isolated fish from their fellows, creating glacial refuges where ancestral salmon slowly set out to become trout. By the time the great floods of a warmer age finally reunited these fish with their long-lost relatives, the offshoots had red spots and were often content to ignore the lure of the sea. Staying in fresh water often meant staying small and spawning in shallower streams than their sea-going cousins; so they continued to seek out their own kind, and never truly interbred again.

Considering how widely it ranges, *salar* can be described as very stable, with remarkably little variation within its species, seeming secure enough within itself to resist any evolutionary pressures to change. To the human eye, Atlantic salmon from both North America and Europe are outwardly indistinguishable, but electrophoretic tests show they differ sufficiently to be informally divided into subspecies – *americanaus* and *europaeus*. The same tests also apparently give good cause to identify at least two distinct races within the European fish. Those of the boreal race were once isolated in part of what is now the North Sea, while the Celtic fish continued swimming freely south of the limits of the ice. Salmon from the Baltic Sea may even constitute a third distinct race, living a peculiarly isolated existence and very seldom straying beyond its brackish borders.

Throughout the brown trout's kingdom there are countless races and subspecies, each created by thousands of generations in isolation. Some of these once-isolated populations were released from the scenes of their evolution as the barriers confining them broke at the end of an Ice Age. Others are still where the forces of Nature dispersed their forebears millions of years ago. In the rivers that feed the Caspian Sea live *S. t. caspius*, up in the Black Sea are *S. t. labrax* and in mountains round the Aral Sea, *S. t. aralensis* may still swim. The marbled trout of the Po River and other mountain streams emptying into the Adriatic look so different from more conventional brown trout that they are often elevated to their own species, *S. marmoratus*. Their exquisite vermiculations give them more of the look of a lake charr, and suggest that they were isolated from other Mediterranean trout millions rather than thousands of years ago. They have more vertebrae and dorsal fin rays than other trout and, with their huchen-like predatory habits, grow far larger.

The distinctions between different forms of the same fish are never more apparent than when two or more share the same lake without interbreeding. By doing so, they loudly proclaim their individuality, proving in practice what is more often only suggested in theory after dissection and microscopic analysis. The inclination to classify these different forms, even as their own species, then seems particularly justified. The trout of Lough Melvin are much quoted as one of the prime examples of different coexisting forms, which still remain reproductively isolated from one another. In northern Italy, a similar scenario exists in Lake Garda. The lake drains into that evolutionary mixing pot, the Adriatic Sea; and, like Melvin, it is also a creation of the last Ice Age.

Inevitably, the presence of different forms of fish in the same lake raises one fundamental question: have they split from a common ancestor since their colonisation or were they already different by the time they got there? The same question can be asked about the Arctic charr in Windermere or Loch Rannoch, the lake charr in the Great Lakes, or the rainbow trout in Kootenay Lake in British Columbia. No answer can ignore the snail speed of evolution, nor fail to appreciate how creatures diversify much faster if one population is geographically isolated from another, and in such circumstances how inevitable diversification will be. So the biological likelihood must be that these different forms of fish were already different when retreating glaciers and floods of melting ice brought them together again, and have remained distinct, perhaps becoming even more so, ever since.

While early *Salmo* were slowly setting off down the evolutionary pathway they still follow today, those same tides of ice that ebbed and flowed in Europe were also shaping the fish, their communities and their habitat in America. The precursors of today's Pacific trout left the ancestral *Oncorhynchus* lineage long before any of its salmon began to show as distinct species. The Gulf of California was perhaps as great a fount of ichthyological diversity as the Adriatic Sea. Cooling waters allowed ancestral Pacific trout to swim further south than they could in warmer times and to enter river systems that were otherwise beyond their reach. There, the cold's inevitable retreat stranded them, perhaps to be released again in a few thousand generations' time, by then fractionally yet critically changed from the fish they once were.

Oncorhynchus australis is only a fossil fish, but it left its skeleton for posterity in Lake Chapala near Guadalajara in south-western Mexico; this is 200 km (125 miles) further south than any trout swim today, and as clear a sign of colder times as the one-time existence of its Taiwanese relative, *O. formosanus*. There are still relict populations of trout all the way up the mountains of the Sierra Madre and in the headwaters of the Colorado River system, long ago left to go their own evolutionary way. The oldest of these relict fish are probably the Mexican golden trout and the Apache and Gila trout, whose ancestors split from the Salmonidae trunk before the other southern trout. They were then followed by cutthroat trout, which, if this is correct, means the Mexican and Colorado trout are more closely related to cutthroat than to rainbows. The last rainbows to branch away were the coastal subspecies, their sea-going habits placing them closer than any other rainbows to the Pacific salmon (see Chapter 8).

The formal recognition in 1989 that North American trout belonged in *Oncorhynchus* rather than *Salmo* implied a general agreement on the occurrence of one critical event in the family's evolution. If Pacific trout were to sustain their place in *Salmo*, they must obviously have left the *Salmo* line after this had split away from the family tree trunk. Their current classification as *Oncorhynchus* now recognises that in fact they did not. Instead, they appeared on the *Oncorhynchus* branch only after the Pacific and Atlantic fish were well and truly separated from each other. With hindsight, linking Pacific trout to faraway fish of the Atlantic, largely because they could all breed more than once, rather than to their Pacific salmon neighbours ignored not only the shape of the world but also fundamental similarities of bones and teeth. As long ago as 1914 the succinctly logical Tate Regan pronounced from the ivory tower of the British Museum that if 'cranial characters warrant its separation from *Salmo* . . . *Oncorhynchus* will include not only the Pacific Salmon but the Pacific Trout also'.

So today, all Pacific trout belong in *Oncorhynchus*. Cutthroat are at least fenced in fairly securely by the boundaries of their species, even if within those boundaries there is the inevitable disagreement over how *O. clarki* should be subdivided. There are perhaps as many as fourteen formal subspecies, but no suggestion that any of them are distinct enough to be any more than that; one is extinct and others have even reached that status without a name (see Chapter 9). The rainbow trout region is much less clearly demarcated, and the current thinking tends to leave Mexican golden and Gila trout outside the *mykiss* boundary, in their own enclosures. Of course all these fish need names, but however confused these names may be, it should not mask the natural reality. This is quite simply that in the cold streams and lakes from Mexico right up beyond the Alaska Peninsula and down much of the western Pacific coast swim trout in all their myriad shapes, sizes and colours, from tiny little cutthroat of the desert, never growing longer than 20 cm (8 in) to great steelhead of the sea that may reach 20 kg (44 lb).

Pacific trout have changed much less than Pacific salmon, which have evolved a variety of very different lifestyles, almost all culminating in death after they have bred for the first time. Masu salmon provide occasional exceptions, and also show how closely related they are to trout by often feeding in fresh water on their way up to spawn. They were next to shoot off the ancestral branch and are taxonomically more confusing than any of the other salmon in that they are sometimes split by the presence or absence of red spots into two species, masu (*O. masou*) and the usually fresh-water amago (*O. rhodurus*). Both are exclusively fish of the western Pacific and their link with the trout is also enhanced by skeletal similarities.

Over the classification of the other Pacific salmon there is no confusion. All five species have quite clear taxonomic boundaries with probably nothing as distinct as a subspecies inside any of them, not least because they are all younger than the trout and masu, and so have had less time to divide. This is not to deny the vast genetic diversity within each species, nor the highly distinctive genetic profiles of many of their populations. But perhaps fish that always go to sea are inevitably more homogenous, even though different populations theoretically remain reproductively isolated from one another by nearly always returning to spawn where they were born. The chinook and sockeye come nearest to some form of internal subdivision. Chinook are divided into either stream or ocean types, each with quite different life histories, while stocks of landlocked kokanee have evolved independently, and frequently, from sea-going sockeye.

Coho and stream-type chinook are perhaps the most typical salmon – if such a thing exists – certainly more akin to Atlantic salmon in their early behaviour than to any other Pacific salmon. Together, coho and chinook form a sub-group within their genus, and coho were next to bud off the main branch. Young coho and stream-type chinook spend at least a year in fresh water, establishing trout-like territories and living off invertebrates brought down by the current. These early territorial instincts make them individuals, not creatures of the shoal, and in that they differ from the other three species.

Chum and pink salmon are often grouped together with sockeye, the three species united by the shoaling instincts of their young. Chum and pink together are also distinguished by the haste with which their newly emerged fry head down to the sea. Whether hatched over 3,000 km (1,900 miles) up the Yukon River or downstream of the limits of the high tide, they launch themselves into the current as soon as they have exhausted their own in-built food supplies. These two species mark one end of a spectrum of sea-going behaviour with lake charr at the other, although for all their reliance on the sea, both pink and chum remain able to complete their lives without ever scenting the salt, as the pink salmon introduced into the Great Lakes have so readily demonstrated.

Like coho and chinook, most sockeye also spend at least a year in fresh water, but their young nearly always start life in lakes, not rivers. Their behaviour is remarkably varied, maximising the chances of the species' long-term survival by keeping open several different evolutionary options. In the absence of a nursery lake, the young may rear in rivers, and occasionally even head straight down to the estuary after emerging. Some populations breed in still, not running, water, and the non-migratory kokanee never go to sea at all.

Sockeye are perhaps the newest species of *Oncorhynchus*. The timing of their divergence from the pink salmon lineage is uncertain, but may have occurred around six million years ago. This would place all the other evolutionary milestones in the genus's history before that date, but after the split with *Salmo* around twenty million years ago. Like most other cold-water fish, sockeye may have been further divided by the chaotic upheavals of the Ice Ages, which separated fish from their fellows, although seldom long enough for them to emerge as distinct species by the time warmer weather reunited them. Genetic analysis recognises at least two distinct groups of sockeye. These are thought to be the products of thousands of generations of isolation in two separate glacial refuges with the fairy-tale names of Beringia and Cascadia. For the last 12,000 years the two groups have mixed freely in the Pacific Ocean, but seem to have retained their genetic identities to such an extent that they are still distinguishable. The north-western Pacific group embraces sockeye from Kamchatka, western Alaska and northern British Columbia, and the more southerly group takes in those from the Fraser and Columbia Rivers.

Whitefish, grayling, huchen, charr, Atlantic trout and salmon, Pacific trout and finally Pacific salmon: so goes the branching order as constructed by a consensus of different techniques, all ultimately attempting to describe the evolution of the Salmonidae family and the interrelationships of its species by creating a phylogenetic tree. The branching order becomes particularly significant when different life history traits are overlaid upon it to paint a picture of evolving behaviour, as well as gradual changes in form and physiology.

Much of a species' behaviour and life history derives from the strength of its migratory instincts. The ancient genera of whitefish and grayling are generally much less inclined to migrate than are the more recently evolved salmonids. A few whitefish go to sea, usually in the far north of their range, but often no further than the estuary, and grayling seldom even get that far. Some species of *Hucho* and *Salvelinus* are more determined sea-goers, although none of them ranges far from the river mouth. Only in the youngest genera of the Salmonidae family, *Salmo* and *Oncorhynchus*, has the sea-going habit become fully developed, to such an extent that at the end of the migratory spectrum not only do all natural populations of chum and pink salmon migrate to sea, but they all do so as quickly as they can.

Those fish in the middle of the sea-going scale, particularly the single migratory species of huchen, *Hucho perryi*, and the migratory charr, hardly ever overwinter at sea. This seldom gives them more than six months there, and therefore very little time to stray far from the estuary. They all spawn more than once, although not always in successive years, and live to much greater ages than fish which spend longer periods at sea. Migratory brown trout and cutthroat trout are slightly more compulsive migrants; they may not live as long as huchen and charr, and often spawn every year once they mature, although sea-going *Salmo trutta* occasionally miss a year and spend the winter at sea.

As a species, *Oncorhynchus mykiss* is about as migratory as its place on the phylogenetic tree would suggest – more so than cutthroat but less than masu salmon. Steelhead combine elements of the lives of salmon and trout. They can breed more than once,

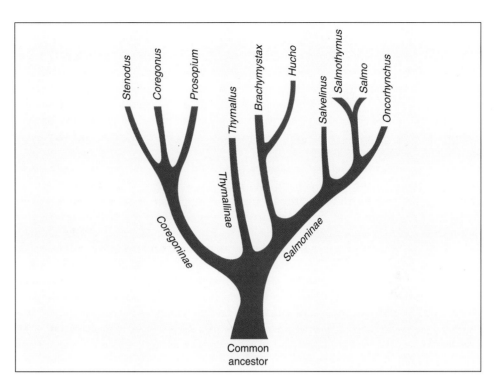

A phylogenetic tree for the Salmonidae family showing the suggested branching sequence of different genera.

although seldom do so, and when they reach the sea, set out to spend two or even three years on oceanic odysseys which take them further than almost any salmon. Masu salmon neatly link the habits of Pacific trout and Pacific salmon. Their restricted distribution in the western Pacific is clear evidence of very localised migrations, which have never taken them far enough to expand their range over to America; indeed, a large proportion of masu salmon never even set off to sea. There are also records of their surviving to spawn again and feeding in fresh water, but these are scant enough to keep masu firmly with the salmon rather than the trout.

As well as being able to overlay a migratory spectrum on the family tree, it is possible to discern the evolution of a distinct trend away from simply broadcasting eggs over the stones towards nest making and defence. Some species of whitefish are stream spawners, others lay their eggs on rocky lake beds, but none of them makes nests. Female sheefish splash noisily around on the surface of the swift upper reaches of Arctic rivers as they release their eggs to be fertilised by the males swimming just below them. Grayling are much more careful spawners than whitefish, but can still hardly be called nest builders. They seek out clean gravel in streamy water, where the males establish territories which they defend, like bull seals on a beach, against the incursions of others – as do Arctic charr. The female grayling then make brief sallies into the males' territories, mate and retreat again to deeper pools after laying some of their eggs. The male uses his fins to push the female's vent onto the gravel and in so doing often creates a slight depression in which the eggs may be partly buried.

By the time huchen left the Salmoninae branch, nest making was beginning to emerge as part of the ancestral fish's breeding strategy, and has continued through into the lives of the most recent species. Lake charr still broadcast their eggs over rocky shoals, but Arctic and brook charr make nests and breed with equal ease in still and running water, and all species of *Salmo* and *Oncorhynchus* are confirmed nest builders. With the gradual movement away from open-water spawning to nest building, other changes in behaviour evolved. The extra energy invested in making nests would be wasted if later spawners arrived and dug up the eggs in the course of their own breeding efforts, and so the females began guarding their nests. Having started doing so, it was no great behavioural shift for them to take over the role of establishing territories. Amongst the salmon and trout of *Salmo* and *Oncorhynchus*, the males compete for females which have already secured spawning sites, rather than the other way round.

Perhaps the most fundamental physical change to accompany the gradual shift towards nest building was a concomitant reduction in numbers of eggs, as fish diverted energy from their production to their care. To maintain a population of any creature at its existing level requires each female to produce two offspring which survive to breed successfully themselves (assuming an equal proportion of the sexes, and that as many males as females are necessary for successful reproduction). Oysters lay as many as 500 million eggs a year, and clearly invest very little energy in each. Gorillas and chimpanzees produce one infant every four or five years. In between these two extremes are animals which seem to have adopted almost every other conceivable alternative breeding strategy, at least with enough success to ensure that they are still with us today. In general, fish are nearer the oyster extreme, but within the five taxonomic classes into which they are usually divided, there are fish breeding in a variety of amazingly different ways – even, like the coelacanth and many species of sharks and rays, producing live offspring.

It is far more usual for fish to lay eggs than bear live young, and the number they lay reflects the degree of care afforded to the newly laid eggs, and occasionally even to the offspring. A female bitterling extrudes her eggs down a long tube which emerges out of her body, and will only do so between the valves of a fresh-water mussel; protecting her eggs so well means she only needs to lay about sixty of them. Cod squirt their eggs straight out into the sea; a large female may produce over five million, which float around in the open water until those that are fertilised and have escaped hungry predators hatch. One in a million may survive to maturity. Somewhere in between comes the Salmonidae family, and during its history, species have gradually emerged which lay fewer and fewer eggs, but ensure that they are increasingly well protected.

Sheefish are the most abandoned spawners of their family, and large females of 10 kg (22 lb) or more may lay over 300,000 eggs. Furthermore, sheefish, like most whitefish, often spawn several times in their lives, perhaps producing over a million eggs by the time they die, in their subconscious mission to ensure that two of their offspring survive to breed. Grayling are more careful spawners and the Arctic species have been found to lay between 6,000 and 16,000 eggs per kilogram of body weight. These figures are many times greater than those for the more recent genera in the family, and salmon, trout and charr produce between 1,000 and 1,500 eggs per kilogram of their own weight. So egg numbers and spawning habits are a function of one another, leaving unanswered the conundrum of whether fish lay fewer eggs because these are well protected, or learn to protect them well because they are few. The benefits of protecting eggs in a gravel nest are clear, but one further variable needs feeding into the equation: that is how long eggs take to incubate and therefore how well developed young alevins are on hatching.

There is a direct correlation between egg number and size, and fewer means larger. Salmonid eggs are large, as fish eggs go, and filled with yolk which sustains the young until they are comparatively well developed, so there is little need for any larval stage once they hatch. Large eggs take much longer to hatch than smaller ones. The tiny eggs which sprats lay in the open water hatch four days later; however, their young are then far less developed than those of salmon, trout or charr, whose eggs have taken anything from 30 to 150 days to hatch, depending on the temperature. At 9°C European grayling emerge from their egg shell in sixteen to eighteen days, while at that temperature brown trout eggs would hatch in about forty-five days. As well as being smaller, newly hatched grayling spend far less time – usually four or five days – in the dark security of the gravel before starting to feed for themselves. A grayling's yolk sac is much smaller than that of any salmon, trout or charr, which take almost as long to absorb theirs as they did to hatch. This gives the alevins time to gain confidence and strength, gradually substituting their initial aversion to the light above for a positive attraction, which finally lures them towards the surface.

That incubation periods are under thermal control was soon brought home to the first exporters of brown trout ova to Australia, who had to delay hatching for at least the hundred days they took to get there. The lower limit for successful hatching varies slightly from one species to another, as does the time it takes eggs to hatch. For most salmonids, success rates begin to decline below 4°C, although there is no physiological reason why eggs should not eventually hatch even in the 150 days or more they need at 1°C or 2°C. Equally critical is the upper limit: above 10°C hatching rates start to drop off, until at 15°C the chances of any young surviving are remote unless fish are specifically, and unusually, adapted to spawn at such temperatures.

Parental care of any kind is rare in the fish world. Several diverse species keep guard over their eggs until they hatch, but very few actually care for their young as female cichlids and sea catfish (Ariidae) do, incubating eggs in their mouths and even sheltering offspring there in times of danger. For them, producing a few hundred eggs is enough to maintain a static population. Salmon, trout and charr are not unusual in never seeing their parents, and having to rely exclusively on their instincts to guide them through their lives from the time they hatch – although of very few species can it be said, as it can of Pacific salmon, that by then their parents are always dead.

To breed successfully, most salmon, trout and charr need cool water running over gravel beds, and if this is not to be found there are no fish, however ideal the lakes or streams may otherwise be for daily life. Water temperature is critical to every aspect of all salmonids' lives and so to their distribution, although this is ultimately controlled by the need for much cooler water in which to spawn successfully. Fish can flourish and grow in water that is far too warm for their eggs to hatch in, and trout often drift downstream to feed where they could never breed. Usually though, if streams are cool enough through winter and spring for eggs to survive to hatching, the summer highs are tolerable for the growing young.

The desert streams of Oregon and Nevada once fed the great glacial lakes at the head of the Columbia River, but now empty into dried out depressions and may never reach the sea. There both rainbow and cutthroat trout survive summer temperatures often exceeding 25°C, after spawning in the thermal safety of spring when it is never above 15°C. At the polar limits of the planet's land mass, the only restriction on the northward spread of Arctic charr is temperatures so low that the fresh-water streams never unfreeze, even in summer. And in between Baffin Island and the Oregon desert or the Atlas Mountains are trout, salmon and charr of one kind or another filling fresh-water niches

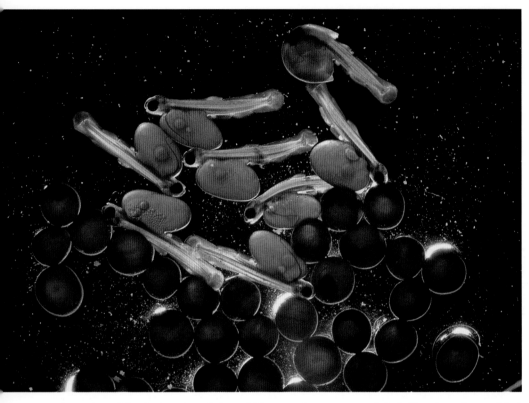

Life begins – Pacific salmon eggs and alevins.
(Natalie Fobes)

throughout North America, Asia and Europe, the patterns of their lives largely moulded by the temperature of the waters in which they live.

Fish isolated in southerly mountain retreats, like the brook charr in the Appalachians and rainbow trout in Mexico, cannot reach the sea simply because it is too warm downstream. Likewise, the migratory urges of the relict population of masu salmon in Taiwan are totally suppressed, and very few of those in southern Japan migrate either. Arctic charr, too, never leave fresh water towards the south of their range, and only surrender to their sea-going inclinations further north. For those fish that do migrate, temperature also largely determines the age at which they do so. Salmon hatched in warmer rivers tend to turn into silvery smolts, ready for salt water, far sooner than they do in colder ones. This may be a consequence both of reaching a given size sooner on better food, and of longer summers in which to eat it. Atlantic salmon from rivers in Spain often move down to the estuary when they are just over a year old, but above the Arctic Circle they may be six or seven before they are ready to leave fresh water. Ocean-type chinook, which head to sea soon after they are born, dominate stocks from British Columbia southwards, while northwards, throughout Alaska, nearly all chinook are stream-type and spend at least a year in their native river.

In general, trout can live in warmer water than either salmon or charr can, which in part accounts for their amazing success as exotic introductions into strange habitats all over the world. The maximum temperatures most rainbows and cutthroat can tolerate are around 25°C, but those living in generally hotter climes are more at ease at these levels than fish brought in from colder waters. Charr may not survive above 23°C, but their comfort at almost zero is quite apparent from their occupation of a great slice of territory north of the Arctic Circle, where the only other salmonids are whitefish.

No aspect of breeding or the hatching of eggs escapes the all-pervasive influence of temperature. Warming or cooling water is almost invariably accompanied by changes in both day length and barometric pressure, and it is difficult to dissociate their respective effects. However, there is no doubt that falling temperatures, in part at least, trigger the spawning urges of salmon, charr and brown trout, while rising ones prompt rainbows and cutthroat to breed – as they do grayling. So in general, spring spawners breed later further north and autumn spawners earlier, not only because the critical temperature is reached later or earlier respectively, but also because eggs take so much longer to hatch in colder water.

The responses to changes in temperature and to its reaching specific levels contribute to the distinctive characters which fit different stocks of the same species for the Arctic-draining Tree River, the highland lochs of Scotland or the Alpine lakes of Austria and Switzerland. The temperatures that trigger the spawning urges of Lake Windermere's Arctic charr may be higher than fish in Baffin Island ever experience, and brown trout in northern Norway are by now programmed to breed at different temperatures from those in the chalk streams of Normandy. Some of these responses are genetically controlled and stay with fish wherever they are taken – and often contribute to their failure to survive in an environment which is markedly different from the one in which they evolved. Frequently though, it is clearly the environment itself that conditions the behaviour of fish, and when stocked into strange waters they can adapt quickly to a new thermal timetable. This may demand that they spawn in early December rather than at the end of October, and ready themselves for a marine life at the age of two, not seven, or head down to sea even though their parents never did. Brown and rainbow trout exported to the southern hemisphere had to change their inherent spawning timetable by six months, and soon proved that they could easily do so.

Fish destined to spend their whole lives in a river must either tolerate its temperature or die. They may be able to adapt to gradual temperature changes over epochs or eras, as the cutthroat of Nevada or rainbows of Mexico have done. However, these have now moved upstream as far as they can, and if the Earth is still retreating from the last Ice Age, then they will eventually disappear, with or without a push over the brink from mankind. Much further north, most salmonids are migratory, allowing them to move from one river to another via the sea. They are already so far within their ideal environment that when they nose into strange estuaries they are unlikely to be searching for more comfortable conditions; rather they may be lost, or on some unrecognised mission in search of new spawning grounds where there may be less competition for their young than they experienced themselves. After all, that is just how salmonids have spread over the last 12,000 years, and perhaps this is what chum and pink salmon are still doing along the north coast of Alaska. Arctic charr, too, despite being comparatively uneasy at sea, have conquered new territory within the last 1,000 years, and if the world warms still further, salmon may follow them.

2
To sea or not to sea

No aspect of a salmon's life raises more unanswered questions than the workings of its migratory instincts. From the shallow fresh-water riffles to the larders of the sea and back, the salmon's migrations still remain a source of absorbing speculation. Their journeys combine great feats of open-ocean navigation, largely unaided by the visual cues which help birds on their way, with equally spectacular homing powers to guide them to the gravel of their birth. For some salmon, and also the less compulsive migrants like brown trout and Arctic charr, there are even more unanswered 'whys' and 'hows' about the alternative lifestyles seemingly offered them. In particular, why do some members of a species migrate to sea, while others live out their whole lives without ever leaving fresh water?

Salmonids are far from alone in being able to exploit both fresh-water and marine environments, and there are several other families of fish, many of whose members do so with equal ease. Like the Salmonidae, most of these are anadromous, in that they breed in fresh water and then migrate to sea to feed. In the families of lampreys (Petromyzontidae), shads (Clupeidae), sturgeons (Acipenseridae), smelts (Osmeridae) and sticklebacks (Gasterosteidae) there are migratory species whose young seem to cross the salt-water frontiers with little apparent difficulty. A few fish live their lives in reverse, breeding in the sea but spending the rest of their time in fresh water. The greatest exponents of this lifestyle are the eels (Anguillidae), all of whose fifteen species are described as catadromous.

Dividing migratory fish into fresh-water spawners which feed at sea, and marine spawners which feed in fresh water, risks the implication that they are all easily and distinctly pigeonholed as being anadromous or catadromous. In reality, however, eels and salmon are at either end of a migratory spectrum in the middle of which is a whole range of fish at ease in both fresh and sea water, and which exploit both environments at different stages of their lives. Salmon may appear to be the true champions of an anadromous way of life, but while all salmon, trout and charr are confirmed fresh-water, or occasionally intertidal, breeders, the patterns of their seaward migrations are extraordinarily varied – if indeed they migrate at all.

Where the evolutionary path to an anadromous life begins must depend for each fish upon the origins of its family. Did the forebears of Atlantic salmon, Allis shad or beluga sturgeon first migrate from the sea to breed in fresh water, or from fresh water to feed in the sea? If a fish's ancestors originated in fresh water, then the pressures of overpopulation, poor feeding or uncomfortable water conditions in rivers and lakes may have slowly squeezed them further and further downstream, seeking food, space or more congenial temperatures right to the limits of the high tide and then into the estuary. These tentative early explorations may gradually have become more focused forays, eventually

Sockeye beginning their journey upstream to spawn.
(Greg Syverson)

taking fish out to the open sea. At first, as one generation after another pushed back its feeding frontiers, fish still clung to their ancestral fresh-water diets. Then, as evolution continued favouring those that exploited the sea to the full, increasing numbers of the species started to spend more and more of their adult lives there. Eventually, time at sea became an integral part of their life-cycle, what was once exceptional behaviour became the rule, and so finally an anadromous species emerged.

If the family's early history was a maritime one, its members may first have moved into fresh water in search of sanctuary from the predations of larger fish, or in some subconscious quest for more secure spawning grounds, giving their young better chances of survival. Through successive generations evolution continued favouring the fresh-water spawners; these ultimately became so successful that they finally eclipsed any fish which had continued breeding in their original habitat. Still, wherever their origins and whatever the pressures that drove them down to the sea or up the river, the ancestors of the salmon, trout and charr eventually acquired the complex abilities allowing them to move from one environment to another and live easily in both.

One of the most convincing clues to any fish's ancestral environment is likely to be found in the nature of its present spawning habitat. Reproduction is any creature's most fundamental act, and from an evolutionary perspective, the last to change. The suggestion that Salmonidae originated in fresh water gains great support from the fact that every single member of the family spawns in fresh, or occasionally brackish, water. Often this means right at the source of the river, where mosses are the only aquatic plants, and in the clear, fast flowing streams there is just enough food for the young, but not for their parents. The journey to the redds may be long and tortuous – chinook and chum salmon spawn over 3,000 km (1,900 miles) up the Yukon River – and yet the fish seem driven out of the sea up to the freshest, cleanest, coldest and most distant waters before they are prepared to breed. This is compelling evidence in favour of fresh-water origins; so is the fact that in every genus of the Salmonidae family there is at least one species, some or all of whose members never leave fresh water.

Within the family, it is also possible to trace a distinct evolutionary trend away from an almost wholly fresh-water existence towards increasing dependency on the sea (see Chapter 1). When the branches first appeared on the trunk of the Salmonidae family tree is impossible to estimate accurately, but the most ancient families appear to be whitefish and grayling, and their migratory instincts are distinctly muted in comparison to those of the most recently evolved species of chum, pink and sockeye salmon.

A further contribution to the case for fresh-water origins is provided by a strange attachment to many fish's stomachs known as the swimbladder. Its function is still much debated, but whatever its other uses, it certainly helps regulate a fish's buoyancy. Salt water is denser than fresh, and fish need less help in floating at sea, so the well-developed swimbladder of the salmonids suggests that this organ evolved to support fresh-water, not marine, fish.

Arguments in favour of the salmonids' maritime beginnings focus on their extensive distribution throughout the northern hemisphere, clearly showing the ease with which they pushed back the frontiers of their range in time with the retreating ice. To have spread so far and fast on the floods of meltwater after successive glaciations, finally to reach their present homes at the end of the last Ice Age, 10,000–15,000 years ago, certainly required considerable tolerance of salt water – even if the sea at the edges of the ice was then much more diluted. Yet this need not necessarily imply that the Salmonidae sprang from the sea, only that most of them survived easily in salt water by the end of the last Ice Age. Brown trout, Atlantic salmon and Arctic charr have all colonised the lakes and rivers of Iceland, Greenland, the Orkneys, the Shetlands and most of the Scottish Hebridean islands. Reaching Iceland, in particular, entailed much more than just a quick swim through brackish water, and the only other fish to have made that far-off landfall are sticklebacks and eels, both of which can also survive in fresh waters and the sea. Other truly fresh-water species slowly felt their way northwards, up continental coastlines where the thawing ice and melting snow reduced the sea's strength to levels even they could tolerate, but never reached islands far offshore.

Not only do all members of the Salmonidae family spawn in fresh water, but so too does almost every species of the other seven families usually grouped within the sub-order of its closest relatives. Ayu, icefish, Tasmanian whitebait and nearly all the rest of the diverse collection of fishes in these families breed in lakes and rivers, only some aberrant smelts, like the capelin, spending all their lives at sea. This is probably the strongest of all pointers to the origins of the Salmonidae, indicating that the great ocean-bound migrations of the Pacific and Atlantic salmon were born of their ancestors' first tentative movements out of fresh water in search of a more hospitable environment. Moreover, all these families are confined to the polar and temperate zones in the northern and southern hemispheres. At these latitudes, the sea is a much richer source of food than fresh water, and if the search for nourishment is the spur to their migtations, fish are most likely to swim down the river to feed in the sea. Closer to the equator, the opposite situation prevails, and it is not surprising to find a greater number of tropical species breeding at sea and then moving upstream to feed in rivers.

The habit of migrating between fresh and sea water has evolved quite separately in many different families of fish. Closely related families may already have acquired anadromous tendencies by the time they went their separate ways, but when, for example the long-distinct lineages of sticklebacks and salmonids diverged, anadromy was very unlikely to have been part of their lives. Of the eight species of sticklebacks only two are anadromous. This implies that the three-spined and nine-spined sticklebacks began to appreciate the advantages of exploiting both fresh-water and marine environments well after sticklebacks became sticklebacks.

Only one out of the fifty-five or so species of cod (Gadidae) leaves the sea to breed. This is the tomcod, which is a winter spawner in the fresh waters of eastern Canada and the USA, and must also have opted for its distinctive lifestyle very recently. The same can be said of the only fresh-water species of cod, the burbot, which is probably now extinct in Britain; otherwise it is widespread around northern latitudes, and obviously abandoned its affinity for a marine life long after cod became cod.

The emergence (or re-emergence for those who contend that the Salmonidae originated in the sea) of true sea-going species within the family has been a long and gradual process. Ancestral fish must have been able to tolerate some salt in their water, even before the family began to diverge, because there are many exponents of the sea-going life within the sub-order to which Salmonidae and the seven other families belong, despite all the families being generally fresh-water breeders. It is difficult to account for the distribution of these families in the colder latitudes of both northern and southern hemispheres. Perhaps their ancestral line began to divide in time with the original break-up of the earth's surface, when fish were carried off on slabs of Gondwanaland and Laurasia. The scope for speculation on their evolution seems almost unlimited. It has even been seriously suggested that all salmonid species evolved to live anadromous lives in parallel, quite independently of one other, after each had already become the fish it is today. This almost implies that going to sea is no harder for a fish than it is for a man in a boat – that it is no more than a question of evolution of behaviour – and seems to ignore the considerable evolution of body that is also required of a fish before it can survive on both sides of an estuary.

Unlike the cod, with their single anadromous representative, time at sea has become increasingly important for the Salmonidae family in the course of its evolution (see Chapter 1), and probably continues to do so. All three genera of whitefish contain sea-going species which at least reach the estuary, as occasionally do grayling. The Far Eastern species of huchen, *Hucho perryi*, grows to great size on an inshore diet, and of the salmon, trout and charr, only lake charr seem to be resisting the familial trend.

To say that a species is anadromous may suggest that it must migrate between fresh and sea water at some stage in its life, if not to survive, then at least to complete its life successfully (which implies producing offspring). It may also understandably suggest that all members of the species behave the same way. Swallows, for example, *must* migrate south in the northern winter, and they *all* do. But where salmonids are concerned, both implications may be very misleading, and one of the most perplexing aspects of anadromy is the selection by fish of the same species, which may even be siblings, of totally different patterns of life. Overlay on this conundrum the existence of specific non-migratory populations of a species like Atlantic or sockeye salmon, which are otherwise confirmed sea-goers, and the whole question of migration to and from the sea becomes as confusing as it is intriguing. No group of fish displays a greater range of migratory options, or of differing dependence on a sojourn at sea, than the salmon, trout and charr.

Pink and chum salmon are at the saltiest end of the spectrum. Pinks often spawn in brackish water as, less often, do chum, and the young of both species are genetically programmed to set off downstream as soon as they emerge – a journey of minutes for fish hatched between the tide's limits. On returning to the estuary these fish are already close to maturity, and so fresh water is only important to them at the very end of their lives. Perhaps only the lure of the cleaner gravel beds in the river mouth, which the alternating currents of the sea's tide and river's flow keep free of sand and silt, prevents them from exploring the sea for alternative spawning grounds – as of course does their inherent

Chum salmon spawn in this intertidal stretch of Tonsina Creek, close to Resurrection Bay, Alaska. (Author)

attachment to their birthplace. It is not hard to imagine pink or chum salmon laying their eggs on gravelly wave-washed beaches, as capelin do, in 10,000 generations' time.

Despite their close affinity for the sea, both pink and chum salmon can complete their lives while completely confined to fresh water, although none do so naturally. Pink salmon now live easily, but artificially, in the Great Lakes. The angling and fish-farming fraternities hold chum salmon in lower esteem, and have made no real effort to extend their natural range, but the fish have shown, at least in aquaria, that maturing in fresh water is not beyond them. If pinks seem set towards an even more marine existence, they may soon no longer be able to survive in fresh water. Evolution is sparing in its grant of powers. Hard-won though they may have been, abilities must be used, and those superfluous to survival start to disappear – birds that seldom fly soon cannot do so, and the human sense of smell is far less acute than it was when man depended on it for successful hunting.

The sea is only marginally less important in the lives of chinook and coho salmon. No populations of either species live out their lives in fresh water, although young residuals mature in fresh water and spawn successfully. In contrast to pink and chum salmon, there is a distinct fresh-water phase in the lives of young coho and stream-type chinook, both of which establish territories soon after emerging, occasionally spending even a second year in their river before heading down to the estuary and out to sea.

Most young sockeye salmon spend their first, and sometimes their second, year in a lake, quickly moving down their natal stream after emerging. *Oncorhynchus nerka* is much the most versatile of Pacific salmon. Some sockeye also rear in running water for a year if they have no access to nursery lakes, and a few even go straight down to the sea at the speed of pinks. There are also many distinct populations which never leave fresh water. These are called 'kokanee' and spend their lives in ignorance of the benefits of the sea, although none of them seem to have lost the ability to survive there, nor to navigate their way back home if they have to. To complete the range of lifestyles, a few young sockeye – not kokanee – mature in fresh water as residuals, sometimes spawning with sea-going adults but seldom reaching the sea either.

Of all the Pacific salmon, masu retain the greatest affinity for fresh water, and, by so doing, show that they are the salmon most closely related to the Pacific trout. Masu are only found round the coast and in the rivers of the western Pacific, and many never leave the river of their birth; if they do, they only spend a year away, seldom straying far from the estuary, and even feeding sporadically in the river on their way back up to spawn. Of those that opt for a fresh-water life, the majority is usually male, as it is with other salmon. The proportion of fresh-water-maturing females increases towards the southern end of the masu's range, where entire populations perpetuate themselves without any of them ever reaching the sea.

The existence of so many distinct stocks of Atlantic salmon which, like kokanee, have voluntarily adopted fresh-water lives without any coercion from the forces of geography, topography or mankind, pushes them further towards the fresh-water end of the migratory spectrum then they would otherwise be. Perhaps they are about on a par with sockeye. Some residual males mature before they leave fresh water, and are fully able to mate with larger females, but generally the Atlantic salmon is seen as epitomising the sea-going habits of its family – the ultimate ocean wanderer, with an almost magnetic attraction for its place of birth. Its only congener, *Salmo trutta*, is much less predictable, and does its best to confound attempts to draw any reasonably firm conclusions about the migratory behaviour of the Salmonidae. All brown trout are perfectly able to live their whole lives in fresh water – which most of them do. Yet there is an internal mechanism within each of them, which, when triggered, sends them off to sea.

Unlike brown trout, the migratory and resident populations of both rainbow and cutthroat trout are much more distinct from one another, genetically and geographically – coastal cutthroat even have a different chromosome count from their inland kin. Still, as a species, rainbow are about level with brown trout on the migratory scale, with cutthroat just below them. Pacific trout from short streams seem more inclined to migrate than those whose seaward journey would be more arduous. Once at sea, cutthroat wander far less than migratory rainbows (steelhead), which travel just as far as any Pacific salmon. Sea-going Arctic charr and Dolly Varden seldom range much beyond the estuary. Their systems seem unable to tolerate the sea for very long, and this, coupled with the shortness of the Arctic summer, means they spend very little time feeding at sea, and have hardly ever been found to overwinter there.

The brook charr of eastern America is very like the cutthroat from the west coast in its subdued sea-going instincts, and it is the lake charr which rests firmly at the bottom of the salmon, trout and charr's migration league. It shows such a disregard for the potential attractions of the sea that it can scarcely be described as anadromous. The species still remains tolerant of mildly salty water, which probably accounts for it having been able to colonise some of the islands in the Canadian Arctic, but for most lake charr the ability to live in brackish water is a superfluous aid to survival.

So, at this moment in their evolutionary history, salmon, trout and charr are all able, in varying degrees, to tolerate both fresh and salt water, and all need fresh, or occasionally brackish, water for successful spawning. At either end of the migratory continuum created by the overlapping behaviour of all these fish are species whose life patterns are fixed – without options. Lake charr are no more likely to feel urged to head for the open sea than perch, pike or crucian carp. At the other extreme are young pink or chum salmon whose inclinations detain them in fresh water no longer than the current takes to carry them out of it. In between, though, are many more versatile species, which almost seem confused as to which evolutionary pathway to follow, whether to heed the call of the genes or the messages from the environment.

Some stocks of otherwise migratory fish have even begun living preordained fresh-water lives, and whether their destinies are controlled by genes, topography or temperature, they never reach the sea. They are often described as landlocked, which risks the implication that some impassable obstruction prevents them from reaching the sea, or if not, then at least from returning to where they were born. In fact there is more often no physical barrier to their return journey, and some other influence is suppressing their urge to migrate.

The distinctions between the genetic profiles of distinct migratory and non-migratory populations of a species are usually clear-cut, even when these share the same river system. This should theoretically help to explain the tendency to adopt one life pattern or another. However, such genetic distinctions as there are do not actually contribute much to answering the question of why some fish go to sea and others do not, because much more than just differences in migratory behaviour contributes to these distinctions. Until it is possible to identify the genes controlling migratory instincts, it remains impossible to define the specific influence of genes on these instincts over that of any other factor.

Kokanee – non-migratory sockeye – are genetically closer to migratory sockeye from the same lake system than to kokanee from other lake systems. The same can be said of Atlantic salmon, although far less often do sea-going and resident populations live in the same waters. This shows that the tendency to live fresh-water lives has evolved repeatedly, and frequently, ever since sea-going sockeye (from which kokanee are descended) and Atlantic salmon first reached the homes their descendants now occupy. As this was only 15,000 years ago at the most, no more than minor differences in genetic profiles have had time to emerge. Yet these genetic differences are clear, and if the next Ice Age is far away in the future, and landlocked fish are left where they are for long enough, then continued genetic isolation will make them ever more distinct from their sea-going fellows from the same lake or river.

Landlocking is common in many other anadromous species. The boneless, jawless sea lampreys provide one of the best quoted examples, having found their way up the Welland Ship Canal from Lake Ontario to the upper Great Lakes. There they established non-migratory populations which gradually ate their way through most of the indigenous lake charr (see Chapter 6). Fresh-water-dwelling twaite shad live in Lough Leane in Ireland and also in several of the larger Alpine lakes such as Como and Garda; otherwise this is a marine species which only enters rivers to spawn, just above the high-tide mark. It may be that these fresh-water populations of fish, which otherwise spend most of their life at sea are, like similarly isolated stocks of salmon, trout or charr, founding new lineages. In some cases adopting fresh-water habits may already have resulted in the creation of a distinct species. Brook lampreys are small eel-like fresh-water fish, which may be only recently derived from the sea-going, and thus larger, river lamprey; the larvae of the two species are indistinguishable and apart from their size, only minor differences in fins and teeth set them apart.

Fish living above waterfalls or dams become landlocked simply because any that migrate downstream are unable to return, and instincts to head seawards are totally incompatible with those driving fish back to breed where they were born. To endure, the population above the falls or dam is therefore totally dependent on non-migratory fish, and over the generations evolution selects against fish which are inclined to swim to sea. Below the falls, fish retain the option to migrate or not, and comparisons between the genes of populations of a species living above and below impassable barriers often show distinct differences.

Rainbow trout from above waterfalls in Kokanee Creek in British Columbia can be distinguished both genetically and physically from those below. The Arctic charr population in Alaska's Sagavanirktok River, which flows north off the Brooks Range into the Arctic Ocean, is divided by a stretch of rapids impassable for the sea-going Arctic charr living below them. Atlantic salmon in Norway's River Namsen can easily reach the sea, but the unjumpable Aunfoss waterfall bars their return. The fish above are dwarf fresh-water salmon, genetically quite distinct from the sea-going stocks below the falls, their existence preserved by thousands of generations of selection against downstream migration.

As well as the genetic differences between the above- and below-waterfall populations, and occasional differences in numbers of gill rakers or fin rays, fish sometimes show other, more significant physical or physiological distinctions. Those above falls have been found to react more positively to water current, and to show greater stamina in countering its effects, than those below. They also appear to hatch out later in the year, perhaps thereby avoiding the worst of the spring floods which might otherwise carry them over the lip of the falls. These distinctions are now genetically fixed, and further serve to emphasise the influence of genes in controlling migratory behaviour. None the less, a stock of fish above a fall can quite easily afford to lose a considerable proportion of each generation downstream and still remain self-sustaining, so the continued exercise of both life options by above-falls fish is not necessarily inconsistent with the survival of the population.

While the genetic profiles of many specific migratory and non-migratory stocks of the same species are now distinct, this is certainly less so of residual fish, which are often the progeny of two sea-going parents, but mature in fresh water. The young of many truly migratory fish, that spend the first year or more of their lives in fresh water, are forced to decide whether they should go to sea one spring or postpone their downstream journey for a further year. For Atlantic salmon, sockeye, brown trout and Arctic charr in particular, there may be a further choice: that is not so much when to go to sea, but whether to go at all. Having emerged out of their gravel and gradually familiarised themselves with their home stream, there comes a time when the systems of these fish must set them off on one life journey or another. The temptation to become too anthropomorphic about their voyage into the unknown vastness of the sea needs to be avoided. The fish do not toss coins nor debate among themselves the dangers of life in the ocean, but yet there is an internal mechanism which prompts them into staying or going, the precise workings of which are still unclear.

If the inclination to migrate evolved from the gradual discovery of better feeding at sea, then it is reasonable to assume that the main benefit of going there remains the opportunity to grow much bigger than fish which stay behind. Despite the hazards of a marine life and of the journeys up and down the river, these wanderers may have an edge over their fellows that never migrate. Yet the edge must be a thin one, because while most Atlantic salmon or sockeye seem sure of the benefits of migration, a few are pushed into a fresh-water life which ensures that they never reach the sea.

Salmonids which are to migrate prepare for the marine environment by their transformation into smolts. Once smolting starts, the tendency to mature is suppressed, and fish are set irreversibly on a sea-going life. Smolting takes place in fresh water and is therefore, crucially, not prompted by any contact with the salt of sea or estuary. Instead, other factors must induce it. The most fundamental of these may be reaching a given size, which for Atlantic salmon seems to be about 10 cm (4 in). Salmon hatched in French or Spanish rivers are usually this size within a year, and start smolting when only fourteen months old. In Greenland and Ungava Bay, where the feeding season is very short, it may be six years before they are ready for the sea; by then they may be much larger too – 15 cm (6 in) or more – which is often the size of brown and rainbow trout before they start smolting.

It is not reaching a specific size alone which induces smolting. Having reached that size, environmental triggers, perhaps particular day lengths or the water rising to a specific temperature, actually activate the first signs of a fish's preparing for the sea. It also seems that if fish are to smolt in a given year, they have to reach this optimum or minimum size by a particular time that year, and for those that do not the opportunity to migrate is lost and they must wait out a further year in fresh water. Seldom do all the fish from a single hatching smolt in the same year, but instead stagger their downstream migration over two or more years. This adds credibility to the idea of a minimum smolting size, and also buffers the population against environmental catastrophes.

The environment presumably exerts similar influences on all fish in a river at the same time, whether they migrate or not. If one or more of these influences – days of a particular length or water warming to a certain level – were responsible for triggering smolting, all fish that had fulfilled the necessary preliminary requirements, such as reaching a given size, would presumably smolt. But they do not necessarily do so, which could point to some sort of inherited, as well as environmental, control over smolting, and thus over the migration that almost inevitably follows.

Young brown trout born of sea-going parents and translocated to a Scottish hill loch with no outlet began developing the silvery sheen normally associated with preparation for a marine life. Those reared in tanks never began to smolt, nor did the young of non-migratory trout raised in the loch in parallel. Surely the early influence of genes on the migratory behaviour of trout is also apparent in their leaving their nursery streams – and perhaps many of their siblings – and moving further downstream long before they start to smolt. All of this implies that, as is so often the case – and as is so often suggested to be the case for want of any better ideas – it is the workings of the environment on the raw material of inheritance that ultimately influences behaviour.

Whatever it is that prompts most young fish to smolt fails to touch others, which then set off down the pathway of fresh-water maturity, not migration. These residual fish are often faster growing than their fellows, and maturity therefore overtakes them before they ever reach the smolting stage. Maturity, and so reproduction, is the aim of their species, and in the right conditions some of its members will mature as quickly as possible, even if this means not going to sea. This is particularly evident when the conditions in a spawning stream start to improve, usually as a result of a decrease in the fish population giving young fry better feeding and more space. It has been repeatedly demonstrated that, in such circumstances, more fish mature early and live out fresh-water lives. This also fits well with the idea that seaward migration was originally driven by overcrowding in fresh water and competition for its limited supplies of food and space.

By far the greater proportion of these residuals are male. Environmental pressures affect males in just the same way as they do females, and the imbalance between numbers of migratory males and females is therefore most likely to be genetically influenced. These residual males should be able to pass on their stay-at-home habits by sneaking in to release their milt as the older fish reach mutual spawning climaxes. In this way the population can retain the ability to adapt to a full fresh-water life if circumstances ever require it to do so. This is probably how the various stocks of kokanee began to emerge, as well as the above-waterfall populations of otherwise migratory fish. Even today, residual fish may still be the guiding influence in the foundation of landlocked populations. In New Zealand, where transplanted salmon seem to be able to reach the sea but hardly ever find their way home, the survival of each individual population is entirely dependent on fish which never develop migratory urges, as was its foundation.

The preponderance of migratory females suggests that females gain greater advantages from migrating than males do. This then raises the whole question of why fish migrate at all. Initially fish may have been driven downstream by an urge to escape from extreme water conditions or an overcrowded home stream, where aggressive competition turned survival into just too great a struggle for too many fish. To this could be added the search for better feeding, and the most obvious advantage to be gained from migrating to sea remains the opportunity to eat more and grow larger. Paradoxically, this is often emphasised as much by the habits of fish which do not migrate as of those that do. The Atlantic salmon that once inhabited Lake Ontario are reputed to have reached weights of over 20 kg (44 lb) on their fresh-water diet, and seem never to have headed down the St Lawrence River to the sea. Salmon introduced beyond their natural range have frequently taken up lake-dwelling lives. If they can find their food without having to migrate, then this represents the best of all possible worlds – rich feeding without either the dangers of the sea or the physiological stresses of entering and leaving it. Often fresh-water lakes seem to provide a perfectly acceptable alternative to the sea, as if it was the environment of a large area of food-filled still water that was important to fish, rather than anything to do with its salinity *per se*.

If conditions are generally much better at sea, why do so many fish remain behind in fresh water long after hatching, rather than moving down to the estuary at the earliest possible opportunity? Young pink and chum salmon set out to sea as soon as they swim up from the gravel, so do a few sockeye, but most other salmon and trout wait much longer. Charr spend up to thirteen years in Arctic lakes before heading down to the estuary for the first time, and in the north of their range Atlantic salmon may be seven before their systems send them seawards. Of course the salmon have not reached the critical size of 10–15 cm (4–6 in) until this age, but why do they need to grow so large at all if pinks and chums can go to sea when they are only 3 cm (1 in) long? If food is really the driving force, why do not all members of all anadromous species at least eventually set their sights on the sea, even if not as soon as they emerge? It is certainly true that if at least some fish out of a population go to sea, this leaves more food than would otherwise be available for those that stay behind, but at best this is only part of a complex, many-sided answer to a complex, many-sided question.

Meanwhile, it seems that, along its evolutionary road, each species has balanced the advantages of early migration and faster growth against the price of greater dangers at sea and the strains of entering it at a young age. Some species have decided this is a price worth paying, while others have decided it is not. The optional migrants in between are still deciding, and in the meantime some from each species migrate and others stay behind where they were born.

The timing of their movements between fresh and sea water seems to suggest that, while better feeding may be an important component in a fish's urge to migrate, it is not the only one. At polar and temperate latitudes, where the differences between summer and winter are far more extreme than they are closer to the equator, the changing climate affects the food supplies of almost every creature. Ducks, geese and wading birds, which have moved up to the Arctic to breed, fly south as soon as their young have fledged – being able to fly allows them to reach the tropics in a few weeks. Caribou move south too, down to the tree line where they can scrape a winter's existence out of the meagre vegetation. Other less mobile animals simply go to sleep – which is almost the way of many fish. Yet, far from leaving the sparser environment of fresh water when its food supplies begin to dwindle, this is precisely when sea-going fish choose to return, starving themselves in the process and thus often hastening their deaths. Their return is presumably timed to try and ensure that their offspring emerge the following year, at the same time as most insects hatch. This usually works out, but then the next year or the year after, just when the feeding in the river is approaching its richest, the great exodus of silvering smolts begins.

It may be fair to assume that all aspects of a creature's life strategy have evolved as aids to successful breeding and the production of the most offspring. No salmonids spawn in the sea, and those that have been wandering the ocean are driven back into fresh water by the urge to reproduce close to where they themselves were hatched. By then they are far larger than they would have been had they remained in fresh water and this in itself confers many reproductive advantages, particularly, it seems, on females. Eggs are much bulkier than the male's sperm, which in itself allows small males to fertilise the eggs of large females. Larger females lay larger eggs. From these hatch larger offspring, which are more likely to survive than the young of females stunted by a lifetime's dependence on fresh-water food supplies. Larger fish can bury their eggs deeper in the gravel. They are also likely to be more successful in securing territories and mates, and then able to defend their nests against subsequent spawners for longer.

Sometimes these large sea-going fish, particularly the Pacific salmon, appear to have become victims of the success of their own way of life. When thousands of breeding adults eventually arrive at the gravel beds together, the competition for spawning space is intense. Eggs may fail to hatch and many newly emerged alevins die. Then one is tempted to wonder whether, in fact, the interests of the species would not be equally well served if they all remained in fresh water, not growing so large and laying fewer eggs. Still, on balance, the price of going to sea seems to be worth paying – only marginally, but it is on the narrowest of margins such as these, that evolutionary success ultimately depends.

Their popularity as game or food fish, as well as their amazing adaptability, has meant that no fish have been more widely distributed around the world than brown and rainbow trout. There are also populations of Pacific salmon far beyond their natural boundaries, and odd outposts of brook and Arctic charr. Whether stocked in pursuit of profit or pleasure, one could still hope to find some clues in the behaviour of these colonists to the role of genes in triggering the migratory urge. But if there are any such clues, they are proving almost impossibly elusive. When fish are transplanted to strange waters, the conditions in their new environment nearly always seem to override any genetic predisposition to behave in a particular way.

There are not enough records of introduced rainbow trout having taken up steelhead habits from which to draw any conclusions at all. Probably the only sea-going populations of introduced Atlantic salmon are in the Faroes, other than those re-established in the course of river restoration programmes. Despite the massive effort to persuade the various species of Pacific salmon to set themselves up in alien territory, there remain very few stocks which actually satisfy their migratory urges by going to sea, rather than simply passing their growing years in a fresh-water lake. Only brown trout have shown something of their versatility in taking their migratory capabilities with them when transported to new environments, and starting truly self-sustaining sea-going populations. In the process they have also emphasised that fish born of sea-going parents are scarcely more likely to migrate than if they were the offspring of small resident fish with no discernible trace of sea trout in their lineage.

Tweed sea trout provided the eggs for the second successful shipment of trout ova to Australia in 1866. From the 500 that hatched are descended many of the trout in Australia's rivers today, almost none of which migrate to sea. New Zealand also relied on this stock for its first trout. After countless subsequent importations of eggs from both migratory and non-migratory parents, it now has several self-sustaining stocks of sea-going fish, particularly on South Island – although fish in many apparently suitable rivers still do not migrate. Introductions into the rivers of the Falkland Islands, Tierra del Fuego and southern South America have been generally successful in establishing self-sustaining populations of sea trout. These are principally descended from ova of non-migratory Chilean stocks, although in all these rivers there are also many small fish which never leave fresh water. In the northern hemisphere, brown trout introduced into several

Canadian rivers have found conditions conducive to the development of their sea-going habits, but there is barely any correlation between the behaviour of parents and offspring. Other species show the same disregard for the habits of their parents, and the self-sustaining populations of introduced Pacific salmon have nearly all suppressed their migratory urges, seeing out their lives in fresh water despite being descended from thousands of generations of sea-going ancestors.

Amidst all this confusion it is at least possible to point with more certainty to the influence of temperature on migratory inclinations. These warm water undoubtedly curbs, whether the fish are indigenous or introduced. Towards the southern end of their native range, brown trout are much less migratory than they are in more northerly latitudes, while in New Zealand and South America the reverse is the case. None of the Arctic charr from British or central European lakes goes to sea, nor do those from New England or southern Canada. The most distinctive populations of non-migratory Atlantic salmon are those from Maine, and no brook charr south of Maine migrate either. Even amongst masu salmon there is a marked tendency for both males and females to complete their lives in fresh water towards the warmer end of their range, while further north, only males do so.

In all these cases the higher temperature of the lake outflow or of the river's lower reaches seems enough to tip the scales in favour of staying put, and the danger or discomfort from warm water clearly outweighs the perceived advantages of a spell at sea. When water temperatures rise the dissolved oxygen content falls, and as salt water contains less oxygen than fresh, even if fish can tolerate conditions in the river they may become too distressed at sea. Thermal regimes may also affect the timing of migrations. Atlantic salmon in France must time their passage through the Loire to ensure that they reach its cooler headwaters before the summer overheats the lower reaches. Pink salmon returning to spawn in Arctic streams are genetically programmed to reach them before the water begins freezing solid, as are their young to move south before the sea ices over.

This downstream inhospitability, which seems to confine European Arctic charr to the depths of glacial still waters and deters Atlantic salmon from leaving lakes in New England, may sometimes be responsible for landlocking populations of introduced Pacific salmon. Where fish are already close to their upper thermal limits, the extra degree or two of the river's temperature may be enough to suppress the urges of even these most committed migrants, and keep them in the lake over the summer. Yet while a warming world may very gradually be curtailing the sea-going inclinations of some fish in the south of their species range, it also unfreezes northern waters which were once inaccessible. Animals must continually adapt to changing climates, and salmonids and their ancestors have been doing so for tens of millions of years. Birds respond in the same way, only faster and more visibly. Curlews and lesser black-backed gulls are now far more inclined to overwinter in Britain than they were thirty years ago, shunning the dangers of migration, as are many British breeding ducks like wigeon, gadwall, teal and pintail.

Much more than high or rising temperatures is needed to explain the near-total failure of Pacific or Atlantic salmon to establish sea-going populations anywhere outside their native range. Of the millions of pink salmon ova introduced along the coasts of northern Russia, Scandinavia and eastern America, only round the White Sea and off the Norwegian coast have there been any signs of the beginnings of a permanent population. Coho may be breeding in the Kerguelen Islands, which are in the far south of the Indian Ocean on the same latitude as the Falklands, but information on their status there is hard to find. All deliberate efforts to bring chinook into Europe and South America failed totally, as did those to introduce them to Australia. In a great victory for hope over expectation, chinook were also released in many of the same New England rivers from which their Atlantic cousins had been almost driven to extinction.

It is possible that chinook are now gaining tenuous holds in some Chilean rivers after escaping from fish farms. With the expansion of salmon ranching on both sides of the equator there are countless other opportunities for exotic species to get out of the confines of their cages and head up strange fresh waters with every intention of trying to breed in the wild. No doubt, after all the massive deliberate efforts to expand the range of these exotic fish, some of these escapees will now set themselves up, without any further human help, just where they are not wanted. But it takes several generations to be able to say with any certainty that a fish population looks set for survival, and it remains the case that the only firmly established stock of sea-going salmon in the southern hemisphere are the chinook of the South Island of New Zealand.

The New Zealand chinook are known as 'quinnat', and are largely descended from fish introduced just after the turn of the century. They run mainly up east coast rivers from north of Christchurch down to the southern tip of South Island. It is suggested that the particular characteristics of the Southland Current favour the salmon when at sea, and are also conducive to their finding their way back home again. Huge amounts of money and energy have been spent in trying to introduce other species of salmon into New Zealand. These have resulted in founding a fairly secure stock of lake-dwelling sockeye, a rather tenuous population of landlocked Atlantic salmon and no populations of migratory rainbow trout at all. So unless there is something about the sea that particularly favours chinook over other species of fish, the Southland Current seems unlikely to have contributed to the quinnat's success, and its reasons remain tantalisingly obscure – as do the reasons for the failure of the other transplants.

The comparative ease with which transplanted brown trout take up sea-going habits has prompted the suggestion that longer-distance migrants, like most salmon, may become disoriented at sea; rainbow trout wander far out to sea too, and the dearth of steelhead in the southern hemisphere supports this idea (see Chapter 8). No matter how perfect the fresh-water environment is for the early stages of their lives, these far-ranging fish may simply be unable to find their way home. Another reason put forward to account for the chinook's success in New Zealand is that the fish are all descended from ocean-type stock (see Chapter 10), which do not usually wander far from the estuary and so are less likely to get lost. Against this, however, are arrayed the results of experiments involving the importation of Atlantic salmon of Baltic origin into New Zealand; these are not natural long-distance migrants either, but wherever they went once they reached the sea, they never returned. Similarly, nowhere beyond the boundaries of their native range have brook charr adopted a migratory life, and they too never naturally stray far from the estuary.

From the failures and successes of all these translocations of different trout and salmon, what conclusions can be drawn? Almost none, except to stress that whether born of fresh-water-resident or migratory parents, all salmon, trout and charr appear to be able to lead a different life from the one their parents led. They also all still retain the ability to live out their lives in fresh water. At the edges of their range, warmer waters often seem to stifle migratory inclinations, but otherwise the comparative influences of genes and environment, or the specific pressures which coerce fish into one life or another, remain little understood. Where migratory fish have failed to establish themselves, it is not usually

for want of satisfactory breeding grounds nor because conditions do not favour the young – and if Nature is deemed deficient, fish can be reared to any size artificially anyway. Millions of young fish have reached the sea, having gone through the smolting stage first, and naturally hatched fish may still be doing so, but once they get there, some other forces take over. These either so disorientate the fish that their otherwise extraordinary powers of navigation are rendered utterly useless, or simply sweep the smolts off so fast and far that they are physically unable to return. Salmon have been liberated into New Zealand's rivers at every stage in their lives, from eyed ova to mature adults. Yet despite this colossal effort, the numbers that have found their way home are now scarcely even consistent with the random returns from trial and error. Only in the case of the South Island quinnat have enough come back to found self-sustaining populations.

How fish navigate their way for thousands of kilometres around vast areas of open, featureless water for up to four years, often at depths where light hardly penetrates, continually changing direction in search of food or to flee from bigger fish, is still a mystery. Their success is patently obvious, but the faculties and abilities they use to achieve it are not. The workings of their homing instincts and the forces guiding them back to their birthplace once they fall under the influence of the estuary are perhaps more easily explained. Yet to what extent these are genetically or environmentally controlled is not yet understood.

The instinct to return to breed in fresh water is certainly inherited, but how much further environmental conditioning is needed to imprint upon the fish the idea of a 'home stream'? And when does that conditioning begin? If salmon inherited pre-programmed notions of the specific attractions of their natal streams, then it would have been impossible to introduce them into streams other than those for which they were programmed. Atlantic salmon may certainly have proved impossible to establish south of the equator. However, in the course of river restoration programmes within their native range, fry or ova from one river system introduced into another have repeatedly come back to the river of their introduction and founded self-sustaining populations, rather than pursuing some inherited vision of a far-off Shangri-La and never being seen again.

Few fish ever know their parents – young cichlids cared for in their parents' mouths are probably the best example of those that do – and all Pacific and most Atlantic salmon are actually dead before their eggs have hatched. When fry first emerge from the gravel, experience has yet to temper their actions, and their first movements must be born exclusively of instinct. So many generations have passed since the end of the last Ice Age, which left most fish where they are today, that trout hatched above waterfalls must generally inherit tendencies not to migrate downstream. Fish bred in feeder streams running into a lake gradually move downstream to reach it, and this seems so obvious as to hardly require even instinct. Yet those born in the outflow need to inherit a very positive inclination to swim upstream, otherwise they too will be lost to the population for ever. And if, as they grow and start to head down their natal river, young salmon must rely on clues from the environment to enable them to return, they certainly inherit much of the ability to programme these clues for later use.

When fish finally abandon the last influences of fresh water, they must have some inherited idea of how they will exploit the ocean. Arctic charr or cutthroat trout are programmed not to stray far from the estuary, not least because they almost always return to their home river in the autumn. They may never even move beyond the river mouth's influence, and so possess less refined navigational skills than the true wanderers. Ocean-

Chinook spawning on Double-Hill flats, New Zealand.
(Andrew Hendry)

type chinook and coho go further, but often not beyond the edge of the continental shelf. If the poorer navigators among them can still find their way home, natural selection will not have favoured those with the spectacular orientation powers of steelhead, sockeye and Atlantic salmon.

True long-distance migrants clearly know they are destined to travel far out into the ocean's vastness. They may also have some inherited idea of their ultimate destination, and use their navigational powers to reach it. Alternatively, they may simply surrender to the ocean's forces, which carry them in a great circle, eventually returning them back where they started. This somewhat simplistic sounding idea is the basis of the gyre theory, which seeks to explain both the success of marine migrations in the northern hemisphere and the failure to establish migrating populations of salmon in the southern. The earth's rotations set up a series of circular currents, shaped, in the north, by the continental land masses on either side of the Atlantic and Pacific Oceans. In the southern Pacific, the African and South American boundaries are so far from New Zealand that there are no really distinct circular forces around its shores, and, so the theory continues, once the sea-bound smolts get into the current, it carries them off on a one-way journey from which they have no way of return.

The particular characteristics of a current are especially apparent at its edges, where salinity, temperature or turbidity is in most obvious contrast to the water beyond. These contrasts help keep fish within the current, and by joining these circulating gyres salmon may be able to complete successful migrations around the Atlantic and Pacific Oceans. The gyre theory allows fish to leave the current to exploit particularly rich feeding areas, before rejoining it again, and eventually being delivered back where they started. Once they near their home stream, a highly developed sense of smell may then tell them it is time to abandon the current in exchange for the influence of the estuary once again.

Salmon have been shown to possess many other powers of navigation, and it would be surprising if their possession was superfluous to survival at sea – which blind reliance on the gyre theory suggests they are. Exactly which of these other powers is most important is not known, and may never be. Probably it is their combination which works so effectively. The difficulty with demonstrating the importance of, say, the sun in helping fish find their way is the need first to deprive them of all other possible aids to successful navigation. This means somehow preventing them from detecting changes in magnetic fields, temperature, pressure or the water's chemical composition, and is usually impossible — or can only be achieved by first rendering fish near-senseless wrecks.

As a fish swims through the marine wasteland, it almost certainly uses a combination of environmental cues, interpreting them with the aid of different skills and faculties. Some of these cues will be more important than others, and some skills more critical, and in the end a successful return to the stream of its birth is a victory for the co-operation of its senses.

In the course of its oceanic odyssey, a fish may be able to pick up and retain information which is stored, sequentially, on a mental map that the fish is then able to reverse on its return. Rolling up the outward journey is an attractive idea although there is now no doubt that, even if they can do this, fish can still find their way home by using other skills. Although most sockeye smolts leaving the Fraser River move northwards through the Strait of Georgia, between British Columbia and Vancouver Island, many of them then return through the Juan de Fuca Strait, between the island and the coast of Washington. The route they choose seems to be affected by the temperature in the Gulf of Alaska, which itself largely determines where the salmon are when they begin their return journey. In warmer years sockeye are inclined to close into the shore further north, and return down the Strait of Georgia. They also tend to reach the river later than usual, presumably because they were further away when they began to head home.

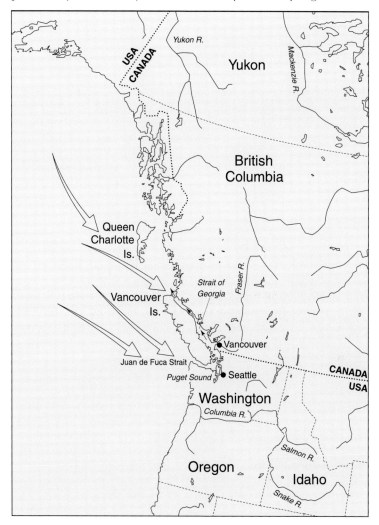

The outward (small arrows) and return (large arrows) migrations of Fraser River sockeye. Nearly all smolts reach the open ocean via the Strait of Georgia, but as adults may return through either the Strait of Georgia or Juan de Fuca Strait.

It is no use fish being able to create a mental map without having the power to read it, and to orientate along the paths it dictates. The sun, and even the moon, may help salmon on their journeys, but on their own these are useless aids. Just as someone trying to navigate by the sun also needs a watch or a way of measuring shadows, so fish must be able to compensate for its shifting position throughout the day. This implies that they have some internal biological clock, and possibly also a calendar, to help them interpret the signs from the sky. Anyway, there is a limit to the use of celestial cues, because they are so often hidden by horizons or clouds, and blinded fish have shown that they can continue finding their way at least around inland waters.

As if in defiance of these attempts to desensitise them, fish deprived of the powers of both sight and smell show that they are still able to orientate themselves. Magnetic particles have been discerned along salmon's lateral lines and magnetic-sensitive receptor cells in their nose, and their existence could point to the contribution of magnetic or electric fields to successful navigation. Is it even possible that in fact the whole essence of fish migration is still hidden in some set of environmental signals whose modes of transmission and reception as yet both remain undetected? Is there a sixth or seventh ichthyological sense which its possessors have yet to reveal?

Science may be on surer ground in stressing the role of the salmon's olfactory powers in guiding fish once they reach the influence of fresh water. Salmonids have prominent twin nostrils on the front of their heads, leading into nasal cavities where water is swilled around, stimulating the epithelium. These transmit messages to the brain, which then initiates any necessary response – eat, do not eat, swim on up the river or hold up where you are. There is no denying the efficiency of this sense of smell, but the possible role of the sense of taste is often ignored. There is no anatomical link between mouth and nasal sacs, but the connection between a fish's senses of taste and smell is much closer than it is in other vertebrates. Both can be stimulated by substances dissolved in the surrounding water. By using their sense of smell fish can detect food without being able to see it, and they may also be able to taste it from a distance with the help of some sort of taste buds in their skin.

The abilities of trout, charr, and particularly salmon, to find their way home have long been recognised although how they do so with such precision is still not proved. Cro-Magnon man may not have asked himself whether the Atlantic salmon he had just scooped out of the gravel shallows of a Pyrenean stream with his bare hands was actually born there too; but at least by 1653 Izaak Walton was able to write in *The Compleat Angler* of 'tying a riband . . . or thread in the tail of smolts and catching them again when they came back to the same place'. That their sense of smell is crucial to a successful return seems to have been generally accepted since Frank Buckland, always far ahead of his time, expressed the thought in *British Fishes* (1880) that:

> Doubtless, to the fish each river has got its own smell; taste, flavour it has hitherto been called, but this, I think, is a wrong expression, as a salmon's tongue has hooks upon it and is not so sensitive as the tongue of land animals; in fact it is more an organ of prehension than of taste. When the salmon is coming in from the sea he smells about till he scents the water of his own river. This guides him in the right direction, and he has only to follow up the scent, in other words to 'follow his nose', to get up into fresh water, i.e., if he is in a travelling humour. Thus a salmon coming up from the sea into the Bristol Channel would get a smell of water, meeting him; 'I am a Wye salmon,' he would say to himself. 'This is not the Wye water: it's the wrong tap, it's the Usk, I must go a few miles further on' and he gets up steam again.

There must be a moment in any salmon's successful migration when it first senses its natal stream – a final endorsement of its phenomenal powers of navigation and a signal that its oceanic wanderings are nearly over. From that moment on, a fish can shelve away many of the abilities it relied upon in the open sea, and start using its sense of smell to detect the chemical composition of its ancestral waters. Experiments to test salmon's sensitivity to particular odours have proved that they respond to concentrates of human, bear, sea-lion and many other creatures, as well as to artificial compounds to which they were introduced as smolts. Salmon have been shown to recognise their home water in extraordinarily weak dilutions, and may in fact be able to sense that they are nearing their own estuary from hundreds, perhaps thousands of kilometres out to sea – even while still coasting along on their oceanic gyre.

Returning fish often appear to 'sample' nearby estuaries. Interpreting this as an indicator of olfactory confusion, suggesting that in fact fish are not so adept at finding their way home after all, is risky. It assumes that fish up the 'wrong' estuary have indeed made a mistake, and are not about some other deliberate business, like escaping from what they perceive as unfavourable conditions in their natal stream. Anyway, most of these fish sampling strange estuaries eventually return to the 'right' one, and on average – a very sweeping average – less than 5 per cent carry on to spawn in a different river system from the one in which they were born.

Straying is actually as critical to the future of a species as homing. If fish were fixed unerringly on the stream of their birth, and refused ever to enter any other, they would never have moved out of the refuges to which the Ice Ages confined them. It is the very act of ignoring their birthplace, either deliberately or accidentally, which has made them so successful. For all the strength of their homing instincts, the various species of salmonids also seem to have been urged to follow the retreating Ice Age, dropping populations off as they continued pushing northwards and expanding their ranges. For fish so strongly programmed to return to the redds of their birth, spawning elsewhere seems to require them to suppress their natural instincts in an apparently unnatural way. Yet only by having done just that do salmon, trout and charr come to be where they are today.

Almost the whole of their present range has been colonised within the last 15,000 years, and the process still goes on. As a result of the untypical actions of a small proportion of strayers, salmon, trout and charr have spread over much of the northern hemisphere. The future of a species is never better secured than by its being scattered widely across the Earth's surface, and the far-ranging distribution of many salmonids is largely due to their being able to survive in both fresh water and the sea. True fresh-water fish, unable to tolerate more than slightly salty water, were certainly able to expand their ranges by riding on the floods of melting snow and glacial ice – and many members of the carp family reached Britain that way. However, they are not nearly so widespread as anadromous fish, and few fresh-water species are found on both sides of the Atlantic.

Straying has also helped fish to recolonise rivers from which they have been driven by earthquakes, volcanic eruptions and other environmental upheavals, as well as to expand into new areas. Atlantic salmon strayed from the River Leven and repopulated the upper reaches of the Clyde after the treatment of sewage and other effluent had made these tolerable for fish once more. Pink salmon are sometimes said to be the least faithful of their genus to their natal stream, perhaps because they spend so little time in it. Their rapid spread throughout the Great Lakes was certainly inconsistent with any degree of fidelity to the area of their introduction; so was their expansion around the White Sea from the stocking sites on the Kola Peninsula. Pink salmon also recolonised the Fraser River after the Hell's Gate landslides in 1914. Perhaps salmon gradually start to forget the scent of their home stream as they get older, because evidence points to older salmon straying more than younger ones. This would seem to make the eighteen-month-old pink salmon less prone to wander. As with all other migrants which stray into strange rivers, the crucial, unanswered, and perhaps unanswerable, question is are they actually lost or have they found conditions in the new river preferable to those where they were born?

What is certainly not yet identified is the actual essence in the home stream waters that stimulates the fish's senses – a substance with near-mystical properties that so often has to proclaim its presence through the obfuscating dilution of human and industrial waste. After up to four years at sea, fish must still be able to scent this essence, and because mature fish usually return to a river later in the year than they left, its production must be constant enough for them to home in on it at any time of the year. Yet, for all its attractions, this elixir must only lure back those fish born under its influence, not those that were not.

The old idea that fish are imprinted with the distinctive scent or flavour of their own river – a chemical cocktail derived from the plants and rocks which the water washes on its way to the sea – still seems to retain most credibility. The existence of any detectable distinction between the waters of adjacent rivers flowing out of geologically similar catchments is almost incomprehensible to humans, conditioned by their own very limited powers of smell. However this lack of any significant difference may be exactly why fish often seem to make false starts up the 'wrong' river.

A further popular theory proposes that fish are drawn back to their natal stream by pheromones secreted by the mucus of others of the same population. The thought that salmonids may be attracted by the secretions of their own young is especially appealing. It seems particularly valid for fish, like Arctic charr, which regularly breed more than once, and may still find the offspring of their first spawning in the river when they return to spawn again. For those species that die immediately after spawning, the pheromone theory requires that the juveniles of a specific population of a river are able to emit their own distinct chemical signals, even when at sea, which are only recognisable by returning adults of the same population. The evidence for this theory is somewhat tenuous. It is not supported by the many instances of fish returning successfully after being introduced into previously fishless rivers, nor by the homing of pink salmon. When these return to spawn towards the end of their rigid two-year life-cycles, there are often no other pink salmon of any age in either the river or the estuary.

Small upland streams are as close to pure as running water ever is. They are scarcely tainted by dissolved substances to guide a fish back home. Further down, the current slows and the stream is joined by others, each adding its own distinctive contribution to the water's make-up. By the time a returning fish nears the estuary, it is likely to find the influence of its natal trickle on the water's chemical composition almost unrecognisable. Therefore being able to detect the scent of the water in which they were born seems of very little use to fish without a similar ability to identify the lower stretches of their river, which will be what they first sense on coming back to spawn. Fish then need to be able to recognise the different scents of the water at every junction on their upstream journey. In fact what they need to have done on their way down is to have absorbed – sequentially imprinted – a map of the river's changing chemistry, which they can then reverse as they make their way back home. Fry trapped at the top of their river, and then released near the estuary, become confused on their return, almost certainly through having been denied the sensory clues on their downstream journey.

Nearly all experiments support the importance of the smolting stages of a fish's fresh-water life as a period when it is supremely receptive to the chemical signals from the river. Increased levels of the hormone thyroxin may be largely responsible for raising the fish's sensitivity. Fish hatched in one stream or stretch of water and released in another almost invariably try to home to the scene of their release, only moving on to their birthplace if this is further up the same stream. However, important though the smolting period almost

Atlantic salmon returning to spawn in Canada's Dartmouth River.
(Gilbert van Ryckevorsel)

certainly is in imprinting young fish with the distinctive character of their natal stream, evidence from the first fresh-water migrations of sockeye suggests it is not the only critical period.

As soon as most sockeye have emerged, and are no longer dependent on their yolk sacs for food, the current carries them down to the lake which is to serve as their nursery for the next year, and sometimes two. Then they smolt and head to sea. On their return as mature adults, sockeye nearly always manage to find their way back to their natal stream to spawn. Yet when they left this stream they were only hours out of their gravel. It therefore seems that, at least to some extent, fish become ingrained with the character of the water while they lurk, as tiny alevins, in the darkness amongst the stones. Coho and Atlantic salmon may also move some distance downstream from their birthplace before their spring smolt, and still manage to return to the stretch of river from which they emerged.

The first outward sign that a fish is set for the sea is the gradual coating of the parr's distinctive fingermarks with guanin, a light-reflecting substance secreted by guanophores. Thyroid activity is likely to prompt the silvering, but whether this hormonal output results

from, or causes, the start of smolting, is not clear. Guanin's secretion increases in time with reductions in the production of other pigments, and so fish gradually lose the browny hues that allowed them to shelter against backgrounds of rocks and stones, and take on silvery-blue colours to camouflage them in the open sea. At the same time they begin to acquire a more streamlined shape, and also show changes in behaviour. Gone is the aggression with which salmon and trout defended their territories, its place taken by a more sociable nature, causing them to seek the company – and perhaps the protection – of other members of their species. The tendency to face into the current and watch for food is replaced by a gradual surrender to its downstream forces, and the acceptance that where it leads is where the fish should go

Fish which live in both fresh and sea water need much more than just the inclination to move from one to the other, and a change in colour. They must also be physically and physiologically able to cope with the two environments. In streams and rivers, all fish's body fluids are much more chemically concentrated than the surrounding water. A fish therefore automatically absorbs water osmotically through the thin permeable linings of its mouth and gills. This excess fluid needs to be excreted, and is filtered through the kidneys and then expelled as very dilute urine. In the sea, the direction of osmotic flow is

Sockeye massing before spawning in one of the feeder streams of Lake Iliamna, Alaska.
(Greg Ruggerone)

reversed because the water is now chemically much stronger than the fish's body tissue, and the natural tendency is for the fish to lose fluid. To compensate for this, it needs to swallow sea water, which is then absorbed into its system through stomach and intestine. The kidneys are thus required to reverse their function, expelling the excess salt in small quantities of very concentrated urine and conserving the swallowed water to make up for the extra loss. To help the kidneys, salmonids have evolved specialised gill cells, whose function is also to secrete surplus salt at sea.

Some fish just go as far as the estuary and are able to survive there without passing through the smolt stage. Brown trout that make these limited migrations are called 'slob' or bull trout, and seem to reap the benefits of richer feeding without undergoing any of the changes normally associated with the movement from river to sea (see Chapter 4). Full-strength sea water is about three times more saline than a trout's blood, so if estuary water is more than a third sea, trout start to lose water. By remaining in fresher water than that for most of the time, perhaps only straying into saltier water at very high tide for a few hours, their bodies will not be required to make any great concessions to these brackish conditions.

All animals are able to respond to changing environmental pressures — and their evolutionary histories show them continually doing so. The end of the Ice Age was a cataclysmic event that could be exploited to the full by creatures able to do so, but threatened others that could not. That salmonids were able to respond in spectacular fashion largely explains why they are where they are today. Then fortune favoured the anadromous. Now fish in the middle of the migratory spectrum, which show genuine versatility in their choice of life options, may appear unsure whether their destinies lie upstream or down. On the other hand, they may be in the process of perfecting this versatility, and if evolution allows them to retain it their chances of survival can only be enhanced. Being able to complete a life without ever going to sea, and yet to be able spend time there if circumstances dictate, can only be to a species' advantage.

The habits of other fish which exploit both fresh-water and marine environments give an idea of the evolutionary alternatives which may be open to salmonids, and also place their lives in a wider perspective. In some part of the world or other, fish seem to be using both environments for breeding and feeding, in almost every conceivable combination.

With teeth specifically designed to scrape algae off stones, ayu are the most popular fresh-water fish in Japan. They spawn in the lower reaches of rivers, and immediately after hatching the larvae are swept down to sea where they spend the winter. In spring they leave the sea and swim back up the river, far beyond their birthplace, to feed for the summer, before dropping back down to spawn – and die – near the sea. The migrations of the ayu transcend the boundary between fresh and sea water, and yet they are not specifically driven by either the feeding or the breeding urge, and as such are particularly unusual. Normally, migrations entail a more specific movement between a breeding and feeding environment, even if they take fish no further than the estuary. Barramundi (Australian sea bass) are close to living catadromous lives, but they only come downstream as far as the estuary before spawning. There the young spend their first year before heading up river, sometimes as far as 800 km (500 miles), to feed and fatten to maturity.

Far more species of fish visit the estuary to feed rather than to spawn, either from further out at sea, or from up the river. Sheefish seldom move very far beyond the brackish waters of northern river mouths on their feeding expeditions, before returning back upstream to breed; nor do most sturgeon. Other species approach the estuary from the other direction; many young mullet (Mugillidae) and flounders are hatched in the open ocean, but move quickly inshore to nourish themselves on the rich feeding to be found there. A few species can tolerate waters of varying strengths of salinity, but use the ability to help them survive in extreme environments rather than to cross the boundaries between sea and fresh water. Desert pupfish are able to live in the trickles of the Arizona desert, where at some times of the year the water is fresh and at others much saltier than the sea.

The sturgeon family is an ancient one. Fossils over 100 million years old are little different from some of the twenty-five species in the four genera which today comprise Acipenseridae. They grow to a huge size, reportedly over 1,000 kg (2,200 lb) and may live beyond a hundred. Like the Salmonidae, all species spawn in fresh water, but several spend most of their lives at sea. The young of some species mature in rivers and lakes for several years, while others, including apparently the beluga, head almost immediately down to sea after hatching. The only species which occasionally turns up in British waters is the common or Baltic sturgeon, with habits very similar to those of the Atlantic salmon. It stops feeding as soon as it enters fresh water and spawns on gravel beds, relying on the sticky surface of the eggs to keep them there rather than excavating a nest. After spawning, the spent fish then drift back down to sea, sometimes dying on the way. There are several landlocked populations which never go to sea, and all species of the genus *Scaphirhynchus* spend the whole of their lives in fresh water. As a family, the sturgeon are less marine than the Salmonidae, and unlike most salmon, adult sturgeon tend not to stray far from the river mouth.

Perhaps most intriguing of all anadromous fish are the much studied sticklebacks, which show a range of salt-water tolerance and migratory behaviour very similar to the Salmonidae. Both families are also noted for the variety within a single species, which has made the description of those species such a contentious issue. Sticklebacks breed when they are one or at the latest two, and then die, so completing their generations much faster than most trout, salmon or charr. This makes their evolutionary paths much easier to follow than those of longer-lived species like chinook salmon, which could be six or seven when they spawn, or Arctic charr from the far north that may be thirteen before doing so for the first time.

There are arguably eight species of sticklebacks. They are diverse enough to be divided into five genera, mainly distinguished by the number of their spines. The fifteen-spined (sea) stickleback is a totally marine species which never enters fresh water at any stage of its life. Other species are partially or totally dependent on fresh water. The three-spined is probably the most versatile and adaptable fish in the world, and, like brown trout in particular, varies as much in colour as it does in its life.

Three-spined sticklebacks are spread through the combined ranges of the Pacific and Atlantic salmon as well as round some of the northernmost territory of the Arctic charr. They are likely to have followed the retreating ice in much the same way as the salmonids did. Defying its name, this species may have as many as four spines or none at all, as well as varying numbers of rays in its fins. Instead of scales, their bodies are covered in a series of bony interlocking plates, of which there may be up to twenty-five, although occasionally they are absent altogether. Whether environment or heredity governs the numbers of spines or scales is as unclear as it ever is, but they vary consistently between fish with different habits.

The typical stickleback of childhood is a fresh-water creature that may turn up in

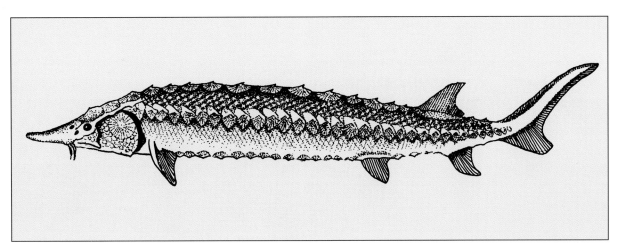

Common (Baltic) sturgeon.

almost any lake, river or ditch. It is renowned for the male's brilliant spawning dress and some of his extraordinary breeding habits, particularly his nest building and the unusually conscientious care of his offspring (which may even extend to rounding up any strays in his mouth and spitting them back into the nest). But three-spined sticklebacks are equally at home in the estuary, and, unlike trout, there are also some populations that spend all their lives at sea. These are usually much better endowed with bony plates and spines than their fresh-water fellows, and while their nest-building habits bring them into coastal pools and estuarine shallows to breed, their home is otherwise the open sea. On account of these differences, sea-dwellers were given their own species and called rough-tailed sticklebacks (*Gasterosteus trachurus*) to distinguish them from the fresh-water smooth-tailed sticklebacks (*Gasterosteus leirus*). There are other populations which are truly anadromous, adults overwintering at sea and then migrating into fresh water in late winter or early spring. Being so small they do not usually travel far upstream to breed, the young then returning to sea in the autumn together with any adults that have survived spawning.

Nine-spined sticklebacks are even more widespread than their three-spined cousins. They seem less tolerant of full-strength sea and more at home in underwater vegetation than in the open streams which the three-spined favours. Otherwise they too certainly deserve to be described as anadromous and have used their sea-going faculties to great effect, spreading all the way round the shores of the Arctic Ocean as well as far down the Atlantic and Pacific coasts.

Like the Salmonidae, Gasterosteidae is a family of fish showing almost the whole range of migratory behaviour, the advantages of tolerating sea water being only too self-evident from the distribution maps of the anadromous species. The sticklebacks, particulary the three-spined, stretch the range of life options even wider. At one end are fish which even breed at sea without any recourse to fresh water at all, while at the other are fish that never leave fresh water. Yet for all the versatility of the species, three-spined sticklebacks, as individuals, adapt less easily than salmonids to the different environments of sea and fresh water, and depend on quite drastic internal physiological changes to ready them for the move from one to the other. The species which is today a three-spined stickleback may be even closer to fragmenting into two or more pieces than the brown trout is – and incidentally perhaps then reverting to the nomenclature of old which divided fish into smooth- or rough-tailed sticklebacks, according to their affinities for fresh water or the sea.

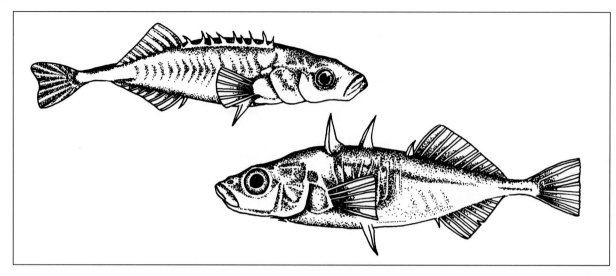

Changing climates are one of the most powerful forces driving evolution, compelling creatures to expand and contract their ranges, dividing and merging populations. Where life is easy, and fish are not coerced into change then, like coelacanths which have scarcely altered in the last 350 million years, they can afford the luxury of staying as they are. However, just as salmon, trout and charr have done, sticklebacks have surged back and forth on the frontiers of melting ice rather than resting on their fins on the bottom of the tropical Indian Ocean. They have had to change and adapt and are still doing so. Three-spined sticklebacks are even more flexible than brown trout, but Nature seems reluctant to tolerate too much flexibility for long, and there are few real generalists in the underwater world. So perhaps the price of true eventual change is that the individuals of a species must lose the very versatility which once allowed them to change, and the salmon, trout and charr will have to opt for either fresh-water or marine lives.

Nine- and three-spined sticklebacks.

Yet there are unavoidable paradoxes in these evolutionary stories. At one end of this continuum of migratory behaviour are pink and chum salmon, whose young rush to leave fresh water with an urgency that suggests the future of their species must lie in the sea. At the other end are lake charr, only a genus away from these salmon, for which evolution seems to be planning a fresh-water life. If every aspect of a creature's life is ultimately designed to improve the chances of the continuation of its species, how can evolution have driven such close relatives to reach such different conclusions as to what will best serve the interests of their descendants; and how could brown trout appear so confused over what is most advantageous for them? And when the Atlantic salmon is setting off on its ocean voyage, or as the lake charr is cruising around in the fresh-water gloom, either of them might pass European or American eels, convinced by the forces of their own evolution of the advantages of living and feeding in fresh water and breeding out at sea!

3
Atlantic salmon

There is just a chance that anyone crossing the Thames on one of London's bridges on a grey winter's afternoon may be passing over a salmon edging its way up river on the incoming tide. After 150 years of such pollution at the river's mouth that fishermen had as much chance of catching a swordfish as a salmon above its tidal limits, the Thames may now be entering the last phase of one of the most successful river restorations in the world. That ruination must inevitably precede restoration is a sad truism, but no river is ever dead; at worst it is merely comatose, with no sign of life but its flow, still nurturing the hope and possibility of revival – and thousands more miles of river all over Europe await the salmon's return.

Before the great technological leaps of the nineteenth century and the ensuing urbanisation and intensive farming, salmon swam up almost every northern Atlantic river they could breed in. From Portugal's Dourado northwards round the Atlantic, North Sea and Baltic coasts as far as the rivers emptying into the Barents Sea, salmon fulfilled their destinies in a world which had scarcely any use for the word 'pollute'. The Rhine was then the greatest of all Europe's salmon rivers, filling the nets of fishermen in Holland, France and Germany with huge harvests of returning fish. Even distant, landlocked Switzerland boasted salmon in some of its streams, as did the Czech Republic, whose melting snows nourished the Elbe and Oder.

On the other side of the Atlantic, the first humans to reach the east coast found streams thronged with prolific runs of sea-going shad, sturgeon and salmon. The Indians never over-exploited the resources upon which their very survival depended, and when the Europeans arrived salmon swam in the rivers of Connecticut, Massachusetts, New Hampshire and Maine, and as far south as the Housatonic River running into Long Island Sound. In Canada, the fish surged into almost every suitable east coast river as far up as Ungava Bay on the northern tip of Newfoundland at a latitude of 60°.

Despite the restoration of many one-time salmon rivers, today's map of where salmon swim is still so unlike Nature's original as to be almost unrecognisable. If there is any part of the Atlantic salmon's eastern range where its runs are still relatively unaffected by the industrial and commercial ravages of the last 200 years it is along the northern coast of Russia. There, extensive river-mouth netting has so far made little impact on salmon stocks, nor have the activities of visiting sport fishermen on the Kola Peninsula, who are required to return almost every fish they catch. Salmon range as far east as the northern spur of the Urals. Beyond this the sea is frozen for most of the year and there are several thousand miles of salmonless Asian coastline; this eventually merges into the western end of the Pacific salmon's range, where chum and pink salmon have colonised some of the rivers flowing into the East Siberian Sea.

Salmon stake nets on the Kola Peninsula in Russia.
(Peter Hutchinson)

Norway's Atlantic coast is riven with short, rushing rivers which have gouged out the deep valleys and fjords that now give the country such a jagged western outline. A combination of climate, geography and topography has kept these rivers free from industrial development and human overpopulation. In a country which is cold and dark for so much of the year, and average domestic electricity consumption is among the highest in the world, the rivers' potential for hydroelectric power could never have gone untapped, but with fish-ladders and dam bypasses many wild salmon still reach their ancestral gravel.

In the Baltic Sea, there is scarcely a trace of Finland's natural runs of salmon, their migrations having been brought to a shuddering halt by impassable hydroelectric dams. Much the same has happened on many of the rivers in northern Sweden, but to compensate for the destruction of natural stocks, Swedish power companies release huge numbers of reared smolts to be harvested as mature fish on their return to breed. Now over 90 per cent of the Baltic salmon catch is made up of ranched fish. This is a simple and highly effective method of exploiting the Baltic's rich marine life, even though other countries reap much of the benefit by netting fish in the open water. The smolts are released in the second spring of their lives and hardly ever venture out of the brackish Baltic waters, and nor do any of the fast-dwindling numbers of wild fish. The one great drawback to the ranching scheme, and to similar schemes involving different species of Pacific salmon in Alaska, Canada and Japan, is the unavoidable by-catch of wild salmon in the nets set for ranched fish (see Chapter 12). This can endanger the precious wild stocks which have managed to survive the construction of the dams, and which the ranched fish are intended to supplement, not replace.

There is hardly a salmon left in any of the rivers of the Low Countries of the Baltic, from Estonia right down to Denmark. With the turbulent political and economic histories of all the more easterly states, it is sad, but not surprising, that conservation of natural resources is so low on their list of national priorities. More could be expected of Germany and Denmark, and there are signs of concerted efforts to clean up many of their more polluted waterways, even though neither country is blessed with short fast-flowing rivers which are much easier to restore than those with long sluggish lower reaches.

The Rhine died a slower death than the Thames. As early as 1798, Samuel Taylor Coleridge was writing, on returning from Germany:

> The river Rhine it is well known
> Doth wash your city of Cologne.
> But tell me nymphs, what power divine,
> Shall henceforth wash the river Rhine?

Yet in 1885 at Kralingen, near Rotterdam, the nets still took 69,500 salmon averaging 8 kg (18 lb) each, and a few fish were still managing to struggle up the river at the end of the Second World War (apparently aided upstream by allied bombers' destruction of a huge weir that had once blocked their way!).

The Rhine's restoration is inevitably hampered by the international co-operation required from all the different countries whose streams ultimately find their way into that huge aquatic artery. The same must be said for many of Europe's other great river systems, but the unifying influence of the European Union may help reconcile competing national interests. This influence has also done much to raise environmental standards, with or without the additional powers of statutory sanctions, and may help even out the financial burden of expensive conservation controls.

The cool, short rivers of Brittany and Normandy provide France's finest natural habitat for salmon, and small numbers still find their way up to spawn each year. The once grossly polluted Elorn, discharging into the Rade de Brest, is an example of the potential for restoration that lies just beneath the oily surface of so many of Europe's waterways. Further south, in a triumph of the possible over the probable, a few salmon still struggle over fifteen dams, 800 km (500 miles) up the Loire to its headwaters in the Massif Central. They must now time their return to reach their natal stream before the summer heat, when the torpid lower stretches of the river warm to over 30°C, and become far too deoxygenated for salmon to negotiate.

The earliest scientific reference to salmon, in the first century AD, comes from the writings of the great Roman natural historian, Pliny the Elder. His extensive travels, either as soldier or scientist, took him all over Europe, and in his *Historia Naturalis* he describes how, even then, Gauls in Aquitaine extolled the gastronomic delights of the salmon. Perhaps they caught them in the Dordogne, which is now the subject of an ambitious programme to restore its long-gone salmon and sturgeon. Further south, the waters flowing quickly down from the chill heights of the Pyrenees are more hospitable, and on both sides of the Franco-Spanish border there are short rivers which salmon can still swim up to breed.

Spain is unique among European countries in continuing to forbid salmon netting in sea, estuary or river, but despite this – or perhaps perversely, even because of it – numbers of fish in the country's rivers are minimal. General Franco was a notoriously enthusiastic salmon fisherman, and along with the rest of his draconian social legislation, banned all commercial or subsistence fishing. The ban remains in force today and almost every pool on every river is watched continually throughout the season – as it needs to be, because during almost every hour the watcher watches, the fisherman fishes, and the angling pressures are now intense enough to threaten the future of the Spanish salmon as much as the nets ever did. Further round the Atlantic coastline, in Portugal, a few salmon still survive, and conservationists are endeavouring to re-establish them in many of the rivers where they once spawned prolifically.

As it rode the waves of national prosperity through the Industrial Revolution and beyond, Britain seemed quite content to offer up its natural aquatic inheritance in the cause of national affluence. Now, as if to atone for the sins of the fathers, the sons are often seen in the vanguard of attempts to conserve what has escaped the destructive power of industry and urbanisation, and even to try recreating the environment this replaced. Wolves, bears, beavers and elk are never likely to roam what is left of Britain's wild places again – they are simply not wild enough. Yet as long as rivers keep flowing there remains the possibility of reintroducing their original inhabitants, and no country in Europe has brought the salmon back to its rivers more effectively than England. There are no human costs, no communities to be moved to create national parks, only money to be spent. Bringing back salmon also often means regulating capitalism, and this may sadly be a political price that few governments are prepared to pay.

Defying the pessimists who predicted that the construction of the Kielder reservoir would destroy any chance of restoring Northumberland's Tyne, in the space of thirty years it has risen from near-death to take its place as one of England's most productive salmon rivers. (Comparing average annual rod catches since 1990 it ranks fourth after the Wye, Eden and Lune.) In 1871, 121,600 salmon were netted out in the river or its estuary, and anglers caught thousands more; yet in 1959, there was no netting and not a single report of a rod-caught fish. The salmon probably never completely disappeared from the river, but they now swim conspicuously up both North and South Tynes, aided by a statutory enhancement scheme to compensate for the lack of any fish-pass round the Kielder dam, which adds nearly 200,000 parr to the wild stocks.

Twenty miles further south, autumn runs of salmon and sea trout now migrate up the Wear as soon as there is enough water to cover their backs. Over the Durham moors, in the neighbouring valley, the efforts which have gone into cleaning up the Tees may yet tempt migratory fish back into the foothills of the Pennines. Ironically, within 10 km (6 miles) of the mouths of all these rivers, is the scene of one of the most controversial of all offshore fisheries, where great curtains of invisible monofilament ensnare returning salmon. Perhaps with even greater irony, the success of these restoration programmes in the face of the drift nets may only serve to support the cause of continued netting.

From a glance at the Clyde in Glasgow, that river would still seem as unlikely as any other in Britain to lead salmon back to their spawning grounds. At one time a highly productive salmon water, during the sixty years after 1905 not a single fish was seen upstream of the city. Now, since the installation of sewage treatment works and the

Salmon spawn in this stretch of the North Tyne just below Kielder reservoir.
(Author)

closure of most of the more poison-producing industries, when the flow is good there is enough dissolved oxygen in the water for migratory fish to reach the river's upper stretches once again. Salmon reappeared above Glasgow in the late 1970s entirely of their own accord. The first fish were most likely strays from the River Leven; this drains Loch Lomond, and because it joins the Clyde estuary well below Glasgow, never lost its runs of migratory fish.

Despite these success stories, the overall outlook for Britain's salmon can be viewed with no more than guarded optimism, and, as if balanced on some giant Gaian scales, triumphs seem inevitably to be matched by disasters – real, impending or sometimes just imagined. Now the country appears to be locked into a dangerous cycle of lower annual rainfall, which means greater domestic, industrial and agricultural demand for an already diminished resource and, inescapably, lower river flows all over the country. Scotland escaped the full force of industrialisation in the nineteenth century and its human population has never impinged on the natural environment as it has done south of the Border. The Tay, Dee, Tweed and other long east coast rivers can still provide some of the finest fishing in Europe; however, there is little room for complacency, and even they are far from immune from the effects of low summer water levels, distantly generated acid rain, power-generation schemes, coniferous afforestation and interceptory netting.

Ireland plays a dangerous game with the wild salmon passing its shores, especially on the west coast, legalising a thriving drift-net fishery (amongst which illegal netters also operate with apparent impunity), as well as salmon farms in almost every suitable inlet. While the negative effects of farming (such as they may be) are felt mainly by locally bred fish heading out to sea, the nets are indiscriminate in their catch, much of which is headed for distant rivers elsewhere in Europe. Like so many other countries, Ireland seems to have decided to offer up its stocks of wild salmon on the twin altars of employment and localised economic prosperity. In doing so, it appears determined to ignore the international condemnation of its offshore fishery, as well as the much further-reaching economic benefits to be gained from encouraging more fish back into the rivers for visiting anglers to catch.

To salmon conservationists, the Faroe Islands were once also a pariah, but that changed when they began to accept recommendations for the conservation of the salmon feeding round their coasts, and then to sell their offshore fishing quotas each year. Their contribution to the salmon's welfare was further boosted when the fish began to breed in several Faroese rivers, as the result of enhancement schemes begun in 1957, using ova imported from Iceland. It is notoriously difficult to convince salmon of the attractions of new environments (see Chapter 2), and this little-publicised extension of their range (they never bred there before) has been an outstanding success.

Iceland is well north of the tip of Greenland, but is warmed by the waters of the Gulf Stream, and if both were up for rechristening, the two countries should exchange names. Iceland has long been a prime destination for wealthy anglers, and the fishing in its sixty or so salmon rivers remains carefully controlled. Most of the rivers are short, and the salmon's efforts to exploit their full length are often hampered by impassable falls (*foss*) although ladders are now helping fish past many of these. Pollution is almost unknown in Iceland, and with no netting at sea and only minimal harvesting at the mouth of one or two glacial rivers, if salmon numbers have declined over the past century it can only be from causes far beyond the island's control. Very few Icelandic salmon ever turned up in high seas fishery nets and stock fluctuations often mirror those in the rivers of the Kola Peninsula. Iceland also ranches salmon, harvesting the returning fish close to the site of their release, and this may be starting to have negative effects on wild stocks.

Greenland, on the other hand, for all its vastness, has only one river with a proven breeding stock of salmon. This is the Kapsigdlit, which flows out of the west coast harbour of Godthaab at 64°N. There is no obvious reason why some of Greenland's more southerly rivers should not support fish, but although the odd straggler turns up in estuary nets, it has yet to be proved that salmon breed anywhere else.

From Godthaab to Ungava Bay in Newfoundland is a leap of less than 1,000 km (600 miles) across the Davis Strait – a simple straight line over an innocuous looking patch of blue on the map, but in reality the most significant stretch of water for *Salmo salar* in the world. Here many of the larger European fish, which spend two or more winters away from fresh water, mingle with most of North America's salmon, all drawn there by better feeding than they seem to find anywhere closer to home.

Salmon once swam up Canada's east coast rivers, particularly those flowing into the St Lawrence and Lake Ontario, in numbers that could almost compare with the great runs of Pacific salmon on the other side of the continent. An 1869 report to the Department of Marine and Fisheries gives an idea of the staggering abundance of fish which once spawned in Wilmont Creek, Lake Ontario, as well as a portent for the future of fish, that

Salmon water in Iceland.
(Peter Hutchinson)

were so plentiful . . . that men killed them with clubs and pitchforks, women seined them with flannel petticoats, and settlers bought and paid for farms . . . Later they were taken with nets and spears, over 1,000 being often caught in the course of one night.

The Hudson Bay Company exploited Canada's natural resources for much more than fur, and made fortunes for its investors both from its own fisheries in Labrador and Quebec and from trading goods for salmon at its stores. In the fertile, more hospitable lowlands of Canada, one salmon run after another was systematically ravaged; and if overfishing did not kill off the breeding stocks, it was left to the usual melange of human destruction to exterminate salmon from the rivers flowing into the lower St Lawrence. Still, while there are many rivers in Canada from which no one alive can remember seeing a salmon taken, especially in Quebec and Nova Scotia, elsewhere a carefully enforced fisheries policy has preserved rivers in their near-pristine state, helped by the revenue from relays of visiting anglers who fly north for their annual holidays. On Newfoundland Island, Labrador and the islands in the Gulf of St Lawrence, salmon continue to return to the rivers they first colonised at the end of the last Ice Age. That they may longer do so in an unbroken stream is more a reflection of harassment at sea, or other more global influences, than of any ruination of their fresh-water homes.

In the USA, conservationists are trying to repair some of the devastation wreaked upon the environment by their forebears, who treated Atlantic salmon with the same callous indifference they showed for bison. Logging operations, a proliferation of dams to power textile mills and the other inevitable consequences of industrialisation slowly drove the salmon out of one river after another. After visiting the Concord in 1839, Henry David Thoreau could only hope that

> Perchance after a thousand years, if the fishes will be patient, and pass their summers elsewhere, meanwhile nature will have levelled the dam and afterwards the canal . . . and the . . . factories, and the . . . River run clear again, to be explored by new migratory shoals.

Fortunately many people are not prepared to wait a thousand years for Nature to take her revenge on mankind, and if it were not for the sustained effort of intensive restocking programmes, sea-going salmon would probably be extinct in the USA. As it is, there are hardly enough salmon to allow them to be fished for, and well over half the fish returning to the twenty or so 'salmon rivers' on the east coast run up the Penobscot in Maine – and most of these are hatchery products. Fish are also being coaxed back into the mouth of Long Island Sound and up the Connecticut. This is the longest and most southerly of these salmon rivers, and until 1798, when the Upper Locks and Canal Company proudly constructed a dam right across it, was among the most prolific. Longer rivers, near the limits of the salmon's temperature tolerance, are often too warm to swim up in the summer, and fish are harder to encourage back into them than into the shorter faster streams further north.

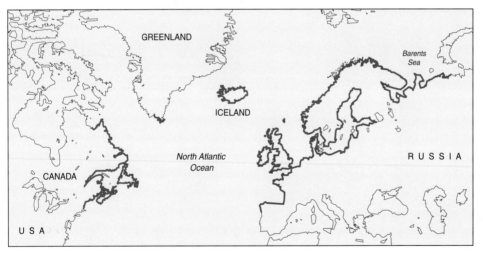

The natural distribution of Atlantic salmon.

Wherever they may be, the single characteristic that most sets Atlantic salmon apart from their Pacific cousins is their ability to survive the stresses of spawning and breed again. Such survival is in fact largely theoretical, because surprisingly few fish actually do breed more than once. Spawning might appear to require much more effort from the female, not least because of the far greater bulk of her eggs over the male's sperm, and thus her greater loss of weight when these are shed. Yet males use far more energy on the redds than females, pursuing and securing mates, and nearly all those fish which make it back up the river again are females.

The length of the river can also affect the likelihood of salmon spawning more than once, although a long journey is not necessarily an arduous one. Where the rigours of reproduction follow on a punishing upstream migration, salmon may be so exhausted that they can hardly recover enough strength to edge their way back into the winter current and be eased downstream, spent, drained, but still alive. If they do not die immediately after spawning, the sooner salmon reach the sea and start feeding the more likely they are to make a full recovery and eventually to return and spawn. Perhaps a quarter of all spawning adults will make it down to the estuary (then known as 'kelts'), but less than a quarter of these will live to breed again. About 5 per cent of British salmon breed more than once, and in the Loire only 1 per cent of fish show any sign of spawning marks on their scales. When they reach the sea, some kelts do not stray much beyond the estuary, growing and gathering strength for their return to the river in the autumn. Others find their way back to Greenland's shores, and only come back after eighteen months. Neither Atlantic nor Pacific salmon feed in fresh water, and the stresses of spawning are finally borne by bodies already weakened by many months of starvation.

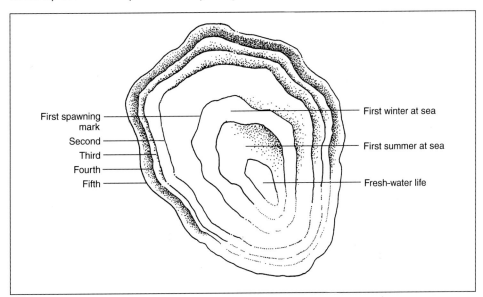

First spawning mark

Second

Third

Fourth

Fifth

First winter at sea

First summer at sea

Fresh-water life

A simplified drawing of a scale from an Atlantic salmon found dead in the River Cothi, in Wales. It had spawned five times.

Despite the relatively few Atlantic salmon which survive to pass on their genes more than once, those that do are clearly the more vigorous creatures and exert a disproportionately strong influence on future generations. Their vigour is apparent in the return of some fish to spawn three or four times. The scales of a Welsh fish, found dead in the River Cothi in 1997, showed it to have bred five times before finally giving up its life to the waters where it was born. In Britain, kelt fishing has long been illegal, but on the Miramichi River in Canada there is a 'sport fishery' that specifically targets 'black salmon' in the spring. This is largely justified on the grounds that few of these fish would have survived in any event, which is true, but it is a strange fisherman who derives any pleasure from killing a weakened, shapeless salmon with as little taste as edible flesh. Some of the efforts to conserve endangered stocks of salmon in Maine and Quebec involve reconditioning wild kelts, which are caught up at the river mouth and then used as hatchery broodstock.

Atlantic salmon spawn in typical salmonid fashion, excavating nests in the gravel of swift, often very shallow streams. Cutting the nest and repeatedly testing its suitability with her anal fin is the female's task, while the male hovers in attendance, guarding her from the attentions of intruding rivals. His repeated quivering may be a sign of aggression towards other males, but if the female is nearby and nest-cutting is finished, it is more likely to signify impending orgasm and ejaculation. Once the spawn is shed and fertilised, females cover it over with small stones displaced from just upstream of their nest and then, in Izaak Walton's words, '. . . leave it to the Creator's protection'.

The role of precocious male parr – parr that have become sexually mature before leaving the stream of their birth and heading to sea – is among the most intriguing aspects of the Atlantic salmon's spawning behaviour, and one with parallels in the lives of many related species (see Chapter 2). In some streams, all male Atlantic salmon mature early, while in others only a small proportion do so. These young males are able to fertilise the eggs of large sea-going females perfectly effectively. Early researchers concluded that parr were incapable of stimulating the female to orgasm by themselves, and that to shed her eggs successfully she needed the attentions of a large sea-going male, the little parr then nipping in and adding their sperm to that of the larger fish. Now, from more detailed observation of salmon on the redds, it is clear that, in the absence of mature males, a parr on his own can in fact mate successfully with a female, although his usual role remains that of an intruder on the stage. Sometimes several parr leave their milt in a single nest, perhaps providing some sort of biological insurance against the unsuccessful efforts of the older male, as well as enlarging the genetic diversity of the offspring. Young parr hanging around the redds also take full opportunity of the frenetic spawning activity to snap up any loose fat-laden eggs bobbing down in the current. One of the more remote consequences of overfishing may actually be to enhance the role of male parr on the redds in the face of decreasing numbers of sea-going fish which return to breed. It is not unusual to find populations of brown trout where the only migratory fish are females, and in some streams salmon may be headed that way too.

The strange intrusions of these precocious males into the culmination of the lives of the older fish may have been one reason why early ichthyologists for so long regarded parr as a separate species, *Salmo salmulus*. As late as 1836, the formidable naturalist William Yarrell continued to contend, in his *History of British Fishes*:

> That the Parr is not the young of the Salmon, or indeed of any other of the larger species of *Salmonidae* as still considered by some, is sufficiently obvious from the circumstance that Parrs by hundreds may be taken in the rivers all the summer, long after the fry of the year of the larger migratory species have gone down to the sea; and the greater part of those Parrs taken even in autumn do not exceed five inches in length, when no example of the young of the Salmon can be found under sixteen or eighteen inches.

It is easy to see that, so long as Yarrell assumed young salmon fry were down the river and out to sea by the end of their first summer, any fish left behind which were not young trout must be something different. Sir William Jardine was another respected authority who promoted the specific status of the parr in *British Salmonidae* (1839), but by the middle of the century some sort of consensus had emerged as to its true identity as a young Atlantic salmon. Even one of the greatest of all species splitters, Dr Albert Gunther, admitted the parr to the ranks of *Salmo salar* (although failing to appreciate that he should have done the same with kelts, which he called *Salmo argentus*).

A shortage of adult males is the most likely reason why a full-grown female is induced to mate with a mature parr weighing a few grams against her several kilograms, and the same reason may explain the occasional hybridisation with brown trout. The presence of a large salmon-like sea trout seems more likely to encourage an adult female salmon to shed her eggs than the attentions of tiny fresh-water-resident brown trout, which usually contribute their milt furtively in between scavenging for salmon eggs. Hybrids occur in varying proportions amongst populations of wild salmon, ranging from none to over 7 per cent, and are almost always found to be the product of a union between a female salmon and a male trout. The bull trout of the rivers of Britain's east coast estuaries are often considered to be salmon x brown trout hybrids. The Tweed bull trout were renowned, and while some may have been hybrids, most were probably brown trout that never got as far as the open sea (see Chapter 4); Tay bull trout appear more likely to have been salmon.

How long Atlantic salmon parr spend in fresh water varies enormously from river to river, and seems to depend largely on how quickly they reach a length of about 10 cm (4 in) or just over. Having attained this size, parr are then likely to head to sea the following year. They usually grow more slowly in the colder fresh waters at the north of their range. In Arctic Norway, Greenland and Ungava Bay it may be as many as seven years before parr take on their silver sheen and move out into salt water. In Iceland and Scotland fish go to sea after two, three, four or five years in their rivers. Yet in the Hampshire Avon and the rivers of France and Spain, most young salmon are ready to face the hazards of marine life by the spring following the year of their birth, when not much more than fourteen months old.

Salmon parr moving down the St. Mary's River, Nova Scotia. (Gilbert van Ryckevorsel)

A long journey from redd to sea may prolong parr's river lives, and where the sea is only faintly saline they often leave the security of the river as much smaller fish. In some of the Kola Peninsula rivers, smolts are only half their normal length on entering the brackish waters of the White Sea, where they stay for the summer before heading out to the salty wastes of the Barents Sea. The Baltic is equally brackish, but smolts are usually normal length and three or four winters old when they get there. While there may be a standard age at which a particular river's salmon migrate to the sea, fish of other ages are always doing so at the same time, and this helps buffer stocks against the effects of environmental catastrophes. Even in the long and languid Loire, where salmon usually become smolts after one year, 20 per cent wait until they are two before doing so.

In the context of their migratory habits, Atlantic salmon are less dependent on their time at sea to complete their life cycle than chum and pink salmon, and can remain in fresh water all their lives, even if they seldom actually do so. Many of the mature male parr that join in the mating activities of their elders do not reach salt water, and most Swedish salmon never taste the true saltiness of the open ocean as they mix with the eclectic community of fresh-water and marine fish that feast off the Baltic's bounty. There, among the cod, sprats and herring are vendace, smelts and even pike and common bream, and it is no great environmental leap from conditions in the Baltic to those in a large inland lake. The half-size smolts that summer in the White Sea may be scarcely aware of having left fresh water. It is not surprising, therefore, that on both sides of the Atlantic there are natural communities of salmon, with ready access to the sea, but which choose instead to treat the lakes that first gather up their spawning streams as alternative grazing grounds.

It may be tempting to think of these landlocked fish as salmon quite distinct from their truly migratory fellows. To do so would imply that stocks of landlocked fish are genetically closer to each other than to the migratory fish from the same watershed, and this they almost certainly are not. Instead, each landlocked population is likely to have evolved separately, from sea-going ancestors, in response to particular environmental conditions which, over the generations, have favoured the strategy of remaining in fresh water. In most cases these landlocked fish have only been where they are since the end of the last Ice Age, which is not long enough for significant genetic differences to have emerged. A similar scenario persists amongst sockeye salmon. The landlocked kokanee are always genetically much closer to sea-going sockeye in the same lake system than to kokanee in other lake systems (see Chapters 2 and 10).

Towards the more southerly end of their range, where salmon may have to face hundreds of kilometres of warm sluggish polluted water before reaching the sea, there are obvious deterrents to migration and incentives to adopt a fresh-water life in cooler cleaner waters at higher altitudes. That said, landlocked fish live easily in Norwegian, Swedish and Russian lakes, as well as in many North American ones. In all of them the temperature throughout the whole length of the outflowing river is well within the salmon's tolerance, and yet they simply opt for life in the lake rather than going to sea. Fish that complete their lives without migrating stand a much better chance of survival, and to a greater or lesser extent this compensates for their usually not growing so large, and therefore laying fewer eggs.

Some of the most unusual landlocked salmon live in Norway's River Namsen, and owe their fresh-water existence to the impassable Aunfoss waterfall. Below the fall, sea-going salmon pursue normal migratory existences, but above are *smablank*, dwarf salmon which spend their whole lives in the river, not even in a lake. Because any fish migrating to sea have been lost to the population above the waterfall, over thousands of generations evolution has selectively favoured those that remain behind in the river. Brown trout are often similarly divided, as occasionally are Arctic charr.

Landlocked Atlantic salmon are much commoner in North America than in Europe. For all the scarcity of sea-going salmon in New England, landlocked fish thrive in many of Maine's inland lakes, where they are often called 'sebago' after the one in which they were first identified. There are many other indigenous landlocked populations in North America, as well as others established by mankind's efforts. In Canada landlocked salmon are known as 'ouananiche', and Lake Ontario was once home to huge numbers which would spawn in its feeder streams in autumn, and yet never showed any inclination to head down the St Lawrence River and out to sea. The first Europeans in Maine arrived to find landlocked fish weighing up to 9 kg (20 lb), while specimens from Lake Ontario were said to reach double that weight. The Ontario fish are now long gone and in Maine sebago average around 1 kg (2 lb).

It is easy to understand that if salmon could reach these huge sizes in fresh water, there was little advantage in their risking a danger-fraught journey out into the open sea. In these large lakes, prey fish were plentiful and varied, and in smaller lakes salmon may owe their presence to the parallel distribution of rainbow smelts, often introduced into waters newly stocked with salmon. The landlocked salmon of Lake Vanern also eat smelts, which in Sweden are usually more at home in brackish estuaries or the Baltic Sea, but there are also landlocked.

The only successful attempts to induce Atlantic salmon to live south of the equator have founded populations of landlocked fish. Atlantic salmon seem unable to adapt their spectacular ability to navigate around their native ocean to any other. Wherever they have left southern hemisphere rivers they have simply disappeared, and none is known ever to have returned to its stream of birth or introduction. Although there are now self-sustaining populations of Atlantic salmon in New Zealand and Patagonia, they never migrate down to the sea, or if they do they simply disappear once they reach it.

For most salmon, the lure of the open ocean and its nutritional riches is irresistible, and in the spring young smolts are ready to begin their marine life. Their spots and parr marks have been gradually disappearing, to be replaced by the layer of guanin that eventually colours them for survival in the open water, and signals the complex physiological changes readying smolts for their move from fresh to salt water. No longer do they seem inclined to fight the forces of the river, which sweep them downstream tail first until, in more sluggish stretches of water, they turn round and swim. They are still feeding as they go, often hungrily and conspicuously, as if determined not to miss the last chance of a fresh-water meal. But there is no temptation to linger, and the smolts seem driven by an urge to leave the fresh water for which their silvered bodies are now so ill-suited, and to exchange the river's current for the push and pull of the tides.

The estuary provides an ideal environment for smolts to absorb the shock of salt water and ease their way gradually into the sea. Young fish transferred straight from fresh to full-strength sea water would probably die. Some rivers have no real estuary, just a long tidal pool, which many young salmon swim straight through, but the river's plume dilutes the nearby sea, giving them a chance to acclimatise themselves not only to the salt but also to the bewildering changes in their diet and the dangers that threaten them. Gone is the stream of current-carried insects which drifted uninterrupted through their fresh-water lives, where the chances of underwater attack were remote and competition from brown trout or brook charr only occasional. Once a pike was the largest fish they might ever see – and smolts raised in fast rocky rivers would not even have seen that – but now a whole array of bigger fish appear out of the gloom, each of which must be treated as a potential killer. Those fish too small to be killers are probably competitors, busy searching for the same food as the young salmon.

While they remain in the estuarine shallows, feeding on or near the surface, young salmon are particularly vulnerable to airborne attack. Round Scottish shores, gannets, cormorants and various gulls all exploit the early summer arrival of the silvery smolts. In the Baltic Sea, Caspian terns snatch them up without wetting a feather, while in North America, double-crested cormorants pursue smolts under water at great speed. Ospreys breed throughout the northern hemisphere and would not miss a chance to seize a young smolt in their talons, although ideally they would prefer something larger. Fish between 200 and 300 g (7–10 oz) seem to offer ospreys the best balance between being reasonably easy to catch and big enough to be worth eating.

The list of fish that eat salmon is a long one, made so simply because the sea is full of so many different species, and most of the larger ones are piscivorous. This makes it particularly difficult to assess the impact of any one species on salmon numbers; so does the comparative rarity of salmon in the sea compared to the huge numbers of true marine fish. At the early stage in their marine life, salmon are also easy prey for cod, saithe and pollack, but these appear to be less destructive predators once the smolts reach the open sea, even if they are then still small enough to be swallowed. Bigger salmon are far from immune from attack, but little is known of their enemies. Large cod and various sharks, whales and dolphins have all been caught with the remains of partly digested salmon in their stomachs, as have skate and ling. Greater danger comes from different species of seals, which usually feed close inshore, and often on salmon thronging the estuaries and waiting for a spate to take them back up to spawn.

When sea-bound smolts reach the estuary there will only be the occasional wind-blown insect to remind them of their fresh-water fare, and they must start to feed off shrimps and other crustaceans. They are already large enough to swallow young sand-eels and herrings, and will soon be able to eat sprats and three-spined sticklebacks. As the salmon grow, so does the size of their preferred prey – the size of creature that is most efficient in terms of energy expended in its capture and the nutritional benefit derived from eating it. Sand-eels are crucial to the healthy growth of Atlantic salmon and of many other species of fish. The continued exploitation of vast sand-eel shoals for industrial use as animal feed (and ironically also to be fed to farmed salmon) is put forward as one of the main causes of periodic crashes in sea-bird populations – particularly of puffins and Arctic terns, which also rely heavily on these tiny fish to nourish them and their young. However, birds are far easier to watch than fish, and it is almost impossible to isolate the effect on salmon of any one of the many destructive influences on their lives. So the responsibility of the sand-eel fishermen for any decline in salmon stocks has yet to be proved, but at least Denmark no longer fuels its power stations with sand-eel oil.

Off the Canadian coast capelin are a vital source of energy-rich winter food for salmon, which pursue them almost to the exclusion of any other prey – as does practically every other large sea fish. Closely related to the smelt, these are small big-eyed, fierce-looking fish sought by tuna, cod, herring, flounders, puffins, guillemots, terns, gulls, seals and salmon – and also Canadians, who use them for garden fertiliser, fish bait and dog

Canadian salmon on their way up the St. Mary's River, Nova Scotia.
(Gilbert van Ryckevorsel)

food, as well as for their own consumption. The capelin's near suicidal spawning habits make them easy prey for the idlest of human fishers as well as for hosts of shore birds. When the female is ready to shed her tough sticky eggs, she rides in on a wave to join one of the males waiting in the shallows. Together they swim up onto the beach, and after hollowing out a shallow scrape with fins and tails, spawn together as fast as they can before trying to catch a life-saving wave back out to sea. As with sand-eels, over-exploitation has threatened populations of both prey and predators, but the Canadian government is able to control the fishery, which is mainly exploited by the country's own boats – a far simpler scenario than exists off any European shores.

Scientific research into the salmon's life continues to replace mystery and speculation with knowledge and understanding, and so, theoretically at least, to improve the prospects for the fish's conservation. Yet knowledge brings the power to exploit as well as to protect. It is not difficult to argue that the salmon's interests would have been far better served if fish had continued disappearing out to sea, to destinations unknown, then returning after one, two or three years spent harvesting the ocean's goodness with the secrets of their wanderings still intact. European eels need no statutory protection as they swim off to their distant breeding grounds somewhere in the Sargasso Sea. However, the details of the salmon's marine life are secret no longer; and for the last thirty years they have been caught, like so many other creatures, between the poles of exploitation and conservation, too often a victim of their own migratory habits and the taste of their flesh.

Although aided by science, it was essentially the search for food that gradually unveiled the salmon's feeding grounds in the 1960s. As commercial fishing methods improved, salmon appeared more and more often in nets set for other fish. So fishing effort began to shift, and to focus on salmon to the exclusion of these other species. Salmon became the specific target for increasing numbers of fishing boats, and as a result the fish slowly started revealing how and where they lived at sea.

While fishing boats exploited the oceanic phase of the Atlantic salmon's life, they concentrated their efforts in three main parts of the ocean, which were generally thought to correspond to the fish's principal feeding grounds – off south-western Greenland, north of the Faroe Islands and near the coast of northern Norway. It now appears likely that salmon exploit a much wider area, along a broad front where the interface between the south-moving Arctic Front and the warmer North Atlantic Drift causes an upwelling, and feeding is particularly rich. Pacific salmon exploit a similar phenomenon in their native ocean, as cool sub-Arctic water is swept down to confront the warmth of the California Current. However, there is so little high-seas fishing now that, for the time being at least, knowledge of the fish's sea-feeding habits remains almost suspended as it was twenty years ago.

It still seems certain that more salmon congregate off the south-west coast of Greenland than anywhere else. For Canadian fish this is not a dramatic journey, and is born of the much richer feeding to be found in cooler northern latitudes. Yet why should so many Scottish, French or Spanish salmon shun the shorter safer journeys to other marine feeding grounds in favour of the hazardous voyage to Greenland's distant shores? This is one of the secrets the salmon have yet to surrender, and one factor which may be crucial to the course of their oceanic wanderings is the length of time they spend at sea. Whether this itself is influenced by environmental or genetic factors is another mystery. As nearly always seems to be the case when comparing their relative effects, science has currently reached the conclusion that the environment triggers behaviour which is otherwise under genetic control.

Salmon returning to spawn the year after they first entered the sea are scientifically one sea winter (1SW) fish and colloquially 'grilse'. Despite their smaller size, they are mature in every respect, and just as likely to die after spawning as older fish. However, their shorter stay at sea inevitably restricts the distance they can travel between leaving and returning to their native river. It also gives them less growing time than those salmon which spend longer at sea. No grilse are found feeding off Greenland's shores, and salmon from the British Isles usually first head up north of the Faroe Islands, where they mingle with others from non-Baltic Sweden and southern Norway. If they are to return after only one winter, these fish may not even go this far, but those that are destined – or decide – to remain at sea for two years or more (MSW fish) have time to travel much further, some moving up towards the north Norwegian coast, while the rest set their internal compasses for Greenland.

Migratory routes are easily charted on maps, but the strong black lines tend to give a misleading impression of scientific certainty. Whenever a clear pattern seems to be emerging from the fog of conflicting evidence, salmon turn up in unexpected corners of the Atlantic, as if determined to confound all attempts to convert speculation into fact. A fish tagged in Britain may be caught off the Canadian coast, ones from North America are recovered in Norway or the Faroes, and there is very little predictable pattern to the migrations of French fish, which seem to head either north or west when they reach the sea.

The suggested advantage to *Salmo salar* of the females being bigger, and thus able to lay more and larger eggs, is supported by the high proportion of females of European origin taken in Greenland nets. It is dangerous out at sea, and therefore the interests of future generations seem better served if males return to spawn after only a year away, leaving the females behind to carry on growing. The salmon that spend two or three winters at sea make up the bulk of the runs of spring fish, and any grilse among them are usually male. In smaller rivers, where most of the salmon are grilse, the ratio between the sexes will be much more even.

Not surprisingly, the later fish arrive in fresh water, the bigger they are likely to be, and grilse leaving the sea towards the end of summer may weigh 4 or 5 kg (9–11 lb). This is almost as much as a spring-run 2SW fish, the first of which may actually start arriving at the same time as the last grilse, so in fact belying their description by spending most of their second winter in the river. These early spring fish may stay almost a year in fresh water before spawning, during which their condition slowly deteriorates. By spending so much longer in the river than later arrivals do, they are particularly vulnerable to the

Salmon in the estuary of the Grand Cascapedia River, Quebec.
(Gilbert van Ryckevorsel)

predations of the angler, which may be one reason why there seem to be fewer of them each year. Why they feel the need to enter the river so early is another of the salmon's mysteries. Most Atlantic salmon rivers are comparatively short, and even though the first fish to arrive usually spawn furthest from the sea, the journey from estuary to redds need never take longer than three weeks in good water conditions.

Man was catching salmon long before he was able to leave lasting evidence behind of his doing so. It is inconceivable that such an omnivorous creature would have ignored this annual bounty, as the salmon proclaimed their return by hurling themselves at waterfalls, splashing around in holding pools and darkening the stream beds while they spawned. In Europe, the oldest clues to man's interest in salmon come from Stone Age caves on either side of the Pyrenean border. An etching of a salmon on a piece of reindeer antler found in Santillana del Mar may have been carved more than 20,000 years ago, when the last Ice Age pressed down on the habitable frontiers of Europe, and there were salmon all the way along the Portuguese coast and proably in many Mediterranean rivers too. However, salmon must have sustained thousands of earlier generations of humans. Cro-Magnon man emerged, probably from Africa or Arabia, to displace the Neanderthals at least 45,000 years ago, arriving with a technology that may have included the ability to use tools to fish; and even before their eclipse, there is no reason why the Neanderthals could not have been using their more primitive stone implements to kill fish in the shallows or below falls. If those other great omnivores, the bears, could scoop spawning salmon out of the shallows with their paws, surely early man could have done the same with his much more prehensile hands?

The first humans may have arrived in North America, crossing the Bering land bridge or edging round its shores in boats, about 14,000 years ago. However, they only seem to have reached the east coast within the last 2,000 years, bringing with them relatively sophisticated fishing techniques to exploit the huge runs of salmon and Arctic charr that formed the very foundations of their existence. The earlier American arrivals may have been blamed for the extinction of mammoths and sloths, but Atlantic salmon stocks remained quite unaffected by the subsistence fishing of the Inuit, even given that once they were able to smoke, salt or dry fish they needed to harvest enough to see them right through the winter. Fish stocks are remarkably resilient to overfishing, and to fish a fish to extinction by conventional means in a river is almost impossible. Even after the Europeans appeared with their advanced fishing methods, which soon began to supersede traditional native ways, and over-exploitation threatened salmon runs on both sides of the Atlantic, the salmon still swam, bred and swam again. It was the dams, poison and pollution that really drove salmon out of so many of their ancestral streams, not too much fishing.

Traditionally, fish were trapped in weirs, dams or baskets, and often caught by less subtle means like gaffs, spears or snares, but nets were far the most effective means of catching migrating fish. Sea-going species are always in danger of falling foul of their own breeding urges, easing the work of the fisherman by swimming into a stationary net, rather than his having to move the net, as in trawling, to catch a stationary fish. By the biodegradable nature of nets, archaeological evidence of their use is hard to find, and the earliest, from Peru, probably date back about 8,000 years. Moravian missionaries are said to have brought nets to the Inuits of eastern Canada in 1770.

The oldest evidence of net use in Britain derives, not from archaeology, but from 1376 reports of Edward III's parliament; this was concerned about 'meshes the length and breadth of two thumbs', which caught so many fish that fishermen 'feed and fat their pigs with them to the great damage of the Commons of the realm and the destruction of the fisheries'. Since then, pole nets, poke nets, stake nets, haaf nets, whammel nets, bag nets, fly nets, seine nets, draft nets, drag nets, bow nets, click nets, cairn nets, shoulder nets, bend nets, snap nets, set nets, hoop nets, gill nets and many more have combined to provide a fine testimony to the ingenuity of a hungry Briton bent on feeding his family off the huge shoals of migrating salmon.

Until the middle of this century, netsmen all focused their efforts on salmon moving from feeding to breeding grounds. The first floating nets were usually operated from boats in estuaries, and even when these evolved into more conventional drift nets a hundred years ago, they were always set close to the shore to intercept fish approaching the river mouth. No one thought of hanging a net in the open sea to catch feeding fish, but this changed in 1956, when a salmon tagged in Scotland swam into a net close to Greenland's shore. Soon afterwards fish marked in North America and elsewhere in Europe also turned up in the Greenlanders' nets.

Suddenly the mystery was no longer a mystery: the secret of the salmon's feeding grounds was out, and the salmon were fast into the net. Within ten years this was a monofilament drift net. Within another ten years salmon numbers had declined so dramatically that only international co-operation and national restraint prevented what then looked likely to be the near-destruction of the stocks of wild fish. At that time, the link between Greenland's fishing and the disappearing salmon seemed absolute and inescapable, but the continuing fall in salmon numbers has subsequently shown that other more fundamental influences must also have played their part.

Until monofilament nylon replaced manilla, sisal, tarred cotton or hemp, fishermen usually had to set their nets at night or in stormy weather; they were then invisible to moving fish that would swim straight into the mesh. In daylight, or on calm moonlit nights, the nets were easily avoided, and their bulk also restricted the length which it was practical to operate. So in the early years of the Greenland fishery – hard though it is to believe in the light of today's methods of indiscriminate global fish slaughter – these physical difficulties kept catches at generally acceptable levels. But it was not to remain this way, and by the end of the 1960s monofilament 'walls of death' were being unfurled all over the world's oceans. At a stroke, technology had made fishing both far easier and frighteningly effective.

Mesh size varies, and its control is one way of restricting a net's efficiency. Because of the nylon's elasticity, one size of mesh can still trap fish of very different weights, ensnaring them behind the gills. The whole net is supported by buoys or a floating rope, with a weighted rope at the bottom to make it hang almost vertically in the water. The nets are now all but invisible, allowing fishermen the luxury of operating them in the brightest daylight, and their lack of bulk makes it more appropriate to measure them in kilometres than metres. The advent of monofilament has also incidentally made illegal netting infinitely easier, and far harder to detect, all over the world.

With only one salmon river of its own, Greenland was angrily accused of overharvesting fish destined to spawn in European or American waters – and thus incidentally to provide the Greenlanders with still more fish for their own nets. Had they been spared, these salmon would nearly all have spent more than one winter at sea, and would have been much larger by the time they returned to their birthplace. As in any other open-sea fishery, the harvest was inevitably random, and there was no way of protecting individual stocks from particular rivers where fish were scarce. The countries where salmon spawned argued forcefully that their efforts to enhance breeding stocks were largely wasted if the mature fish were to be netted out of the high seas. The Greenlanders countered that without the rich feedings in their own territorial waters the fish would not grow to breed anyway, or at least would be much smaller. They also pointed to the gross pollution of so many European rivers, and, with equal justification, to the damage inflicted on fish stocks by other drift-net fisheries, legal or otherwise, off the coasts of Britain and Ireland.

In 1976, foreign-registered boats were prohibited from exploiting the salmon in Greenland's waters, and for many years the North Atlantic Salmon Conservation Organisation (NASCO) continued to settle Greenland's annual quota, based on a baffling matrix of past statistics and future predictions. In 1993 and 1994 all netting off the Greenland coast was suspended except for a small subsistence harvest, and since then Greenland has fished a quota which, in the face of the assaults on the salmon's welfare from other directions, should scarcely be cause for as much concern as it seems to be. Its 1997 quota of 57 tonnes amounted to not much more than 20,000 fish – compared to a record catch of 2,689 tonnes in 1971 – and a small fraction of the normal take from Ireland's drift nets. In 1998 Greenland agreed to less than a subsistence quota of 20 tonnes. That there should ever have been sufficient international co-operation to control the deep-sea harvest of Atlantic salmon says much for the flexibility of the countries involved, even though agreements may have been easier to reach in the face of the collapse in salmon prices following the massive expansion of salmon farming. The fact that there is only one member of NASCO for the whole of the European Union, instead of one for each sovereign country within, may also have helped decision-making.

Canada now outlaws monofilament, and seems committed to preserving its salmon stocks, having banned almost all commercial fishing round its shores, except in parts of Quebec. The social consequences for local communities are dire, as they were when the cod fishery closed down, but the revenue and employment opportunities which recreational angling create are now much better appreciated. The USA only allows recreational fishing and its reported 1997 catch of 333 fish were all returned to their rivers.

Norway banned its drift-net fishery in 1989, a year after prohibiting the use of monofilament. The Baltic states all fish with drift nets within the Baltic Sea, but much the most contentious drift nets are those that hang off the coasts of north-western Ireland and north-eastern England. Ireland's monofilament drift nets are set off the rocky promontories jutting out into the Atlantic and ensnare fish swimming within 2 km (1 mile) of the shore on their way to English, Scottish, Welsh, French and even Spanish rivers. Ireland has difficulty not only enforcing existing fishing regulations but also controlling a rampant illegal drift-net fishery, which is not afraid to compound its illegality by the use of equally illicit fishing methods. Since 1997 it has been confined within 10 rather than 20 km (6 rather than 12 miles) of the coast, and to daytime fishing only. These changes do little more than tinker with the edges of the problem, and are unlikely to reduce catches down much below the 700,000 fish the nets are estimated to ensnare each year. Scotland flirted briefly with drift nets in the early 1960s, when they were still made of hemp, but banned them long before monofilament really took over. That perhaps as much as three-quarters of the salmon currently taken in the nylon drift nets off the Northumbrian and Yorkshire coasts are destined for Scottish rivers is particularly galling to those concerned with the conservation of salmon stocks north of the Border.

Commercial fishing regulations are continually adapting in response to pressures from national and international conservation organisations, as well as to estimates of salmon stocks and other variables. Off the English coast no drift netting is allowed further than 11 km (7 miles) from the shore, otherwise the limit is generally double that. Mesh size is also carefully controlled, as are the length of nets, fishing hours (usually 4.00 a.m. to 8.00 p.m. in England) and the issue of licences. Even so, the north-east of England's fishery is harshly criticised by those other countries which nurture stocks of breeding salmon, and its continued existence makes it almost impossible for Britain's voice to be raised in complaint of overexploitation elsewhere. The social consequences of its closure, in an area long haunted by the history of declining industry and job loss, certainly cannot be ignored. None the less, all those other countries that closed long-established fisheries faced similar repercussions, and the harm that indiscriminate interceptory netting causes stocks of wild Atlantic salmon is now better acknowledged than ever before.

Fish are far more vulnerable to netting as they are funnelled into the narrows of their river mouth from the vastness of the ocean, so why was there such an outcry against netting them on their feeding grounds? Offshore fisheries cannot be selective in their catch, and are as likely to kill salmon returning to rivers, where stocks are precariously low, as fish destined for more prolific waters. Moreover, fish caught while they are feeding are still putting on weight, but on reaching the estuary they are as big as they will ever be before they spawn, and in prime condition for harvesting. Inshore fishing methods are also usually simpler and more ecologically defensible than those used in the open sea, where large fuel-burning boats often operate the nets. More importantly, by fishing close inshore

Netting salmon at the mouth of the River Tweed.
(Author)

it is easier to target fish destined for specific river systems, even if not for a particular tributary of the arterial river. Controlling the catch also implies controlling the numbers of fish that are not caught, and thus go on to spawn. These fish are known as the 'escapement'. They survive to sustain or enhance the population within the whole river system – and to satisfy the demands of sport fishermen, who want to catch salmon in fresh water migrating upstream to spawn.

Through the eyes of commercial fishermen, the pressures to reduce catches in the name of stock conservation inevitably appear as a thinly veiled pitch for the promotion of angling interests and the further enrichment of riparian landowners. That nearly all the effort and finance to preserve salmon stocks comes from anglers and fishery owners, rather than from pure conservationists, may only serve to enhance this perception. But conservation for conservation's sake, particularly of unobtrusive fish usually lurking hidden below the water's surface, remains pitifully low on most personal agendas, and it should be no surprise that those who shout loudest are those with most to lose.

Much has also been made of the supposedly far greater 'value' of a salmon caught by an angler against one taken in the nets (except apparently in Ireland, where the figures are strangely similar). There are any number of ways of calculating these values, but nearly all seem to ignore the fact that as more fish are caught by anglers, the average value drops very quickly. Almost everywhere that salmon swim an infrastructure is already in place to service and support visitors, who seem prepared to pay huge sums of money for a few days' fishing as long as there is even the remotest chance of success. It costs no more to catch ten fish in a week than two (except that rents may rise next year, providing economic benefit to no one else but the landlord). Therefore if increased success can be achieved at very little extra expense the average cost of an angled salmon will drop dramatically, and its edge over a netted one will soon be eroded.

The purchase of commercial netting rights by conservation groups, which then allow such rights to lapse, has become increasingly popular and may suit both sides equally well. Such schemes certainly allow more fish up the rivers – and therefore more to make themselves available to anglers. From the conservation perspective they rely for their success on the simplistic assumption that more fish spawning in the river's headwaters will mean more hatching alevins, and thus more fish reaching the sea and returning to breed. Yet this is not necessarily so. An average female Atlantic salmon may lay 5,000 eggs, and even in a healthy stable population of salmon there is enormous mortality amongst young fish, particularly at the stage when, having swum up from their gravelly nursery, the fry then disperse throughout the riffles to begin feeding. Out of every hundred eggs a female lays, one or two smolts may survive to taste the sea. From the simple standpoint of the salmon population the wastage is enormous, but then so too is the potential for numbers to recover. If relatively few salmon are breeding in a river, more fry from each nest will have space to grow and feed and to rebuild the depleted population, which may therefore return to its optimum level without fishery managers having to let any more adult spawners up to crowd the redds.

Most British netting rights are purchased from long established, small-scale inshore fisheries. The Canadian government has also been buying back fishing rights, sometimes on a voluntary basis and sometimes compulsorily, but it was the buy-out of the Faroese deep-sea fishery quotas that really showed there was no limit to the concept's potential. Since the late 1960s Faroese fishermen had fished the coastal waters around their islands using, instead of drift nets, floating long lines, from each of which dangled as many as

4,000 hooks baited with sprats set to catch salmon just below the surface. There they intercepted small first-year salmon, mostly from Scotland and Ireland, until they discovered older, heavier fish from Norwegian rivers feeding further north. The smaller British fish then found themselves spared at the expense of their larger fellows of Scandinavian origin.

After the foundation of NASCO in 1984 the Faroese fishermen were confined to their own territorial waters, and their catches began to decline. With falling profits they were ideal targets for an offer to purchase their NASCO quotas, and in 1991 signed an agreement for the sale of a three-year quota with a consortium of organisations under the umbrella of the Committee for the Purchase of Open-sea Salmon Quotas. There has been no fishing since then, other than from research vessels, and although the Faroese still argue strongly against any lowering of their quotas, they have actually agreed to substantial reductions, and their 1998 allowance was 330 tonnes. The willingness of the Faroese to sell their quotas was compounded by the crash in salmon prices resulting from the huge increase in salmon farming over the last fifteen years. Lower returns have affected many marginal commercial fisheries, and should also have meant that the rewards from illegal fishing are now increasingly outweighed by the risks. None the less, annual unreported catches still exceed 1,000 tonnes, which would imply that somewhere there is still a good profit in a poached salmon.

Atlantic salmon farming is a complicated operation involving, as it does, raising the young fish in fresh water before transferring them to cages in the open sea. It is a relative newcomer to the aquacultural scene, having been pioneered by the Norwegians in the 1960s, but is now probably the most technologically advanced of all fish farming. In 1982 farmed output first caught up with the total catch of wild fish and the gap between the two has been widening dramatically ever since. The 1997 production of farmed Atlantic salmon in the North Atlantic area was around 480,000 tonnes – over 200 times the reported harvest of wild fish – of which Norway produced very nearly two thirds. Driving around the north-west coast of Britain, it is hard to believe Scotland is responsible for less than 15 per cent of this total, although placed second in the production league, with Chile third, just ahead of Canada.

Farming animals in all but the most confined artificial circumstances is always going to have some environmental impact, and rearing salmon is no exception. In many ways water is a more sensitive element, less forgiving of abuse, than earth or air. The salmon farmer argues that no one has a greater interest in preserving the aquatic habitat than he does. This may be true, but the farmers still have many charges to answer, which they usually do by hiding behind the verdict of 'not proven' – as high-seas fishermen also once did. Unfortunately, it is often almost impossible to dissociate the effects of fish farming or open-sea netting on individual salmon populations from the consequences of climate change, disease, predation, sport fishing, declining water quality or estuary netting. So the debate about the effect on stocks of wild fish of rearing salmon in the sea is prolonged, and the acceptance of the 'precautionary principle', which suggests taking remedial action before conclusive proof of damage, is indefinitely postponed.

The build-up of chemical or organic waste around sea cages is an obvious target for concerned criticism. The highly publicised collapse of Irish sea trout stocks has been blamed almost exclusively on infestations of sea-lice (*Lepeophtheirus salmonis*). These attach themselves to untreated wild smolts passing the cages on their way out to sea, but the case is still unproven and populations of wild salmon initially seemed much less affected. The salmon farming industry can less avoid the finger of guilt which points to its responsibility for the spread of the viviparous fluke, *Gyrodactylus salaris*. So far, its catastrophic effect on both wild and farmed salmon stocks has been largely confined to Norway, but if it ever reaches Britain the fluke could kill off one river's fish after another, and undo all the benefits that river restoration schemes have brought the country's salmon.

The escape of farmed fish into the wild is another unavoidable consequence of raising salmon in the sea. The impact of these interlopers on the gene pool of individual populations of wild salmon is causing much concern. Although sea cages are more secure than they were, and are inspected far more frequently, storms, loose moorings and predators all seem likely to continue to liberate farmed fish into the wild, unless on-growing in enclosed areas of fresh water ever becomes economical.

It can be argued that over a long enough period, the influence of introduced and potentially unsuitable genes should be swamped by the stronger genes of native fish, whose genetic make-up is a consequence of natural selection over thousands of years. Yet the sheer numbers of farmed fish that sometimes find their way into a single river system – up to 90 per cent of fish in some Norwegian rivers were hatched in darkened rows of trays, not the gravel of a spawning stream – will make it very difficult for the genes of the few remaining native fish to triumph over those of the invading hordes of escapees. The genes of salmon bred for their appeal on the supermarket slab, or to mature late and thus direct their energies into growth rather than reproduction, will need to be squeezed out of the populations they have infected. It may be many generations before they are, and until then fish may prove particularly vulnerable to disease, drought or other environmental catastrophes which the original native stock could better have countered. The bird world provides a salutary story of the potential dangers of unleashing unwanted genes. Ruddy ducks were accidentally introduced into Britain from the USA in the late 1940s. They are now alarmingly well established, and are interbreeding with rare white-headed ducks in southern Spain, to such an extent that this species is now threatened with being hybridised into extinction.

One suggestion for preserving the genetic integrity of at least some salmon stocks is to establish farm-free zones, but because farmed fish have not been subjected to the conditioning influences of a natal stream they appear to have no particular attachment to the estuary from which they escaped and are often found several rivers away. If the effects of genetic contamination are eventually shown to seriously damage wild salmon, the only answer may be to farm sterile fish. Doing so may become even more critical if the futuristic experiments involving the transfer of genes from the chromosomes of one species to those of another show this to have commercial potential. In an attempt to produce salmon that can be farmed in even colder waters than they naturally tolerate, they have received anti-freeze genes from winter flounders, and also genes from ocean pout to promote growth all year round. The consequences of such creatures escaping to infect wild fish with their altered DNA are terrifying – and no consolation for the rapid disappearance of natural genetic diversity!

For all the environmental hazards it may pose, salmon farming has driven down the price of salmon to such an extent that many commercial netsmen have either been forced out of business, or proved receptive to buy-out offers they would otherwise never have entertained. Salmon now swim the high seas in comparative safety, even if they return home to greater risk of disease or the contamination of their progeny with alien genes. Pressure from sport-fishing interests and other conservation organisations may ultimately close the English drift-net fisheries as well as other netting stations closer inshore. Yet it will be a sad day for Europe if the only legitimate way to take a salmon is with a rod on a river – if the interests of both commerce and the consumer (who may be deprived of the chance of ever eating a wild salmon) have been sold out to the guardians of the fish's fresh-water life. The pendulum may now already have swung too far in favour of the comparatively elite band of sport fishermen, and if conservation for its own sake will not look after the salmon's interests, morally there are far better reasons for its future to hang in the scales of commerce than those of sport. But that the pendulum has swung at all is itself a victory for the processes of national and international dialogue and co-operation, from which there need be only one winner – *Salmo salar.*

There are now many more kilometres of salmon-swum river than there were twenty years ago, and the same may well be said twenty years hence: that is cause for celebration. Now the high-seas fishery has virtually closed down, fishing rights have been bought out, and fishing boats and fishermen sit idle. The salmon continues to leak out more of its life's secrets to science, through improved tagging technology and detailed research, and sport fishermen are now responding to calls to return many of the fish they catch to the water. And yet, year after year, numbers of salmon returning to spawn continue tumbling from one record low to another. Either enough is still not being done to conserve wild Atlantic salmon or, much more likely, the problems besetting the fish are simply too fundamental for humans to do anything more than contemplate. If changes in climate or in oceanic conditions are hurting the fish, then mankind must just ride out the cycle, and make sure that once they reach the rivers, as many salmon as possible are given as much help as possible to produce the next generation.

4
Brown trout

If *Salmo* looks a simple genus today, with only two species resting side by side within it, this has certainly not always been so. The road to this uneasy, current consensus is strewn with the reputations of eminent Victorian naturalists, particularly those who dissected *trutta* in search of aberrant numbers of vertebrae, gill rakers and pyloric caeca upon which to base their revelations. Yet the efforts of these Victorian species-splitters cannot be too lightly dismissed, nor their conclusions automatically consigned to the Flat Earth scrap-heap, because current biochemical evidence now seems to endorse many of these conclusions, and the tide of taxonomy may actually be turning once more.

The great nineteenth-century undercurrent of amateur scientific enquiry, which laid the foundations of the whole modern study of natural history – and of one of London's greatest buildings – was dominated in its early years by a deluge of discovery of new plants and animals. Researchers at home were not to be outdone by others who wandered further afield, and were also swept up with the excitement of the day for naming new species. Even alive, brown trout from a peaty highland loch looked astonishingly different from fish hatched in the gravel of a meandering chalk stream, and when the scalpel revealed occasional internal differences too, the temptation to proclaim a new species was often irresistible. If some of these early ichthyologists were victims of their own enthusiasms, that still only served to stimulate others of a more rational disposition, and anyway, there remains no satisfactory delimitation of a species. Today the brown trout is described as polytypic – a single species of many forms – but with the full panoply of modern research techniques at their disposal, some scientists are edging back towards the conclusion that, after all, there may indeed be more than one species within the boundaries of *Salmo trutta* (see Chapter 1).

Birds can fly over deserts, insects get blown across seas, while mammals swim rivers and find their way over mountain ranges. These animals can all spread their genes far afield, creating a sameness among their species over a wide area. Fresh-water fish are restricted to their own lake or river systems, which in most of northern Europe are the ones their ancestors first colonised on the flood waters at the end of the last Ice Age. Geographical isolation implies reproductive isolation. Even if they migrate to the sea, brown trout nearly always return to breed in the streams of their birth, their reproductive isolation thus preserved by their homing instincts. Over time, small differences appear in a population of fish restricted to a particular water, which slowly begins to diverge from the common stock as it attempts to fit itself better for its own environment.

No brown trout has been in a British or Irish lake for much more than 12,000 years, and even assuming an average breeding age of three, this only represents 4,000 generations. With the speed at which the wheels of evolution turn, this is scarcely long enough for fish to change so much that they merit the distinction of their own species. Yet genetic analysis repeatedly reveals such marked variations between the genotypes of different trout populations that it is almost impossible to avoid one conclusion: distinct races of trout had already diverged from their common ancestor long before they colonised their present ranges.

There are many examples of different forms of a single species sharing the same lake, while at the same time still continuing to retain the peculiar characteristics which mark them as being of one form or another. Lake Superior was renowned for its different races of lake charr, although many of these have now been sucked to extinction by the invading sea lampreys. Four distinct races of Arctic charr can be recognised in Lake Windermere, and at least two in Loch Rannoch in Scotland. This scenario is much less common among brown trout, and the most quoted research has focused on the trout of Lough Melvin in western Ireland, where at least three quite distinct forms of trout live – sonaghen, gillaroo and ferox.

Sonaghen are open-water fish, feeding off midges and water fleas, which they filter out of the water by swimming along with their mouths open. Gillaroo nibble snails, shrimps and caddis larvae off stones round the margins of the lough and its islands, digesting them with the help of thickly muscled stomach walls. They are pale sand-coloured underneath, with lots of red spots on their flanks – as unlike the steely blue sonaghen in colour as they are in behaviour. Both these forms are themselves quite distinct from the third, the ferox, which turn piscivorous as soon as they are large enough to prey upon charr, perch and young trout. All three forms spawn in quite separate habitats, sonaghen in small inflowing streams, more typical of brown trout's normal breeding habitat, gillaroo round the lough edges and in the outflowing river, and ferox in the deep pools of the largest feeder stream. Despite living in the same lough, the three forms almost never interbreed, each treating trout of the other forms as if they belonged to different species; and this they may do, so genetically distinct are they from each other.

There have been many glaciations during the last two million years of the Pleistocene Age, each of which could have isolated populations of ancestral trout as the landscape thawed and froze and thawed again. Being confined to lakes or river systems during the climatic upheavals between one Ice Age and the next may have given fish the time and the isolation to evolve into distinctly identifiable races or subspecies, before the floods at the end of the last Ice Age finally left them where they are today. There are also gillaroo in Ireland's Lough Neagh and in some northern Scottish lochs, and ferox are found in many of the deep glacial still waters throughout the British Isles, usually together with whitefish or Arctic charr. So far as is known, sonaghen are endemic to Lough Melvin. There are also charr in Melvin, which only reinforces the argument that the sonaghen could not have evolved into the plankton filterers they are today since arriving there, because that niche was already occupied by the charr. Instead they were washed into the basin of Lough Melvin, perhaps 12,000 years ago, more or less in their present form, and then set about competing with the charr as best they could.

To acknowledge that these Melvin fish are actually distinct species would largely vindicate the arguments of Dr Albert Gunther, the keeper of the British Museum's zoological collection, who produced a catalogue of its fishes in 1866. In this he included, among ten species of trout, great lake trout (S. ferox), Irish gillaroo (S. stomachicus) and Welsh black-finned trout (S. nigripinnis), which are superficially quite similar to sonaghen, although genetically very distinct. One of the last great Victorian species-splitters,

Gunther was slower than his contemporaries to react to the theories Darwin expounded in *The Origin of Species by Means of Natural Selection* (1859). These suggested that ancestry, rather than commonality of physical or physiological characteristics, should be the critical factor in determining inter-species relationships. If this was so, then the most critical question to ask in classifying a creature was how far had it travelled down the evolutionary road since diverging from its ancestral line.

Francis Day emerges as one of the greatest early authorities on salmon and trout, although his *British and Irish Salmonidae* (1887) was written with the full benefit of both a lot of research by other ichthyologists and twenty-five years in which to assimilate the full impact of Darwin's theories. Day was the first to assert with real conviction that all European trout belonged to the same species. Even if modern research is on the verge of shattering the species into many small pieces again, for his views to have survived intact in the face of over a hundred years of intensive research is itself an achievement:

> I find myself unable to accept the numerous species that have been described, believing those ichthyologists more correct who have considered them modifications of only one, which as *Salmo trutta* includes both the anadromous and non-migratory fresh-water forms.
> For it must be evident when looking through the works of systematic zoologists, that the greatest number of false species among fishes are local varieties . . . and that local races have been taken for distinct species. If among certain specimens an example is found similar to what exists in another so called distinct species residing in a different locality, this individual specimen might be an indication that both were descended from a common origin, in short how it may be an instance of atavism, of reversion towards an ancestral form.

This also shows Day's appreciation of the fact that sea trout and brown trout were most likely to be one and the same species, a view that today is strangely less contentious than the question of speciation within the non-migratory forms of brown trout. Day went on:

> As to the varieties and hybrids of trout. If, as seems probable, we merely possess one very plastic species subject to an almost unlimited amount of variation, that its largest race is found in the ocean, while in order to breed, it ascends streams . . . we at once obtain a clue to the characters of the various so-called species, and relegate these different trout to a single form, in which numerous local races are to be found.

'One very plastic species' the trout may be, but how plastic can any species be before those individuals on its fringes edge over into the boundaries of another? That question looks set to occupy scientific minds for as long as animals need names, but for the purposes of this book almost all trout occurring naturally east of the Atlantic are grouped within *Salmo trutta*. As with so many aspects of salmonid biology there has to be a qualification, and trout in remote corners of Iran or Turkey may be just too different for even the most committed 'clumpers' to include within *trutta*, and deserving of their own species, *S. platycephalus*.

The brown trout's plasticity allows it to be squeezed into many different shapes and still remain a brown trout – that is the very essence of a polytypic species. Its variety is also a sign of its adaptability, and that in itself is what has allowed the fish to be introduced so successfully beyond its native range. Colour and spotting patterns are the most striking sign of this variety, both influenced by a combination of light, diet, inheritance and changes in the fish's life cycle. How much importance should be attached to colour in

Brown trout.
(Richard Grost)

determining taxonomic status is still debated, and naturalists extracting trout from the lakes and rivers of Britain 150 years ago were understandably bewildered by the differences in their colouration.

Brown trout are essentially European fish which have spread as far north as Iceland and the White Sea. Their southern limits are broadly described by Europe's Mediterranean coastline. There are probably still a few left in North Africa, but they are hard to find, and in many of their former streams in the Atlas Mountains they have been displaced by introduced rainbows. It is difficult to be precise about their eastern limits, which are continually contracting in the face of one environmental disaster after another. The salinity of the Aral Sea has trebled over the past thirty years – whether because of a leak in its basin or the diversion of its waters by melon and cotton growers still seems uncertain – and brown trout have probably disappeared from much of its wider catchment area as well. One can only guess how they are faring in Lebanon, Iran and Afghanistan, where the survival of some fragments of the human population is equally precarious.

There are relict populations of very unusual forms of trout around the Adriatic coast.

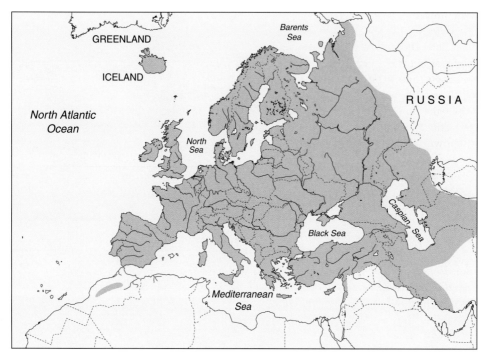

The brown trout's present approximate natural range.

Marbled trout have no black or red spots, but rather a web of pale lines over their darker bodies, making them look more like lake charr than brown trout. If any trout look set to secede from the species it is these beautiful fish, or otherwise perhaps the deep-water dwellers of Italy's Lake Garda, which drains into the Po, and where there are two distinct forms of trout. One lives a conventional trout-like life, and used to reach weights over 10 kg (22 lb); the other, once known scientifically as *Salmo carpio* and colloquially as *carpione*, is a plankton eater, and said to spawn as deep down as 200 m (650 ft), some at the end of summer and others in early winter.

Russians may have made the earliest efforts to introduce brown trout beyond their natural boundaries, in the middle of the last century, but a wealthy Tasmanian sheep farmer, James Youl, is credited with the first successful attempt, in 1864. Given the distance from London to Australia, this success was no small achievement, and had been dearly paid for by several years of expensive trial and error. The spread of trout around the world must be seen in the light of colonial expansion and of the activities of the various acclimatisation societies, particularly in Australia. These tried to ease the lives of early settlers by softening the shock of an alien environment and imposing familiar plants and animals on the local landscape. Importing rabbits, blackbirds, starlings and sparrows was relatively simple, but fish posed different problems as the Secretary of State pointed out in a letter to the governor of Van Diemen's Land in 1850:

> The obstacle to the proposed plan has been the apparent impracticability of carrying the fish in the mode you suggested, namely in tanks placed in the poop of the convict ships . . .

The journey to Australia by clipper took nearly three months, and providing trout with cool fresh, well oxygenated water, and subjecting them to minimal stress for so long was quite impossible. Perch did actually reach Australia in an aquarium mounted on gimbals, otherwise 'apparent impracticability' was more than an understatement, and the trout would have been dead long before the Bay of Biscay. However, while transporting live fish may not yet have been feasible, fish breeders were beginning to fertilise trout eggs artificially, and it soon became apparent that the only hope of getting trout to Australia was to export eyed ova, timed to hatch well after their arrival.

Whether in the wild or in captivity, brown trout nearly always spawn in the early winter. The effect of high summer temperatures on incubation periods was therefore quite unknown to early breeders whose endeavours to expand the trout's range began by dispatching unrefrigerated eggs on a clipper and a prayer. These hatched after a month. Trout eggs hatch in ninety days at a steady temperature of 5°C. At lower temperatures hatching is less successful, but takes much longer. Therefore, reducing the temperature to 3°C would give the importers more than enough time to get the eggs settled into the Tasmanian hatchery. After three costly failures, when the ice melted too quickly, the clipper *Norfolk* left London on 21 January 1864, loaded with 181 boxes of salmon ova and 2,700 trout eggs from the Rivers Itchen and Wey, all packed in ice imported from the Lake Wenham Ice Company in Massachusetts. None of the eggs had hatched by the time the ship reached Melbourne eighty-four days later, and there was just time to trans-ship them to the hatchery outside Hobart before the first alevins appeared on 4 May.

In 1866, 15,000 sea trout eggs from the Tweed arrived safely in Australia, and that same year adult fish from the original shipment were also stripped of their eggs and milt – although allowing them to breed naturally in special ponds with gravel beds eventually proved more successful. From these two consignments trout were dispatched all round the Australian mainland, and descendants of the Tweed stock provided ova for most of the exports to New Zealand in the 1870s. Not until 1883 did New Zealand first bring in trout ova direct from England, the same year as rainbow trout eggs also reached its shores from America.

Steamships could carry cargo far faster than clippers, and with better refrigeration the export of ova soon became much easier. The trout's range appeared to be expanding even faster than the British Empire. At the receiving end were well established hatcheries, and immediately the fry emerged trains, and later cars, were waiting to transport them to distant streams. Europeans reached southern Africa before any other part of the continent, and so did trout. The Mediterranean climate and extensive mountain ranges made it ideal for the fish, and the hatcheries that sprang up in Natal and the Cape later spread their stock around Rhodesia, Nyasaland and Basutoland (now Zimbabwe, Malawi and Lesotho). East Africa initially imported eggs from Britain, and around 1905 both brown and rainbow trout ova are supposed to have been planted directly into the gravel of the Gura River in Kenya's Aberdare Mountains – the first of many successful stockings that gradually spread trout all over the country's highlands. From Kenya, they were taken to the cool equatorial streams of neighbouring Uganda and Tanzania, and little more than thirty years ago reached Ethiopia, where they still thrive in the Bale Mountains.

With America's wealth of indigenous salmon, trout and charr it may seem extraordinary that brown trout ever found their way across the Atlantic. Yet fishermen are seldom satisfied with Nature's endowments and brown trout came with a fine sporting reputation. The temptation to see what they could do for the entertainment of early American anglers was too much to resist (as eventually was the allure of rainbow trout and brook charr for British fishermen). Even if Fred Mather, an American fish breeder, had not met Lucius von Behr, a German fish breeder, at the Berlin International Fisheries

Exposition in 1880, brown trout would have reached America sooner rather than later. As it was, in 1883, just when New Zealand was buying rainbow trout ova from the west coast of the USA, the first of several consignments of von Behr's brown trout eggs was reaching its east. This was divided between three different farms, and soon after hatching the first fry were released into Michigan's Pere Marquette River. A year later, Loch Leven ova arrived from the Howietoun hatchery in Scotland, and for some time the two lineages remained quite separate, their distinctive liveries proclaiming their origins as loudly as if they could talk. The pale von Behr fish were known as 'German' brown trout and the silvery Scottish imports as 'Loch Leven'. Inevitably the two lines began to lose their identities, and by the time the distinction was formally dropped during the First World War, (when the word 'German' was lopped off everything it had once described), they had become almost indistinguishable anyway.

Loch Leven trout reached Canada at about the same time. Brown trout are now spread widely around its provinces, only Yukon, the Northwest Territories and Prince Edward Island having turned their backs on the imports – as has Alaska – all preferring instead to rely on indigenous fish to provide their sport. In South America brown trout have adapted spectacularly well to life in rivers flowing off both sides of the Andes, and if Antarctica is the only continent without them, in Tierra del Fuego they are not far away. There the sea trout reach prodigious sizes, as they do in the Falkland Islands. In both these treeless wind-blasted lands some of the trout never leave their natal streams; others head seawards to feed on the krill, which supports such a spectacular diversity of wildlife in the freezing sub-Antarctic seas.

Brown trout in an Idaho stream.
(Richard Grost)

Kashmir, Sri Lanka, Pakistan, Japan, New Guinea, Madagascar – these and many other countries have all tried to encourage brown trout to adapt to life in alien waters. Sometimes the attempts have withered in the face of the rival attractions of rainbow trout, which are freer feeders and seem to tolerate marginally higher temperatures. Never the less, there are still self-sustaining populations of brown trout in almost every part of the world for which they are well enough suited except, as in the wilder parts of Asia, where difficulties of access have preserved the pristine, often fishless, state of the waters.

The ease with which *Salmo trutta* has slipped into so many foreign streams clearly demonstrates its adaptability. This in itself is largely due to its catholic feeding habits. The brown trout, like all its closest relatives, is a carnivore, and within these flesh-eating parameters will snap up almost anything that lives in or lands on the water. For much of the year trout cannot afford to be too selective. Certainly there are times of bounty, when there is more food than fish can eat; then Nature allows them the luxury of choice. However, for much of their lives trout must take what they can find and are physically capable of catching, so any description of what they eat is largely an analysis of available prey.

When they hatch trout are endowed with their own in-built food supply; this can last them between three and twelve weeks, depending on the temperature of the water. Like most fish, young trout never see their parents and must rely entirely on inherited instincts to guide them through the first conscious contact with their environment. Having no need to go out and search for their own food, yet at the same time being aware of their surroundings, gives young alevins time to find their fins, to orientate themselves and to gather strength for the next stage in their lives, when they must leave their gravel nests and swim up to begin feeding for themselves.

Perhaps only a quarter of hatching brown trout alevins survive to establish territories. Then, if they are among those strong enough to do so, they must start to rely for their food on the current – that great conveyor belt of invertebrate drift. At this early stage in their lives, trout grab at anything small enough for them to swallow which might possibly be nutritious. For every midge larva that comes floating by, they will gulp down any number of air bubbles or particles of vegetation, but slowly experience tempers instinct and there are fewer wasted snaps at passing debris. The most successful feeders will grow larger and expand their territories as they do – at the expense of the weaker individuals which, in true Darwinian fashion, are driven away from their feeding stations to their deaths so that the strong can survive.

By the end of their first summer, as the supply of current-borne food declines and the young trout have begun to identify what is good for them and what is not, they start drifting away from their territories, downstream to the lower reaches of their natal stream or perhaps to the larger river into which it flows. There, while still maintaining some sort of territorial instinct, they forage much more for their food and begin to exercise some degree of preference between alternative prey. Trout born in lake inflows may let themselves be carried down into the still waters much sooner – perhaps by midsummer and only a month or two after emerging. Down in the lake there is no help from any current; trout will have to seek out every mouthful of food for themselves, and not until the following year will they be large enough to take adult insects off the surface.

In North America 'mayflies' are any insect of the order Ephemeroptera, and so to read that these may account for as much as 80 per cent of a trout's diet is much less surprising than it would sound in Britain, where the word is usually used more precisely. There are

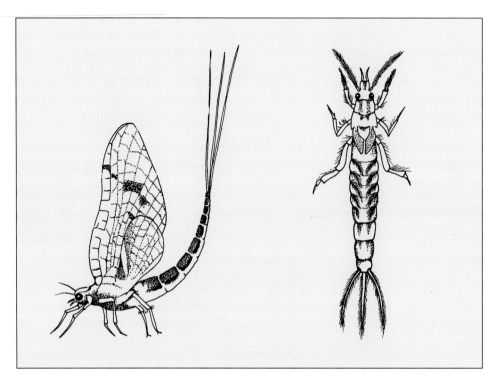

Dun (sub-imago) and nymph of mayfly – Ephemera danica.

strictly just three species of British mayfly, only two of which (*Ephemera danica* and *E. vulgata*) are at all common; these are found in rivers and lakes with muddy or sandy banks, where the nymphs can excavate their underwater homes.

The distribution of aquatic insects mirrors the habitat's suitability for the developing young. On rocky streams in northern England, March browns (*Rithrogena haarupi*) and yellow uprights (*R. semicolorata*) may be clinging to stones smoothed by thousands of years of strong currents. In these tumbling waters there are as likely to be tsetse flies as true mayflies, which has allowed local fishermen to christen emerging stoneflies (Plecoptera) 'mayflies' without any fear of confusion. The larvae of caddis flies (Trichoptera) protect themselves with their distinctive cases, and their distribution is critically affected by the availability of building materials. Young sandflies (*Rhyacophila dorsalis*) need sand and gravel for their protective cocoons, for which great red sedges (*Phrygania grandis*) must have vegetation that only grows in more sluggish waters.

There are over 500 species of ephemeropterans in America, and about fifty in Britain. With so many members of the order, there is almost sure to be an American mayfly of one species or another wherever there are trout. The same is largely true of ephemeropterans in Britain, despite the paucity of species, and taken over a whole year, on most waters on either side of the Atlantic, they will top the brown trout's nutritional league tables. Including, as they do, the olives and duns this is no more than a function of their being the most widespread order of insects in Britain and America. There are far more species of caddis fly in Britain (around 200) than ephemeropterans, with at least one or more species filling every available aquatic niche in the country. These are specialised insects and it is their inimitable larvae that are most important to trout rather than the adults (sedges), which only emerge in small numbers, instead of proclaiming their arrival in spectacular swarms, like true mayflies.

Aquatic insects may spend up to three years under water, as eggs, larvae or pupae, and only a few hours or days above its surface, before collapsing from the exertions of breeding, and drifting down to die – echoes of the lives and deaths of Pacific salmon. Generally, larger insects mature more slowly; some of the bigger stoneflies emerge into the open air after three years under water and true mayflies after two, while tiny little *caenis* complete a generation in only six months. Sedges retain the vestiges of a mouth, which allows them to absorb small amounts of moisture during the final stage of their lives. They thus experience airborne life for much longer than ephemeropterans, some of which are granted as little as two hours to fulfil their destinies. Even though many of them can only flaunt their breeding beauty so ephemerally, the synchronised emergence of mayflies and olives is spectacular to the human eye, and their lingering waterborne deaths present trout with an unrivalled opportunity for massive overindulgence.

There is much more to a trout's diet than just stoneflies, sedges and mayflies in the various stages of their lives, even if these are what most trout eat most of the time throughout their natural range and beyond. The two-winged Diptera is a wonderfully varied order of insects, which includes the non-biting chironomid midges as well as many insects of terrestrial origin. The larvae of reed smuts (Simuliidae) and other chironomids are vital food for young trout during their territorial feeding phase, when they can only eat what the current brings them. Bloodworms are also chironomid larvae, so called because they are among the very few insects with haemoglobin in their blood, enabling them to survive in thick deoxygenated mud. Terrestrial Diptera can be important to trout too, depending, like every other supply of invertebrate food, on the time of year, and also on the nature of the bankside vegetation. Black gnats, hawthorn and heather flies *(Bibio johanis, B. marci* and *B. pomonae)* may all find their way onto the water's surface with the help of a strong breeze or heavy rain; so may a wide assortment of other land-born insects which often contribute much more to the sustenance of trout than their terrestrial origins would suggest.

Caddis larva emerging from its protective case and sandfly adult.

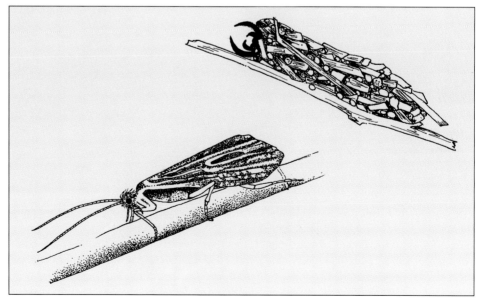

The acidity of water is measured by its pH (potential or *potenz* of hydrogen), a scale that runs from 1 to 14. At 7.0 water is neutral, and pure rain falls at 5.6. The ideal range for trout is between 6.0 and 9.0, levels below 5.0 often proving fatally acidic. Alkaline waters have often travelled far underground, dissolving calcium carbonate, sulphates, nitrates and phosphates on their journey. Thus enriched, such waters are far better able to nourish underwater plant life, which in turn is home to complex communities of aquatic invertebrates. These offer trout rich feeding, and the fish fatten much faster than they would in more impoverished environments. It is unlikely that the alkalinity of the water in itself makes trout grow any better, although the dissolved calcium may contribute to stronger bones and thicker scales. However, there are numbers of other creatures for whom a good supply of calcium is vital for the growth of their shells, and many of these are food for hungry trout.

Pristine chalk stream – the upper reaches of the Foston Beck in Yorkshire. (Author)

Molluscs and crustaceans are usually much less seasonal in their appearance, making them a particularly important food source when no insects are hatching and trout may be recovering from the rigours of spawning. They all need calcium for their shells and so are often more prolific in hard alkaline water, although aquatic snails can survive in any but the most acidic conditions. The snails prefer to live on the stems of thick underwater vegetation, but if the water is not nutrient-rich enough for plant growth, they are content to graze algae around the lake edge where trout, particularly gillaroo, nibble them off the stones. Some snails are so small that caddis larvae construct cases from their unbroken shells. *Daphnia* are tiny water fleas which live suspended in rich still waters, where they feed off minute particles of plant plankton. A sonaghen can filter *Daphnia* out of the water as it swims, but most trout only find them worth eating when they are concentrated in blooms and so can be snapped up, one after the other, with minimum effort. *Gammarus* shrimps offer a much better all-round source of food, particularly in the winter. They are at home in still and running waters, and come in a variety of sizes as if to accommodate the catching capabilities of trout of all ages. The shrimps are well suited to softer, less acidic water, and the carotene in their shells gives a pinkish tinge to the flesh of fish that eat them.

Trout eat frogs, newts, small rodents, fledgling birds and a host of other occasional prey, which demonstrates their opportunistic feeding habits. Of course in their native waters brown trout also eat other fish, especially sticklebacks and minnows, as well as the fry of perch and of any other summer-hatching coarse fish which may be around. Surprisingly, though, fish feature remarkably seldom in the diets of trout, except those of ferox, which reach a stage in their lives when they eat almost nothing else. It is their catholic feeding habits which have served brown trout so well whenever they have been introduced into foreign waters. Trout must survive off whatever lives in their new environment, and they are adept at doing so. Crabs and crayfish and a whole host of other creatures which brown trout never encounter in their native domain, sustain them in the African highlands or the foothills of the Andes. Like rainbows, brown trout are true carnivorous generalists, and when the periodical cicada (*Magicicada septendecim*) hatches in America every seventeen years, the exotic brown trout will be in on the feast.

It now seems likely that ferox are not simply ordinary trout which have grown big enough to eat other fish. Instead, they are a genetically distinct race of trout, and ferox from Loch Ness, for instance, are more closely related to ferox from Lough Melvin than to the smaller trout in Loch Ness. This would allow for the existence of similar specific characteristics within all ferox, which might include tendencies to live longer than other trout, to grow larger, to turn to a diet of fish at a relatively early age, and perhaps to mature later and not to breed every year thereafter (thus diverting more energy into growth rather than reproduction). To a predator, fish have an enormous nutritional advantage over other food, not least because the prey fish have done all the exhausting work of catching thousands of tiny invertebrates and converting them into fish flesh ready to be snapped up by a ferox. If a large trout could contemplate the comparison between the effort it expends in seizing a 15 cm (6 in) charr and the energy needed to catch the 4,500 midge larvae weighing about the same, it would certainly never eat another midge larva again.

Trout which are going to become piscivorous, whether because they are genetically programmed to do so or simply because they grow large enough to catch other fish, seem to change their diet once they are about 35 cm (14 in) long. In the barren lakes that are often their home this may not be until they are six or seven. That first taste of fish flesh is a turning point in the lives of all ferox, signalling a dramatic change in hunting techniques and subsequent growth. Prey of about one third their own length seems to be ideal, and having begun to eat fish, they may double in size in the first year of their new regime. British ferox feed almost exclusively off charr, although in their absence powan or the much rarer pollan are acceptable alternatives. This is especially true in Scandinavia, where the whitefish are more common, and ferox also eat vendace and smelt. All these prey fish live mainly in the open water, grazing on water fleas and other zooplankton, which they then convert into fish flesh for the ease of their predators closer to the summit of the food pyramid.

As well as in Scandinavia, ferox are found in deep lakes on either side of the Alps. British ferox are generally smaller than their continental kin, and nothing over 9 kg (20 lb) has been taken in recent years by the small band of fishermen for whom their pursuit is as much a religion as a sport. So far, the largest fish that conforms to the accepted idea of a ferox seems to be one of 23 kg (51 lb) from Norway. One of the heaviest verified trout of all is probably that of 25 kg (55 lb) found on draining Lake Lokvara, in former Yugoslavia, but this was most likely not a ferox. The Russian ichthyologist L.S. Berg refers to 'Caspian salmon' (describing them as *S. t. caspius*) exceeding 50 kg (110 lb). If these are actually brown trout, then the record looks unbreakable by fish from anywhere else, but they do not appear in any of the lists of large trout.

Apart from ferox, most other large brown trout outgrow their fellows by leaving home and disappearing downstream to reap the benefits of the richer feeding at sea. A small male brown trout, which spends all its life in a highland stream and grows to weigh no more than 250 g (9 oz), bears very little superficial resemblance to the 3 kg (7 lb) leviathan which appears in his own stream in October, but this may be his sister! It is hardly surprising that Linnaeus gave sea trout their own name, *Salmo eriox*, and it says much for Francis Day that he recognised both brown and sea trout as one and the same fish. Tate Regan was a less specialised ichthyologist than Day, and in his *British Freshwater Fishes* (1911) brought out an elegantly simple rationale to support the contention that they were both the same species:

> The distribution of the Trout is sufficient evidence that the migratory and non-migratory fish are not distinct species, nor even races; there are no true freshwater fishes – Roach, Perch, etc. in the Hebrides, Orkneys or Shetlands; yet in these islands every river and loch is full of Brown Trout, which is only to be explained by the supposition that the latter have been derived from the sea-trout, which have lost their migratory instincts and at different times.

There is actually far less genetic difference between sea trout and resident brown trout in any one river than, for example, between the different races of trout in Lough Melvin or Lake Garda. However, there are thought to be at least two distinct races of sea trout, each having colonised the waters of Europe at different stages in the continent's turbulent glacial history. The ancestral race may have edged its way slowly northwards as the ice first began receding 15,000 years ago. They live long and grow slowly, and genetic analysis shows that they may be similar to ferox, which could be landlocked descendants of these early arrivals. As the Ice Age finally lost its grip on Europe a second influx of faster growing, but shorter lived, fish arrived from elsewhere in northern Europe to colonise Britain on the warmer tides of meltwater. Today, the features that characterised these races can be easily recognised in different populations of sea trout around Britain and Ireland. Smaller older fish make up most of the runs in western Ireland, while sea trout from Wales or eastern Scotland are usually much larger. Two distinct races of Atlantic salmon, boreal and Celtic, are also often recognised, and the same geological or climatic upheavals may have split both the salmon and the trout.

The modern map of the sea trout's distribution largely resembles that of the Atlantic salmon in the eastern half of it range, except that there are still trout going down some of the rivers feeding the Black and Caspian Seas. There would have been sea trout in the Mediterranean when it was cold enough, but as it warmed fish were forced to retreat into cooler highland streams, the changing climate effectively preventing them from migrating back to sea. Sometimes other pressures confine trout to a fresh-water life. Sea trout once travelled nearly 1000 km (600 miles) from the Baltic Sea through Gdansk, Warsaw and Cracow up to the headwaters of Poland's Vistula River until pollution, and finally a dam, barred their way – and there are many other European rivers of which a similar story can be told.

In a population of trout where only some migrate, males are much less likely to do so than females, which return to be fertilised either by small resident males or larger migratory ones. This has an obvious parallel in the Atlantic salmon's life, although unlike brown trout, precocious male salmon parr usually try and reach the sea once they have matured. Sea trout seem to find spawning less of a drain on their inner resources than salmon, and far more of them manage to breed at least twice. Exactly how many times depends largely on how arduous the journey is up to the redds and then back to sea. No trout were ever known to travel the Vistula more than once, often spending up to four years at sea and reaching weights of 15 kg (33 lb) in preparation for their great journey home. Yet once they mature, sea trout in short Scottish rivers seem to spawn every year until they die. The highest recorded number of spawnings is twelve, and two fish from Scottish rivers were both found to have spawned eleven times, each weighed 5.5 kg (12 lb), and one was fifteen and the other eighteen years old. These are unheard of ages for Atlantic salmon, very few of which spawn more than once, and also for sea-going rainbow trout (steelhead), for which spawning as many as three times is very unusual.

On reaching the sea, trout often travel no more than 30–40 km (19–25 miles) from their estuary. Some more intrepid individuals may forage further, and fish from Scottish or Northumbrian rivers have been caught in nets off the coasts of Holland, Denmark and even Norway. There are also a lot taken in nets round the Wash and off the sandy shores of East Anglia, which are far from any sea trout river. Despite their unpredictability, it is safe to describe sea trout as far less migratory than Atlantic salmon once they reach the sea, but more so than Arctic charr, brook charr or cutthroat trout, none of which really overwinter beyond the estuary. Apart from anything else, salmon have colonised both sides of the Atlantic while their own efforts have only got brown trout as far as Iceland.

Because they remain closer inshore, sea trout may be tempted to slip back into their natal river in the autumn, and shoals of smolts which summer around the estuary often return to fresh water weighing no more than half a kilogram (1 lb), as finnock, peal, whitling or herling. Rainbow trout in Oregon and northern California also run some way up the stream of their birth as 'half-pounders'. Finnock may overwinter in the river and some even try to breed, but their eggs are small, and these fish do not journey upstream with any specific intention of spawning. It may be tempting to think of finnock as sea-trout grilse, but any comparison is misleading. Grilse have all spent one winter at sea and are returning to the river as mature adults specifically to spawn, not just to dally with fresh-water life for a few months before going back out to sea.

Some trout are able to adapt to life in estuaries without undergoing any dramatic physiological changes. These are the light-coloured bull trout (slob trout, grey trout, whitling or roundtails), which in the last century were common enough to arouse the interests of fishermen as well as taxonomists. They were inevitably ascribed to their own species, *Salmo eriox*, which was the name Linnaeus originally gave sea trout. The arguments over whether they were stay-at-home sea trout which never went further than the estuary, or brown trout that had edged beyond the boundaries of their normal domain, were never resolved. Minute anatomical distinctions were pounced upon to vindicate one theory or the other, but no one focused on the most interesting aspect of their lives – that they reach the estuary without going through the silvering stage of smolts, suggesting that this is not a prerequisite for coping with life at least in brackish conditions, if not in full-strength sea water.

Bull trout are particularly susceptible to pollution. Migrating fish passing quickly through an estuary to and from the sea can almost hold their breath as they do so; but for bull trout to spend the whole summer there, the water must be uncontaminated. Nothing now remains of the prolific runs of large bull trout that swam up east coast rivers in such numbers that Lord Home was prompted to write in 1885 of the runs up the Tweed:

> The second, and by far the most numerous shoal, come late in November. They then come up in thousands, and are not only in fine condition, but of much larger size, weighing from six to twenty pounds.

Whether they linger in the estuary or migrate further afield, trout that risk the greater dangers of a life at sea reap an almost instant benefit from the richer feeding there, and may grow twice as much in the first year of their marine life as they did during their whole time in fresh water. The trout's diet at sea is the same as the salmon's. They are both opportunistic feeders, only restricted in choice of food by their own size and their physical ability to grab and swallow what they want to eat. At the river mouth familiar insects will still be arriving on the current, but once smolts venture further out into the estuary they will have to take their physical sustenance from the variety of strange new creatures the sea has to offer. Initially, only molluscs, worms and crustaceans may be within their grasp, but before very long on this diet, they should grow large enough to graduate to a regime of sand-eels, sand-smelts, sprats, sticklebacks and young herrings. Sea trout much prefer to exploit the easy feeding offered by shoals of smaller fish, but if these are not around they will prey selectively on young pollack or hunt the bottom for plaice, flounders and small crabs.

All fish that move between fresh and salt water spend some time in the estuary to ease the shock of having to reverse the direction of osmotic flow. On the way home, sea trout swim up and down with the tide as if gathering impetus for the start of their run upstream. Sea trout depend much less than salmon do on a full river to carry them away from the sea, perhaps simply because they are usually smaller. They tend to move at night unless the river is very swollen, and may then lie up in deep holes for weeks or even months, waiting for their eggs or milt to ripen and enough of a flood to help them reach the redds to spawn.

While the salmon's refusal to eat anything once it leaves the sea is undisputed, the sea trout's half-hearted efforts at feeding in fresh water make it difficult to draw any worthwhile conclusions about this aspect of its life. Finnock certainly feed in the river, often rising to flies floating down on the current, but older fish are much less enthusiastic feeders and although they are sometimes found to have eaten insects or other fresh-water prey, their stomachs seem to contract once they leave the sea. Anyway, if shoals of large sea trout needed to feed on their way up to spawn, they would soon strip the river of its food supplies. In Ireland sea trout are lured up to the surface by dapped crane flies (daddy-long-legs – *Tipula* spp.), and in Scotland by large fuzzy creations bobbed across the surface of a loch, but this may be no better evidence of serious fresh-water feeding than a salmon's snapping at a pickled prawn or a hookful of worms.

Large sea trout and salmon often choose similar, and even the same, redds on which to lay their eggs, and it is surprising that hybridisation is not more common than it is. Salmon, sea trout and small resident brown trout all spawn in similar fashion, but because usually far fewer male trout go to sea, the large sea-going females sometimes have to rely on small resident males to fertilise their eggs (further confusing the theories to explain any inherited tendency to migrate). A dearth of large males may be why two or three migratory females occasionally share a nest, the same male fertilising each lot of eggs, one after the other.

The journey to the redds would, if anything, seem to be more punishing for sea trout than for the larger salmon, and the actual spawning is equally strenuous for both, so why do sea trout seem to recover so much better? Steelhead show an equally muted inclination to feed, but just enough to provoke the thought that even an occasional meal in fresh water may be enough to help trout back to the sea – in obvious contrast to Pacific and Atlantic salmon.

By the time they reach the redds browny, spotted sea trout are usually easy to distinguish from red, less marked salmon, but when they are fresh into the river identifying the two species is much harder. The heavier spotting may be apparent even then, as may the salmon's distinctively forked tail and much thinner 'wrist' in front of it. The scale count on a line angled forwards from the back of the adipose fin to the lateral line ranges from ten to thirteen on salmon (eleven is most usual), and thirteen to sixteen (typically fourteen) on sea trout. Occasionally it may be necessary to examine individual scales for clues to the fish's life history, and so to its species. If scales from a smallish fish show it to have spawned more than once, they are most likely to have been taken from a sea trout. Those from a larger fish which is found to have bred once or not at all would almost certainly be the scales of a salmon.

There are other ways of trying to distinguish younger fish, although it is still very difficult with only a single wriggling little creature in the hand and nothing else with which to compare it. Numbers of distinctive parr fingermarks are not a safe guide; individuals of both species have as few as eight or as many as thirteen. Perhaps the most reliable pointer is the relative positions of mouth and eye. Young salmon have smaller mouths than trout, and their upper jawbone only extends as far as the pupil, while a trout's reaches the back of its eye. Trout often have more red spots on their bodies, and also a red tinge to their adipose fins. The pectoral fins of salmon parr may be larger than trout's – like butterfly wings – and designed to help them hold their position as they feed.

Salmon parr may provide growing trout with the most intense competition they ever experience, but Nature still contrives to ensure that it is not so direct as to threaten the future of either species where they both share streams. Trout usually spawn first, and therefore also hatch first, giving them an overwhelming advantage over their rivals in the first weeks of life. Trout can also excavate their nests in much shallower water than salmon, which therefore often breed lower downstream. Having swum up from the gravel, both trout and salmon must rely on the current to bring them aquatic insect larvae and other tiny creatures, but while trout are fighting for their lives to establish territories, young salmon find greater safety in loose groups of siblings. As a species, salmon are strongly pre-programmed to head down to sea, and so the security of their own feeding territories may be less important to newly hatched fry, or perhaps the collective strength of a shoal simply allows them to invade other fish's territories with impunity. As the schools of slimmer, more streamlined young salmon move downstream they tend to feed near the bottom in the shallow riffles, which trout have left unoccupied in favour of deeper slower water where they use less energy in countering the current.

In the lower reaches of trout rivers, the water is often warmer and slower flowing, and even though various different species of fish may be competing for space, many of them are largely herbivorous, and competition is actually less intense than it was higher upstream. Grayling are frequently an adult trout's most direct competitors, the two species brought together by the overlap in their ranges, diets and preference for cool streamy water. However, different breeding seasons and the catholic appetites of both species allow them to coexist in relative harmony. Those trout which move downstream of the cool stretches of water where they were hatched will meet different members of the carp family (Cyprinidae). This is the largest fish family in the world with over 2,000 species, sixteen of which occur in the British Isles. Most of them are herbivorous, although dace rise freely to surface flies, as do the larger chub. Some cyprinids might also snap up a young trout, but when they are older trout will have the chance to feed off the shoals of these summer-hatching, coarse fish fry. This complex web of inter-relationships, in which competitor grows into predator, predator becomes competitor, and throughout their lives trout compete with each other, has so far combined to ensure the continued existence of *Salmo trutta*, and to entrust its survival to the strongest members of the species.

When man introduces trout into foreign waters, where Nature never dispersed them, then its laws have less control over the consequences (see Chapter 8). In barren upland waters, which 12,000 years ago were even colder and more isolated than they are today, there may be no fish of any kind, and the habitat is as ideal as any can be for the introduction of exotic species. Many high mountain lakes were above the levels of the floods that accompanied the end of the last Ice Age, and have remained beyond the natural reach of fish ever since. Some of the remote Himalayan lakes in Kashmir, where trout now thrive, were totally fishless before the exotic imports appeared. In Kenya, a series of huge waterfalls have long prevented any fish from moving up into the headwaters of Mount Kenya and Aberdare Mountain streams, so newly arrived trout were granted the rare luxury of establishing themselves free from the pressures of competition.

Not always though, do brown trout slip into their new home with such little impact on the native fauna. If there is only one species of indigenous fish awaiting their arrival, the ensuing competition may be particularly unsettling for a resident species that has previously only had to vie with its own kind for food and *lebensraum*. Thus, in the Falkland Islands, native zebra trout have all but vanished from the rivers to which brown trout have adapted so well. Where several species of fish already coexist, the introduction of one more may have a less dramatic effect, but the new arrivals will still need space and nourishment, both of which can usually only be secured to the detriment of the native inhabitants.

Of the twenty-seven species of indigenous fish in New Zealand nearly half belong to the Galaxiidae family, which is actually quite closely related to the Salmonidae. Now members of both families find themselves sharing a river, and some galaxiids have undoubtedly suffered from predation by, as well as competition from, brown trout. Lake-dwelling koaro were once so abundant that Maoris harvested them like whitebait, but when trout arrived the galaxiids began to disappear from their ancestral still waters, just as fast as the indigenous cichlids did once Nile perch appeared in Lake Victoria. Trout seldom trouble the lives of the small non-migratory galaxiids, which live in tiny forested headwaters inaccessible to larger fish, but other more migratory members of the family face a hazardous seaward journey through the fresh-water domains of one huge trout after another.

The original importers of brown trout into America dreamed of little more than improving their fishing, and gave no thought to the possible impact of their efforts on the native brook charr. Not only are brown trout and brook charr quite closely related, they have also evolved to occupy almost identical niches, and to exploit parallel food supplies, on either side of the Atlantic. They are far too similar ever to have emerged from the same environment, and there was very little chance of the two species settling into lives of peaceful coexistence once they found themselves sharing streams. The early signs were not encouraging and while human hands were helping establish brown trout in eastern America, brook charr seemed to be fast disappearing from much of their original range. It was inevitable that the one should be perceived as a direct consequence of the other, but the actual scenario has more dimensions (see Chapter 7). Even before the competition arrived, brook charr were besieged, fighting against the usual tide of pollution, dams, warming waters and the other consequences of European 'civilisation'. The same surge of scientific and industrial progress that brought brown trout to America was busy wrecking the very streams for which they were destined, and it was the native brook charr that suffered first.

However much the desecration of their environment may have driven brook charr into retreat, their cause was certainly not helped by the arrival of brown trout. The two species may appear to have reached some form of mutual *modus vivendi*, allowing them to exploit their minimal differences to the full, but this has only been achieved at great cost to the charr. Now brook charr seem to feed in deeper stiller water than brown trout, although often closer to the surface. They are much less wary and far freer feeders, both of which make them easier to catch, and if brown trout appear to fare better it is largely because they are less vulnerable to all forms of predators, especially humans with fishing rods. Brook charr mature earlier than the introduced fish, and do not live so long. If, for whatever reason, they fail to breed for two consecutive years, the consequences for the population can be dire, giving the longer lived brown trout an advantage which they may never concede.

While brown trout have wreaked considerable ecological havoc beyond their native European stronghold, they still manage, at least in Britain, to remain remarkably unaffected by competition from exotic North American imports. Brook charr never managed to out-compete brown trout, and any self-sustaining populations in Britain owe their success to the charr's ability to breed in still waters with no running inflow. Rainbow trout have surprisingly fared no better, even though they often dominate brown trout in environments where both species are strangers. Their spring spawning season may put rainbows at a disadvantage against the earlier spawning, and therefore earlier hatching, brown trout (see Chapter 8). Where brown trout have been replaced by rainbows, it is usually after stocking fully grown fish, which bully out the smaller native trout. This is the scenario in many of southern England's chalk streams, where catching a wild brown trout is cause for comment and congratulations. As long as fishery managers continue pandering to the whims of fishermen for whom size and numbers are all, no matter what the environmental cost nor how artificial the production of their fish, there is little likelihood of brown trout reclaiming any of the territory they have surrendered.

The first successful trout hatchery was probably established in Huningue, France, in 1852, but Britain was close behind in the race to breed trout artificially. The varied repercussions of the Industrial Revolution provided much of the necessary impetus. Fish were needed to repopulate streams and rivers desecrated in the name of commerce, and to stock new ponds and lakes, often constructed with the profits from the very same commerce. The urge to spread animals beyond their natural boundaries was not confined to the colonies, and the modern maps of the distribution of different fish throughout Britain owe as much to the efforts of man as to the patterns of Nature. Above all, people wanted to fish, and had the time and money to spend on stocking any troutless water bigger than a puddle in the name of sport.

Conditions in Scotland were generally more conducive to successful fish breeding, and the first commercial operation in Britain was a salmon farm on the Tay near Perth which opened in 1853. Demand fast fuelled supply and hatcheries soon appeared on other river banks. Frank Buckland was one of the pioneers of aquaculture and was involved in several of the early attempts to send ova to Australia. He raised fish in southern England and his *Fish Hatching* (1863) was the first treatise on the subject:

> Man has dominion given him over both land and water. Of the former he has taken every advantage . . . however the human race seem to have entirely forgotten the second item . . . they take no pains to cultivate the largest portion of their earth . . . we have been asleep, we have had gold nuggets under our noses and have not stopped to pick them up.

There are now more than 200 trout farms in Britain trying to pick up these nuggets. Some only hatch ova and bring on young alevins until they are able to feed for themselves, then passing them over to other enterprises to raise to the required size for eating or stocking; other farms undertake the whole operation. Brown trout grow too slowly to be worth farming for the table, but there is still a demand for fish of all sizes to satisfy the needs of fishermen.

The Victorians viewed Nature's bounty as inexhaustible – a huge well that, no matter how deep it was dipped into, would always return to its original level. Given long enough, it usually did, but fishermen were fewer then; they also had more time to travel to remoter areas and demanded less instant results. Now, throughout much of Europe, too many fishermen have raised their expectations far above the natural productivity of the waters they fish. It seems impossible to modify these expectations, and to meet them means providing unnatural numbers of outsized fish.

There are many ways to enhance natural fish stocks. Ideally this is best done by improving the aquatic habitat so that it can support more trout. Encouraging healthy underwater vegetation, creating pools and building fish passes and groynes can all help to increase numbers of trout in rivers or lakes, but often not enough to satisfy the fishermen who want to fish them. More dramatic, but usually easier, is to destroy pike, sawbill ducks, cormorants and other predators, or to remove different species of fish that compete with brown trout for space and food. The lazy chalk streams of southern England are natural coarse fisheries. Their reputation as the trout fisherman's Mecca is only maintained at the expense of the resident grayling, chub and dace, which are often netted out to make room for trout. Likewise, many lowland reservoirs are the natural homes of roach, not trout which cannot breed in them. But even tampering with the underwater community in this way may not provide enough extra fish to catch, or they may not be large enough, and so the fishery manager's cure-all is invoked, and suddenly one day all the fish in the fishery are no longer wild.

The labyrinthine channels of the Berkshire Trout Farm near Hungerford on the River Kennet. The farm produces both brown and rainbow trout.
(Michael Stevenson)

There is a limit to the amount of trout flesh any stretch of water can support (its carrying capacity). Under natural circumstances, if this is exceeded trout begin to deteriorate and die, and in time the balance is restored. Artificially, it is possible to exceed the carrying capacity in the certain knowledge that man, the most efficient of predators, will quickly reduce the numbers of fish back down to levels the environment can sustain, and then it is time to stock again. This is the rationale behind the 'put and take' principle, which, although it may be disconcerting, is probably the best for heavily fished waters. The whole practice raises a tangle of moral dilemmas, but at least where the trout are unable to breed the ecological consequences are far less dangerous than when stocking hatchery-bred brown trout among populations of wild fish with entirely different genetic profiles. Letting farmed salmon escape may have similar repercussions on stocks of wild fish with which the domestic fish interbreed (see Chapter 3).

Trout from a small barren upland loch, where there are few predators and the only other fish are Arctic charr, have evolved very differently from those lower down the neighbouring valley, which nibble their food off the stalks of aquatic plants and breed in slow flowing feeder streams they share with pike and perch. Domestically raised trout need an array of very different strengths from those fish born in the wild. They need to grow fast on a concentrated diet and to be able to resist the diseases that spread all too easily through shoals of tiny fish tightly confined within vertical walls of cement. They may also need to be coloured to please the human eye, rather than to hide among the stones of the stream bed. The urge to feed throughout the year will have served them well below the inexhaustible supply of fish pellets, but will be of no advantage during a winter in the wild, where searching for food often uses more energy than is gained from eating it.

Adulterating a gene pool, that has been naturally selected over thousands of years, with the genes of hatchery-bred fish is almost as certain a way of driving a population of wild trout to extinction as draining its lake or poisoning its river. Even if, over the course of the next millennia, the alien genes are slowly suppressed and the wild fish gradually begin to resemble their ancestors, their genetic profiles may never be quite the same again. Extinction is irreversible and for ever. Many of these isolated populations of brown trout may be well down the evolutionary road to becoming fully fledged species, and it could be contended that their preservation is almost as important as if they had already reached the end of that road.

The most effective way of spreading few fish among many fishermen is to adopt a policy of pure 'catch and release'. This is acceptable to many American fishermen, but less popular in Europe where anglers want the tangible edible evidence of their success that only wanton stocking can provide. Fortunately, there is now a more general acceptance of the application to stocks of wild trout of the precautionary principle, which justifies protective action even before there is conclusive proof of irreversible damage to the particular gene pool. It is also more generally accepted that, if at all possible, waters are best stocked with fish from the same river catchment system. Thousands of races, strains, forms and varieties of brown trout may already have disappeared in the rush to profit from the enthusiasms of fishermen; perhaps even subspecies have been swamped by the tide of unwanted genes. However, just as gillaroo seek to spawn with their own kind, and ferox will not breed with sonaghen, so if the genetic identity of a population is well enough established, fish may survive the arrival of a foreign strain and be able to continue undisturbed on their way to full genetic independence.

To most fishermen a brown trout is a brown trout, and arguments for the conservation of specific stocks or races sound like little more than ecological scaremongering. In southwestern America, the efforts and expense which go into conserving subspecies of cutthroat trout may seem excessive and overly unnatural. However, the USA has at least recognised the diversity of its trout stocks, and what the mindless stockings of non-native fish have done to them. Furthermore, its Endangered Species Act enshrines in statute the concept of protecting not only subspecies of fish but even distinct populations if these are 'evolutionarily significant units'.

The brown trout within Britain's shores may be a more homogeneous lot than rainbow and cutthroat trout are throughout their native range. Many stocks of Pacific trout have been isolated far longer than 12,000 years – which is about as long as any population of fish has been established in northern Europe – and so have had much greater opportunity to diverge away from their ancestral line. None the less, this should not detract from the remarkable diversity which lies within what is currently still considered the single species of *Salmo trutta*, and which so overwhelmed the naturalists of the nineteenth century. It is time to create a much greater collective awareness of the existence of such diversity.

5
Arctic charr and allied species

Throughout most of Europe, anyone who knows Arctic charr thinks of small, deep-dwelling fish from dark remote glacial lakes, occasionally caught by trout fishermen. Those delving a little deeper into fish ecology might know charr as the main prey of ferox trout. Izaak Walton wrote of their rarity, which made them 'of so high esteem with persons of great note'. To Inuits in northern Canada, Arctic charr were fundamental to the survival of their families and dogs, and they trapped migrating fish between two low stone dams. On one of his polar expeditions, Robert Peary collected Arctic charr from Lake Hazen on Ellesmere Island, north of 82°. In Maine, early European settlers netted lake-living Arctic charr spawning in the shallows, and smoked, dried or salted the flesh to tide them through the winter. Commercial charr-fishing still provides many coastal villages of northern Labrador with their main source of income; and in northern Norway, Quebec, Baffin Island and the Northwest Territories, anglers fish for sea-going Arctic charr often weighing over 5 kg (11 lb). One fish, with so many faces?

The taxonomies of brown, rainbow and cutthroat trout are all contentious entanglements of inter-relationships, but no more so than the Arctic charr's. None of the trout is nearly so widespread as Arctic charr, which are found all round the Arctic Circle, and as far south as the Alps in Europe, Maine in America and southern Siberia in Asia. Living over such a great area, and yet often being confined to large inland lakes from which, short of waiting for the next Ice Age, there is no escape, isolated populations of charr are slowly becoming increasingly different from one another. Inevitably, there are suggestions that some of these populations now deserve the distinction of their own species.

Subspecies are continually being moved around on the end of the *Salvelinus* branch of the Salmonidae family tree, and in some lakes charr even seem to have begun splitting into distinct stocks since they reached their present homes. Some of this may be scientific semantics, but if any creature is to be preserved, its existence first needs to be established; and what the arguments over classification reveal above all else is the great diversity of fish within *Salvelinus alpinus*, and around its edges. This diversity is certainly remarkable, but perhaps even more so is the fact that fish from Lake Frolikh in Siberia, from Baffin Island in Arctic Canada and Lake Geneva in Switzerland could ever still be sufficiently similar to belong to the same species!

The Arctic charr's taxonomic history in Britain has run a very similar course to the brown trout's. In 1758 Linnaeus christened it *Salmo alpinus* – Alpine salmon – which, given its similarities to the trout and salmon with which he was also familiar, was perfectly reasonable. It then lived briefly under the name *Salmo salvelinus* before becoming *Salvelinus alpinus* in 1836, and thereafter gradually absorbing peripheral so-called species under its umbrella. When Dr Albert Gunther catalogued the fishes of the British Museum in 1866, he named six species, but was derided by Francis Day in *British and Irish Salmonidae* (1887), who felt that local variations had 'deceived many ichthyologists who have studied these fishes more in museums than in their natural haunts'. Day's views prevailed and over the past century there has been a general consensus that all of Britain's 200 or so populations of charr belong to the same species.

Round the Pacific rim is a much greater variety of Arctic charr-like fish. The Dolly Varden charr is superficially almost identical, but has always refused to surrender its specific status to the Arctic charr despite repeated efforts to link the two. It began its taxonomic existence in 1792 as *Salmo malma*, before joining *Salvelinus* along with the other charrs. Exactly where Dolly Varden live round the Pacific depends on which charr are classified as Dolly Varden and which are not. Up the Canadian coast and round into south-western Alaska, most charr are considered to be Dolly Varden, but further north Arctic charr appear in the rivers and lakes, and the overlap between the two seems to be genetic as well as geographical. There is also a general consensus that the true charr of the Arctic islands and most of the Arctic Ocean coastline are Arctic charr and not Dolly Varden. In 1978 bull charr (or bull trout and not to be confused with estuarine brown trout of the same name) became its own species, *S. confluentus*, on the grounds of a larger broader flatter head, and other more subtle physical differences. Now most of the inland charr in the north-western USA are classified as bull charr, and it is sometimes suggested that they may actually be more closely related to lake charr than to Dolly Varden.

Dolly Varden were probably first brought to the attention of the Western world by George William Steller, whose name is still carried by eider ducks and sea-lions (Steller's sea-cow is now extinct). As the naturalist attached to Vitus Bering's exploration of Siberia and the whole northern Pacific rim in 1741, he wrote detailed accounts of the fishes of Kamchatka. Dolly Varden apparently take their name from a character in Charles Dickens's *Barnaby Rudge* who wore a pink-spotted dress and hat. They are said to have more, smaller spots than Arctic charr, although these are far less distinct on the silvery sea-going fish of both species. Otherwise differentiating between the two in the hand is almost impossible. The green or brown backs of fresh-water fish and the brilliant orange bellies of spawning males are characteristic of both species; so are the vivid white lines down the edges of their tails and lower fins, which also mark the other charrs. Internally, numbers of vertebrae, pyloric caeca and gill rakers are often distinctive, although these latter also vary enormously within each species. There is no doubt that the two are so closely related that they may even form a super-species – which is another way of saying they are only just distinguishable as separate species, and that they only split from their common ancestor very recently.

Over in the western Pacific, the taxonomic confusion is no less. In Japan, there are thought to be Dolly Varden and a further distinct species, the white-spotted charr, *S. leucomaenis*, to which other researchers suggest bull charr are most closely related. In Kamchatka, the stone charr is sometimes given its own specific name, *S. albus*, and from Lake Elgygytgyn in north-eastern Russia comes not only a possible new species of charr – the smallmouth charr, *S. elgyticus* – but also a suggestion that a further type of charr, so far only found in a the stomach of another fish, deserves a genus of its own; it has tentatively been named *Salvethymus svetovidovi*.

These close relations of the Arctic charr may swim under different names, but their behaviour and life histories are still very Arctic charr-like. If they differ, it is more because

Bull charr.
(Richard Grost)

White-spotted charr in Jape
(Kazutoshi Hiyeda)

of environmental influences than genetic ones, and in this chapter 'charr' refers to the Arctic charr and its allied species. Where it is necessary to be more precise, then more precise names are used – as they are to avoid any confusion with lake and brook charr.

Looked down upon from above the North Pole, the Arctic Ocean appears almost entirely ringed by land, except for the gap between Greenland and Europe, and small outlets through the Bering Strait and the jumble of islands north of the Canadian mainland. Round the whole coastline within the Arctic Circle there are both fresh-water and sea-going populations of charr – often no other species of fresh-water fish has reached the particular lake or river which is now their home. Sometimes only the absence of dry land, and therefore fresh water in which to breed, has prevented them spreading any further north. Sea-going stocks of Arctic charr extend southwards to just below the line where the sea freezes in winter; from there on, the only Arctic charr are non-migratory, although sea-going Dolly Varden are found as far south as Washington and Korea.

On both sides of the Atlantic, the southern limits of migratory charr are several degrees south of the northern boundaries of the salmon's range, and both fish run up many of the rivers of Labrador, Iceland and northern Norway. Round the Scandinavian coast, the warming currents of the Gulf Stream create congenial conditions for Atlantic salmon well above the Arctic Circle (66°), and also confine migratory charr more or less within it. In the western Atlantic, the southbound Labrador current cools the Canadian coast to such an extent that a comparable climate prevails down at 49°, where Newfoundland's Gander River marks the southern limit for sea-going charr.

As a genus, *Salvelinus* is far less at ease in salt water than *Salmo* or *Oncorhynchus*, and neither lake nor brook charr have established colonies further away than some of the islands off the North American coast. Arctic charr and their allies seem much more adventurous and have spread easily round the Pacific rim, colonising one river system after another. The waters of Stanwell-Fletcher Lake on Somerset Island in Canada's Northwest Territories only freshened a thousand years ago, and now there are charr there. Jan Mayen Island is about 750 km (470 miles) north of Iceland and the same distance east of Greenland. On that island, Nordlaguna is the only fresh-water lake, formed as a sand-bar finally filled up, enclosing the waters behind it. The lake has certainly existed for no longer than 4,000 years, and quite possibly less than half that time, and now both migratory and non-migratory charr live and breed there, which they could never have done before the sand bar closed. This suggests that even now, the fish are still probing at the frontiers of their natural limits, and that if the world gets still warmer, setting rivers flowing and unfreezing lakes, charr will continue to discover new homes in Greenland and elsewhere beyond the Arctic Circle.

The approximate range of sea-going Arctic charr and their allies (their distribution at some of the northernmost limits is unknown).

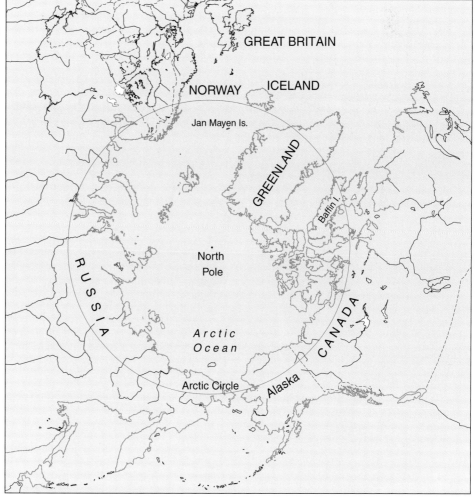

This has been the Arctic charr's history, retreating and advancing in front of great tides of ice, first contracting their range and then surging back again on the floods of meltwater. As the tides ebbed and flowed, charr left their kind behind them in remote watery outposts. Eventually these populations were isolated by warming downstream waters, which not only prevented them reaching the sea again, but perhaps forced them even higher if impassable falls did not bar their way. The brown trout in the mountains round the Mediterranean tell the same story as the charr in the Alps; and most of the Atlantic salmon in Maine are confined to fresh water for the same reasons that stop the neighbouring Arctic charr reaching the sea. In the Alps charr are found as high as the Schwarzsee in Austria at nearly 2,800 m (9,200 ft), although man may have been responsible for stocking most of the charr-filled Alpine lakes above the tree line. Still, Nature, not man, is known to have left them in lakes draining into the Rhine, Rhône and Elbe, invoking scenes of tumultuous geological chaos as the last Pleistocene Ice Age drew to a close.

The more southerly relict populations of landlocked Arctic charr were the first to be marooned by the retreating ice. They have had longer than those further north to adapt to their own environments, but they live precarious existences. At the maximum extent of the Ice Age, the climate in Maine, Quebec and New Brunswick was as it is today round the shores of the Arctic Ocean. Then charr could have swum up and down the rivers linking their present-day homes to the sea, just as Atlantic salmon still did until the outpourings of industrialisation effectively barred their way. Now the charr's New England habitat is so marginal that of the two forms of charr in Maine, sunapee are confined to one lake only, and blueback to about a dozen. Both forms are continually being translocated to other suitable habitats in an effort to extend their range, usually starting off well in their new environments but often seeming reluctant to spawn.

Sunapee take their name from Sunapee Lake in New Hampshire, where they apparently reached weights of over 5 kg (11 lb) on a diet of rainbow smelts and sticklebacks. The smelts were deliberately introduced as prey food, and news of the charr's size attracted anglers from all over New England. Before long, this gilded creature became a celebrity for anglers and ichthyologists alike, drawn by a fish that:

> As the October pairing time approaches . . . becomes richly illuminated with the flushes of its maturing passion. The steel-green mantle of the back and shoulders now seems to dissolve into a veil of amethyst, through which the daffodil spots of midsummer gleam out in points of flame, while below the lateral line, all is dazzling orange.

So wrote John D. Quackenbos in *The Geological Ancestors of the Brook Trout* (1916), before the sunapee set into decline, hastened on their way to local oblivion, not by overfishing but the deliberate introduction of lake charr. These competed for the smelts, preyed on the young sunapee and interbred with the adults, with the result that this piscine gem is now confined to just one lake, Floods Pond: this provides Bangor with its water supply and the pond's health is probably more closely monitored than that of any other still water in America.

Bluebacks are more dependent on plankton, and are therefore usually smaller. To the astonishment of early European settlers, the fish would appear from the depths of their lakes in vast shoals on about 10 October each year to spawn in shallow inflowing feeder streams. For the rest of the year they were almost never seen, but this did not prevent an autumnal orgy of overharvesting, after which the catch was smoked or salted and then sent off to New York's fish markets. Again, though, it was not really the overfishing which spelt the end of what became known as *Salmo oquassa* after the town of Oquossoc near the Rangely Lakes. This time it was the introduction of Atlantic salmon, and perversely also the smelts which had nourished the sunapee so well. The salmon ate the charr, the smelts actually competed with the charr for plankton, and, not being piscivorous, the charr never ate the smelts. Soon there were no bluebacks left in the Rangely Lakes, but the race's future was saved by the later discovery of other populations, and, for the time being at least, these relict charr rest secure in a dozen or so lakes in northern Maine. In southern Quebec there are also landlocked charr, locally called 'red trout'; closely related to the bluebacks they have bigger teeth and often share their native lakes with brook charr, cruising around in more open water and leaving the brook charr to exploit the shoreline.

These landlocked charr, isolated from their fellows for several millennia, are intriguing not just for the clues they give to the patterns of the retreating ice. The degree of difference between fish from individual lakes is also remarkable, as is the existence in many different still waters of two or more distinct stocks of charr. Despite occupying the same area of water and having every apparent opportunity to interbreed, the stocks continue to retain the differences of form or habit which mark them apart from one another, as the lake charr of the Great Lakes once so vividly demonstrated (see Chapter 6). Does this imply that they were distinct before the ravages of the melting ice thrust them together, or have they diverged since then? If geographical separation is a prerequisite for genetic separation and eventual speciation, then any two stocks must already have been on their separate evolutionary trails long before they ended up together. If it is not, then the possibility must exist that they have split off from a common ancestor without any physical barriers to help set them on their way, and in several lakes charr are now thought to have only begun diverging since they arrived there. First minor differences in behaviour start to show, perhaps connected to their migratory inclinations, then more obvious physical characteristics emerge, and ultimately distinct genetic profiles.

The retreating Ice Age left Arctic charr in much of Ireland and the north of Scotland, but only in scattered lakes in south-western Scotland, north-western England and north Wales. Britain is well south of the limits for migratory charr and none of the British fish goes to sea; nor do any of them live permanently in rivers, although sometimes fry linger on in running water for several months after hatching. The best-known charr in Britain live in Windermere in the Lake District, and for hundreds of years sustained a thriving commercial fishery. The Freshwater Biological Association also happens to be on the lake's shore so these fish are well studied, but the existence of two distinct forms of charr in the lake was observed at least 300 years ago, when they were colloquially referred to as 'case' charr and 'gelt' or 'silver' charr. A local naturalist, Thomas Pennant, then correctly concluded that the key difference between the two forms was in their breeding seasons, commenting that 'this remarkable circumstance of the different season of spawning in fish apparently the same . . . puzzles us greatly'.

Arctic charr can breed in still or running water. Fish from Windermere's case stock spawn in shallow water in November and December, while the others wait until February or March to lay their eggs on gravel 20–30 m (65–100 ft) below the surface. Some of the autumn breeders travel a few hundred metres upstream to a large pool on the inflowing River Brathay, and this is the only site outside the lake where Windermere charr are known to spawn. Apart from the different spawning sites and times there are no other

significant ecological differences between the two stocks. Superficially, the differences between them also appear minimal. However, the larger size of mature spring spawners and their extra, longer gill rakers is enough to identify a fish as deriving from one stock or another with near certainty. Perversely, at the alevin and fry stages, autumn- not spring-spawned charr are larger, perhaps giving them an early advantage which accounts for their comprising 95 per cent of Windermere charr.

The two Windermere stocks are genetically very distinct, and tagging experiments have shown that these charr adhere rigidly to their established times and places of spawning, and also produce young with similar habits to their parents. The distinction between the two populations is therefore retained from one generation to another, despite their intermingling outside the breeding season, and this may in time allow other more obvious differences to evolve. Different stocks of lake charr in the Great Lakes preserved their genetic integrity in the same way, by homing back to spawn over the same reef where they were hatched. In Windermere, the north and south basins of the lake each contain stocks of spring and autumn spawners, thereby effectively creating four reproductively isolated

The pool on the River Brathay where some of Lake Windermere's 'case' charr spawn in the autumn.
(Author)

populations; these could theoretically all go on to become distinct races and eventually species, if they are left where they are for long enough, just as the cichlids have done in Lake Victoria.

Distinct breeding seasons or spawning habitats are probably more likely to encourage the gradual emergence of separate races of Arctic charr than any other subtle differences in form or habit, but the two stocks in Windermere are still unusual in that so little else distinguishes them. This in itself may simply be a sign that they have only recently diverged, and if 'recently' means since they occupied their present home, it supports the suggestion that the seeds of speciation can be sown without the need for populations to be geographically isolated. In many other lakes, especially in Scandinavia, fish from different populations may also be identified by their relative size at maturity, their tendency to migrate to sea, and most significantly, their different distributions within the lake, and therefore also their diet. These more distinctive stocks may have diverged from their common ancestor much longer ago.

Two discrete stocks of Arctic charr have been known for some time to coexist in Loch Rannoch in Scotland, and there may in fact be as many as four. Like the Windermere fish, these also spawn in different sites, the one round the loch edge in mid-October, and the other at the mouth of the inflowing River Gaur a few weeks later. The loch spawners conform to the general perception of British charr, spending most of their lives deep down in open water, feeding off zooplankton, and very seldom growing to weigh more than 500 g (18 oz). Their pelagic habits set them apart from fish of the other stock (now actually thought to comprise three distinct forms), which graze most of their food off the loch bottom and even eat fish, growing noticeably larger as a result. Lochs Tay and Earn may also hold more than one different form of Arctic charr, as many other Scottish lochs may be found to do once they are better investigated.

In the Bodensee, on the Swiss/German border, there are also two forms of charr, a 'normal' form which lives down at about 60 m (200 ft), and a smaller form lurking in the near total darkness below 90 m (300 ft). It was once suggested that the smaller fish were simply stunted either by infestations of *Taenia* tapeworms, which did not affect those living closer to the surface, or as a result of having to compete for zooplankton with whitefish. However, the two forms are distinguished by differences in numbers of gill rakers, and the deep-water fish also appear to have slightly larger eyes and are particularly pale in colour; so there are good reasons to consider them as literally races apart.

The choice between migrating to sea every summer or remaining all their lives in fresh water is often made for Arctic charr by the inhospitability of conditions downstream, as it is for many other salmonids. Warm water is one of the most powerful deterrents to migration, and water temperature effectively demarcates the ranges of migratory and non-migratory charr. These are only likely to alter in response to long-term changes in climate. Non-migratory charr also occur throughout the range of migratory fish, and, like brown trout, often alongside them. Are these two genetically distinct races or is there simply one common stock from which some fish go to sea while others do not. Here again the Arctic charr's ecology seems to mirror the brown trout's or sockeye salmon's. Generally there seems to be less genetic difference between migratory and non-migratory charr from the same stock in a given lake system than there is, for example, between non-migratory charr from neighbouring stocks. Studies of charr in northern Norway, in Nauyuk Lake opposite Victoria Island on the north coast of Canada and in the Arctic islands of Spitzbergen all found no genetic distinction between migratory and non-migratory fish; nor were there any physical differences between them other than those resulting directly from their alternative lifestyles. Distinctions in colour, shape or size were all easily attributable to the influences of environment, and the thicker 'wrist' of many sea-going fish probably developed from their feeding more actively and often having to swim against stronger currents than the lake-dwellers ever had to contend with.

For any fish living above waterfalls the urge to migrate is quite incompatible with the ability to return to their birthplace. While fish below the falls theoretically have the choice of either migrating or not, those above do not, and there are often distinct genetic differences between the two populations. The Sagavanirktok River flows north off Alaska's Brooks Range, reaching the Arctic Ocean at Prudhoe Bay, where the trans-Alaskan pipeline starts. In the river's lower reaches, there are migratory charr which seem deterred from swimming any further upstream by a stretch of fast-flowing rapids. Above these rapids the charr are all non-migratory, and the differences in numbers of gill rakers and pyloric caeca give good enough grounds for splitting the river's fish into distinct stocks, irrespective of any genetic disparity. The fish above the rapids are similar to those from other stocks in the eastern Arctic, while those below are more akin to charr from further west, suggesting that in this case the two populations may even have derived from separate invasions, rather than their differences having evolved *in situ*.

Not only have Arctic charr and their allies spread much further than brook or lake charr, they also use their greater tolerance of salt water to take more advantage of the better feeding at sea. In the far north, the Arctic summer is over almost before it has begun, giving sea-going charr very little time to reap the benefits of their migrations. None the less, the dearth of insect life in many of their rocky fresh-water homes must have been a powerful impetus for the first charr to start searching elsewhere for food, and their spectacular growth clearly shows the benefits of even a few weeks on a marine diet.

The movements of Arctic charr between fresh and sea water are driven by very different instincts from those that urge most other salmonids back home. When trout and salmon return to fresh water, they usually do so to spawn – fresh water holds no other attractions for them. A few brown trout in the finnock stage flirt with the river, as do 'half-pounder' rainbows in Oregon and California. Cutthroat trout also often need a second summer at sea before spawning, but essentially trout and salmon will not leave the sea until they are ready to breed. Arctic charr have different motives, and for them the river is often also a refuge from sub-zero temperatures. Salt water freezes at a lower temperature than fresh, and fish's blood is one third as salty as the sea. With no special adaptations for living in sub-zero water – unlike winter flounders, wolf fish or polar cod, which all generate their own anti-freeze proteins for release into their blood plasma – charr would run the risk of literally freezing to death if they overwintered at sea. So in northern latitudes their upstream journey may be borne of necessity rather than the urge to breed, taking them to the safety of a winter spent below fresh-water ice, where the temperature will never fall below zero, while they wait for spring.

There is no evidence of Dolly Varden or Arctic charr ever having overwintered at sea, although white-spotted charr have recently been observed doing so in southern Hokkaido, where the sea's winter temperature never falls much below 5°C. At the southern limits for sea-going charr, the sea does not ice over and they share rivers with Pacific or Atlantic salmon, neither of which feel compelled to head back to fresh water in winter. Therefore something other than the discomfort of low temperatures or the risk of death must drive these charr back up the river after their brief sojourn at sea. This seems to be essentially an inability, or at least a reluctance, to tolerate salt water for any length of time – something that is borne out by the pattern of their growth rates at sea and by experiments with charr farming. Charr also pass through a very muted smolt stage, in which colour changes are far less dramatic than the silvering of young sea-bound salmon and trout. The actual urge to get to sea is also much less marked, and young smolts often hang around the lower reaches of the river without going as far as the estuary.

The age at which young charr are first prompted to explore beyond their fresh-water horizons varies greatly both between and within different populations. Atlantic salmon seem to head to sea when they reach a size of about 10 cm (4 in); this in itself means that those hatched in colder, more northerly rivers generally spend longer in fresh water than juveniles raised on the richer feeding further south. Charr are less predictable, and while on average they spend the first four or five years of their lives in fresh water, it may be as little as two or as many as nine. Once sampled, the sea's attractions appear irresistible, and charr then return every year thereafter until they spawn. This may not be for another three or four years, with a similar interval between each subsequent spawning; again much depends on the latitude. The time it takes charr to mature, and the intervals between their spawning, means that only a small proportion of each run of returning fish are actually breeding. It is therefore misleading to think of charr running upstream to spawn, salmon-like, when in fact perhaps 90 per cent of them are not returning to breed at all, merely to overwinter.

Shoaling Arctic charr in northern Labrador.
(Gilbert van Ryckevorsel)

Not only does the changing temperature urge charr back to fresh water, it also triggers their spring migrations down to the sea. All through the winter, charr may be resting on their fins on the stones at the bottom of lakes, for most of the time in complete darkness, sealed into their world by a lid of ice and snow several feet thick. Even if they were then inclined to stray away from their refuge, its outlet would probably be frozen solid, or else dried up altogether. Only when the snow starts to thaw and the ice melts, and the first trickles begin to flow, will charr once again be in reach of the sea.

Spring comes suddenly in the far north as the rim of the sun edges above the horizon, bringing first light then warmth to the frozen landscape. Each day, the sun climbs a little higher in the sky, and the Arctic quickly begins to emerge from its hibernation, mammals climbing out of their burrows and insects hatching out of their unfreezing ponds. Yet true summer is frighteningly short, squeezed by spring and autumn into a few weeks of continuous daylight, and a frenetic haste to feed and breed seizes all the Arctic's creatures. Even the plants seem infected with a sense of urgency, as if only too aware that there is so much to do and so little time to do it. So too are the charr, which are not given the opportunity to spend more than two months away from fresh water, even if they felt inclined to do so. Some fish cannot even leave their lake before the end of June, and must start returning in early August, and are therefore only able to migrate if the sea is very close by.

Given how little time they can spend at sea, charr grow almost unnaturally fast once they get there, and for them eventually to reach weights of 5 to 7 kg (11 to 15 lb) is quite normal. The rod-caught record for Arctic charr is just over 13 kg (29 lb), but relatively little effort is spent on fishing for charr in the remote inaccessible areas where they live, and compared to brown trout, rod catches give little indication of average or maximum sizes. Arctic charr may live to great ages, by fish standards, and thirty is not unusual. They continue growing, at least in length, every year; but for each fifty days at sea, 315 are spent in fresh water, during which they may lose up to 25 per cent of their body weight if they are not spawning, and much more if they are. Sea-going charr eat very little in fresh water; in energy terms it is simply not worthwhile for large fish to cruise all over the lake in search of tiny mouthfuls of food, always assuming they could see them, which much of the time they cannot. So each subsequent migration, each frantic fifty-day dash around the larders of the sea, not only has to make up this lost condition, but must fuel nearly all their growth as well.

Once spring has arrived and the rivers start running, charr have no time to lose, and larger fish, their confidence perhaps enhanced by experience, are the first to start moving down towards the sea. They are followed shortly afterwards by smaller adults, and finally by a distinct migration of smolts for which this is all a new adventure. The first visit to the sea shocks the systems of all fish, and not the least of all the surprises which the ocean has in store is the opportunity for unrestrained feasting. Young charr, raised for perhaps five years on a diet of tiny animal plankton, suddenly find themselves confronted by an array of marine creatures as spectacular in size and variety as they are in numbers. There are *Mysis* shrimps and a great range of amphipods and molluscs throughout northern waters, and these are the staple food of small charr at sea.

The choice of fish prey around the North Pole is much less than it is further south, where the sea never freezes; however, in summer there is enough to satisfy the hunger of all the marauding charr, which grow even faster once they are big enough to be piscivorous. Larger charr, over 50 cm (20 in), can eat small polar cod, and further south

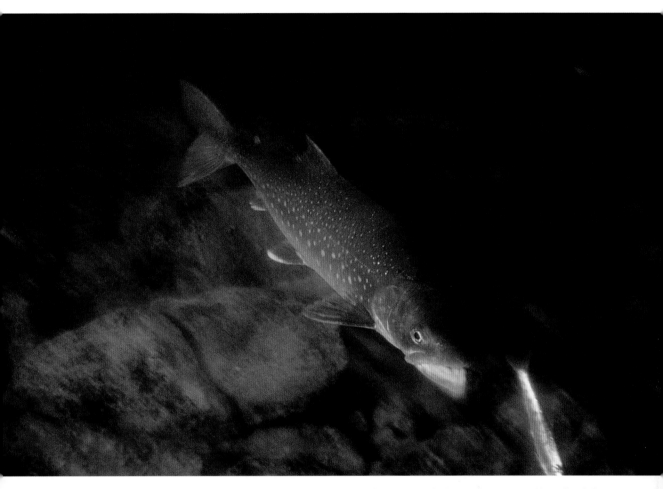

Arctic charr chasing sockeye smolt.
(Greg Ruggerone)

search for herrings, sand-eels and, most favoured of all sea prey, capelins. Sculpins (Cottidae) are interesting little fish, so ugly that the French called them *crapauds de mer* (sea toads), and much sought out by charr and other salmonids. There are both fresh-water and marine species, the best known in Europe being the bullhead. The sea-dwelling species live in coastal shallows, where they try to escape the predatory searches of charr by blending, often unsuccessfully, into the mosaic of pebbles on the sea bed.

The Dolly Varden's reputation as a devastating predator of young salmon, particularly coho, appears to have been unjustified – but only after a massive campaign was mounted to reduce its numbers through the use of a bounty system. For twenty years the charr's tail earned a reward of between two and five cents. Only when this had been paid on over six million fish were most of the tails found to have come from rainbow trout, or even from the very coho salmon the whole system was designed to protect. The payment ceased in 1940, and now whatever harm Dolly Varden may do to shoals of young coho in estuaries – and there is no doubt they chase them aggressively if they get the chance – is thought to be outweighed by the benefits they bring to salmon redds by eating up unburied eggs. If they were not eaten, these loose eggs might well become infected with fungi which could then infect healthy eggs buried in the gravel.

Even though charr grow so fast when they first reach the sea, their growth rate soon slows. This implies they have difficulty adjusting their systems to cope with life in salt water for any length of time. Fish often go back up their river after two or three weeks at sea, and then, if there is enough summer left, head down again for a second bout of feeding, apparently fortified by their brief return to fresh water. This behaviour tends to contradict the charr's undeniable success in expanding its frontiers and occupying new territory. Their summer salt-water feeding forays are usually very local, yet colonising Jan Mayen Island entailed a journey of at least 450 km (280 miles), and two Dolly Varden tagged in the Wulik River in north-western Alaska were recaptured over 500km (310 miles) up the Anadyr River in Russia after crossing the Bering Strait.

Larger fish tend to move further from their estuary than smaller ones, perhaps because being first down the river they can spend longer at sea, and also because they travel faster. From recaptures of tagged fish it appears that only a small proportion move further than 100 km (60 miles) from their home estuary – the one found 420 km (260 miles) off the Kamchatka coast was most likely lost – and many go no further than 25 km (15 miles) in search of food. They seem to move in shoals of similar-sized fish, often cruising together close inshore. There they are easily visible as they forage around for prey in clear, almost waveless water – and are also easily speared by Inuits standing in the shallows.

There is very little time for charr to take advantage of this great marine cornucopia, even if their systems are not demanding their return to the river. If rivers are late in thawing, fish will not reach the sea until well after midsummer; unbroken sheets of ice still cover much of the sea, and time may be too short for them to travel far beyond the estuary. Even feeding through the continuous daylight may not give them enough time to recover the weight they lost in the depths and darkness of their fresh-water winter. The temptation to linger on in the sea must be almost irresistible, especially if they have the glimmer of a memory of the empty larders of their home lake. Yet resisted it must be, and some internal trigger, probably pressed by falling temperatures or shrinking days, stimulates them to return to fresh water while the connecting river still flows and before the sea becomes too cold.

If 'return' implies that charr all go back up the same stream they came down, then it is misleading, for one of the most intriguing aspects of their northern lives is a tendency to settle for different winter retreats. It is as if, when that internal clock strikes the time to leave the sea, they play a game of musical rivers and simply head up the nearest one to find a lake for the winter. These journeys are not born of the urge to breed, and will not culminate in spawning; nor is there any suggestion that the fish have lost their way or cannot identify the river they came down earlier in the year. Rather, they seem to be a response to the precariousness of the charr's Arctic existence, and an opportunistic reaction which strengthens their chances of surviving the winter.

There are clear advantages for charr in severing any attachment to the river they came down. In exceptional years their original stream may be too low for them to swim back up, and they will need to find alternative routes out of the fast-freezing sea. At polar latitudes, the slightest shifts in climate can suddenly open up new streams and lakes that may make better homes than the ones the fish left. Swimming back from good feeding grounds to a particular estuary uses precious energy. Time at sea is so short that, even if they are not growing as fast as they did when they first arrived, charr can only benefit from the opportunity to spend more of it feeding and less travelling. By late August the Arctic snow has melted and the first frosts are already icing up the summer trickles; if charr can then still find a good flow of fresh water, it is almost certain to be draining out of a large lake in which they can overwinter at ease.

In the lakes of Norway there are more indigenous populations of Arctic charr than in the whole of the rest of the world, and the fish in the Vardnes River have received more attention than most others. This has helped to establish certain patterns of behaviour which researches in Nauyuk Lake have largely supported, as have studies of Dolly Varden in south-eastern Alaska. For the first few years of migratory life, most charr return to the river they know, but as they grow and can travel further afield, they become more adventurous and confident in their ability to survive at sea. A large number of fish were tagged in the Vardnes River, 271 of which were recaptured in fresh water – 99 in the Vardnes itself and 172 in neighbouring rivers. Of these wanderers, 27 found their way up rivers more than 100 km (60 miles) away, while the rest settled for rivers inside that distance. The long-distance record was held by a charr which had migrated up and down the Vardnes in at least four previous years, before travelling 940 km (580 miles) to the Tuloma River near Murmansk, covering the distance at a minimum speed of just under 10 km (6 miles) per day. Of the total number tagged, more were recovered at sea than in fresh water, but such marine recoveries are misleading as they give no indication of the river for which charr are headed, nor of whether they are moving into or out of a particular area. Much also depends on the relative effort put into the netting which collects the fish, and it is difficult to extrapolate useful conclusions from the fact that of all marine recoveries, 74 per cent were made within 25 km (15 miles) of the Vardnes estuary.

While many charr seek shelter in unfamiliar rivers, just as many seem to arrive from afar to take the place of the *émigrés*, and so numbers of each age group remain remarkably constant. Yet this should not imply that fish from different populations interbreed; and when they are ready to spawn, charr usually give a glimpse of more typical salmonid behaviour by returning to the lake or stretch of river where they were born. Whether they spawn on exactly the same redds as their parents is less certain, because a magnet-like attachment to these is scarcely compatible with the urge to push back the boundaries of their range.

To breed successfully, *Salvelinus* has much less need of running water than either *Salmo* or *Oncorhynchus*, for both of which still-water spawning is exceptional. A few populations of sockeye spawn near upwelling springs, and brown trout occasionally find that wave-washed loch shores reproduce conditions in running water well enough for some of their eggs to hatch. However, all the charrs can easily spawn in still waters – lake charr seldom do so anywhere else – and Arctic charr and their allies spawn more often in lakes than in the streams flowing into or out of them. This is particularly so in the Arctic, where the rivers freeze solid in winter, and if their eggs are to hatch charr have no choice but to spawn in lakes. Further south, instead of icing solid, inflowing streams may be too warm, again giving the charr no option but to exploit the cooler waters of the lake depths. In between these two extremes, temperature has less influence on where they spawn, and given a choice, as they are in Britain, they usually opt to breed in their lake. A few of the Windermere charr provide an exception, as do at least some of those in Ennerdale Water, also in the Lake District, which spawn in the River Lisa.

Extrapolating even general conclusions as to where charr might spawn, given how they lead the rest of their lives, is almost impossible. It would be neat at least to be able to say that all sea-going charr spawn in still water, but this is far from so, and in Norway's Salangen River they spawn in fast flowing riffles, as they do in many of the rivers on

Baffin Island. Sometimes geography imposes its own limitations on their spawning habits. Round much of the Canadian coast, from Yukon to Labrador, there are charr rivers that neither originate in nor pass through lakes, and therefore give fish no choice of spawning grounds. The best known of these is the Tree River in the Northwest Territories with only 11 km (7 miles) of river between the sea and 7 m (23 ft) high falls which block the way of migrating fish and force them to breed below it. This stretch of water is probably the best charr sport fishery in the world, and their river-spawning habits effectively keep the charr within easy casting distance all summer long.

Charr's breeding habits are further complicated by their erratic spawning seasons and the fact that, as in Windermere, there may be two or more distinct populations distinguished by when and where they spawn and very little else. Throughout other parts of the Lake District, variations in breeding seasons are also apparent between neighbouring lakes. Coniston charr spawn in spring, Ennerdale fish in the autumn while those in Haweswater, Crummock Water and Buttermere do so in midwinter. Elsewhere, individuals from the same population may spawn any time over a three- or four-month period, and in some Alpine lakes, where fish also usually spawn in the depths of winter, maturing charr seemingly about to breed have been taken almost throughout the year. The breeding seasons for sea-going charr are less variable, and it can be said with some certainty that most are autumn spawners, whether in still or running water. It is also fairly safe to say that all charr spawning in running water do so in the autumn.

Charr returning from the sea to breed advertise their intentions with the brilliant orange and green colouring that so dramatically sets them apart from the silvery non-breeders – and gives them their name, probably from the Gaelic *ceara* meaning 'blood-red'. They are usually first back up the river, avoiding any risk of ice or dwindling trickles keeping them from their chosen spawning grounds, even if this means less time at sea to build up their strength. Fish opting not to migrate to sea in their breeding year must spend at least two consecutive winters in fresh water. In the Nauyuk Lake system in northern Canada, charr overwinter in the main lake before setting off up Willow Creek into Willow Lake when the ice melts, readying themselves to spawn in the autumn. They will therefore only be able to return to sea the following summer at the earliest. Two years with almost no food, their energies further drained by the exertions of spawning, is too much for many of the older fish, and they never reach the sea again, often making easy meals for predatory gulls that peck out the eyes of charr flapping feebly around in the shallows.

Most charr usually need to spend at least two summers at sea before they are strong enough to breed again. If the ice breaks up early and fish that bred the previous autumn are able to stay a good fifty days at sea – perhaps made up of two separate visits – they might just manage to spawn again the following year. The river-spawning charr of Norway's Salangen River seem to breed every year, like sea-going brown trout, but otherwise migratory charr usually only do so every three or four years. On average they might live to fifteen, and if maturing at seven, this will allow them to spawn three times in their lives. At their northern limits they mature even later, and in Nauyuk Lake no fish was found to spawn before it was ten, and the normal age at first breeding was thirteen, suggesting a lifespan of around twenty. Dolly Varden from more southerly rivers, where life is softer, mature sooner but seldom live beyond ten.

The combined effect of maturing late, and then only breeding occasionally thereafter, is that a very small percentage of any given population of charr spawns in any one year. In the far north, this is seldom more than 10 per cent, and a particularly short summer

Arctic charr leave Summit Lake on Baffin Island and migrate down the Weasel River below Mt Thor, the highest continuous rock face in the world.
(Paul Clarke)

the previous year, giving fish very little time at sea, may halve this figure. Fresh-water populations seem to find spawning less exhausting, and are almost oblivious to short-term aberrations in the climate. Tiny stunted fish from an Alpine lake and large bull charr in the rivers of Montana or Idaho usually recover quickly enough to breed again the following year. They obviously find it easier to regain their condition from the limited local food supply than do charr which depend on supplies of marine food to restore their strength. However, ten would be a good age for non-migratory charr, which are more likely to live to six or seven, and therefore in the end probably spawn no more often than their sea-going kin.

Wherever they choose to spawn, charr show a distinct preference for beds of marble-sized gravel, although bigger fish can obviously displace larger stones with the flexions of their tails. Even in still waters they will try and find an area where currents have swept away the silt that might otherwise choke the incubating eggs. Watching charr spawning on lake beds, often in near-total darkness, is almost impossible, and observations of them on their redds are usually made in running water or round lake edges. Excavating the nest is the female's task, as it usually is with salmonids, but the charr's earlier behaviour on reaching their breeding grounds is quite unlike that of any salmon or trout.

Males appear first on the scene, and divide suitable spawning areas into distinct territories – as, incidentally, do grayling. While they wait for the females to arrive, males have to defend these territories, often aggressively, against the incursions of others which have missed their chances to mark their own claims. The first female to approach a male's territory may be rebuffed and chased away, but gradually the male becomes more receptive to her advances, and soon after she has dug her nest they mate, squirting eggs and milt into the gravelly scoop. Charr often breed several times in the same nest before the female covers it in, usually with gravel from a subsequent nest she digs next to the previous one. In the end there may be as many as ten nests in a line. The female's urge to continue digging seems so strong that if she runs out of space, she sometimes returns to the area of her earlier nests and begins to dig them up again, scattering the first-laid eggs into the water to be greedily eaten by other charr. Male charr are highly sexed, and after breeding several times with one female may then turn their attentions to another. Because each male can fertilise the eggs of more than one female, fewer males are needed on the redds, and while on some the ratio is more or less even, females greatly outnumber males on others. As when salmon spawn, small resident males sometimes seem to sneak in between the spawning frenzies of the larger sea-going fish.

Like the eggs of all their close relatives, charr's take longer to hatch in colder water. Figures are conflicting and detailed experiments in the wild are often frustrated by the ice that invariably covers the redds. When the average temperature is 4°C they may need about ninety-six days, and at 12°C, thirty-six days. The brown trout's range is much wider – from 108 down to twenty-seven days between the same temperatures. At 6°C, just above the charr's optimum incubation temperature, the hatching time is the same for both species. Charr egg mortality begins to increase above 7–8°C; this is much lower than the marginal level for brown trout ova, which are usually kept at 10°C in hatcheries.

Temperature has a crucial effect on growth as well, but despite generally living in much colder climates, charr can tolerate water as warm as 20°C, and even 23°C if it is flowing fast and is therefore well oxygenated. This is slightly lower than the upper limit for brown trout, although the optimum range for both species is similar at 12–16°C. Charr are not specifically adapted to withstand low temperatures, but that they are far more at ease in very cold water than either brown trout or Atlantic salmon is all too apparent from the respective distributions of the three fish.

Charr seem to have gentle natures, which they first show as fry after absorbing their yolk sacs and starting to seek out their own food. They are much less territorial than brown trout, and, resting on the bottom behind a stone, will easily tolerate the intrusions of other young charr swimming by in search of prey. Often young fish group together, distinguished from similarly aged trout not only by their shoaling habits but also by their overall silvery sheen and ten to eighteen slender parr marks. Despite being less aggressive, young charr seem to put on just as much weight as brown trout fry when the two species share the same nursery, although when they all disperse the trout then begin outgrowing the charr. Much of the characteristic behaviour of different populations of Arctic charr has been attributed to competition from brown trout – from breeding habits and seasons to the particular part of a lake that charr are supposedly forced to occupy. Comparing the ecologies of Arctic charr in lakes with and without brown trout suggests that trout do indeed force charr to adopt a very different way of life from the one they would select in the absence of such direct competition.

The European perception of Arctic charr as small plankton-eating fish cruising the deep open waters of remote glacial lakes is mainly gained from an experience of environments where the piscine community consists of charr and at least one other species. The luxury of life without competition is seldom granted to creatures not sitting at the very apex of their food pyramid, except in areas of climatic extremes, and there are not many lakes in Britain or central Europe in which charr are naturally the only fish. Few animals have been able to adapt to life in very hot or icy cold environments, and at these extremes numbers of species are low. Thus it is perfectly realistic to imagine charr at polar latitudes living in splendid Arctic isolation. Further south, such Utopian circumstances seldom exist, and the charr are forced not only to coexist, but also to compete, with other fish.

Arctic charr are the only fresh-water fish to have reached the scattered archipelagos of northern Scandinavia and the great jigsaw of islands north of the Canadian mainland, except for occasional sticklebacks which provide food rather than competition. Even at sea most fish are smaller than the charr, allowing the migrants to feast with little fear of being preyed upon themselves, except perhaps by seals. Other mammals, like wolves, otters and bears, never shun the chance to snatch a spawning charr out of its stream – on such opportunistic feeding reactions their survival depends – but they make very little impact on fish populations. Edging south, the climate becomes more hospitable and the environment less exclusive; then other fish begin to impinge upon the lives of charr, as competitors, predators or prey, until at the warmer end of their range they may be sharing a lake with up to ten different species.

It is generally easier for fish to avoid others in still than running water, and stream-hatched Dolly Varden often face competition from young coho salmon. When the two are competing for their first territories the more timid charr may be edged under the banks and into the quieter backwaters, leaving the young coho to take up stations on the more productive edges of the current. As they grow older, charr seem to assert themselves more, and the two species reduce direct energy-consuming competition by charr feeding closer to the bottom and salmon in more open water. That the competition is none the less real is shown by the behaviour of either fish in the absence of the other, when the prevalent species feeds both on the bottom and in the open water. Life for indigenous charr is sometimes made much harder by the introduction of exotic fish. Bull charr, in particular, have suffered from the unnatural arrival of brook charr, which mature earlier than the native fish as well as interbreeding with them. The introduced fish also often gain an edge by seeming to tolerate some degree of environmental degradation much better.

Both Atlantic salmon and brown trout have found their way up the rivers draining northern Norway and western Russia, but climatic extremes still help preserve an exclusive competitor-free domain for the charr in the headwaters and in more inaccessible lakes. Iceland is a long swim from the nearest land, and it is not surprising that the only fresh-water fish to have made it are salmon, trout, charr, the ubiquitous three-spined sticklebacks and eels. They were either true explorers, with no possibility of knowing when they set off that Iceland was there at the end of their journey, or simply bad navigators that got lost on their way elsewhere. In Canada Arctic charr sometimes provide the piscivorous lake charr with their main source of food, although in very few lakes are these the only two species. The little four-horn sculpins and nine-spined sticklebacks, which have a similar circumpolar distribution to Arctic charr, are reliable sources of food in the north. However, throughout America, Asia and Europe the fish which most impinge on charr's lives, usually as competitors for both food and space, are whitefish.

Charr have proved how well they can adapt to rocky tundra lakes, as well as to more luxurious environments. Their widespread distribution throughout the northern hemisphere is ample evidence of their flexible appetites. Never the less, one of the biological costs of such catholic feeding habits is that when a generalist is forced by circumstance of mutual distribution to compete with a specialist in a narrow niche, the specialist is likely to prove better able to exploit the food there. Whitefish are specialised plankton eaters. Pollan have forty-one to forty-eight gill rakers, and vendace thirty-six to fifty-two, as against the Arctic charr's nineteen to thirty-two, and the large shoals in which the whitefish gather to feed must prove intimidating to the passive, less communal charr.

The precipitate arrival of a new species in a lake is likely to be particularly unsettling to the native inhabitants, which have exploited the food supplies undisturbed since the end of the last Ice Age, and in several Swedish lakes stocked whitefish have quickly driven charr to extinction. Where whitefish and charr coexist naturally, they have almost by definition done so for at least the last 10,000 years, and so have obviously reached some sort of mutual *modus vivendi*. In Britain, whitefish are generally uncommon, and the overlap in the distribution of charr and whitefish makes it impossible to escape the conclusion that they both arrived together on the same great floods of melting ice. In all the powan's British strongholds – Lochs Lomond and Eck in Scotland, Ullswater and Haweswater in the Lake District and Lake Bala in North Wales – there either are, or almost certainly were, charr. Pollan are even rarer than powan and there are both charr and pollan in Ireland's Lough Erne, but now only pollan in Lough Neagh, where the charr have long been extinct.

If there are more than just charr and whitefish in a lake, the presence of an additional species seems to ease the strain of coexistence, reducing the potential for confrontation. In Sweden's Lake Vattern, smelts provide an alternative source of food for the charr, which thus compete much less with whitefish for the open-water plankton. The equation is inverted over much of North America; there whitefish often distract predatory lake charr away from Arctic charr, which may owe their continued survival to the presence of the alternative prey. If they live with lake charr, Arctic charr tend to eat plankton, and only in the larger fish's absence do they become piscivorous. In the very few northerly lakes where lake charr and Arctic charr are the only species, the large lake charr usually prey heavily on their smaller congeners until these migrate to sea and then grow too big to be eaten. Generally, though, lake charr are far more dependent on whitefish, whether or not there are also Arctic charr in the lake, and are seldom found without at least one species to provide them with easily captured prey. In Maine there were no whitefish in any of the sunapee's lakes, which helps explain why they disappeared so quickly once lake charr arrived.

In very few British lakes can charr choose what they eat and where they live, unhampered by interference from brown trout. Loch Meallt lies exposed to the elements on top of a wind-blown sea cliff on the Isle of Skye, and the only fish to have reached it are charr and three-spined sticklebacks. With no competing species to constrain them, the charr have adopted feeding habits very like the trout's. Shunning the effort of filtering plankton out of the open water, they concentrate instead on nibbling insect larvae and other invertebrates off the loch bottom, occasionally indulging in a stickleback or mouthfuls of its eggs.

The ease with which charr can breed in still water, provided there is good gravel, should give them a huge advantage over brown trout, which must spawn in a flowing stream; but for reasons unknown it is an advantage largely unexploited. Throughout the British Isles and much of the rest of Europe, charr are forced to cohabit with brown trout, usually reaching a compromise by surrendering the territory on the fringes of the lake and moving off to cruise around the open water in the middle. In this way they capitalise on the marginal advantage they have over trout in being better able to filter out plankton with their extra gill rakers. Very occasionally, charr may gain the edge over trout and become the dominant species. In some particularly barren Scandinavian lakes charr seem to cope more easily with conditions that are almost too extreme for trout. Moreover, in artificial reservoirs charr are less affected by fluctuating water levels that may kill off invertebrate trout food round the edges, although falling levels can destroy their spawning grounds.

It is simplistic to regard charr as almost exclusively plankton feeders in the presence of trout, and when larger prey is plentiful they often move into shallower water to share the bounty without provoking the aggressions of satiated trout. Late on summer nights charr rise up to take insects off the surface, which they can do without fear of confrontation. In some of the lakes with two or more forms of charr, although not Windermere, each is often identified by its feeding habits. Loch Rannoch's forms differ markedly in what they eat, the pelagic form conforming largely to the accepted eating habits of British charr, with over 95 per cent of its food consisting of *Daphnia* and other water fleas. The benthic form has a much more trout-like diet, in which water fleas scarcely feature and at least a third consists of caddis larvae. There are plenty of brown trout in Rannoch as well, and so some direct competition between them and benthic charr seems inevitable. Two forms of charr are also found in Korsvattnet in Sweden, but there are no trout in the lake and a neat scenario has evolved whereby the larger form tends to occupy the niche normally taken up by its competitor.

The stomachs of charr taken from other highland lochs are often found to contain little else but hundreds of pea mussels (*Pisidium*) or the larvae and pupae of non-biting midges (Chironimidae). *Gammarus* shrimps may be a particularly important source of food for charr in the leaner winter months, just as they are for trout. On the Pacific coast charr are never far behind breeding salmon, waiting to snap up unburied eggs, and on their own breeding grounds they are not averse to eating other charr's ova. After the salmon have spawned and their carcasses begin to float back down the river, charr feed on pieces of rotting flesh. They also display their opportunistic feeding habits by lurking below fish-breeding cages in Scottish lochs and picking up pellets and other fish waste, as well as the odd escaping fish – incidentally reaching sizes far greater than truly wild fish ever attained in Britain and throwing the records into complete disarray. Perhaps the apogee of opportunism is reached in the recently formed Nordlaguna on Jan Mayen Island; there the production of fresh-water food supplies lags far behind the charr's needs, and mature fish survive largely off seagull droppings.

If they grow big enough, even non-migratory charr may become piscivorous. This is unusual, but certainly not unknown, in Britain, where a fish of over 500 g (1 lb) which has not experienced the dubious benefits of life under a fish cage is noteworthy. (Until 1985 the record rod-caught charr weighed just over 800 g (2 lb) and was taken on a worm off the bottom of Loch Insh.) Out of over 1,000 charr sampled in Windermere, where there are minnows, three-spined sticklebacks and bullheads for them to eat, only one had the remains of a fish inside it. Yet in nearby Ennerdale Water, 19 out of 109 dissected charr had been eating fish. The geology of this impoverished lake encourages the suggestion that these charr are quite distinct from all others in the Lake District, and may be descended from an invasion of fish which reached Ennerdale but none of the other waters nearby. (The lake is also home to two other extraordinary relict populations of marine creatures, one the opossum shrimp, *Mysis relicta*, and the other a copepod crustacean, *Limnocalanus macrurus*, neither of which is found anywhere else in the Lake District.)

In Europe and Canada it is not unusual to find Arctic charr turning to a diet of their own kind, and thereafter growing at the prodigious rates more normally associated with ferox trout, reaching weights up to 10 kg (22 lb). Although there is no suggestion that these large charr derive from a different race, as there is in the case of ferox trout, this cannibalistic behaviour seems more prevalent where there are two forms of charr of disparate sizes, and mature individuals from the one are already much larger than those of the other. Bull charr, with their large broad heads, are determined piscivores. Most of them live too far from the sea to reach it and in Montana, Idaho or southern Canada they can only become as big as they do by eating other fresh-water fish – one from the Lardeau River in British Columbia weighed over 18 kg (40 lb).

If charr are slow to cultivate a taste for other fish, ferox trout are certainly not, and in Britain at least, these trout usually become dependent on Arctic charr. Ferox essentially prefer to prey on fish of whatever species inhabit the lake's open waters, and which are about one third their own length. These are usually charr, and in their absence whitefish, and ferox are seldom found in lakes without one or the other. Very occasionally, as in Norway's Lake Jolster, if there are neither charr nor whitefish, a distinct form of trout emerges to exploit the vacant, open-water niche, and, as a somewhat unjust reward for its adaptability, also takes on the role of ferox prey. Burbot are probably extinct in Britain, but wherever they have had 10,000 years of uninterrupted feeding on charr in Norway it has produced a population of fewer, larger prey. Elsewhere, pike are great charr predators, particularly when the pike are stocked. Nature never introduced them to Ireland, nor to much of Scotland, but fishermen did and the pike's senseless spread in the name of sport has played havoc with indigenous fish faunas.

Inevitably heading the list of charr predators comes man. Some men fish for fun and others fish to sell what they catch. The Inuits around the shores of the Arctic Ocean fished to stay alive. The first humans may have arrived in America between 10,000 and

20,000 years ago, and set off south, where of all the hardships of life in a strange land, at least almost permanent cold was not one of them. So until a second migration crossed the Bering Sea 3,000 to 4,000 years ago, the Arctic lands may still have been devoid of human life. The new arrivals brought with them the technology to survive in polar extremes, although the earth was much warmer by then than it had been when their predecessors arrived, and headed east. They may have taken 2,000 years to reach Labrador, Newfoundland and Greenland, and it is quite likely that without charr in the rivers they would never have been able to spread in the way they did, leap-frogging from one stream to another along the Arctic coastline. Man is an omnivorous predator, and even in the hostile northern environment there were also seals, whales, caribou, musk-ox and perhaps an occasional polar bear to help Inuits through the year. But the runs of charr were as dependable as the seasons – far more so even than the appearance of the caribou – and it was no coincidence that Inuits always made their camps by rivers where charr swam. There was also no greater incentive to maintain the prey/predator balance than knowing that survival depended on being able to catch them.

Inuits spearing charr between stone dams. (Canadian Museum of Civilization – photo 37081)

For all their supreme ability to survive in the Arctic, Inuits arriving in Alaska probably never had nets, and so could not fish in the open sea. Their inventiveness was constrained by the raw materials available to them, and in the sparse tundra they lacked the vegetation to weave the mesh – unlike their ancestors who had turned southwards and eventually arrived in a landscape where they could make nets from stinging nettles and the inner bark of cedar trees. Like all fish that migrate between fresh and sea water, Arctic charr are most vulnerable as they move from one environment to the other, particularly on their return to the river, whether to spawn or just overwinter. Then Inuits would trap them with a system of two stone dams (*saputit*), ingenious in its simplicity. Jens Haven, one of the first

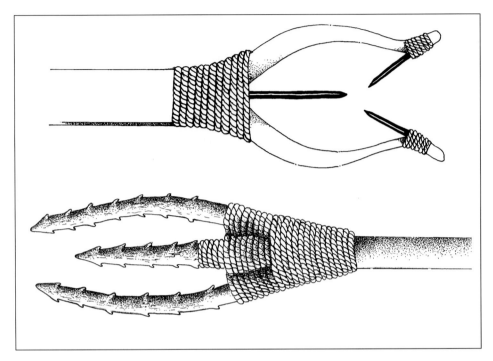

*Inuit spears (*leisters*) used for killing charr.*

Moravian missionaries to the east coast of Canada, described in 1773 how

> a stone dam was made to hinder the charr from running too far up with the flood [tide], and another dam lower in height downstream over which the charr can get with the flood. At the ebb, charr are kept within the two dams and speared.

The spearing was a community affair, and groups of villagers of all ages and both sexes would form a semicircle between the two dams, using barbed spears (*leisters*) to kill the trapped charr before they could escape back towards the sea on the outgoing tide. This way of fishing only worked in small rivers, but was so effective that it may not have been sustainable for very long. Probably it was not, and once they could no longer catch enough fish to feed themselves and their dogs, the Inuits moved their village to a new stream, like pastoralists moving on to better grazing. Because charr are so slow to mature in the far north, and then only breed intermittently thereafter, depleted stocks take a long time to return to their natural levels, and this rotational system of overfishing followed by complete rest seems to have allowed them to do so.

When charr were not migrating, Indians further south might catch them through holes in the ice or round lake edges. At Arctic latitudes charr become lethargic in the winter, their animation suspended as they rest on the lake bed, and they are unlikely to feed until the ice starts to break up. Sometimes Inuits used baited hooks made of bone or wood, later copper and finally iron, but more often the bait was simply dragged through the water to lure fish within spearing range. On the Coppermine River near Great Bear Lake in the Northwest Territories, charr massed in such numbers below Bloody Falls that they could be caught with a fish rake on the end of a very long pole – a devastatingly effective device wherever fish were forced to wait for the right water levels before they could continue on upstream.

Over on the west coast of North America the huge runs of spawning salmon overshadowed the return of the charr, which were largely ignored in the excitement of the salmon's arrival. On the other side of the continent, there are salmon all the way up through Labrador as far as Ungava Bay at the entrance to the Hudson Strait, but this did not deter the Inuits from continuing to exploit runs of other fish. While they slowly stretched their territory along the Arctic shoreline, Inuits relied entirely on charr, giving the fish a prominence in their culture which was not to be displaced by their first encounters with Atlantic salmon. The regular runs of migratory Arctic charr remained crucial to Inuit survival wherever man and fish coexisted. So long as Inuit communities remained self-sufficient and relatively isolated from each other they could never risk depleting the stocks of creatures on which their survival depended. Arctic charr were one of their staple foods, and in those days of economic autonomy this alone was enough to ensure that human predators did not exhaust their supplies of piscine prey, even if it required voluntary restraint to keep prey and predator in balance.

Anthropological evidence suggests that the idea of net fishing spread across the Bering Strait from Siberia around the end of the fifteenth century. To isolated fishing villages the first appearance of nets must have been as dramatic as the arrival of the wheel was elsewhere in the world, and net fishing spread quickly along the north coast of Alaska, at least as far as the Mackenzie delta. Yet the scattered nature of the Inuit population along the Arctic Ocean shores and beyond, or perhaps the jealousy with which they guarded their secrets, seems to have kept all the communities further east in technological darkness until Moravian missionaries landed on Labrador around 1770.

Like so many of their kind, both before and since, these central European Christians saw their remit as extending far beyond the spiritual nourishment of the Indian populations, to include responsibility for their economic welfare as well as for the overall administration of northern Labrador. The Bible may have nurtured the mind, but the net certainly fed the body, and at a stroke opened up the sea to Inuit fishermen, extending their fishing season throughout the summer, instead of it being confined to the spring and autumn runs of migrating fish. The Moravians discouraged other settlers, fearing that the rough frontiersmen would contaminate both the minds and bodies of the missionaries' *protégés*, and it was nearly a hundred years before the first cod-fishing boats from Newfoundland appeared on the horizon, effectively signalling the end of the Inuits' isolation. The boats began to put into shore, trading stations sprang up, fur trappers appeared, and with the insidious influences of the Hudson Bay Company, the Inuits could no longer escape the currents of nineteenth century commerce. Slowly the autonomy of the Inuit communities began to disappear, closed societies opened, and with the European methods of hunting and fishing came the real possibility of upsetting the balances between man and animal which had been nurtured for so long.

The missionaries saw that once the dam was breached, the tide of European influence was unstoppable, and that it was best to flow with rather than against it. Having experimented with pickling salmon and charr for international consumption, they bought two boats to collect barrels of fish along the coast, launching their enterprise unashamedly into the world market-place. Pickling gave way to smoking and finally to deep freezing. This tended to concentrate fishing effort around freezing facilities, but the fishery continues to thrive and there is little sign of a serious decline in stocks. Charr prices fluctuate in response to changes in the price of salmon, and have been kept up by the drastic collapse of the Atlantic cod fishery. Other commercial charr fisheries still operate on Baffin Island, and particularly in Cambridge Bay on Victoria Island, where nylon gill nets ensnare charr in estuaries and river mouths, on their way both down to and back from the sea.

It was not only large migratory charr that were considered worth harvesting. In Europe the fish was regarded as such a delicacy that good profits could be made from netting small fresh-water charr out of the lake depths. The earliest evidence that commercial fishermen operated in Windermere dates from at least 700 years ago and is in Latin, headed with the seal of Edward I. In the fifteenth century the fishery was restructured into the form that was to last for the next 400 years. This divided the lake into three 'cubbles', in which there were a total of twelve separate fisheries, each conferring the right to net spawning charr and to fish for other species in a particular part of the lake. A 1697 sale deed of half a cubble referred to 'all charr roades, settings, fishing places, landings, landing places, places for hanging nets and lines in, with half of the boat'.

Charr were most vulnerable on their spawning grounds (roades) round the lake edge, and were netted out with draft nets attached at one end to the shore and at the other to a boat. These nets, being made out of cow or horse hair, were light and easily operated by just two fishermen. Mesh size was carefully regulated by the proprietors, who allowed different sizes according to the time of year. Even more effective were gill nets set close to the shore to catch fish driven into them off their spawning grounds, but these 'case' nets were banned before the end of the seventeenth century.

By closing parts of the lake during the breeding season, the proprietors at least showed they knew how vulnerable charr were once they deserted the relative safety of deeper water and headed for the shallows to spawn. None the less, greed still got the better of good management, especially once the railway arrived in 1847. This brought tourists who took away pastry-topped charr pies and spiced charr, sealed with butter in decorative pots. The fish these pots contained were often neither charr nor from Windermere, but became so fashionable that within fifteen years a correspondent to the local paper was expressing his fears for the fishery's future after seeing a basket of 1,000 tiny charr 'not bigger than your little finger'. The letter was anonymous, ending 'I dare not sign my name, or I should get a stone at my head some night.' He was not alone in appreciating the disastrous state of the charr fishery, and in 1863 all netting was banned for five years. Fishermen were then confined to using lines; these were sometimes nearly a kilometre long, with hooks hanging off droppers every few metres.

When netting resumed again, the minimum mesh size was increased, and a close season imposed a few years later. Catches still declined and the management of the lake was surrendered to a Board of Conservators, who eventually banned all netting in 1921. Since then any charr caught other than by anglers have been taken on plumb lines, which happily combine sport and commerce. Regularly netting out pike and perch has also helped charr stocks recover.

Charr were netted in one or two Welsh lakes as well, although nothing like as enthusiastically as they were in Windermere, and also in the north of Ireland, especially in Lough Neagh, whose fishery was so efficient that no one has seen a charr there since 1824. The fish still survive in Lough Melvin, where there are no records of commercial netting, perhaps because direct competition with sonaghen has always prevented the charr population expanding to an extent worth exploiting. Charr were also netted in Loch Leven, but their disappearance was more likely due to the water's over-enrichment than to

St Mary's Loch in Scotland where overfishing probably drove the charr to extinction.
(Author)

overfishing – although overfishing may have finished off the population in St Mary's Loch in Selkirkshire, where the locals dried the fish 'in chimneys like red herrings'. Fortunately the seine net fishery in Loch Rannoch seems to have had no adverse affect on numbers of charr, which are now enthusiastically studied and fished for.

Not surprisingly, the gastronomic delights of charr have not been lost on the rest of Europe either. Many pony-drawn cartloads of charr fry were tipped into Alpine lakes, so long ago that no one knows whether the charr in some of the remoter ones are there because of man or Nature. Old manuscripts from the beginning of the sixteenth century record the enthusiasm of Emperor Maximilian for stocking Tyrolean mountain tarns, clearly far beyond the reach of the floods of melting ice and snow, which spread charr around the northern hemisphere as the last Ice Age ended. Since then, commercial fisheries in the Alps have come and gone in time with repeated cycles of overfishing and recovery, fluctuating prices and changing tastes. Fishermen still net charr in some Austrian lakes, and if catches are declining, intensive agriculture rather than overfishing is more likely to blame.

There were three, and are now only two, indigenous populations of French charr, and that self-sustaining stocks are now found in nearly 140 lakes says much for the ease with which the fish take to strange environments. Nylon gill nets still catch charr in many Swedish lakes, and where Norwegian charr migrate to sea they are sometimes netted on their return. In Scandinavia, ice fishing can be effective enough to be more of a business than a sport, especially where charr mass at the outflows of hydroelectric dams.

As hatchery fish, Arctic charr have never received the same attention as trout and salmon. They are the trout's poor relation when it comes to fresh-water sport fishing, and there is very little demand for stock fish. Experiments in cross-breeding *Salvelinus alpinus* and *S. fontinalis* have attempted to produce fish superior in one way or another to both their parents. Hybrid charr are often unusually fertile, one of the depressing results of which has been that introduced brook charr have irrevocably damaged the genetic integrity of native stocks of bull charr in Montana and Idaho.

The production of charr for the table has increased significantly, and they now appear in supermarket deep freezes. Being so uncomfortable in salt water for any length of time, they are generally reared in fresh water, although careful stock selection is enabling farmers to make more use of the sea. Charr are hardy fish, not stressed by living in crowded conditions, and grow well in cold water, even when temperatures fall below 5°C. Against that they mature early, which is a great disadvantage when fish are being raised to table size; also pigment does not stay long in their muscle, so they need filling with carotene just before slaughter if the farmer is to pander to the consumer's preference for pink fish flesh.

Physiologically, Arctic charr are highly efficient converters of very limited supplies of tiny invertebrates into fish flesh, and their ability to spawn in still water enables them to live where trout cannot. Brown trout populations all over their native range have been adulterated by the introduction of hatchery-bred stock fish, yet charr remain little touched by unnatural influences, and the pristine environments in which they live are often similarly unaffected. The need to preserve this planet's biodiversity is a concept which has gained general acceptance; and the genetic diversity within the species *Salvelinus alpinus* combined with the undisturbed state of much of its territory creates a unique opportunity to study a fish in a natural laboratory.

Living where they do, charr are generally far less affected by the fallout from Western life than any other salmonids, although static human populations, fast transport to remote areas and limited agricultural and industrial pollution all threaten them in different parts of the northern hemisphere. Often they are probing at the very frontiers of their range, and sometimes even beyond. Living at the limits of their ability to survive makes them particularly vulnerable to the slightest change in these environmental extremes. Yet environmental change can work both ways, and can act to make life easier rather than harder at the fringes of the charr's existence. After all, it has taken charr not much more than 10,000 years to spread from southern Europe and from a line roughly along the USA/Canadian border, almost to the North Pole.

6
Lake charr

Disasters often bring their victims uncalled for attention. Sea lampreys, first given access to the Great Lakes by the Welland Ship Canal, eventually rasped the lake charr into oblivion from every lake but Superior, and now the world knows far more about lake charr than it otherwise would. They lead extraordinarily different lives from all the salmon, trout and other charr, not least through being confirmed still-water breeders, and so ill at ease in salt water that perhaps they will eventually no longer be able to survive in it. Theoretically, being spared the dangers of migrating to sea or upstream to spawn should increase their chances of survival. None the less, growing slowly, maturing so late and living to great ages, they have always been alarmingly susceptible to overfishing, and this may have contributed to their decline in the Great Lakes.

Compared to the Arctic charr's, the lake charr's taxonomy is supremely simple, and a lake charr is always a lake charr – except to those who still prefer to call it a lake trout. Lake charr are spread throughout most of North America north of the USA/Canadian border, as well as down into the Great Lakes and New England. From time to time they have been introduced into other parts of the USA, and experimented with in South America, Europe and New Zealand, especially in troutless lakes with no running inflows. They can be a risky prospect as an exotic introduction to foreign waters: being at the apex of the food pyramid, and usually committed piscivores, they are always potentially damaging to populations of other fish on which they depend to reach the size Nature intended.

Nearly all their present range was under the Wisconsin Ice Sheet until 12,000 years ago, and where they sought refuge during the Ice Age is not clear. Some may have lingered in ice-free areas of Alaska, while others were pushed further south into the Mississippi basin. When the ice began to thaw, the lake charr nosed their way gradually northwards on the floods of meltwater, populating one lake after another along the way. Their intolerance of salt water has meant that they have never crossed the Bering Sea to Asia, nor reached the Island of Newfoundland, but the Arctic Ocean is much less saline and lake charr have made it across narrow straits to some of the islands close to the north coast of Canada. Their general range is very similar to the Arctic charr's in North America. Strangely, though, the two are seldom found together in the same lake, especially if they would be the only two species and there are no whitefish to provide the lake charr with alternative prey. In lakes where they did once coexist, the piscivorous lake charr may eventually have wiped out their Arctic cousins, which disappeared without leaving any sign that they ever lived there. Occasionally the two charrs seem to have settled for more peaceful coexistence, and in northern Canada they have been known to interbreed – as they did in Lake Sunapee in New Hampshire, where introduced lake charr

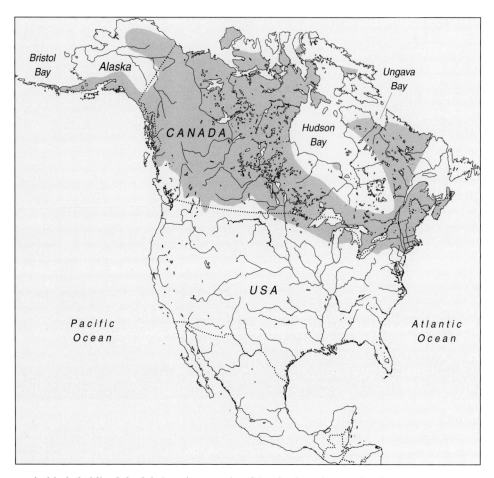

The natural range of lake charr.

probably hybridised the lake's unique strain of Arctic charr into extinction.

Their strong affinity for fresh water means that lake charr seldom exploit the richer feeding at sea which fattens up Arctic charr at such a startling rate. Just occasionally, odd fish are found in northern estuaries, where salinity is lower; lake charr have turned up in nets set for salmon in Bristol Bay in Alaska, as well as in eastern Canada in Hudson and Ungava Bays. Parasites associated exclusively with salt water (e.g. *Brachyphallus crenatus*) are often found in lake charr from coastal Labrador lakes, suggesting that these fish visit estuaries more often than may be supposed. The remains of capelin in their stomachs are also good evidence that they make the most of their piscivorous inclinations once they get there.

Salvelinus namaycush are specialised fish with a narrow niche effectively confining them to deep still waters, cool and rich in oxygen. In summer they may have to chase the layers of better oxygenated water up or down the water column. Their homes are often rocky impoverished lakes, in which they grow very slowly until they become large enough to switch to a diet of fish. Occasionally they move into the rivers which feed or drain their native lake, and in the far north some scattered populations of lake charr spend their whole lives in running water. The lakes they live in need not be very large, although populations are clearly better equipped for long-term survival if many individuals

Lake Charr.
(US Department of the Interior, Great Lakes Science Center, Ann Arbor, Michigan)

contribute to a greater gene pool. They do not have to be very deep either, and the charr are found in many of the shallow depressions in the tundra above the Arctic Circle, as long as these stay cold enough during the summer and do not freeze solid in winter. For much of the year they live on the lake bed, whatever the depth. Great Bear Lake, in the Northwest Territories, is big (over 30,000 sq. km – 11,600 sq. miles) and deep, and lake charr have been caught down in its total darkness at depths of over 300 m (980 ft).

There is not much colour on a lake charr, even when it is about to spawn. The spots are paler than the rest of its greeny-brown body – a negative of the darker-spotted trout and salmon. Its back may be lightly covered in whorls, but less so than the brook charr's, from which lake charr are also distinguished by their deeply forked tails. The spotting often extends over the tail and fins, and distinct white edges line the lower fins, which are sometimes touched with orange too; so is the flesh of smaller individuals which are still on a diet of fresh-water shrimps and other crustaceans. There is little difference between the sexes, even during spawning, although some males then show a darker line along their flanks.

The huge size of many lake charr is all the more remarkable for being reached on an exclusively fresh-water diet, and every gram of their weight is usually hard earned from foraging around the barren waters of a rock-strewn lake. The heaviest on record weighed 46 kg (101 lb), and got tangled up in a net in Lake Athabasca in Saskatchewan. Further north the feeding season is much shorter, and lakes may be covered with ice until after midsummer; they are also less productive and the fish grow far more slowly, exploiting what little food they can find with maximum efficiency. Still, the recent rod record is 29 kg

(64 lb), from Great Bear Lake. Some of the enormous salmonids coming out of Lake Titicaca in Peru are apparently lake charr derived from introduced ancestors, and local fishermen are said to have caught specimens weighing up to 38 kg (84 lb).

To grow so huge, lake charr must live to great ages – far longer than any other salmonids – and their lives can even be measured on the same scale as those longest-lived of all freshwater fish, the sturgeons. There is something almost venerable about a huge fish that has spent sixty-two years in a remote northern Canadian lake – and sad that it had to die to claim the record of the oldest lake charr ever captured. Great Bear Lake has produced one of fifty-three years old of unknown weight, and also a forty-three-year-old weighing 23 kg (51 lb). That growing old does not necessarily imply growing large is evident from the lake charr fished out of Sassenach Lake in Jasper National Park, aged twenty-eight, but only 33 cm (13 in) long. Scales are often poor indicators of age because the fish grow so slowly and the annuli are indecipherably close together. Slightly more reliable, particularly as fish get older, are otolith bones from the ear, although with lake charr aged twenty or more, even these may be difficult to interpret.

Reaching so great a size on such an impoverished diet is superficially something of a biological contradiction. Obviously longevity is almost fundamental to great weight, but so is maximising the sparse resources of these barren lakes with extreme efficiency. The opportunistic feeding habits, which contribute so much to their family's success, were never more vital than to lake charr, especially to those in the far north, whose summer feeding seasons are all too brief. There is no scope for picking and choosing when the menu is so short, and it is hardly surprising that lake charr are forced to eat their own kind where alternative food is particularly scarce.

Their yolk sacs give young lake charr the same kick start to life that any other young salmonid gets, allowing them to stay nestled in their natal crevices for several weeks before setting out in search of their own food. Fish born in rivers usually head downstream soon after they emerge, snapping up any tiny invertebrates they find on the way. Otherwise, lake charr are destined to forage for food all their lives, cruising through the water in continual search of prey as any other still-water fish would do.

In more southerly latitudes, like Ontario, Quebec and the Great Lakes region, lake charr fry are presented with a wide variety of insects, snails and crustacea to set them on their way. The ubiquitous opossum shrimp *(Mysis relicta)* is a mainstay of the diets of many young salmonids all over the northern hemisphere. Up to 20 mm (0.8 in) long, with large black eyes on the end of stalks, it is a relic of glacial eras and crucial fare during the early years of Great Lakes charr, as well as supplementing their piscivorous diets as they get older. There is hardly a patch of water in Alaska and northern Canada from which mosquitos do not emerge in July or August, and their larvae are a boon to many different species of fish; so too are the adults, and in shallower lakes even lake charr abandon the security of the darkness to come up and sip them off the surface. Damselfly and dragonfly larvae shed their skins many times, and during their early instars are easily caught by first year charr – although not at the time the insects are close to emerging, when they may even reverse the pecking order and attack small fish themselves.

Lake charr are particularly intolerant of conditions much outside their ideal range. They start to feel uncomfortable when the water warms above 12°C or 13°C or the oxygen content falls below about six parts per million (ppm) – above 22°C or below 4 ppm and they may die. Temperature and oxygen content are intimately connected in that as the former falls, the latter rises; so usually, but not always, in finding cool enough water, the fish also satisfy their need for plenty of oxygen. In spring, when the lake edges are just starting to lose their winter's chill, conditions in the shallows are briefly ideal for both predators and prey, and charr are presented with an abundance and variety of food the like of which will not come their way again for the next twelve months. Then, as the days lengthen and the sun beats stronger, the shallows gradually become too warm for them, forcing them away from the shore, and from the shoals of smaller fish which so easily sated them, but for such a short time. All through the summer, Nature continues teasing the charr by making them abandon their choicest prey just when they most need it.

In relatively shallow lakes, like Erie, water starts to stratify in summer, and the upper layer (epilimnion) heats up far above the charr's liking. Down at the bottom of the lake bowl is the hypolimnion, which may be only 4°C, the temperature at which water is densest. This is colder than lake charr and much of their prey prefer, and the water is often poorly oxygenated. Charr are therefore forced into the central thermocline, where water conditions may be closest to ideal. There they can rest comfortably throughout the summer, although they continue paying the biological price for doing so, particularly in more southerly lakes, by missing out on the rich inshore supplies of piscine prey. Most insects hatch around the stony shallows and reedy fringes of lakes, and fish catch the adults most easily on the surface; yet in the summer these may also be beyond the reach of lake charr, which are perforce confined to a diet of plankton and any occasional fish that stray unguardedly into the open water. The free floating plankton are apparently taken one by one, rather than being sieved through gill rakers, as Arctic charr feed, and this further slows the lake charr's summer growth.

Deep cold lakes stratify much less. Superior is about 400 m (1,300 ft) deep and stratification is minimal; so it is in Tahoe which is 500 m (1,600 ft) at its deepest, and where the introduced lake charr indulge in the luxury of grazing crayfish (*Pacifastacus leniusculus*) off the bottom all summer long. These exotic lake charr stand accused of

*The opossum shrimp (*Mysis relicta*) is an important source of food for salmonids in lakes throughout the northern hemisphere.*

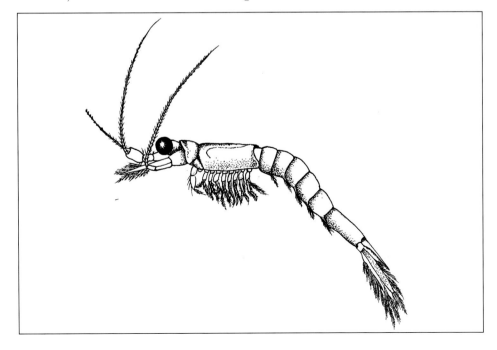

pursuing the native Lahontan cutthroat to extinction. The charr's recent appearance in Yellowstone Lake for the first time could also presage disaster for its huge population of the distinctive subspecies of cutthroat, *Oncorhynchus clarki bouvieri*, variously reckoned to number between one and four million. The lake is the cutthroat's last great refuge, where they are largely unadulterated by the genes of rainbow or other strains of cutthroat trout, and if the lake charr find conditions as ideal as seems likely, the consequences for the native fish could be catastrophic (see Chapter 9).

Despite their preference for the cold, lake charr are sometimes found in the shallows or near the surface, defying their own inclinations in water far warmer than they prefer. Then they are probably on feeding forays, when a few hours of mild distress is fully repaid by the opportunity of much richer pickings than they would ever find in the open water. In the Great Lakes, charr are often lured into the shallows by the chance to gobble up spawning alewives in July; mountain whitefish are worth the discomfort of warm water in Tahoe, and so are grasshoppers hatching in the bankside scrub round the edge of Great Slave Lake in northern Canada.

Lake charr may eventually weigh about 1 kg (2 lb) on a diet of plankton, and in Alaska they were recorded growing larger on a regular supply of tundra voles, but if they are to reach any great size they must eat fish. As it does with ferox brown trout when they abandon their invertebrate menu and start chasing Arctic charr, that critical change to a piscivorous diet sets lake charr growing far faster than they ever did before. What fish nourish that growth clearly depends on the available choice, and the size of both predator and prey. Generally, larger and more southerly lakes have more diverse fish communities than smaller ones further north, although living in more productive lakes may not be so advantageous if much of this diversity stays out of the lake charr's reach in the summer. Nearly 140 different species of fish have been noted in Lake Erie at one time or another, which would give the lake charr something to feed off almost anywhere at any time of year. At the other end of the diversity scale – and of the lake charr's range – the only other fish for lake charr to feed on in Willow Lake, on the Arctic Ocean coast, are Arctic charr and nine-spined sticklebacks. In this desolate area the water is so cold that the predators can forage wherever they like at any time of the year, ice permitting. What they may miss in variety of prey, they make up for by feeding much more consistently than they could if they were forced to retreat from the best feeding areas in the summer.

The fish faunas of the various Great Lakes are each a jarring mishmash of indigenous and exotic species. Some stocks of indigenous fish are shadows of their natural abundance, and, like lake charr, can only be sustained by artificial output; others have simply lapsed into near-obscurity, as lake sturgeon have done. The exotic alewives and rainbow smelts have both adapted so well to their new surroundings that they flourish, for better or worse, with no further assistance from mankind. Sea lampreys are so successful that they need continual control with spawning barriers and poisons. Other exotic species, particularly rainbow trout and chinook and coho salmon, are deemed worth spending huge amounts of public money on, and millions of their domestically produced fry are poured into the lakes every year, usually to satisfy the inflated hopes of fishermen. Rainbow trout are well established and breed freely in many of the feeder streams without any assistance from hatchery managers. This is far outside their natural territory, although not as far as it is for brown trout, which are also quite at home round the edges of the lakes.

The most unnatural of all unnatural fish in the Great Lakes are the splakes, crosses between lake and brook charr, and man-produced to mature early with no other purpose than to attach themselves to a fisherman's hook. Generally it is the populations of large fish at the top of the food pyramid which have been manipulated or interfered with, and many of the species lower down, like nine-spined sticklebacks, still survive easily in the niches they evolved to fill. These little fish continue to be preyed upon, both by indigenous fish such as the remaining lake charr and by introduced species like coho salmon. Provided their own supplies of food are not depleted by human-induced pollution or other environmental catastrophes, they are likely to continue playing their role as forage fish for any predator large enough to seize them.

Bigger charr eat bigger prey – it is much more energy-efficient to catch and consume one large fish than several small ones. Size, of course, is all relative, and lake charr slowly move on to larger prey, shunning the easily caught sticklebacks in favour of whitefish (ciscos), or simply increasing their ideal size of whitefish in step with their growth. Ciscos are also called lake herrings and in many colder lakes are almost the lake charr's only available prey. In the Great Lakes and other southerly waters whitefish search out cooler areas in the summer, and this makes them especially important food for lake charr which are also retreating from the heat. The exotic rainbow smelts are another key prey for Great Lakes charr, as well as for the equally exotic coho salmon, and further north lake charr may be sustained by the supremely elegant Arctic grayling, despite their spiny dorsal fins.

For much of the year, lake charr, especially younger ones, tend to remain on the bottom. There they catch four-horn sculpins, slimy sculpins and other Cottidae that are foraging around among the stones; bottom-dwelling suckers are also easy prey. Burbot are the only fresh-water cod in North America, and take their name from the French *bourbeter*, meaning to wallow in mud. Being particularly active in winter and found down at depths of over 200 m (660 ft) makes young ones natural prey for lake charr where the two species coexist.

As they get bigger, lake charr tend to move off the bottom in search of the open-water food supplies which can satisfy their needs for larger, more energy-saving prey. This almost invariably means other fish, although lake charr once had such a reputation as omnivores that W. C. Kendall wrote in his *Trout and Charrs of New England* (1914) of their eating

> tin cans, rags, raw potatoes, chicken and ham bones, salt pork, corn cobs, spoons, silver dollars, a watch and chain and in one instance a piece of tarred rope two feet long. In the spring wild pigeons were often found in their stomachs. It is thought that these birds frequently become bewildered in their flight over the lakes, settle down on the water and become the prey of trout.

When stocked into strange waters, beyond their natural territory, lake charr must live off whatever they find there, and like all their close relatives usually seem to have little difficulty doing so. Unburdened by any inherited fastidiousness, charr introduced into Colorado took easily to a diet of long-nose suckers or tui chub, and those in Sweden continue to survive off perch and the local whitefish, *Coregonus lavaretus*. Transfers of fish from one lake to another show that genes have very little control over growth. Lake charr whose ancestors have spent the last 12,000 years in a rock-strewn lake, one generation after another stunted by poor feeding, soon respond to a better diet when moved to more fertile waters, just as trout do. Similarly, when exotic creatures like opossum shrimps or rainbow smelts are introduced into their lake, the charr are quick to take advantage of the new-found food supplies.

Eventually, if they survive long enough, lake charr will eat their way to the top of the food pyramid, there to rest as the ultimate predator in their community. In this privileged position they have few natural enemies (leaving aside the sea lamprey, more of which later), and throughout most of their northern range they continue to thrive, despite growing so slowly and maturing so late. Harbour seals have reached Quebec's Lower Seal Lake, but threaten the charr in very few other lakes. Arctic lampreys are also unusual predators and have only found their way into a small number of northern waters like Great Slave Lake. In the sparse conditions of the Arctic tundra, lake charr may be tempted to eat their own kind, and may not survive unless they do. Otherwise, even little fry growing slowly bigger in their deep-water nurseries are often spared the serious attentions of larger fish – although in the Great Lakes, alewives are widely believed to eat newly emerged lake charr, unaware that they are devouring their most potentially devastating predators.

Mature lake charr seldom experience serious competition, but when they are younger might find themselves chasing the same prey as other species of fish – fish which will one day be charr food themselves. Burbot also like whitefish, sculpins and ciscos, and while northern pike (the same species as in Europe) are also theoretical competitors, they ambush their prey in shallower weedier water than lake charr usually haunt.

Staying in fresh water, lake charr miss out on the rich feeding at sea, but by minimising their exposure to marine predators still higher up the pyramid they are able to lead much longer safer lives. Even their breeding habits expose mature charr to less predation than most of their relations, which lay eggs on the gravel shallows in running water. Lake charr usually spawn on rocky shoals in their home lake, and only occasionally swim up the inflows to breed in more conventional salmonid manner. Brook and Arctic charr also sometimes spawn on the lake bed, as do sockeye, which usually seek out underwater springs to keep their redds well cleansed of silt and bits of vegetation. Lake charr rely on wind and waves to wash their ancestral spawning grounds, and, unlike other charr or salmon, make no attempt to excavate a nest in the gravel. Instead, they simply squirt their eggs and milt over the stones, leaving the future of their species with those fertilised eggs that settle into the security of cracks and crevices.

Lake charr are always difficult to watch – their preference for the deep and the dark shields them from intrusive scientific inquiry. Discovering more about them is made no easier by their shrouding not only their spawning in darkness but also much of their daily lives. Most breeding activity peaks between dusk and midnight, and only on grey, windy days may lake charr feel secure enough in the shallows to appear in daylight. Males reach the breeding grounds before females. They appear to mature a year earlier, which helps account for there usually being far more males on the spawning shoals; so does the longer time they spend there, and the fact that females in more impoverished lakes may only breed every other year or even only every three years.

Both sexes seem to mill randomly around the breeding ground, a single female often accompanied by two or three males. One or more of these will brush along her flanks and nibble at her fins before yawning mouths and raised dorsal fins signal brief mutual climaxes. Females appear to lay their clutches in repeated bursts of eggs with no consideration for the suitability of the lake bed beyond the selection of a general spawning area, thereby seeming to leave far more to chance than those salmonids which bury their eggs. On average, lake charr lay significantly fewer eggs per kilogram of body weight than, for example, sockeye, but the salmon only lay them once, whereas a large female charr will spawn several times in her life.

Eggs that miss the stony crevices in the lake bed seldom hatch. Even if they escape the predatory eyes of other fish, the newly hatched alevins do not find the darkness and protection they need just after they emerge. As the eggs sink slowly down from the female's vent, most of them already inseminated by sperm from one of her escorts, some will fall straight between the stones. A lot will miss the cracks and lie exposed on the lake bed, where the ebb and flow of the current may finally push them down into a safe resting place; the others will either die or be eaten. Predation of lake charr eggs is not very significant, and most of the eggs that are eaten by the scourers of the lake bed are destined never to hatch anyway. Suckers of various species have often been found with hundreds of lake charr eggs in their stomachs, and sculpins are just as likely to take charr eggs as their river-dwelling cousins are to feast off salmon's. The same burbot with which lake charr compete as adults also nose around for unburied eggs; so do yellow perch, which are one of the lake charr's most favoured foods, once the predator has grown large enough to catch its prey.

The eggs that end up in the dark safety of a gap between the stones hatch, on average, after four months, sometimes even more. This is longer than trout and salmon eggs take, even granted that lake charr often spawn in colder water than their relatives, where eggs need more time to hatch anyway. After about a month, newly hatched alevins have absorbed their yolk sacs, and then seem urged away from the scene of their birth to exchange the seemingly easier feeding there for the greater safety of the lake depths. At some stage they have to surface to fill up their swim bladders with air. For lake charr born in the shallows this is easy, but for those hatched on deep reefs 90 m (300 ft) down, it entails a journey seemingly fraught with hazards, but apparently accomplished with very little difficulty.

Like other salmonids, lake charr mature later in their lives further north, at four or five in American lakes and between ten and fourteen in the Northwest Territories and Alaska. Reaching a given size may be what presses the maturity button – just as doing so often controls the smolting of salmon. This size takes fish much longer to attain on the meagre diets of the north, where feeding is confined to the short, urgent Arctic summer, than it does in more fertile southerly lakes. However, size at maturity is not absolute, and where lake charr are condemned to a lifelong diet of plankton, and so live much briefer lives, they mature both earlier and smaller than others do.

As well as influencing the age at which they mature, latitude also affects the start of the lake charr's spawning season each year. As it is for other charrs, spawning appears to be triggered by a combination of dropping temperatures and shortening days, and the critical thresholds are reached much earlier in the north. Peak spawning time in the big lakes of the Northwest Territories is mid-September, while lake charr in New York State may not breed until at least two months later. Stretching the season still wider are some of the Lake Superior charr, which breed in June, and those introduced into California's Lake Tahoe, that may not head for the spawning shoals until January.

Spawning usually begins with a distinct movement into shallower water, sometimes scarcely enough to cover the fish's back, but more often between 1 and 6 m (3 and 20 ft) deep. On the rare occasions when lake charr have been seen spawning in streams, they are still usually not far up from the lake. There is some evidence that lake charr tend to spawn in the same area each year, and that this is where they were born themselves. How precise their homing instincts are is not clear, but there is no doubt that they retain a strong affinity for a particular type of breeding habitat, so much so that in some large lakes like Superior several distinct races of charr could be distinguished in a single area. Despite mingling in the open waters of the lake, each race preserved its genetic integrity, and remained reproductively isolated from the others, by always homing back to the same reefs to spawn, often at differing times of year. Salmon, too, mix together in the vastness of the ocean with others of their kind from hundreds of different rivers, but retain their distinct identities by returning to their own natal streams to breed.

Lake Superior is a huge slab of water – at 83,000 sq. km (32,000 sq. miles) easily the largest Great Lake. Its lake charr have survived the sea lamprey's onslaught rather better than those in the other Great Lakes, mainly by dint of the lampreys having taken much longer to reach Superior. It is too late to analyse the genes of many of the different stocks, which were once such a feature of the lake's charr, and now exist only in the memories of old fishermen or historical accounts of the lake's ichthyololgical diversity. Still, there is no doubt that variations in times and places of breeding, flesh and fin colours, feeding habits, shape and weight all contributed to the profiles of distinctly identifiable races of charr, a few of which are still recognisable today. Like the brown trout of Lough Melvin or Lake Garda, some of these are distinct enough to suggest that they must already have acquired their distinguishing characteristics long before they colonised the Great Lakes some 12,000 years ago. This would in turn probably mean that they derived from at least three separate glacial refuges, in each of which they slowly diverged from their common ancestor as they saw out the last Ice Age, or perhaps even an earlier one.

On the deep reefs of Superior, far from human sight, charr spawned as early as June, but the first to announce their arrival by swimming into the shoreline nets, or being seen in the shallows, were small fish moving in to the lake edge or up the inflows in September. Known as 'little greys' or 'blacks', the lake-edge spawners weighed up to 2 kg (4 lb). Time kept them reproductively apart from the larger leaner redfins, which might have spawned on the same reefs but appeared much later. Siscowets were fattier fish, first described by

The Great Lakes.

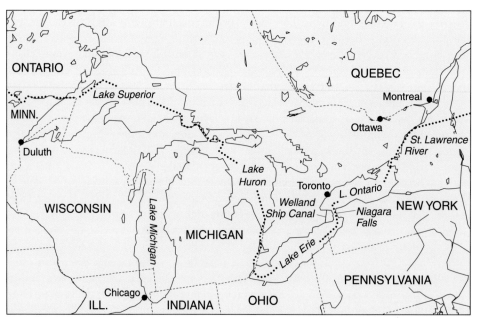

Jesuit priests in 1670 from Lake Huron and named after an Indian word meaning 'cooks itself'. Lake charr were most easily caught as they prepared to breed because they usually did so in shallow water, although in Superior siscowets were known to spawn at depths below 90 m (300 ft). Because the charr bred in well-defined areas and at predictable times, most races became known by their spawning habits rather than how or where they lived during the rest of the year. The larger fish usually spawned later, causing fishermen to move their nets closer inshore and also to fish with much bigger mesh. Perhaps the most easily recognised of all Superior lake charr were the humpers, so called because they lived on submerged humps far out in the lake; they had very pale skin on their undersides, which was so thin that they were was also known as 'paperbellies'.

Today there are only a few fragments left of the once great diversity of Superior's lake charr, the gene pool having shrunk to a puddle. But at least there is still a puddle, because in the rest of the Great Lakes the pool is dry, and the only lake charr outside Superior are hatchery stock or, depressingly seldom, their descendants. The consequences of the sea lamprey's arrival up the Welland Ship Canal were as devastating as they were unpredictable. Perhaps the unpredictability was just as well. It meant no one ever had to take a conscious decision as to whether a huge traditional Indian fishery, thousands of lakeside livelihoods and a spectacular diversity of races and species of fish were all worth sacrificing for a link between the Great Lakes and the sea – echoes indeed of offering up the Columbia River's salmon on the altar of cheap electricity a century later.

Fish have theoretically been able to swim up from the sea, past the sites of Quebec and Montreal to Lake Ontario ever since the retreating ice carved the St Lawrence River valley into the shape it is today. When sea lampreys first reached Ontario is unclear, but they were certainly there by 1835, and even this date gives them near-indigenous status in comparison with their descendants in the upper Great Lakes. Their early arrival in Ontario is very significant. It shows that for some time sea lampreys and large salmonids were quite capable of coexisting in reasonable balance – like all natural predators and prey – until some other force upset the scales, and then the predators wiped out their prey.

It is a long journey down the St Lawrence River, and the Atlantic salmon that once swam up so many of Lake Ontario's feeder streams in the autumn seem to have spent the rest of their lives in the lake, forsaking the journey to sea and back for the greater safety of a freshwater existence – and still reaching weights of up to 20 kg (44 lb). The salmon's 10,000-year tenancy of Ontario ended around the close of the nineteenth century. There is no suggestion that lampreys in any way contributed to the salmon's demise. This is much more likely to have been precipitated by a combination of dams, overfishing and silted-up spawning grounds (see Chapter 3). Lake sturgeon too had virtually disappeared by then, hastened on their way not by lampreys but by being unable to evade the fishermen's nets for up to fifteen years of immaturity before they were old enough to breed. Although lake charr also laboured under the disadvantage of a lengthy adolescence, not until well into the twentieth century were they seen as seriously threatened by the rasping suckers of sea lampreys.

When the salmon disappeared from Ontario, the lampreys lost one of their favoured hosts. So they turned their attentions to lake charr. Paradoxically, the same dams that barred the salmon from their redds, and eventually pushed them over the brink of no return, may also have kept the lampreys from their own breeding grounds, thereby controlling the parasite's numbers. When the dams were gradually removed, it was too late for the salmon, but not for the lampreys. These responded with a population

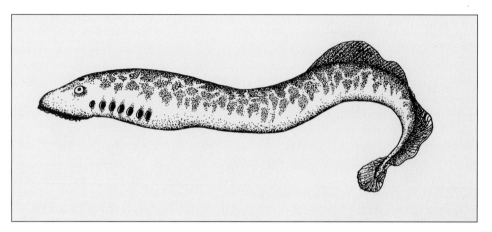

Sea lamprey.

explosion which could only be sustained by the juices of the hapless lake charr. As fishing pressure increased, the lake charr became ever more vulnerable to lampreys, because they never survived to grow large enough to withstand the parasites' attacks. Killing its host is seldom in the best interests of any parasite. If the lake charr had been spared the fishermen's nets long enough to reach a reasonable size, host and parasite might have reached some sort of equilibrium. They were not, and the lampreys were forced to attach themselves to smaller and smaller lake charr, nearly all of which died.

The lampreys' lives are almost as intriguing as those of their salmonid prey, particularly because of the similarities between them. Lampreys usually go to sea too, only returning to spawn in fresh water where they stop feeding. Those in the Great Lakes are as unusual as the ones in Loch Lomond, which are the only sea lampreys known to feed in British fresh waters, fixing themselves to the flanks of one of Britain's rarest fish – the powan. Lampreys spawn in sandy or gravelly stream beds, where they make simple nests by rearranging the stones with their suckers. The larvae, called 'ammocoetes', bear so little resemblance to their parents that, like Atlantic salmon smolts, they were once considered a totally different species and named *Ammocoetes branchialis*. They hatch within two weeks of fertilisation, and after a month in the nest drift off downstream into slacker water, burrowing into silt or sand and living quite blindly off tiny organisms for up to eight years before quickly metamorphosing into adults. Then, almost suddenly, eyes start to show through the skin, and the slit of a mouth develops into a sucker, surrounding rings of rasping teeth. Within two months there is a miniature adult, ready to head to sea, or down to a Great Lake, and to begin an existence where survival depends on being able to suck out the life juices from other, larger fish.

Niagara Falls had kept sea lampreys away from all the Great Lakes above Ontario, just as effectively as Murchison Falls had stopped Nile perch reaching Lake Victoria. Niagara Falls also created a barrier to downstream navigation – the one huge obstacle preventing ships taking the agricultural and industrial output of the Great Lakes basin to the outside world. To circumvent the falls the Welland Ship Canal was completed in 1829, but the price of expanding the horizons of commerce to the ends of the earth was to stretch the horizons of sea lampreys, first to Erie and then to the other Great Lakes beyond. The Nile perch have now reached Lake Victoria too, also as a result of human thoughtlessness, and are busy playing the same sort of ecological havoc with the indigenous fish fauna as the lampreys did once they swam through the last lock of the canal and into Lake Erie.

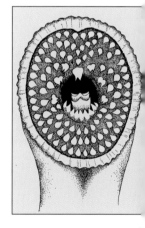

Sea lamprey sucker.

Erie is a warm shallow lake and only the deeper, easterly end was ever suitable for lake charr. It did not take the first Europeans long to set about modifying the surrounding landscape, and both the gradual replacement of vast tracts of indigenous forest with intensive agriculture and the inevitable growth of shoreline industry had a huge impact on the lake and its piscine inhabitants. Being so shallow, Erie was particularly susceptible to eutrophication. With every conceivable form of pollution spewing into its waters, oxygen levels tumbling and intensive fishing, its charr were probably headed for extinction anyway, with or without the help of the parasitic invaders, which were first reported in 1921. This was nearly a century after the Welland Ship Canal's completion had given the lampreys a waterway round Niagara Falls, and perhaps shows that, having eaten Lake Ontario out of most its large prey, they were simply driven by hunger to explore their way up the canal in search of new feeding grounds.

The lampreys never really took to Erie as they did to the lakes beyond – perhaps there were not enough good spawning streams, or they too felt choked by the lake's desecration. It was in Huron and Michigan that they really rasped and sucked their way through stocks of lake charr with such devastating effect. By 1932 they were in Huron and four years later in Michigan, and so deadly was their destruction that the charr had practically disappeared from both lakes by 1955. Only the contribution of overfishing to this annihilation remains in doubt. Were lake charr already threatened by over-exploitation when the lampreys arrived, or are the parasites alone responsible for their extirpation? The 1950s were critical years for fish all over the world as near-invisible nets of synthetic nylon began replacing those of natural fibre. Yet most of the Great Lakes charr had gone by then, and even if some localised stocks might have been fished to extinction if the lampreys had stayed below Niagara Falls, there seems little doubt that much more of the great diversity of lake charr would still be left above them.

The story of lampreys in Lake Superior has a different ending. The lake is at the top of the chain. It is cold, deep and relatively untouched by human activities, and not until around 1950 did lampreys become well established throughout. By then nylon nets were starting to hang down into the lake, and overfishing was almost certainly making its unwelcome impact, but help for the beleaguered lake charr was not far away. Slowly, and just in time, a combination of practical management and scientific research began to turn the tide against the lampreys. First, barriers were built across streams to stop them reaching their chosen spawning grounds. Then biologists experimented with releasing sterile lampreys in the hope that wild ones would dissipate their energies by breeding with them, and finally came TFM, a 'lampricide' which selectively poisoned young ammocoetes. Gradually the lampreys were brought under control, but not before all that remained of the marvellous diversity of Great Lakes charr were a few fish in their ancestral depths in Lake Superior.

As well as almost obliterating a magnificent predator at the pinnacle of the food pyramid in the largest area of fresh water fit for salmonids in the world, lampreys destroyed the livelihoods of thousands of fishermen and a fine source of protein for the local inhabitants. Indians used to fish through holes in the ice, either with baited hooks or by sprinkling bits of fish in the water and then spearing the charr as they nosed up to feed. The first settlers followed their example, or chummed larger areas of lake with pieces of meat for several days, and then tied the meat to hooks once the charr were at ease with the unaccustomed bounty. Generally, though, like their Arctic cousins, lake charr were at their most vulnerable in the autumn as they moved closer inshore to spawn. Round the lake edges they could often be speared by torchlight, or netted with almost ridiculous ease, especially those populations which spawned in the shallows or inflowing streams.

The earliest nets were conventional seines, one end of which remained attached to the land while the other was drawn out into the water, then round in a circle and back to the shore, entrapping fish in a ring of mesh. The charr's breeding migrations into the shallows or up inflowing streams were just as predictable as the great runs of salmon up the rivers of the west coast – if less spectacular. Indians round the Great Lakes had come to rely on the lake charr to sustain them through the winter long before the first black-robed missionaries arrived. They would barter extra fish for essentials not otherwise available to them, but it was left to the Hudson Bay Company to make the first real efforts to exploit lake charr commercially. Scottish immigrants brought the skills to use pound nets, which were supported by buoys and either trapped fish by the gills or in pouches of net into which they were funnelled. These could be used offshore and dominated fishing effort in the Great Lakes until the arrival of the true gill nets, which simply hung straight down into the water waiting for fish to swim into them. Gill nets could be set far below the surface, where the thickest twine was scarcely visible. Even down at 100 m (330 ft) fish were not beyond the reach of the nets, and once fishermen could catch charr without having to wait for them to respond to their breeding impulses, the harvest increased dramatically – just as it did when Atlantic salmon were first exploited in the open ocean, off the Greenland coast.

By 1880, an average of 8,000 tonnes of charr was coming out of the Great Lakes every year, and the catch remained around this level for the next sixty years. Fishing technology fast became more sophisticated. Lighter and more easily manipulated nets were operated from motor boats rather than wind- and man-powered ones, and heavy copper lines sank trolling baits down onto the deep reefs where charr spent the summer. To sustain catches must have meant pressuring easily caught stocks, and also continually searching for others which had been safely beyond the reach of more primitive fishing techniques. It is therefore difficult not to conclude that lake charr were heading for a drastic collapse, lampreys or no lampreys, although only Lake Superior furnishes any really firm evidence to support this conclusion.

Elsewhere, beyond the Great Lakes, Indians and settlers alike took advantage of what was usually the only source of fresh fish available to them. Arctic charr, being strongly inclined to migrate wherever the water was cool enough, were nearly always easier to catch than lake charr, but seldom as large. However, only occasionally do the two charrs coexist and there were often only lake charr for fishermen to catch to feed their families or to barter and sell to their neighbours. The lack of roads, and of any freezing facilities other than those Nature provided through the winter, ensured stocks were never overharvested. So long as their desolate habitat remained inaccessible and fishing techniques stayed simple the lake charr rested secure. Inevitably though, the remote north could not stay remote for ever, and with the great wave of new twentieth-century technology, many subsistence fisheries gradually succumbed to the insinuation of commerce.

By the end of the Second World War enough charr were being netted out of Great Bear and Great Slave Lakes in the Northwest Territories to keep several exporters in business, but the early successes flattered to deceive. Given how lethally efficient fishing became once nylon replaced natural net materials, sustaining these successful commercial fisheries for lake charr was probably an ecological contradiction, and one after another they closed down. Lake charr always grow slowly, especially in the far north where they may not breed until aged ten or more. Even with the application of a more scientific approach to their conservation they are constantly vulnerable to overfishing from which they take a very long time to recover. Their harvest can be controlled by the usual means of close seasons, quotas and limiting mesh size. Most effective is to allow a lake to be fished for a few years and then rest it completely to give stocks a true chance to recover – and make fishermen stick to catching whitefish in the meantime. Full recovery may take a long time though. During the construction of the Alaska pipeline, over twenty years ago, lake charr in Toolik Lake were drastically overfished and they have yet to show any real signs of making a comeback.

While commercial fishing for lake charr has generally declined over the past fifty years, sportsmen remain attracted by the romance of the Arctic and the mystery of hooking a trophy-sized charr far down in the darkness of a northern lake. In distant waters, accessible only by float planes, 'catch and release' rules can help match fishermen's catches with their expectations. Elsewhere, particularly in the Great Lakes, this is often only possible by the dubious expedient of massive hatchery output.

The efforts to reintroduce charr back to the Great Lakes in many ways parallel those to restore salmon to the Pacific North-west – so do the motives, the problems and the cost. The motives are mixed and often confused. On the one hand is a desire to repopulate waters with their original inhabitants – a desire begat of a complex mixture of guilt and environmental altruism. On the other is the avowed intent to give fishermen fish to catch, more often for pleasure than to provide them with a livelihood, at almost any cost and often irrespective of the consequences for other species of fish. Both motives have the same fundamental aim: to establish self-sustaining populations of lake charr, able to survive without never-ending hatchery help.

Two great difficulties still continue to frustrate efforts to bring back lake charr. The first is a lack of genetic raw material. The only wild charr left in the Great Lakes able to provide broodstock for repopulation programmes lived in Superior. Hatchery-bred charr descended from these wild fish have had little difficulty in adapting to the conditions in their own lake, and numbers in Superior have now built up to levels at which artificial input is scarcely necessary, so long as fishing is carefully controlled. Even this limited success is enough to contradict many of the suggestions that a hatchery upbringing ruins fish for life in the wild. Yet, for whatever reason, getting charr from Superior or the Finger Lakes in New York State to breed in other Great Lakes remains next to impossible.

It may be that the genetic make-up of Superior lake charr is simply unsuited to conditions elsewhere. Even so, however distinctive the chemical and geographical characters of the other lakes may be, it seems difficult to believe they are all so unsuitable for non-native fish that with a bit of a genetic shake-up, sufficient numbers cannot settle into these new environments and found breeding populations. The same problem besets schemes to restore salmon rivers. If there are none of the river's original stocks left, then restoration means using salmon from elsewhere. Even though these fish may be obtained from adjacent rivers in the same watershed, where conditions are seemingly almost identical, getting them to breed in the wild is never easy.

The second real difficulty in reintroducing lake charr is that fishermen are not prepared to stop fishing for long enough to let the population become fully self-sustaining; and even if they are the charr may still become the accidental by-catch in nets set for whitefish. Pacific salmon have adapted to life in the Great Lakes so successfully that fishermen can find their sport with these faster growing exotics. This is often much better sport than they might get from lake charr, which are condemned as too easy to hook because of the predictability of their lies, and for struggling very little when they are hooked. When fully grown, these huge numbers of hatchery salmon reach the apex of the food pyramid once exclusively occupied by the charr, adding unnatural competition to the other difficulties charr already face in trying to establish themselves. A decision in the Michigan courts upholding the rights of Indian fishermen to fish with traditional methods, freed from the fetters of state regulations, has made it even harder to protect charr until they are old enough to breed. And so fishery managers go on pumping lake charr into the Great Lakes, perhaps hardly clear in their own minds exactly what they hope to achieve, let alone how to go about it.

The lake charr going back into the Great Lakes below Superior are, it can be argued, no more indigenous to those lakes than the Pacific salmon which now live there. They happen to have the same binomial tag, *Salvelinus namaycush*, as the lake charr which once swam in Michigan, Huron and Erie, but their genetic make-up is entirely different. The original stocks are gone from the lower lakes – gone for good – and in Superior the indigenous charr are now largely self-sustaining. So is it all worth it? The cost is colossal, the results are of little but the most superficial consequence to most fishermen, and lake charr still flourish throughout much of the rest of their original range. Should more effort not focus on educating fishermen to expect less, to take less and to understand more? Could the money not be better spent on trying to preserve endangered stocks of lake charr in other waters, where at least the genetic material is still extant, rather than in continuing to push square genes into round lakes, which are either too polluted or for which these genes are patently unsuited?

7
Brook charr

Somehow, blue pigment has found its way into the brook charr's skin; not much, just enough to ring some of the red spots with delicate haloes. Brook charr are perhaps the most exquisitely coloured fish of their family – even of all the fresh-water fish in the world. Once out of the water, though, their colours seem to fade even faster than those of other fish, as if in silent protest at the death of such a creature. One of their greatest liabilities is that they are far too easily deceived and dragged from their element, and all too often need rules, bag limits, close seasons and closed rivers to protect them. They are also particularly vulnerable to the aggressions of introduced brown and rainbow trout. Yet perversely brook charr seem to flourish in the role of exotic species when stocked into strange waters and forced to compete with other native fish.

The first Europeans into America soon came to depend on the brook charr, which proliferated in the streams of the continent's north-east, as a regular and reliable source of food. Many of the fish that haunted the coastal rivers, from Ungava on the edge of the Hudson Strait down to New Jersey, migrated to sea and were easily harvested on their return. Further inland, naive little non-migratory fish crowded thousands of smaller streams, the Appalachians stretching their distribution all the way down the mountains into the hilly corners of South Carolina, Georgia and Tennessee. Most of the streams flowing into the Great Lakes once nurtured brook charr, and many of them still do; but any fish west of the Mississippi found their way there through man's endeavours rather than on the floods of melting ice. Naturalised populations are now dotted throughout all the states west of the Rocky Mountains, struggling for dominance and domain with the indigenous rainbow and cutthroat trout – as if the charr were trying to make up for all the territory they themselves have surrendered to the usurpers introduced into their own native range.

To these early settlers, brook charr seemed little different in life or looks from the brown trout of Britain and Europe, with which many of them were familiar; and so they first became known as 'brook trout', or sometimes 'speckled trout'. Both species have red spots in common, but the brook charr's spawning colours are more akin to their Arctic cousin's, the male's brilliant red belly contrasting vividly with the white edges to the lower fins. Fine worm-like patterns mark their backs, and often also their dorsal fins. Both vermiculations and spots are lighter than the rest of their bodies, as on all the other species of *Salvelinus*, in contrast to the salmon and trout, whose spots always show darker than their background skins. The charr's coloration varies with area and habitat. Fish are paler in clear water or streams with sandy beds, and more silvery if they take to life in a lake or while under the influence of salt water – although having returned from the sea they quickly become indistinguishable from fish that never went there. Diet affects flesh

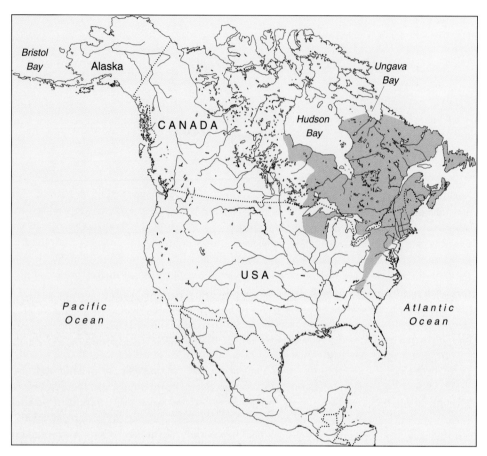

The natural range of brook charr.

colour, which pales as spawning time approaches, perhaps because the carotene deserts the muscle to brighten the skin and redden the female's eggs. Brook charr's tails are much squarer than those of their congeners – 'squaretails' or 'squaretailed trout' were other names they once travelled under – and their 'wrist' in front of the tail is distinctly thicker.

The sea is more important to brook than to lake charr, but is still not the object of focused mass migrations to a great marine larder that it is for many northern populations of Arctic charr. Sea-going brook charr – known along the Canadian coast as 'salters' – seem to swim up and down the river at almost any time of the year, and fish of one age group swimming up from the sea may meet those from another on their way down. Like all their close relatives, brook charr are more migratory further north, where the rivers' lower reaches are still cool enough for them to navigate. In the south of their range they find comfort only at higher altitudes, confined to their mountain refuges all year through by the inhospitability of conditions downstream. Brook charr are no more able to leave the tops of the Appalachians than rainbow trout are to desert the cool of the Sierra Madre, or Arctic charr to set off from the lakes of England or New England in search of the sea.

The climate's annual rhythms certainly influence the patterns of the brook charr's migrations. When the ice melts it frees fish to move downstream, if they are so inclined, and the sea's midsummer warmth may push them back up into fresh water again.

Otherwise, it seems difficult to draw any firm conclusions either as to what age brook charr are when they go to sea or how long they spend there. Some fish seem to taste the salt for not much longer than a month, while others spend the whole winter at sea. How far they roam once they reach the estuary is also questionable. Brook charr are sufficiently adventurous to have made it to Newfoundland Island and to other islands in the Gulf of St Lawrence, but most of the time they appear to remain close inshore, within the reassuring influence of their home river. Their abilities to navigate long distances in the open ocean are seldom put to the test, but what evidence there is suggests that, at least once they reach fresh water, they can find their ancestral patch of gravel or lake-edge stones as well as any other salmonid.

That brook charr tolerate warmer water than other charrs is apparent from their distribution, the shading on their map stretching much further south than the Arctic or lake charr's. The territories of the different species overlap considerably, and even though the inflows to the Arctic Ocean appear too cold for brook charr, they are found in most of the rivers draining into Hudson Bay. They live easily in water temperatures from 10° to 19°C, and appear most comfortable between 13° and 16°C. Their tolerance of unusually acidic conditions gives them an edge over other salmonids, allowing them to live in

Brook charr in the Causapscal River, Quebec.
(Gilbert van Ryckevorsel)

streams where, for example, introduced rainbows struggle to survive. They lead much more flexible lives than lake charr, which very seldom go to sea and are even reluctant to leave their still-water depths except to spawn or forage for smaller fish.

If any brook charr epitomise their species, they are the little fish of rocky headwaters which behave like upland brown, rainbow or cutthroat trout, spending all their lives in the same short stretch of stream. These are the quintessential brook charr, and it is this upland niche that each species has independently evolved to fill in different parts of the northern hemisphere. Hatched in the narrow gravelly sections of small streams, young brook charr waste little time before heading away from their nurseries in search of larger territories and more security. Most of them move downstream, but if spawning has been particularly successful and fry are plentiful, some may explore upstream in the hope of finding less crowded feeding grounds. Whether up or down, these are short journeys, effectively serving to redistribute the new crop of young around the most productive areas of water. There they will usually remain, growing quickly to maturity before migrating upstream again to breed. Even as older fish, they seem reluctant to leave familiar territory, unless they are unsettled by competition or their habitat is disturbed. Once exhausted by their efforts to reproduce, they drop back into deeper pools to rest for the winter, seldom far from where they spawned.

Brook charr water in Great Smoky Mountains at the southern end of the Appalachian Mountains in Tennessee.
(Leslie Todd)

As a species, brook charr are short lived, more southerly populations particularly so. Males have been known to mature at the end of their first summer, only a few months after emerging from their eggs, but nearly all females mature aged two and breed at the beginning of their third winter. Males occasionally spawn more than once by dint of their often maturing a year earlier than the females, but few Appalachian fish of either sex live to see out their third winter. Many of these brook charr are living on the frontiers of their species' range, where conditions one year may be ideal and the next barely tolerable. Like pink salmon, which stick unerringly to their two-year life cycles, the rigid breeding patterns of these southerly fish make them dangerously vulnerable to droughts, floods and other environmental disasters. A whole year's hatching can be wiped out by a weather-borne catastrophe, and with one such disaster after another, the brook charr's range will slowly contract.

Further north the story is very different. Life is less urgent, and fish are born into more predictable environments. They have the time to grow more slowly, they mature at different ages, and often spawn several times during their lives. Males may try and breed every year, and females every other, so fish from one age group are continually mating with those from another. This has the effect of making populations far less susceptible to the dramatic fluctuations in climate that may afflict those further south. Longer life does not necessarily imply greater size, and if they are also stream-bound all their lives, these northern fish will not die much larger than their shorter lived southern kin. Brook charr transplanted into the barren waters of Bunny Lake in California survived to the age of twenty-four, but had still not outgrown their east coast ancestors who usually died before their fourth winter.

If brook charr are to grow beyond the 20 cm (8 in), which is a big fish for a small stream, they need to have natural access to a lake or the sea. Whether born in its inflows or the lake itself, brook charr granted the twin luxuries of ample food and plenty of space grow far larger than those living out their lives in the narrow confines of running water. The largest brook charr on the fishing record books came from the Nipigon River, which links the lake of that name with Lake Superior. Fish could exploit both lakes, as well as the river, and a super-race seems to have evolved there which produced a brook charr of nearly 7 kg (15 lb) for a fisherman in 1916. A dam across the river subsequently blocked the old migratory routes, and may have driven those fish to extinction, but brook charr of 4 or 5 kg (9–11 lb) are still not uncommon from lakes in Quebec. This is especially true of Assinica, in which they may not mature until three or four (when, if they lived in the Appalachians, they would already be dead). However, if the record is to be broken, it will most likely be by a leviathan from one of the cold Andean lakes of Argentina – from which larger fish have probably already been extracted and gone unremarked.

The ease with which brook charr can spawn in lakes as well as rivers is one of their most distinctive features. Arctic charr can also breed in both environments, as can lake charr although these very seldom spawn in streams. Lake charr are generally far less adaptable than their brook cousins, which are as likely to be found in large still waters as in small rocky rivers. The brook charr's spawning seasons are little different from those of any other charr. In the Appalachian Mountains streams may not cool down enough until December, but moving northwards, brook charr spawn ever earlier, and may have to do so before the end of August in the rivers flowing into Ungava Bay. Their eggs invariably hatch quicker than lake charr's at similar temperatures – 140 days compared to 150 at $2°C$, and sixty compared to sixty-five days at $8°C$.

Males usually reach the spawning area first, and in their excitement often try to nudge a female onto the redds before she is ready. Only when the membrane surrounding her eggs has broken and they are all loose inside her body is she truly overtaken by the urge to spawn, and then chooses her nest site and starts to dig it out in true salmonid fashion. *Fontinalis* means 'spring-dwelling', which may be a reference to the fish's preference for spawning where water wells up through the lake or river bed to aerate its eggs. In northern streams, where water is cooler and thus better oxygenated, this is scarcely necessary for the successful incubation of the eggs, but upwelling currents around lake edges allow brook charr to spawn even on sandy bottoms by preventing the eggs from being choked with sediment.

Many salmonids make use of lakes, estuaries or seas at some stage in their lives, and all of them reap the benefit of size from the far richer feeding they find there. In the rivers of the brook charr's birth, food arrives at the whim of the current, and even when fish are older they seldom forage much beyond the borders of a single pool. In the stillness of more open water there is only minimal current, and although the wind sometimes blows adult insects along the surface into a bay, fish must usually search out their sustenance. Feeding in lakes may be more energy-consuming than in rivers, even though fish are spared the exertions of countering the river's current. However, their efforts are more than compensated for by the much more prolific and varied prey, especially once they are large enough to shift to a piscivorous diet.

Being so easily caught shows that brook charr are unselective feeders, simply snapping at whatever comes within their reach. Salmon, trout and charr all owe much of their success as species to their catholic feeding habits, but brook charr seem to feed even more indiscriminately than other members of the family. In small streams where the banks are overhung with oaks, maples, hemlocks and pines, terrestrial creatures make up the greater part of their summer intake. Leafhoppers, ants, bees, grasshoppers, slugs, snails and earthworms are all grist to the brook charr's digestive mill, but caddis flies, either as larvae or adults, are almost always found to dominate the diets of fish living in running water. Lake-living brook charr also feed on free-floating animal plankton, as well as grubbing for shrimps, snails and even crayfish on the bottom, and may grow to weigh 2 kg (4 lb) even if they have not begun to satisfy their appetites with other fish.

The charr that grew so huge in the Nipigon River probably did so on the ciscos and rainbow smelts that spawned in the river or round the lake shallows in late summer and early autumn. In Maine's Rangely Lakes, brook and Arctic charr – there known as bluebacks – had coexisted ever since the vagaries of the melting ice left them there together. For 10,000 years the small bluebacks provided prey for the brook charr, until the introduction of landlocked Atlantic salmon and rainbow smelts so upset the lake's ichthyological equilibrium that the bluebacks disappeared (see Chapter 5).

Brook charr seem decidedly lazy in their pursuit of fish prey, grabbing at a winter alewife which has little energy to resist capture or taking northern redbelly dace (often introduced into lakes by fishermen tipping in unwanted bait at the end of the day) spawning in the shallows. Once they reach the sea brook charr become much more determined piscivores, as if deciding there is little point in getting there if they do no seize the chance to feast. Young hake and eel elvers are common quarry, but from the Gulf of St Lawrence up to Ungava Bay, sand-eels, sculpins and capelin are the favourite food of brook charr – and of the Atlantic salmon with which the young charr may have shared a stream.

Before Europeans began meddling with the fish faunas of the rivers and lakes of

America, brook charr in the south of their range had no competition from any trout or other charr. Elsewhere, different species of *Salvelinus* often naturally coexisted, but just like any other creatures that have evolved together, they generally managed to apportion space and food between them so that direct and damaging competition was avoided. In the Great Lakes, lake charr ruled the deep open waters in which they also often spawned. Brook charr spawned in the inflows, and many of the young migrated down to the lakes, where they kept away from the lake charr by feeding closer inshore, eventually returning to breed several times larger than the resident fish that had never left the stream. Such a partition is typical of the two species wherever they coexist, and is advantageous for both – although in the shallows brook charr become much more susceptible to attacks by divers (loons) and other birds. The harbour seals in Quebec's Lower Seal Lake have made life much easier for brook charr by eating their way through most of the lake charr, but such a scenario is almost unique.

Brook and Arctic charr live together in many of Newfoundland's coastal streams and inland lakes. The two species seem to divide up a lake's resources in the same way as Arctic charr and brown trout do in Europe, the Arctic charr filtering the animal plankton out of the open water, leaving the brook charr to forage round the edges. In many of the larger streams flowing into the Atlantic, young brook charr may find themselves competing directly with Atlantic salmon, but again the two have coexisted long enough to have evolved a way of sharing the same nursery to the obvious detriment of neither species. The salmon seem to stake their claims to shallow riffles in the open, while the charr keep to the shade and shelter of the banks from which they may dare to venture only at dawn or dusk.

Coexistence need not imply competition, for where two or more superficially similar species live naturally in harmony subtle differences in their diets and habits minimise competition between them. Ecologically speaking, competition only exists when there is a shortage of a resource, like space or food, not simply when different species vie for the same one. More specialised fish, like whitefish specifically designed to filter plankton out of the open water or some species of *Haplochromis* that subsist exclusively off the scales of other fish, experience no competition for food other than from their own kind. However, such specialised fish are uncomfortably dependent on the whims and well-being of the creatures that sustain them.

The generalists among fish, which can snap up every passing morsel of invertebrate flesh should, theoretically at least, be better equipped to withstand competition. They only have to compete with the other generalists of the underwater world. Yet, perhaps somewhat paradoxically, they may actually be less resistant to the incursions of exotic imports than those more specialised fish whose niches often appear almost impregnable in the face of invasion.

Food was what the earliest European settlers wanted, and brook charr provided it in plenty. Like the Indians, they had little space in their lives for the luxury of sport, and almost every hour of every day was taken up in the struggle to survive. Whether or not they were familiar with brown trout, so long as the brook charr flourished there was no need to add alien fish to the rivers. Anyway, while the technology for moving fish around the world remained undeveloped, the impossibility of importing trout suppressed any ideas of doing so.

Americans began fishing for fun long before brown trout arrived. While industrialisation brought employment, leisure and enough money to indulge in it, networks of trails and railways began to spread throughout the interior, measuring journeys in hours and days rather than weeks and months. By the time rainbow trout ova reached the east coast from California in 1874, sport fishermen were well into their stride, gleefully embracing the Biblical notion that man was given dominion over the beasts, and also touched with the colonial craze for modifying the environment to suit their own ends. Brown trout arrived from Germany ten years after rainbows, and the same network of trails and railways that led fishermen to the fishing also brought new fish or their eggs to the rivers. The exotic imports took to the new waters as well as if they had been born into them, and ultimately better than the fish that actually were. What began as the brook charr's defence of its territory ended in an almost total surrender to the invaders from the rivers of Europe and the Pacific coast.

Brown trout and brook charr have evolved to fill almost identical niches on either side of the Atlantic. Despite inhabiting different continents, their diets are much the same. They also spawn at the same time of year in broadly similar habitats and tolerate almost identical ranges of temperature. Rainbows and cutthroat occupy similar slots in the streams of western America, and although they are spring spawners, direct competition between the native fish and the new arrivals was almost inevitable. No two species can survive a head-on collision intact, and both brown and rainbow trout were destined to dominate the less assertive brook charr. Rainbow trout tolerate marginally warmer water than brown. This has made them suitable for introduction into the more southerly parts of the brook charr's range, where, in the streams of the Appalachian Mountains, they are still stretching the extent of their dominance further and further upstream.

Brown and rainbow trout were first stocked into new rivers in those places most easily reached by road or rail – usually well downstream, where the valley slopes were gentler and construction easier. If the exotic arrivals were to expand their territories it had to be upwards – further down was too warm – and this is clearly what they did. Where brook charr and trout now share the same stream, their different characters and environmental preferences lead to their partitioning the water into distinct zones of occupation.

The lower reaches of the stream are soon completely taken over by the new arrivals, which quickly displace all the charr. This zone of exclusivity extends upstream for varying distances before gradually merging with the stretch where both trout and charr coexist. These overlap zones are often strangely similar in length, extending for about 3 km (2 miles) before merging with the exclusive territory of the brook charr – now confined to ever-shrinking headwaters of their ancestral streams. There the water is often more acidic than it is lower down, and by exploiting their tolerance of higher acid concentrations the charr may be able to preserve these headwaters as their exclusive domain. Some streams are so short that there is no longer any charr-only zone, and even the uppermost reaches are occupied by both species. Eventually a shrunken gene pool and the unceasing pressures of direct competition may drive the native charr into oblivion. In extreme conditions, where both species are vying for space on the same redds, charr may end up interbreeding with brown trout – an inter-generic cross which may certainly have satisfied the spawning urges of both fish, but only serves to hasten the demise of the charr.

This pattern of eventual domination by the introduced fish is apparent in one stream after another, but why does it happen as it does? Brown trout are marginally more piscivorous – and it is on such narrow margins that struggles for supremacy are ultimately decided – and eating other indigenous fish may ultimately confer a size advantage which the trout retain for the rest of their lives. Slimy sculpins rely on their cryptic colouring to

A brook charr at its feeding station – the large stone provides some shelter from the current.
(Gilbert van Ryckevorsel)

escape the notice of predatory trout, but are easily caught if they suddenly move along the bottom; so are brook charr before their instincts are gradually sharpened up by stream life. The trout also seem more aggressive, and the gentler charr may be pushed aside in the search for food or spawning space. Occasionally they become almost immobile in the presence of brown trout, like mesmerised rabbits in front of a stoat. Otherwise they make for sheltered runs under stream banks, away from the more productive lies on the edges of the current where the trout quickly take up station. Securing the best territories from an early age may also set trout off growing faster than charr, soon gaining an ascendancy which may be further accentuated if the trout then start to eat fish.

Rainbow trout spawn in the spring, and by the time their young emerge to feed for themselves the same generation of brook charr will already be two or three months old. Both species grow at about the same rate for the first twelve months of their lives, but then rainbows seem to start catching up, perhaps because, like browns, they manage to occupy better feeding stations despite their smaller size. If most of the rainbows are removed from a section of river, the charr population rebounds spectacularly, providing some of the most conclusive evidence of the destructive competition that the trout bring with them.

So at home are rainbow trout in the Great Lakes that they could almost pass as an indigenous species, but again their easy existence is often bought at the expense of brook charr. There are impassable falls on some of the rivers feeding Lake Superior, which rainbows have never surmounted. Above them, brook charr still flourish in God-given numbers. Below the falls, indigenous 'coasters', which once reached pound weights in double figures, struggle to sustain their natural population against the intrusions of the rainbows – and a shameful history of overfishing, from which the charr have never really recovered.

It is unfair to point the finger of guilt at the exotic imports without also taking account of how else mankind may have eased their passage up the brook charr's native streams. The very tracks that helped stock these streams with brown and rainbow trout were, as often as not, built to ease the extraction of timber. Used to tan the hides of countless cattle, and as many slaughtered bison, these trees had shielded the water from the sun and kept the streams cool enough for brook charr, while the banks squeezed out water all summer, as if from a sponge. Once the shade was gone, the temperature rose, often critically, and instead of hundreds of steady trickles feeding streams throughout the year, water simply poured off the naked slopes during the storms that brought it. Even before trout arrived, a lot of brook charr were already starting to feel uncomfortable, as the downstream limit of their ideal habitat crept slowly up the hillsides, followed closely by the threshold below which the fish could not survive at all.

Fishing, too, was already taking its toll – a toll which was often more than the river could stand. The early settlers, fishing for food not fun, used to wade in among migrating schools of brook charr and hammer them with clubs. 'Striking of fish' was banned by law in 1696, but other only slightly less drastic methods of harvesting continued for the next 200 years. Brook charr were at their most vulnerable as autumn approached, and netting lake-dwellers at a river mouth on their way up to spawn could devastate the run; so could dynamiting fish on the redds, where they were also snagged with grappling hooks or speared by torchlight. The fish were seldom numerous enough to justify large-scale commercial fisheries, although the charr were often salted and pickled for the winter or sold locally to hotels and markets. Given their innocence in the face of such onslaughts, it was little wonder that by the time brook charr began attracting the attentions of sport fishermen, in the middle of the nineteenth century, their numbers in many lakes and rivers were already down to danger levels.

To some extent, the spread of sport fishing acted to control such mindless destruction, but the sport fishermen were quite unable to control their own kind, and their activities soon began denuding the best fishing streams just as effectively as nets or spears ever did. Buoyed up with the current belief in Nature's inexhaustibility, huge bags of charr were easily caught below falls and at the mouths of lake inflows. Newspapers and travelogues brimmed with tales of charr catches measured in boatloads and wagonloads rather than pounds and ounces, and 'the only fault with the trout fishing is that the fish are too numerous' was a common cry. Nor was the brook charr's cause helped by the taste of its flesh, which was considered 'the most delicious article of food of the fish kind'. It was only a question of when, not whether, the crash would come, and by the end of the century the famous fishing in Lake Superior had collapsed, hastened on its way by the destruction of prime spawning habitat.

In many other waters, particularly those within easy reach of towns and cities, charr were coming under similar pressures. Throughout much of its range, *Salvelinus fontinalis* was fast becoming a victim of the lazy and indiscriminate feeding habits that had sustained it so successfully ever since embarking on its own evolutionary trail. And while populations of fish were rapidly declining, numbers of fishermen perversely seemed to increase. It was as if, knowing that the charr's end was near in many of its native waters, the fishermen felt morbidly compelled to participate in its last rites.

So all was already far from well in much of the brook charr's territory by the time the foreign fish arrived, their introduction into new environments often eased by their ability to tolerate slightly warmer water than the indigenous fish could. But exactly what were the introducers of these exotic species hoping to achieve, and did they achieve it? If the habitat was no longer suitable for brook charr, then replacing them with another species better able to cope with the altered conditions made fair sense. Generally, though, it was thought that, almost by definition, new species meant better fishing and that man could make much more of his environment than Nature had done. Only after brown trout were well established did fishermen realise how good the fishing for brook charr had once been. But then, what is good fishing? To the Michigan Conservation Commission it was lots of easily caught fish – 'A few years of experiment and experience have convinced us that the brown trout is inferior in every respect to the brook or the rainbow'. Other, more pragmatic fishery managers could see that playing hard to catch was not only an advantage to the fish. In an age when every fish caught was killed, it was clear that stocks of imported brown trout were able to stand far more fishing pressure than native populations of brook charr could ever have done.

Often the most obvious cure for the ill of disappearing brook charr was, and still is, to replace them with more brook charr. Hatchery fish used to be selected both to hatch and mature early in the hope that this would give them a head start in the wild. Maturing early usually meant dying early, and small, making these domestic products poor prospects as foundation broodstock for depleted rivers, as well as unpopular with fishermen. None the less, if charr are to be stocked to boost populations in rivers where other salmonids are already out-competing them, they may need selecting to breed early in their lives.

These days, rivers are more often cleared of all unwanted species in preparation for the exclusive restoration of stocks of indigenous fish. Electro-fishing allows the selective removal of a particular species, but a few individuals nearly always slip past the collecting nets. Much more effective, although somewhat extreme, is poisoning every single fish in the river and then setting out to recreate Nature's original design.

Now brook charr are recovering some of the territory they have surrendered over the past hundred years. Trees are planted along the riverbanks, pools are excavated, and the usurpers are being removed, even destroyed, in attempts to restore the underwater community to its natural state. Three generations on, man is now trying to redress some of the more destructive actions of his forebears, but there is an inescapable irony in all this: while brown and rainbow trout are being poisoned out of existence in many of the waters of north-eastern America, so are brook charr in the west, where all too often they have edged native cutthroat into oblivion.

It is easy to appear less critical of the efforts of early ichthyologists to expand the brook charr's range to Europe, quite simply because, at least in Britain, these efforts can generally be said to have failed, and the indigenous brown trout have refused to give ground to the exotic imports. Despite the infancy of the science of fish culture, America wasted no time in setting up hatcheries to breed brook charr, and a full fifteen years before brown trout ova had reached America, the first brook charr eggs were shipped over to

England, arriving in the spring of 1869. Sending these eggs across the Atlantic was a much simpler proposition than transporting eyed brown trout ova from England to Australia – first achieved successfully in 1864 – but still represents one of the very earliest efforts to introduce fish from one continent to another. The pioneer pisciculturist, Frank Buckland, was in the forefront of the importation programme, and the earliest consignment seems to have come from Lake Huron, as does the second. From these enough fish hatched to establish a broodstock for further breeding.

Once eggs reached the Howietoun hatchery in Stirling (where the manifest shyness of young charr on Sundays was eventually attributed to the staff's wearing unfamiliar clothes for church), there was suddenly no loch in Scotland that, with some energy and enterprise, could not be stocked with brook charr. Most of the impetus for propagating different species of fish derived, as it later did in America, from the search for better fishing. All the same, the yearnings of British colonists for the faunal trappings of their homeland were almost matched by the homeland's fascination for the idea of enlivening its rather sparse animal life with some exotic imports. Britain had its own Acclimatisation Society, just like most of its colonies and dominions, dedicated to 'the introduction, acclimatisation, and domestication of all innoxious animals, birds, fishes, insects and vegetables, whether useful or ornamental'. Started by Frank Buckland, it was scarcely surprising that fish were high on the society's priority list.

Beyond their native range – brook charr in Wyoming.
(Richard Grost)

By the time Francis Day's great compendium of science and ideas, *British and Irish Salmonidae*, was published in 1887, brook charr were sufficiently part of the country's fish fauna to merit a chapter. Highland lairds were introducing the exotic species over much of northern Scotland, and the charr seemed to survive effortlessly wherever they were stocked. Yet persuading them to breed was quite another matter. When Sir Herbert Maxwell published his 1904 version of *British Freshwater Fishes* reality was beginning to dampen the wave of early enthusiasm:

> The so-called brook-trout . . . has been reared successfully in great quantities for naturalisation in Great Britain; but something in our waters is displeasing to it, and it invariably disappears, apparently descending rivers and escaping to the sea.

Ever since they first arrived in Britain, brook charr have often been referred to, with a mixture of near-reverence and affection, simply as *fontinalis*. A nod over a distant mountainside, or a finger on the map, pays mute tribute to the efforts of Victorian forebears to stock remote lochs where perhaps, who knows, the fish's descendants still swim. Brook charr were particularly attractive prospects for lakes and lochs without the gravelly inflows brown trout need for their redds, but with upwelling springs or wave-washed shallows which might still create the right conditions to allow the American fish to breed successfully. Whenever they were forced into instant competition with indigenous brown trout, the charr struggled. In almost every still water where they still survive through their own reproductive efforts there have never been any trout, usually because there is no inflowing stream. There are certainly more viable populations of brook charr (although still probably less than a dozen) than of rainbow trout (maybe five or six), but given the effort and money spent in trying to establish them, neither species can be said to have taken readily to the fresh waters of Britain.

One of the best known *fontinalis* fisheries is in Llyn Tarw, near Newtown in central Wales, where, in the absence of any inflow, the fish breed easily in the lake, and have done for so long that no one remembers exactly how or when they first arrived. There is another long-established brook charr colony at the head of Kirkton Glen in Perthshire. Last stocked some seventy years ago, the tiny one hectare Lochan an Eireannaich contains no brown trout either, and has produced a fish of just over 1 kg (2 lb), which was once the British record. It probably still is for a wild fish, but has without doubt been overtaken many times by fattened charr from 'put and take' fisheries. Hatcheries also experiment with inter-generic crosses between brown trout and brook charr. These zebra (tiger) trout are inevitably sterile, and so their breeding in British waters is not just unlikely but impossible. Meanwhile, in a few other small Scottish lochs brook charr survive without hatchery help. There they exploit their tolerance of acidic conditions to the full, and compensate for the shortness of their lives by growing far faster than trout ever could, on diets of tadpoles, water slaters (*Asellus* spp.), caddis larvae and midge pupae.

In other parts of the world, where conditions are more like those in their native North America, and they are not forced to compete with either indigenous or exotic relatives, brook charr have established themselves with much less difficulty. In isolated Scandinavian lakes, and tarns high up in the Alps or Carpathian Mountains, beyond the reach of the forces of natural fish distribution, brook charr reproduce so freely that they never grow more than a few centimetres long. In South America, *trucha de arroyo* have been propagated much more enthusiastically, and have adapted spectacularly well to life in cold mountain

lakes and rivers on both sides of the Andean backbone. New Zealand brook charr had a four-year start over imported rainbows, the first charr eggs arriving in 1877, but more because of a general preference for other species than any lack of suitable habitat, interest quickly tailed away. Nowhere in the southern hemisphere is there any danger to brook charr of competition from indigenous salmonids – there are none – but rainbow trout adapt so easily to new environments, and fulfil even the most unreasonable expectations of fishermen, that the borders of the brook charr's range seem unlikely to be stretched much further.

Llyn Tarw, near Newtown in Wales – home of one of the very few self-sustaining populations of brook charr in Britain. (Julian Watson)

8
Rainbow trout and their allies

Rainbow trout are all fish to all fishermen. Fattening to salmon size and beyond on the goodness of the ocean, adapting to strange environments with an ease that derides the effort and expense of rehabilitating many other species, often dominating the fish which live with them, easily reared in cages, free feeding, fine tasting. These are the true survivors of the Salmonidae, and if the last fish left in the earth's cool waters is not a three-spined stickleback, it may be a rainbow trout.

What is, and what is not a rainbow trout? What are the fish enclosed within the boundary fence of rainbows and their allies? The question is perhaps best answered in the negative, and the current consensus favours the idea of the rainbow group's fence enclosing all those trout of western America which are not cutthroat. One or two remote mountain streams are home to fish which, according to some scientists, teeter on the border fence between the groups, but generally there is agreement as to which fish belong where. Within the fence though, taxonomists struggle with the rainbow's classification just as much as they do with brown or cutthroat trout's – perhaps even more. Fish may be elevated from race to subspecies, and from subspecies to species, and then downgraded again, depending on the latest results of protein tests, DNA analysis or chromosome counts. Much of this sub-grouping may be of mainly academic interest, but it at least shows that a rainbow trout is only a rainbow trout for want of a better description. Fish in the mountains of Mexico and the rivers of western Alaska may both swim under the same colloquial name but they are far, far from being the same fish.

Most firmly within *Oncorhynchus mykiss* are the coastal rainbow trout, which are spread down the edge of North America from the Kuskokwim River in Alaska to southern California, as well as in the fog-bound lakes and rivers over on the Kamchatka Peninsula. Like coastal cutthroats, they are a subspecies unto themselves (*O. m. irideus*) and genetically quite distinct from their inland kin, which are often collectively called 'redbands'. Unlike the coastal cutthroat, whose territory is quite unconnected to that occupied by their relatives in the interior, the ranges of coastal and inland rainbows adjoin, and even overlap.

The tendency to migrate can be a confusing indicator of subspecies. Sea-going rainbow trout are called steelhead; it is their seaward migration that qualifies them as such. Not all coastal rainbows are steelhead and not all steelhead are coastal rainbows. A few migratory rainbows are redbands, like those from the Snake River, which still manage to complete the great return journey from the interior to the sea and back, despite the dams and water diversions that waylay them. Scale counts provide the surest means of identifying one subspecies from another in the field, coastal fish having a coarser feel with fewer scales than those from the interior. The bigger spots, pink and orange tints and oval parr marks

of the inland fish also help distinguish them. However, these are far from infallible guides, especially in the areas of overlap where the two may have interbred, and to identify subspecies with certainty may require dissection and even genetic analysis.

Coastal rainbow in Alaska.
(Greg Syverson)

With their freedom to move up and down the shoreline, occasionally straying from one river to another and mixing genes with neighbouring populations, coastal fish are a much more homogeneous lot than their inland kin. They have not been where they are for long either, and may only have reached Kamchatka some 30,000 years ago when the Bering land bridge stood high above the sea. Rainbows from Russia are still more akin to those from the lower reaches of the Columbia River – so far as there are any wild fish left there – than the trout of the Kern River in California are to others in its tributary, the Little Kern.

The distinctions between these inland populations of rainbow are far more complex, and fascinating, although still not as marked as those subdividing their cutthroat cousins. Cutthroat have penetrated much further from the sea, colonising both sides of the Continental Divide. This suggests that they have been there much longer than the rainbows, as does the frequent separation of rainbow and cutthroat territories by impassable waterfalls. Rainbows never surmounted the Shoshone Falls on the Snake River, nor the waterfall on the Kootenay River near Libby, both of which marked the respective upstream limits of Columbia River rainbows and the downstream limit of cutthroat.

Almost all natural stocks of rainbows occur on the Pacific slopes of the Continental Divide. As usual, there is an exception, provided by fish in Alberta that live in the headwaters of the Athabasca River, which empties into Hudson Bay. These rainbows may have reached their eastbound streams on the floods of Wisconsin glacier meltwater; more likely, though, they were already there before the last Ice Age froze the landscape, and with it the movements of fresh-water fish. South-western Alberta seems to have been an ice-free refuge during the last Ice Age, and the ancestors of these Athabasca rainbows perhaps slipped over the watershed from the headwaters of the Fraser River at the end of an earlier glaciation. They are sufficiently different from the nearest redbands in scale counts and colour to endorse the idea of their having been isolated for much longer than the last 12,000 years; however, for the time being they still remain taxonomically grouped with all those other rainbows whose home streams drain into the Columbia or Fraser Rivers.

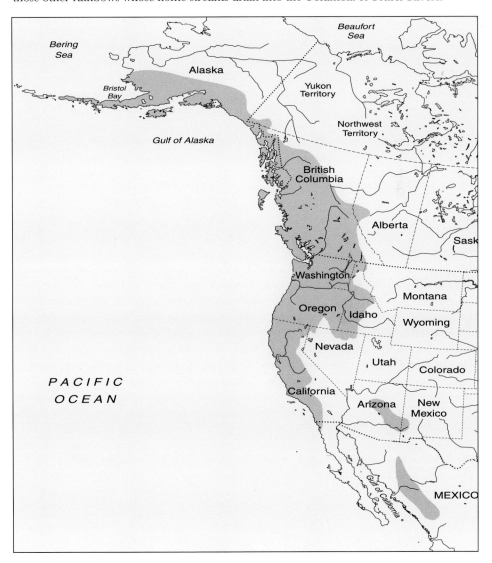

The natural North American distribution of rainbow trout and their allies.

Moving southwards, rainbows, again like cutthroat, become much more diverse and far harder to classify. Their colours range from brassy gold to olive-silver, spots are often few and oddly clustered, and sometimes the finger marks never leave their flanks as they mature. Many populations differ enough from the type specimens, and from each other, to qualify as subspecies, perhaps even species. In Oregon, Nevada, Arizona and Mexico, the warming world has left only headwater trickles tolerable for what are essentially cold-water fish. At the same time, ancient lakes have dried out, isolating their piscine inhabitants in shrinking feeder streams, which drain into desert basins and may never even reach the sea.

The world's most seemingly incongruous natural rainbows live in Mexico, reminders of a long-gone age when the Gulf of California was cool enough for their ancestors to move up and down the coast from one estuary to another. The protective enclosure of the Gulf seems to have been a great ichthyological mixing bowl, which trout deserted when it got too warm, abandoning their sea-going habits to take permanent refuge in the headwaters of coastal streams. There they remained for perhaps thousands of generations, until the planet cooled enough for them to reappear in the Gulf, by then fractionally changed by the evolutionary pressures of their fresh-water life. The next warm spell in the Earth's history might have forced them to return to their original stream, or perhaps to some other one, until the ending of the last Ice Age crystallised the peculiar and illogical distribution of the trout still left in Mexico today.

The most southerly natural stock of rainbows in the world is just north of the Tropic of Cancer in the Rio del Presidio, which drops off the Sierra Madre Occidental. These mountains are flat-topped and the highland tributaries meander through pine-oak forests, which keep the night's chill in the water all through the day. Trout live comfortably up on the plateau before the water tumbles down into sheer-sided canyons, now quite impassable by fish from below. How and when they first reached their highland refuge is hard even to guess, not least because the mountains are far south of the limits of the topographical tumult of the Ice Ages. These fish, and those in the neighbouring Rio San Lorenzo, seem closely related to the trout of the mountains of southern Californian, and appear to combine features from both coastal and inland strains. They remain unclassified, and apart from claiming the southernmost natural record, are remarkable for being utterly distinct from the trout in the three rivers just to the north.

These three rivers are the stronghold of Mexican golden trout, which appear to be descendants of an ancient lineage, long departed from the common rainbow ancestor. They may even provide a link between cutthroat and rainbows, and some genetic analysis suggests that they are actually closer to cutthroat, even though their sixty-chromosome count may indicate otherwise. Never the less, wherever Mexican golden trout should be placed in the larger picture, as *O. chrysogaster* they are different enough from other Pacific trout to rest almost unopposed in their own species. The gold is largely confined to their fins, and the pinky tinge is with them throughout their lives. They only have between fifty-five and fifty-nine vertebrae, which is the lowest average number in any American trout. This may be an evolutionary consequence of having been so small for so long, or otherwise the result of living in warm water which can affect vertebra numbers in developing embryos.

Into the apex of the Gulf of California flows the Colorado River, draining the dry lands of the south-western USA. Far up in the New Mexican headwaters of the Gila River tributary, Gila trout cling to the occupation of their ancestral home in the face of one environmental catastrophe after another – and of the ever present herds of cattle which trample and silt up the stream beds and destroy the bankside vegetation. Yellow in colour, with a yellow cutthroat slash below their gills, and tiny spots, which are largely confined to the upper bodies, they are currently also recognised as their own distinctive species – *O. gilae*. Exactly which waters held Gila trout before European settlers arrived is masked by faded memories, repeated stocking of exotic strains and species, and confusion with their close relations, Apache trout, which also live in Gila River tributaries. Sadly there is much less likelihood of confusion over where pure Gila trout live today. Restricted to five tiny trickles, they are also the most recent trout to rank as 'endangered' under the USA's Endangered Species Act (ESA).

Like the brook charr in the Appalachian Mountains (see Chapter 7) or the Paiute cutthroat of Silver King Creek (see Chapter 9), Gila trout have been squeezed slowly upwards into the steep narrow valleys of juniper trees and Ponderosa pines by the gradual destruction of their downstream habitat. There they live in conditions where survival depends on resources no normal rainbow trout ever need draw upon, and only above waterfalls and stretches of dried-up riverbed do they remain uncontaminated by the genes of their introduced relations. Nature taxes their powers of survival to the limit with an unbroken cycle of droughts, floods and sometimes fires.

Lightning fires are unpredictable and their effects can be devastating when they burn their way through riparian vegetation, raising the water temperature dramatically and stressing fish to the point of death. Floods often follow fires, as rainwater rushes off scorched, overgrazed hillsides, its deluge no longer checked by bankside trees and brush. Ashes cloud the water, and any fish not choked to death may find themselves unable to counter the force of a current, which for most of their lives is so feeble that lack of dissolved oxygen is a much greater threat to survival than being swept away in floods.

Further down the Gila River into Arizona, the more olivey Apache trout survive in larger numbers, although their range is still very restricted, much of it falling within the Fort Apache Reservation. They are probably closer to Gila than to rainbow trout and have suffered particularly from having to compete with brown trout and brook charr. Now propagation programmes are slowly reclaiming some of their original territory, as well as introducing them into virgin still waters. Like all these little dry-country fish, Apache trout are seldom more than 25 cm (10 in) long in their native habitat. Translocated to dams and lakes they may grow twice that length and weigh over 2 kg (4 lb) – clear evidence that their growth remains constrained by their environment and not by any genetic predisposition to stay small.

Of the many other distinctive types of rainbow, California golden trout (*O. m. aguabonita*, or to those that place them in their own species, distinct from rainbow trout, *O. aguabonita*) are perhaps the best known, not least because in many waters they are legal quarry. There is a romance about them generated by their exotic untroutlike colouring and original Alpine habitat in the web of little streams feeding the Kern River. Like most of these other southerly populations, golden trout never grow large, remaining stunted by the impoverished environments in which they live. There they nibble occasional caddis larvae off stones or seize tiny midges out of the current in a growing season, which, for fish up at 2,000 or 3,000 m (6,500 or 9,800 ft), is seldom more than four months long.

When golden trout are introduced into new waters, like Apache trout they are never slow to show how well they can flourish on a richer diet. Having seldom experienced much competition in their mountainous retreats they are ill suited to facing it, and they adapt best to life in upland, previously fishless lakes where the invertebrates' lives have never been threatened by anything higher up the food pyramid than themselves. The largest golden trout on record weighed over 5 kg (11 lb), and was taken from a lake in Wyoming's Wind River Mountains in 1948. This was exceptional, and most of the still waters in which golden trout now live are barren glacial pools in the High Sierras, where growing large trout has been described as like 'trying to raise alfalfa on a tennis court'.

Apache trout.
(Richard Grost)

There are no native trout on the eastern slopes of the southern Sierra Nevadas, and many pony-loads of golden trout fry or frozen ova have found their way over the watershed. The golden trout's present range is largely the result of the efforts of man trying to make up for having obliterated the fish from much of its native territory. Getting them established has not always been easy. Some remote lakes only emerge from the winter shadows of the surrounding mountains in May, tempting trout to spawn in the outflows, which reach the critical temperature of around 5°C long before the inflows do. This often leads to many of the next generation being lost to the lake, as the newly emerged fry chase their instincts downstream rather than up – although if at least some from each hatching move upstream and survive to spawn, a viable population of outflow spawners may eventually establish itself.

The advantages to golden trout, or to any other brightly coloured southern trout, of being so stunningly arrayed are not easy to imagine. What could a fish gain from looking, as American novelist S. E. White described it, like

> the twenty dollar gold-piece, the same satin finish, the same pale yellow. The fish was fairly molten. It did not glitter in gaudy burnishment . . . but gleamed and melted and glowed as though fresh from the mold.

Predators, both feathered and finned, are rare up in those altitudes, and it may be that the male trout could afford to evolve a mate-attracting brilliance, rather than the cryptic colouring that other fish need to merge with their backgrounds. Unlike size, the golden trout's colour is largely a product of genes rather than environment, and transplanted fish retain much of their gold.

The twin luxuries of evolving in a largely predator-free environment and away from any serious competition certainly make life easy for the generations fortunate enough to enjoy them, but leave their descendants hopelessly ill equipped to counter any competition that arrives. Whenever brook charr or brown trout have invaded the natural domains of these isolated trout, the timid indigenous fish have, like the cutthroat of the interior, retreated quickly upstream. Introducing exotic strains of rainbow trout can be even more damaging, bringing the added danger of their destroying the whole population of native fish simply by interbreeding.

Massive human effort and expense is devoted to safeguarding relict trout by catching up fish and moving them to other streams. These thoroughbred stocks are often very susceptible to extremes of weather and climate in their new environments, and whatever may be said about the loss of genetic diversity, there must be a case for diverting limited resources into the conservation of fish whose natural existence is less precarious.

Rehabilitating trout streams to accommodate their original inhabitants can be an alarmingly long and costly process. Restoring the Californian golden trout's original native habitat to its pristine state is deemed a high priority, even though there are now hundreds of unadulterated stocks elsewhere, which can always provide fish for repopulating any other barren streams. Like most such restoration programmes, preparing the water for the trout's return often entails first poisoning every fish in the river, with all the attendant moral dilemmas this creates. It then involves a whole array of other resource-consuming measures, including constructing spawning barriers to stop non-native fish swimming upstream, removing non-indigenous beavers, and even reintroducing the Sacramento sucker (the two species are known to have coexisted for thousands of years and the sucker may in some way have played a key part on the trout's evolutionary stage).

There are golden trout and golden trout, subdivided by waterfalls and tributaries, watersheds and rockfalls. Their subdivision is of mainly academic interest and the confusion it creates reflects the overall difficulty of classifying all the Pacific trout, whose taxonomic roller coaster has much in common with the brown trout's. The greatest of the early American ichthyologists was David Starr Jordan, whose theories carried gospel weight for nearly forty years, despite their remarkable inconsistency. Jordan see-sawed between grouping all Pacific trout within a single species at the turn of the century, and splitting them into thirty-two full species in his final *Checklist of Fishes* (1930). Since then, one-time species have gradually merged with one another once again, but it took until 1989 to agree the significant departure of rainbow and cutthroat trout from the genus *Salmo*.

So long as taxonomy is constrained by the limitations of the binomial system of classification, there is never likely to be unanimity over the shape of the *Oncorhynchus* branch of the Salmonidae family tree. Perhaps the true value of taxonomic research lies in identifying the genetic diversity that actually exists, and so is there to be conserved. Often this diversity is literally only skin deep, and in habit and behaviour one river's trout may be no different from fish just over the watershed. Other populations of trout show more fundamental distinctions in their growth rates or adaptations to climatic extremes. Even though environmental influences may induce similar differences in one generation after another, this does still not mean such differences are necessarily genetically fixed. Southern high desert trout are only stunted for lack of food, and their small size provides no basis for any taxonomic distinction *per se*. On the other hand, thousands of years of natural selection has meant that these same trout now inherit an easy endurance of temperatures well above 25°C, which they take with them wherever they go.

Eagle Lake, near Susanville in eastern California, is still a fair size, but in the context of the Lahontan Basin in which it lies, it is a mere puddle with no outflow. Cutthroat trout were the dominant fish in Lake Lahontan, and there are still relict populations in some of the other puddles and trickles within the lake's original boundaries. Yet in Eagle Lake there are rainbow trout, the only ones within the basin. Suggestions that these may in fact only be descended from nineteenth century stockings are countered by the fish's extraordinary tolerance of alkalinity levels high enough to kill any other rainbows – a tolerance which has evolved in parallel with the slowly shrinking lake and the concomitant increase in its salinity. Being dominated by chub and suckers, Eagle Lake's fish fauna is typical of the other waters of the Lahontan Basin – that is except for the rainbow trout. Because there are no other rainbows anywhere else in the basin, these ones must have arrived in that narrow gap in time after Eagle Lake became a lake unto itself, but before its alkalinity started climbing to the potentially lethal levels of today.

Eagle Lake rainbows used to spawn in Pine Creek, the lake's only inflow. The creek may have provided a link with Pit River on the western side of the watershed, which the rainbows managed to cross during some cold wet interlude in the gradual desiccation of the countryside. Such conjecture rests in the theoretical realms of zoogeography, and of much more practical significance is the fact that Pine Creek spawning grounds have been so ruined by human activities that the fish can no longer breed there. For their continued survival they now depend on being restocked into the lake by hatcheries every year. The ease with which they settle into alkaline waters has made them particularly popular fish for introducing into lakes and reservoirs with higher than average pH levels. Occupying such a unique environment, early ichthyologists placed them in their own species, *Salmo aquilarium*. Undoubtedly they have an inherited, and transportable, tolerance of high alkalinity, which sets them apart from their relatives; but nothing else does, and they may in fact not even merit description as the subspecies, *O. m. aquilarium*.

Upper Klamath Lake, in southern Oregon, is another where trout have to contend with extreme levels of alkalinity, especially in the summer when blooms of blue-green algae (*Aphanizomenon flos-aquae*) coat the water in testimony to its nutritional riches. The rainbows grow to great sizes on their piscivorous diet, which has fattened fish to weights of over 10 kg (22 lb). Steelhead once also reached the lake up the Klamath River, but have long been blocked from doing so by a hydroelectric dam, leaving the lake to resident fish for which access to the sea is, and always has been, superfluous. These fresh-water rainbows may have been genetically quite distinct from the migratory steelhead, and even if both races shared spawning streams, subtle nuances in their breeding habits could have prevented them from interbreeding.

This natural presence of two different forms of rainbow trout in the same water, remaining reproductively isolated from each other despite their coexistence, was by no means unique to Upper Klamath Lake, and in this respect the rainbow trout in Kootenay Lake have much in common with their Klamath kin. Swimming up the murky waters of the Fraser River, through the Hell's Gate Pass, then turning right into the Thompson tributary, a returning steelhead or sockeye salmon eventually reaches Kamloops Lake in southern British Columbia. Surrounded by dry barren hills, dotted with spruce and lodgepole pines, the lake is inhabited by a magnificent strain of non-migratory rainbow trout, *O. m. kamloops*; these reached record sizes by exploiting the rich feeding in their native water with an inherited inclination to feast off other fish.

Despite the heavy fishing which follows from its gilded reputation as a prime trout water, and the inevitable ravages of the timber companies up the banks of the inflowing streams, Kamloops Lake is still home to many of the splendid fish to which it gives its name. But it is not their only home, and in Kootenay Lake, further south and over in the Columbia drainage, live two quite distinct races of Kamloops trout side by side. One is described as the 'standard' race, attaining an age of five or six and a maximum size of not much more than 2 kg (4 lb) on a diet which stops short of other fish. The other rainbows belong to the Gerrard race and probably arrived in the lake on the same post-glacial floods as landlocked kokanee; these the trout now exploit with such prodigious success that fish have reached weights over 20 kg (44 lb).

It seems to take several thousand years of coexistence before rainbows become properly adapted to feeding on kokanee, making that quantum leap from competitor to predator as they do so. Kokanee are popular with fishery managers for their tendency to feed off free floating plankton in open water, which other species with fewer gill-rakers, like rainbows, do much less effectively. Most native rainbows are thus seldom able to flourish in the face of competition from introduced kokanee. However, when Gerrard race Kamloops rainbows are stocked into lakes with a self-sustaining supply of forage fish and no direct competition, the results can be spectacular.

Already moulded to a diet of fish, Kamloops trout introduced into Jewel Lake in Montana are reputed to have weighed more than 23 kg (50 lb), and several fish of over 15 kg (33 lb) came out of Pend Oreille Lake in Idaho, where the kokanee were stocked before the rainbows. In Crescent Lake, on the Olympic Peninsula in Washington, coastal rainbow trout also coexist with kokanee, for which they have to compete with the equally piscivorous coastal cutthroat. Impassable falls bar sea-going fish from returning to Crescent Lake, and both predators have long been renowned for reaching great sizes on their diets of fresh-water fish – and the lake for the destruction of its unique fish fauna by wanton introductions of other strains of trout.

The urge to migrate to sea also seems to be inherited, and steelhead usually breed steelhead. This may seem a statement of the obvious, but where brown trout are concerned the responsibility of genes for their seaward migrations is much less evident. Coastal rainbows comprise distinct populations of fish which migrate and fish which do not, and the behaviour of the individuals making up these populations is remarkably consistent. If steelhead are transplanted beyond their native range, there is a general expectation that they will continue to behave like steelhead, even if their migratory urges must be satisfied by moving down to a lake rather than to sea. Conversely, introduced brown trout have repeatedly shown that they live quite independently of the way their parents did. Steelhead generally behave much more like Pacific salmon, with which they are often loosely grouped, especially as they now all share a genus; but they still remain as much rainbow trout as the tiny denizens of the deserts of Nevada.

Like brown trout, migratory rainbows are confined within a much narrower band of latitude than resident fish. Just as the rivers far below the Alps or the Atlas Mountains are too warm for brown trout to pass through, so are those in the lowlands of Mexico to let rainbows leave their mountain refuges. The sea is also much too warm, but that this was not always so is obvious from the very existence of trout in any Mexican river. Most of the rivers in southern California are also impassable, mankind having contributed to the inhospitability of their lower reaches by either poisoning the water or extracting far too much. Amazingly, a few steelhead still seem to swim up the Ventura River just north of Los Angeles – a winter run of fish which return when the fresh water is coldest.

The southern limit for those steelheads whose inherited timing prompts them to return to their natal stream in the summer is much further north – probably the Eel River, which reaches the Pacific at Eureka, and also marks the boundary for sea-going cutthroat. But from there, all the way up the Pacific coast, steelhead run the streams and rivers as far as Kodiak Island and the Kenai Peninsula in western Alaska. It is occasionally suggested that some of the huge rainbows in the Lake Iliamna system may have come up the Kvichak River in the autumn, and if this is so it would push the steelhead's northern limits over the Alaska Peninsula and into the Bering Sea.

Rainbow trout in Lake Iliamna, Alaska.
(Greg Ruggerone)

Steelhead run into one river or another in every month of the year. The specific timing of each stock's return is likely to have evolved in response to the temperature and conditions in their natal streams, as well as to how far upstream they spawn. Just as with cutthroat trout, the rainbow's breeding urges are triggered by rising, not falling, temperatures and lengthening, not shortening, days. The hormones of rainbows may start spreading their chemical messages as soon as the water warms up to 5°C in icy Alaskan lakes, and when it reaches around 10°C in the rivers of California. On balance, early hatching is in the best interests of the young, and the more of the summer they have left to grow in, the better. This usually puts a premium on early spawning, and eggs and sperm are well developed by the autumn, so fish are ready to shed them soon after their bodies receive the first thermal or day-length signals of spring. Only if the end-of-winter floods are particularly strong, and early-emerging young risk getting swept away, may late spawners gain an edge over earlier ones.

Clearly the water creeps up to its critical temperature much sooner at both lower latitudes and lower altitudes. Steelhead in California may spawn in December, where their redds are close to the sea, but not until January or February if they are further upstream. In Alaska, even spawning areas around sea level will not warm up enough until April, and the temperature may not be right for steelhead travelling to the top of the Skeena River in British Columbia until May or even June. There is very little time to lose once conditions approach the ideal for spawning, and as soon as they do steelhead must be prepared to take advantage of them. The variety of different strategies which ensure that they are ready to breed only serves to emphasise the extent to which each stock of fish is genetically moulded for its own particular environment.

Steelhead are generally split into river-maturing fish (colloquially called 'summer' fish) and ocean-maturing, or winter fish. This is a simplified distinction with innumerable exceptions, but valid nevertheless and with parallels throughout the salmon world. Atlantic salmon rivers often have distinct runs of 'springers', which mature in fresh water, and autumn fish that are almost ready to spawn by the time they get there. Chinook, as well as being categorised by life history as either stream- or ocean-type fish, are also sometimes divided into spring or fall fish, depending on when they start their journey upstream – itself a function of how far they have to travel (see Chapter 10). The same goes for steelhead; if they are returning to redds just a short swim up a coastal stream, they are often darkened, egg-laden and close to breeding as they approach the estuary.

In other environments, steelhead need to be nowhere near spawning when they reach the river mouth. Some Alaskan fish are forced to delay their final migration for no other reason than that their spawning stream is frozen solid through the winter. Then they lurk in deep holes lower downstream, or in a lake if there is one on their way, until the meltwaters of spring finally provide a channel back up to the gravel from which they emerged. Fish starting their spawning migrations up the great arterial rivers of the west coast of Canada and the USA will always find the way open whenever they arrive, but they may still need spates to help them over the stony shallows of little capillary tributaries. If steelhead are only able to negotiate certain stretches of river, or get up otherwise impassable falls, when the water is at a particular level, evolution may have repeatedly favoured those fish which returned at the appropriate time. Eventually this would have created a distinct run that timed its arrival to maximise its chances of reaching the spawning grounds.

Steelhead spawning in deep wide water are less dependent on the whims of the elements to help them complete their journeys successfully. They need strength and size to excavate their nests in the face of the powerful mainstream, and natural selection may have repeatedly favoured large fish which are able to cope more easily with such conditions. Greater size can also help fish through difficult stretches of river and make them less prone to predation, both at sea and in fresh water. Spending a further year at sea may give steelhead crucial extra kilograms, making all the difference between spawning successfully or not. Fish fitted to spawn in swift rivers like the Skeena are nearly all far larger than their fellows elsewhere – a super-race with the strength to resist the currents on their redds.

Most steelhead return from their oceanic wanderings with the intention of spawning – prodigal children coming back for the first time to the mother river which nurtured them to smolt size, and then helped them down to the sea. They usually reached the sea in spring, after one or more winters in the comparative safety of fresh water, and then headed quickly away from the estuary, only returning when urged back to breed. However, in a few rivers, particularly the Rogue River in Oregon and the Klamath and some of its neighbours in northern California, runs of small fish come back for the winter, still immature, as if just testing life in fresh water again. Called 'half-pounders', they feed whenever they can and are the true rainbow counterpart of the brown trout finnock or herling – one of the many parallels in the lives of the two species which kept them in the same genus for so long.

Like sea trout, steelhead can spawn more than once, and are also said to feed sporadically in fresh water. One may be a distant consequence of the other. By the time a Pacific salmon is ready to spawn, its digestive tract, unused for so long, has begun to waste away, and there is no chance of the fish recovering. A trout's continues to function, certainly in a fairly desultory fashion, but at least enough to ensure that it is not through any physical inability to eat that many trout also die after spawning. Whether mature steelhead can be truly said to feed really depends on what constitutes feeding. Trout seldom ignore unburied salmon eggs bobbing down on the current, and, like resident rainbows, steelhead probably snap up bits of rotting salmon flesh, as well as any passing insect larvae. Summer-run fish are presented with a much greater choice of food than later arrivals, and the warmer water is a greater stimulus to feeding. Steelhead certainly feed less urgently and more impulsively than fresh-water-resident rainbows, but they all settle for little more than a subsistence diet in the winter before the urge to spawn finally suppresses the urge to feed entirely.

Spawning is as exhausting for sea-going trout as it is for salmon. Steelhead once swam 1,600 km (1000 miles) up the Columbia River until the Grand Coulee Dam barred migratory fish from the whole network of streams and rivers above it. These fish probably never spawned again, nor did the sea trout which travelled 1,000 km (600 miles) through Poland up the Vistula River to breed in the Carpathian Mountains. No trout whose body is already drained of energy by the struggle to reach the gravel of its birth is likely to survive spawning and live to scent the salt again. However, in short coastal streams, sea-going fish of both species often manage to breed more than once. For them, not only is the upstream journey quick and easy on their egg- or milt-laden bodies, but so too is the downstream drift for their exhausted spawned-out hulks. Neither steelhead nor sea trout seem to resume their half-hearted fresh-water feeding after spawning, and only on reaching the estuary do they really start to regain condition.

So although more fish come back to spawn again in some rivers than in others, it is still

Steelhead water on the Umpqua River in Oregon. (Richard Grost)

possible to make some useful generalisations embracing them all. Very, very seldom does a steelhead spawn more than three times (the record for sea trout, according to scale analysis, is twelve). In rivers where repeat spawning is common, up to 25 per cent of fish may be coming back to breed again; of these, at least 75 per cent will be doing so for the second time and nearly all others for the third.

All salmonids hatch in fresh, or occasionally brackish, water – this is one of the features which unites them – but thereafter their lives are extraordinarily diverse. Young pink and chum salmon instinctively head to sea as soon as they emerge from their gravel nests; ocean-type chinook only wait a few weeks before they do. Migratory rainbows adopt a strategy more like the coho salmon with which they often share streams, and sacrifice a richer marine diet for at least two years in the greater safety of fresh water.

When they first swim up from the gravel, young rainbows shelter together in the security of numbers, but beyond that they are aggressive independent creatures and soon begin to establish territories they can only expand at the expense of their siblings. Predation takes a huge toll on these tiny fry, which in their first fresh-water months behave much like young brown trout or coho. Having only hatched in late spring, rainbows and cutthroat have a shorter summer than their earlier-hatching salmon and charr relations.

Occasionally, a Californian steelhead may silver up in readiness for an ocean life in the same year it hatched; or could it be driven downstream and out to sea by the man-made misery in the lower reaches of its river? On average, though, steelhead will have spent two winters in fresh water, and often three, before hormones send the signals to start smolting and migrate. Like all salmonids, more southerly stocks of rainbows are ready for the sea much sooner than those further north. In the Alaskan panhandle it is unusual to find fish starting towards the sea before they are three years old. On the Kenai Peninsula, where steelhead hatch latest of all, and growing seasons are half as long as they are in the sunny south, most smolts are four or five.

Spring is the season when smolts head for the estuary, there to spend anything between one and six months, fattening on its new-found riches and learning to recognise its dangers. The larger they are when they reach the estuary, the better their chances of survival, but fish grow slowly in the river and cannot prolong their time there indefinitely. All steelhead, by definition, must eventually set off for the Pacific Ocean. Their lives are a great compromise between fresh-water safety and saltwater growth, the one being finally exchanged for the other as they abandon the familiar scent of their natal stream and head out into the void – usually alone.

Out at sea, steelhead's lives are very like salmon's – devoted to harvesting as much of the ocean's goodness as their systems can process in the time available. This varies almost as much as the time spent in fresh water. Californian and Oregon fish may only stay one year at sea, while steelhead from big cold northern rivers spend up to four there. It perhaps seems perverse that fish spending longer in fresh water also remain longer at sea, but they invariably have more weight to show for it when they reach their estuary again. From this follows another generalisation about the size of steelheads, which is simply that, on average, those further north are larger.

No sweeping statements about the steelhead's migratory patterns should be allowed to mask the variety of life histories among fish from the same river, and even from a single distinct population within that river. Steelhead were studied in splendid detail by closing the fishing for ten years in Waddell Creek, Santa Cruz County, California, and taking scale samples from every single fish migrating upstream or down, after trapping them in a dam. The creek is a short coastal one towards the southern end of the steelhead's range. A combination of different influences, like a river's climate and topography, and spawning distance from the sea, has shaped each steelhead population's behaviour over thousands of generations, to the extent that much of it is now genetically controlled. Yet despite the apparent genetic uniformity of any particular population, the complex interaction of a fish's genes with its environment preserves the potential for individuals to behave very differently under similar conditions, and the steelhead of Waddell Creek were still found to be leading widely varying lives.

In Waddell Creek, over 80 per cent of upstream migrants were spawning for the first time and 15 per cent for the second. Of the first time spawners, 30 per cent were 2.1 fish, 26 per cent 2.2 and 10 per cent 3.1. (One of the most concise ways of summarising a fish's life history is to indicate how many winters since hatching it has spent in fresh water and then at sea, and to separate the two with a decimal point). Only 2 per cent had lingered four full winters in fresh water. Once at sea, very few steelhead stayed as long as three winters there, most returning after just one or two. From their measurements it was quite apparent that the length of time fish spent in fresh water had almost no bearing on their eventual size. What really mattered was time at sea. After one year in the river and two at sea (1.2), fish averaged 66 cm (26 in), only 2 cm less than those which had spent an extra year in the river (2.2). The net benefits of a further year in the Pacific were only too obvious, especially early in life, and 1.1 fish measured nearly 40 cm (16 in), as against the 68 cm (27 in) of 1.2, and 79 cm (31 in) of 1.3 fish.

Other figures dramatically illustrate the strains of spawning. Steelhead returning to spawn for the second time, at the same age as others doing so for the first, are invariably smaller. The breeding year produces very little extra growth, because of the drastic drawdown of the body's reserves needed to fuel not only the development of eggs or milt, but also upstream and downstream migrations at a time when the fish are hardly feeding. The small proportion of repeat spawners grow very little each year, just enough to show that a few months at sea leaves some, but not much, surplus energy for growth after sustaining the rigours of reproduction. Steelhead that have bred once very seldom miss a year before trying again, until recovering from their spawning exertions takes more strength than they have, and with their last efforts to create new lives, lose their own.

The scales of steelhead from slightly further up the coast were carefully analysed by other researchers. In keeping with the tendency for fish to spend longer at sea in cooler latitudes, more than 50 per cent of steelhead returning to the Alsea River in Oregon had led 2.2 lives, over 25 per cent spent three years at sea, leaving about 5 per cent to return after just a single year. Most of these, like other Oregon steelhead, were winter fish whose spawning grounds were not far upstream.

Summer fish are overall much less common, and perhaps the most marked distinction between the two forms is in the Columbia River. Fish facing long journeys, perhaps far up the Snake, need to give themselves enough time to reach their redds. They are summer-run steelhead, weighing slightly less than the winter fish, which put on another kilogram or so during their extra months at sea. Almost all these winter fish turn off the main stream below Bonneville Dam. This barrier, together with the rash of hatcheries all over the lower Columbia River system, has contributed to the creation of steelhead populations as far removed from the ones Nature designed as any in America.

In British Columbia and Alaska, scarcely a fish leaves the river until after at least two winters, nor do they return before having spent two or three years at sea. Not only does this mean northern steelhead are generally much larger than their Californian counterparts; also, because they are at least four or five when they first spawn, repeat spawning is far less common. Commercial netsmen have taken steelhead of over 25 kg (55 lb), but now that the fish are often an accidental by-catch, whose protected status demands their return to the water, such captures often go unreported. The weights of sport-caught fish are more often publicised, even though prone to exaggeration, and the record seems to be just short of 20 kg (44 lb). Caught offshore, this fish most likely derived from the Skeena River, whose summer-run steelhead are probably, on average, the largest of all. Even then, despite their prodigious ocean growth, steelhead may never have reached the size of their cutthroat cousins from Pyramid Lake, nor of the Kamloops rainbow trout introduced to Jewel Lake and elsewhere beyond their natural range.

At sea, steelhead sometimes travel in small, loose groups, united by common purpose or common prey rather than an instinct to shoal together for any other reason. They are the true nomads of *Oncorhynchus*, as independent at sea as they were in fresh water. By nature they are loners, from the moment they start establishing their metre-square territories near the gravel nurseries, from which they first emerged, to the time they return there to spawn. So in essence it is on their own that they set off away from the shore into the gaping sea. On leaving the estuary, many southerly fish, especially those spending only a year at sea, stay close inshore, nosing up and down the coastal shelf in search of food. Further north, if steelhead are destined to spend three years in the ocean, they will eventually shun the safety of the shoreline and join the counterclockwise oceanic gyres. These take them on great circuits, loosely bordered to the north by the chain of Aleutian Islands and to the south by isotherms of about 10°C. Steelhead wander even further than salmon, and American fish have been caught close to Kamchatka and south as far as 41°, level with the tip of Honshu in Japan.

All steelhead seem to prefer life in the top 10 m (33 ft) of water where, at least in summer, the light easily penetrates to illuminate the squid, crustacea and other large free floating zooplankton which are their main source of food. Feeding is better in some years than others, and is particularly variable in lower latitudes where sub-Arctic waters drift down to confront the warmth of the California Current. The convergence zone is usually a rich grazing ground and is continually shifting, its crucial upwellings sometimes suppressed by the northward sweep of the El Niño Current. The resources of an ocean are no more boundless than those of a river, only far greater, and their fluctuations could easily affect the size of steelhead returning to fresh water; so could the inevitable competition from Pacific salmon.

Numbers of steelhead are negligible amongst the millions of salmon milling around the ocean, and in terms of naturally hatched fish, there are far fewer of them than of any single species of salmon. If a species' success is measured in numbers, is this evidence of the advantages of fish always dying soon after they have spawned for the first time? Perhaps, but the populations of salmon and steelhead in many rivers are now so manipulated by hatchery output that the biological realities of their lives in the wild are masked beyond recognition.

Steelhead are identified at sea by silvery-blue colouring and spotted backs and tails (as well as by a noticeably smaller anal fin than salmon), and it is only when they enter fresh water that the pinkish stripes start showing on their flanks. Their navigational skills are as spectacular as those of any other members of their genus, perhaps even more so in that many of them appear to head straight back to the estuary without first feeling their way up or down the coast in search of the familiar chemical mixture identifying their home stream. Straying is rare, although up to 10 per cent of steelhead do find themselves swimming up a river other than the one they swam down, and mixing their genes into its pool.

The dangers from infusions of genes of hatchery fish are now fully appreciated (see Chapter 12), and perhaps even too much so. Domestic stock frequently fare so poorly out of their cages that they seldom get as far as interbreeding with any remaining wild fish. Competition from hatchery-bred fry is also mitigated by the practice of releasing steelhead when they are almost ready for the sea, thereby minimising the overlap with wild young in the river. In recognition of the unique adaptations of wild fish to their own environment, hatchery fish now often derive from the river's own native stock – if this can afford to give up any of its fish for artificial breeding.

In many rivers wild steelhead are now protected, and the only fish which sport fishermen are allowed to keep are fin-clipped hatchery products. From the point of view of their own protection, as opposed to that of their environment, steelhead are in an enviable position. Unlike Pacific salmon, which provide the crews of thousands of fishing boats, large and small, with their livelihood, steelhead are of no legitimate value to most commercial fishermen, who are usually banned from keeping them – not that this prevents them from often being taken in nets set for salmon, nor from dying after being thrown callously back into the sea. In theory, wild fish are also given an opportunity to recover long-lost ground by the expectations of tribal and sport fishermen being largely satisfied by artificial output. However, if wild sea-going rainbow trout are really to get a chance to return to anything approaching their former numbers, it will still mean curtailing these expectations, and at present the proportion of wild fish in annual catches continues to decline.

The rainbow's natural flexibility is both a blessing and a curse. Repopulating once-poisoned waters with steelhead fry from neighbouring streams may be relatively simple; so was naturalising rainbow trout in the fishless highlands of Kenya. Yet the same adaptability which eased the rainbow's way into the lakes of Chile and the mountain streams of Morocco also drove the brook charr of the Appalachian Mountains into upstream retreat and some species of Australasian galaxiids onto the danger lists. Although riverfuls of cutthroat have been condemned to oblivion by infusions of rainbow genes, there are now enough lake-run rainbows in the Great Lakes to sustain an Indian fishery. While rainbows and all their half-caste relations are being poisoned out of existence to make way for reintroductions of pure-bred Paiute and Rio Grande cutthroat, *Oncorhynchus mykiss* is being farmed by the thousand tonnes in almost every country in the world with a cool enough climate and some well oxygenated streams. The rainbow's creeping colonisation may have adulterated gene pools and dominated native competitors. Yet on the other side of the strange scales which can weigh damage to Nature against benefit to man, are a lot of fish on a lot of plates or on the end of a lot of fishing lines. One person's piscine problem is indeed another's panacea.

The Thiririka River in Kenya – with no indigenous fish it was ideal for the introduction of rainbow trout.
(Author)

Salmo trutta arrived in Tasmania in 1864. This was ten years before rainbows were first hatched artificially, and reflected both the earlier perfection of the necessary technology in Britain and the easier access to seaports from anywhere in the country. Brown trout ova only got to America in the winter of 1883 (actually from Germany), but the skills required to fertilise and transport eggs had preceded them. Circumstances and the efforts of Mr Livingstone Stone combined to found the first rainbow trout hatchery on the banks of the McCloud River in northern California, and by 1874 rainbows had reached the east coast. (With the trans-continental rail link still too unreliable, trays of eyed ova had to travel by sea, all the way round the coast of South America to New York, where the Caledonia hatchery awaited their arrival.) Two years later eggs arrived in Japan, and from then on the only constraint to the expansion of the rainbow's range was poor land transport at the receiving end.

The McCloud River is filled by the melting snows of Mt Shasta, whose name was used to identify the river's trout wherever they went. In time they became endowed with a sort of informal subspecific status, even though actually no different from other coastal rainbows, and while *Salmo gairdneri shasta* was at least an indicator of their river of origin, it had no other significance. Some way of first identifying the descendants of both sea-going and resident ancestors, and then naming them differently, could have provided vital evidence on the heritability, or otherwise, of migratory instincts. There are both migratory and non-migratory fish in the McCloud River, but whether or not Stone was able to distinguish them, he never seems to have done so.

Like most other members of their family, rainbows fare far better in alien fresh waters than in strange seas. Even amongst the proven descendants of migratory ancestors there are very few examples of rainbows establishing self-sustaining steelhead dynasties anywhere outside their native north Pacific. Odd hatchery escapees often head downstream to the sea, and sea-going rainbows may perhaps be established in Chile, amongst all the other exotic salmonids milling around its jagged coastline. Otherwise, most runs of so-called steelhead in the southern hemisphere are short-lived, and if rainbows reach the sea, they almost never return (see Chapter 2).

The Eerste River runs through South African vineyard country round Stellenbosch, falling fast off the Jonkershoek Mountains into the cold southern sea at False Bay. Rainbows had long bred easily in the upper stretches of the river – so easily that each year many of the young fish always moved downstream in search of more space and better feeding. The river soon warms as the current slacks off, and by the 1940s much of it was being diverted for irrigation. What remained was adulterated with a cocktail of effluent from wineries, distilleries and other domestic and agricultural enterprises, so intoxicating that no rainbow trout could hope to survive there any longer. Fish caught up in this noxious mixture would move even further down, into slower currents and still less oxygen. Before long the rainbows found they had reached the sea, and there they spent the summer months until the river cooled enough to encourage them back upstream again.

False Bay is hoop-shaped, and if the South African rainbows seem to have had none of their species' usual difficulty finding their way home, it is probably because they never even left its sheltered confines. The Eerste River rainbows apparently no longer migrate, and if rainbows reach the sea anywhere else in the southern hemisphere, they never return home. In the northern Pacific, they are inveterate wanderers, and like salmon, perhaps their phenomenal powers of navigation only function in the ocean they have exploited for hundreds of thousands of generations. Brown trout are much less adventurous and seldom feed far from the shore. This may help explain why many long-established runs of introduced sea trout harvest the krill and squid of the southern oceans, even though they are just as likely to be descended from resident as migratory ancestors (see Chapter 4). Rainbows are usually assumed to be less flexible in their choice of life options, and unless urged to sea by the ruination of their habitat, like those in the Eerste River may have been, their migrations are usually seen to be more under genetic than environmental control.

One of the earliest and most successful expansions of the rainbow's range in eastern America, with far-reaching consequences for the fish community of the Great Lakes, was its introduction into the Au Sable River in Michigan. This drains into Lake Huron, which the trout lost no time in setting off to explore, just as they did when stocked into other neighbouring rivers. Before long, rainbow trout had spread all over the Great Lakes, and are now so well established that many fishermen have no idea they were not always there. Their migrations from river to lake and back have been repeated by each generation ever since, and are nearly always attributed to their following an inherited instinct to go to sea. If they had been brown trout, this would have been put down simply to opportunistic behaviour – exploiting the best of life's options. And even if inherited instinct, coupled with an ability to smolt, prompts most rainbows' seaward migrations, opportunism is still likely to play its part in sending at least some fish to sea.

Failure to make the most of the nearest ocean has not detracted from the rainbow's extraordinary success in establishing itself all over the world. On every continent except Antarctica the fish flourishes, its popularity sustained by a combination of being good to eat, fun to catch and easy to farm. With their aggressive nature, tolerance of marginally higher temperatures than other trout, and readiness to shape their diets to the available food supplies, rainbows further their own cause wherever they are stocked. Sometimes success can only be achieved at the expense of indigenous fish, but in many of the streams where rainbows are strangers they have few, if any, native species with which to compete, and on balance the ecological impact of their arrival has often been largely positive.

Surprisingly, rainbow trout have always struggled to maintain their status as a naturalised British fish. They are poured into hundreds of lakes and rivers week after week, year after year, and are continually escaping, or being deliberately released from fish farms all over the country. The rapid retreat of America's brook charr and cutthroat trout in the face of introduced rainbows might have provoked justifiable concern at the possible takeover of England's lowland trout waters by the Pacific species; yet it never seems to have done so. For all the boisterous behaviour of the rainbows, which first arrived in 1884, native brown trout have almost always retained the superiority of an indigenous species, specifically fitted for its environment. Very few waters in Britain are not totally dependent on regular stocking to maintain the rainbow's presence. Some of these hatchery products manage to breed here and there, but the number of proven self-sustaining populations in England can still be counted in single figures, just as it could fifty years ago.

Spawning in spring may account for the rainbow's fortunate failure to drive brown trout out of their own waters. This means rainbow's eggs hatch later than the brown's, so rainbow fry are always smaller, and the natives are given a lead in life which they maintain throughout that first, most vulnerable year. Against this, though, there is always the possibility of breeding rainbows digging up brown trout eggs as they make their own nests – and spring spawning has not stopped them driving brook charr into oblivion in the charr's native Appalachian streams.

The rainbow's tolerance of slightly warmer, and sometimes less healthy, water may occasionally give them a fractional, but none the less crucial, advantage over brown trout, and explain their success in oddly diverse parts of the British Isles. The best known rainbows in England are those introduced into the Derbyshire Wye, where, from 1908 onwards, they gradually began displacing the native brown trout from long stretches of the river and its tributaries. Why should they succeed so well there, and yet in so few other waters? Perhaps because raw sewage from Bakewell degraded the river to such an extent that brown trout could no longer survive in it, but rainbows could, and by the time the sewage began being treated the browns had gone for good. A similar scenario may have helped rainbows breed in the River Chess in Buckinghamshire, where indigenous brown trout were unable to contend with pollution from the uncontrolled discharge of human waste. Rainbows also once bred in the Wey in Surrey, exploiting conditions which were at best no more than marginal for brown trout. Most other self-sustaining populations live in distinctly alkaline rivers, where the environment may give the exotic fish an edge over the native brown trout, which are more comfortable in slightly acidic water.

So, in Britain at least, naturalised rainbows have had a negligible effect on the indigenous trout. This is not something that can be said of the ceaseless stocking of 'put and take' fisheries with hatchery-bred fish, which compete with the native trout for both food and space, particularly in running waters. The expectations of fishermen are raised to a level which can no longer be satisfied by the smaller slower growing, wild brown trout, only by repeated introductions of large free feeding, easily caught rainbows. Any resident brown trout that still survive this mindless manipulation of the river's fish life become objects of academic interest at best. Like dace or chub, which might also be sipping flies along the weed edges, they are seen to be boring to catch, and hardly worth the bother of conserving.

The consequences of trying to improve on Nature by bringing rainbow trout into other parts of America have been nothing less than disastrous (see Chapters 7 and 9), but more so for native competitors like brook charr or cutthroat trout than for the smaller prey fish, which may as well make a meal for a rainbow as for a cutthroat. Elsewhere, introduced rainbows have wreaked just as much ecological havoc, but more often as predator than competitor. There are no native salmonids in Africa (except brown trout in the Atlas Mountains), nor in South America or Australasia, and the exotic arrivals frequently slipped into an unfilled niche, often at the top of a food pyramid. The other smaller fish below may have evolved in an environment free from underwater predation, in which case the rainbows' initial impact on the small indigenous fish may have been particularly damaging. Australasian galaxiids, African *Barbus* and South American *Orestias* have all suffered from the predatory attentions of the northern hemisphere imports, although possibly only the New Zealand grayling, last seen in 1923, has done so to the point of extinction.

In some stark mountainous regions with no native fish at all, the ecological impact of the trout's sudden arrival may have been more abstruse and had surprising consequences for local mammals and birds. An absence of prey implies an absence of predators, and trout first stocked into fishless lakes and rivers may find invertebrates and crustaceans super-abundant, and dangers, even to tiny newly hatched fry, almost non-existent. It was only many years after trout had been introduced into the virgin streams on the moorlands of Kenya's Aberdare Mountains that long-tailed cormorants and giant kingfishers found

English rainbow trout water – a branch of the Wye in Derbyshire.
(Julian Watson)

their way up there. The cry of the African fish eagle never rang out over the Natal foothills of the Drakensberg until trout reached South Africa.

Cape clawless otters had found their way up to the headwaters of both the Kenyan and South African streams much earlier, surviving largely off little purple fresh-water crabs (Potamonidae). Yet for the mammals, the trout were not the instant bounty they might have been. Not only did the otters never seem able to catch the fish, but the potential prey turned out to be true competitors by adapting enthusiastically to a diet of crabs as well. An identical situation prevails in Argentina, where introduced salmonids also provide competition, rather than food, for the local species of otter.

Rainbows prove even more unusual competitors to various ducks. In New Zealand, blue (mountain) duck are said to have suffered from having to compete for the rivers' invertebrate food supplies with introduced trout; so are Salvadori's ducks in Papua New Guinea and the torrent ducks of the rocky streams running off the western slopes of the Andes.

Rainbow trout have done their damage, such as that may be. However, so far and fast have they spread that today, for all the ecological impact of these naturalised stocks, their existence often touches the lives of nearby human communities too. In many of the lakes and rivers where rainbow trout now flourish, there were never any edible fish, and in several parts of South America wild trout provide hungry families with regular protein additions to their otherwise meagre sustenance. In Africa, fish seldom featured in the cultures or diets of any peoples living near montane forests and moorlands – the streams were barren. Now the exotic trout, first regarded as inedible water snakes, are lured from their new homes with worms and grasshoppers on the end of bamboo poles – welcome supplements to the usual maize meal rations of most locals. In the North American Great Lakes, migratory rainbows contribute to a commercial Indian gill-net fishery (once sustained almost exclusively by lake charr), as they also do in Peru's Lake Titicaca.

Today there are few suitable environments left across the earth, other than some remote areas of Asia, which have not already felt the sting of the rainbow's arrival. From Uganda to Yugoslavia, Michigan to Madagascar, through the Horton plains of Sri Lanka, the Bale Mountains of Ethiopia and the island of Kauai in Hawaii, naturalised populations of rainbow trout are freely producing their next generation unaided by mankind. Lions, elephants, and grizzly bears – perhaps still a Tasmanian wolf? – wander the banks of rainbow rivers, while overhead float Andean condors, lammergeyers and Himalayan griffon vultures. Of few other fresh-water fish can it be said, as it can of rainbow trout, that they are now truly fish of the world.

9
Cutthroat trout

When fish were food, not the objects of man's sporting whims, and lived only where the rivers of melting ice had left them, the cutthroat's inland North American territory was much larger than the rainbow trout's. Cutthroat fed far more Indian villages or hungry trappers and explorers. They were the quintessential fish of the mountains, where in most cases they had evolved oblivious of the existence of their rainbow cousins. Other cutthroat lived in west coast rivers, strangely separated from those in the mountains by large expanses of cutthroat-less country. Today, inland cutthroat have been almost hybridised into extinction by the wanton redistributions of America's native trout. The immediate future of coastal fish is more secure, and despite naturally sharing their rivers with the larger, seemingly more aggressive rainbows, they have generally managed to retain their genetic integrity.

The range of coastal cutthroat stretches over 3,000 km (1,900 miles) from the Kenai Peninsula, just east of Anchorage, all the way down the Pacific shores to the Eel River in northern California. Their distribution almost exactly overlaps the belt of coniferous coastal forest, watered by the heavy rains which fall on the western slopes of the Canadian Rocky Mountains and the Cascade Range in Washington and Oregon. The coastal fish are quite distinct from their inland kin, separated not only by tracts of territory originally colonised only by rainbows, but also by differences in numbers of chromosomes. Coastal fish have sixty-eight (others sixty-six or sixty-four) which contributes to their being universally recognised as all belonging to a distinctive single subspecies, *Oncorhynchus clarki*. While the earth's climate slowly mellowed for the last time, these cutthroat nosed their way northwards, as one river after another warmed enough to welcome the new arrivals, probably reaching their Alaskan extremity less than 10,000 years ago.

Far from the sea-edge strip marking on the map where coastal cutthroat live is a huge shaded area of mountains and upland plateau. This identifies the cutthroat's true ancestral home. Its occupation dates back into distant Pleistocene times, when glaciers and ice fields covered much of the land. Great lakes straddled the watersheds and divides, rising and falling, freezing and thawing, discharging first east and then west, capturing streams that once flowed one way and sending their contents the other. Each successive Ice Age ended with massive topographical upheavals, causing devastating floods, while at the same time allowing cutthroat to cross mountain ranges which now appear utterly insurmountable. Finally, the earth's surface breathed a sigh of relief and settled, at least temporarily, into its present shape. Then, as the last Ice Age drew to a close, wherever fresh-water fish were, they had to stay. Cutthroat trout were marooned in the lakes and valleys where their descendants still live. Some of these stocks of fish have changed little since their isolation: there has been no need for them to do so. Others have been

The native range of cutthroat trout.

continually forced to adapt to an environment which sometimes seems to be changing faster than they can.

This Ice Age tumult left cutthroat in the headwaters of rivers that flowed to all points of the compass. Many of these ended up in the Pacific or, via the Colorado River, in the Gulf of California. Others took less obvious courses and eventually flowed into the Missouri and the Rio Grande, and thence to the Gulf of Mexico; a few even passed through Saskatchewan on their way to Hudson Bay. In the north of the cutthroat's inland territory, rivers flow either west or east. Further south the geography becomes more confusing, and watersheds may have three sides, not just two. In Colorado, the melting snow still runs off the San Juan Mountains either east into the Arkansas River and thence the Missouri, west into the Colorado River or south to reach the Rio Grande. When ice dammed up these three-way flows they may have been ideal places for cutthroat to ease into new valleys and so extend their range.

Near Yellowstone Lake in north-western Wyoming is another almost three-sided watershed. Two Ocean Pass was well known to early fur trappers as the easiest way across the mountains down to Jackson Hole. There, according to the diary of early explorer Osborne Russell, was a smooth prairie about two miles long and a half a mile wide lying east and west surrounded by pines. On the south side about midway of the prairie stands a high snowy peak from whence issues a stream of water which after entering the plain it divides equally one half running west and the other east, thus bidding adieu to each other, one bound for the Pacific and the other for the Atlantic Ocean.

The eastbound waters in Two Ocean Pass follow Atlantic Creek down into Yellowstone Lake, home of the largest near-pristine stock of cutthroat trout in America. If any of these fish felt the urge to head to sea they would end up swimming down the Missouri and out into the Gulf of Mexico. Waters eventually destined for the Pacific flow into the Snake River; this makes a huge loop through Idaho before joining the Columbia, whose headwaters were also full of cutthroat. In colder, wetter times, cutthroat may easily have crossed the watershed at Two Ocean Pass. From there it is only a few kilometres down to the start of the Green River; this is a cutthroat water too and points south, joining the Colorado and finally emptying into the apex of the Gulf of California.

The most potent signs that an Ice Age had just ended were the huge lakes cupped in every valley, hollow and depression that would hold water. As the earth warmed, these lakes began losing more water to the sun and the sea than they gained from rain and snow. Almost imperceptibly each year they shrank, becoming ever more alkaline and less hospitable to their fish. Today, Great Salt and Utah Lakes show as the only traces of Lake Bonneville, once nearly 300 m (1,000 ft) deep and the size of today's Lake Michigan. The Lahontan Basin, which at its greatest extent covered most of northern Nevada, is now flat scrubby semi-desert, watered only by a few tiny upland trickles. From these great inland seas, the cutthroat gradually retreated into whatever streams still flowed, and there they have survived, from one generation to the next, amongst cacti and brush, slowly creating a diversity of stocks, now only too well recognised but woefully ill conserved.

The latest consensus seems to accept fourteen different stocks of cutthroat, each distinct enough to merit subspecies status. Some are identifiable by distinctive numbers of chromosomes or of gill rakers and teeth, others by less fundamental differences in meristic characteristics or even just scale numbers, spotting and colouration. Four of these subspecies have no scientific names yet, a fifth is extinct, and others are almost so. The inter-relationships between these taxonomic fragments are complicated, and despite modern techniques of gene and chromosome analysis, still owe much to guesswork. So do the suggested explanations of how and when these cutthroat first reached some of their more remote outposts. Could they have crossed the Continental Divide at this pass or did that river once flow down a different valley than it does today? Never the less, the Ice Age history of the landscape is not all based on guesswork, nor is the cutthroat's family tree, and four distinct lineages are quite easily recognisable – coastal, Westslope, Lahontan Basin and Yellowstone, from one or other of which all others have diverged.

Coastal cutthroat are clearly and easily distinguished by their sixty-eight chromosomes and by having easy access to the sea. They are probably the descendants of the original cutthroat, some of which explored their way inland on post-glacial floods to found new colonies, each gradually evolving its own specific identity. From one such colony began another lineage, also easily identifiable by a distinctive chromosome count, and to the more casual naturalist by the small spots with jagged edges and their absence from much of the body below the lateral line. This is the Westslope cutthroat (*O. c. lewisi*) with sixty-six chromosomes, to which all the inland fish of northerly rivers belong. 'Westslope' is a

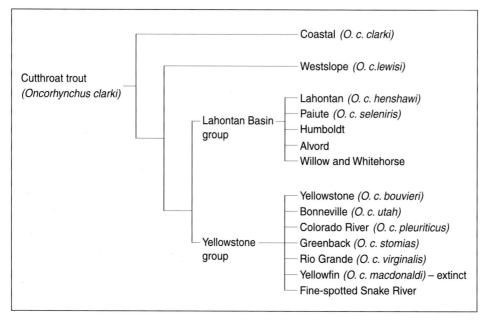

Cutthroat trout
(Oncorhynchus clarki)

Coastal (O. c. clarki)

Westslope (O. c.lewisi)

Lahontan Basin group
- Lahontan (O. c. henshawi)
- Paiute (O. c. seleniris)
- Humboldt
- Alvord
- Willow and Whitehorse

Yellowstone group
- Yellowstone (O. c. bouvieri)
- Bonneville (O. c. utah)
- Colorado River (O. c. pleuriticus)
- Greenback (O. c. stomias)
- Rio Grande (O. c. virginalis)
- Yellowfin (O. c. macdonaldi) – extinct
- Fine-spotted Snake River

A 'species tree' showing the four major lineages of cutthroat trout and the suggested subspecies within them.

confusing term because some of the streams where they live flow east; those in Alberta end in Hudson Bay and others further south drain into the Missouri. At some stage in their turbulent history, some of these trout crossed the Great Divide. Today, its mountain ridge looks as though it must have separated the fish on either side from each other for millions of years, but their genetic make-ups are still so similar that they probably only diverged just before or just after the last Ice Age.

These Westslope trout first found their way to their mountain retreat up the Columbia River. Carrying a volume of American water second only to the Mississippi, its tentacles reach far inland and would have given cutthroat an easy route to much of Montana, as well as to southern British Columbia, where there are still many isolated populations left today. When Flathead and other lakes in what is now Glacier National Park were much higher than they are now, some of their waters might have spilled eastward, introducing the first trout to the South Saskatchewan drainage, in which they have remained ever since.

Today the Columbia gathers up the Snake River too, although whether this was always so is unclear and the Snake might once have found its own way to the sea through Oregon and northern California. Whatever its original course, it opened up the more southerly hinterland to the explorations of other cutthroat ancestors, which probed their way all over the south-west. Now there is little doubt that all these southern fish are descended from the other two main lineages of Lahontan Basin and Yellowstone cutthroat.

These southern cutthroat are all connected by a chromosome count of sixty-four, but beyond that they are a diverse lot, made so by occupying very different habitats, where one stream's fish may be hundreds of kilometres from their nearest neighbours. The upheavals of the Ice Ages allowed them to cross from the tiny southern tributaries of the Snake over into the Lahontan Basin in what is now Nevada and which once held a slab of water as large as Lake Erie. The ancestors of the Yellowstone cutthroat explored their way up easterly tributaries of the Snake. Some of these streams gave them access to the

Westslope cutthroat.
(Richard Grost)

Yellowstone River across Two Ocean Pass; others may have provided a link with the Colorado River system. From the Colorado, fish might have leap-frogged into the upper reaches of the Missouri-draining Arkansas River through Twin Lakes near Leadville.

The Lahontan Basin group unites all the trout living around the former limits of Lake Lahontan and smaller satellite lakes. There are no lakes now, only flat, high-desert basins rimmed with low cliffs. In the sloughs and streams remaining, as many as five distinct subspecies of cutthroat still cling to an existence in habitats defying description as trout waters at all, their evolution seeming to lag far behind the changing climate. Sometimes they hang on in hundreds, not thousands, having at least changed enough to survive temperatures high enough to kill any ordinary trout. Their tolerance of the otherwise intolerable has also helped to protect their genetic integrity from destruction by exotic outsiders, although the distinctive genes of the Alvord Basin cutthroat have probably already been irreparably diluted. The Paiute cutthroat (*O. c. seleniris*) has only just escaped the same fate.

Within their native range, Paiute cutthroat only hold out in Silver King Creek in Alpine County, California, where receding lake levels marooned a single stock of Lahontan cutthroat in a 6 km (4 mile) stretch of creek between two falls. In the course of perhaps a thousand generations there, they have lost all their spots, and now remain with only vague

Paiute cutthroat.

blotches on their bodies. The fish had never got above the upper (Llewellyn) falls, and below the lower falls interbreeding with introduced rainbows soon dissipated the Paiute cutthroat's uniqueness.

In 1912, a shepherd collected up a few cutthroat in a can and carried them up above the Llewellyn Falls where, although seldom growing to weigh more than 250 g (9 oz), they flourished. Some time later, rainbows found their way above the lower falls, leaving the transplants as the only guardians of their genetic integrity left in the world. Eventually the insidious rainbow influence even penetrated above the Llewellyn Falls, but still never as far up as two small feeder creeks where pure Paiutes still clung to their identities. So dire were their straits that they received 'endangered' status under the Endangered Species Act. But there was an odd contrariness to this protection. The best way to obliterate the rainbow genes from above the Llewellyn Falls was to wipe out every adulterated fish and let the purebred Paiutes gradually restock the whole stretch with their own offspring. Wiping out meant poisoning, which was only possible if the Paiutes were no longer classified as 'endangered', only 'threatened', so 'threatened' they became. In went the rotenone poison and out came most of the fish. Most was not enough and in went more poison, but still some survived and slowly the spots on the Paiutes – incontrovertible evidence of the rainbow's continuing influence – began to reappear.

The status of the Lahontan cutthroat (*O. c. henshawi*) was also downgraded, and it too became 'threatened' so it could be fished for. Before Lake Lahontan finally dried up, these fish, with their large evenly spread spots, cruised its open waters, filtering animal plankton through their many gill rakers, and also exploiting the diversity of other species of fish to the full. As the lake shrank, the trout were forced to adapt to ever saltier and more alkaline conditions, until eventually there was nowhere else for them to live but the high desert lakes in Nevada like Pyramid, Walker, Summit and Tahoe. And in these unlikely waters, Lahontan cutthroat, genetically almost indistinguishable from the Paiutes, found an environment so ideal that some of them grew to fifty times the size of the little fish from Silver King Creek.

The biggest cutthroat of all came from Pyramid Lake, fattened largely on a diet of tui chub. Tahoe was also renowned for its large fish. The spawning runs had provided a dependable source of protein for the local Indians, probably ever since they first arrived there. They trapped them with a series of dams on their way upstream, much as the Inuit did Arctic charr – although the cutthroat would have been even more useful if, like charr and salmon, they had spawned in the autumn rather than the spring, and so fed the Indians through the winter! Early European writers inevitably compared them to salmon, even if not always describing them as such elsewhere:

> Their flavour was excellent – superior, in fact, to that of any fish I have ever known. They were of extraordinary size – about as large as the Columbia river salmon [chinook] – generally from 2 to 4 feet in length.

So wrote John Fremont in 1845. On an expedition with frontier folk hero Kit Carson, he was one of the first Europeans to come across these great leviathans, ducking the challenge of their classification by describing them as 'salmon-trout'. Later taxonomists thought they might be landlocked salmon, and it was only in 1878 that Mr H W Henshaw's name was formally tagged on to that of the species in recognition of his submitting the type specimen from Tahoe.

The trout in Tahoe and Pyramid Lake were large and abundant enough even for commercial netsmen to find them worth exploiting, and in the 1880s catches measured in tens of tonnes were being exported. Nor could sport fishermen resist the lure of such specimens whose free-feeding habits usually justified the arduous journey to these remote waters. The largest recorded cutthroat ever extracted with rod and line from Pyramid Lake weighed over 18 kg (40 lb), but other much bigger fish were recorded in the memories of Indians and fishery officers. Fishing pressure quickly began to affect catches, although it took much more than overfishing to drive the Lahontan cutthroat in both lakes to extinction.

A dam killed them off in Pyramid Lake. Nearly all the trout spawned in the one main feeder – the Truckee River – and from 1905, when a dam was constructed to divert most of the flow in the name of the Newlands Irrigation Project, they were doomed. Initially, some water still splashed over the dam, but this quickly shrank to a trickle, the lake level fell by over 20 m (65 ft), and 1938 witnessed the last spawning run of the great cutthroat of

Lahontan cutthroat.

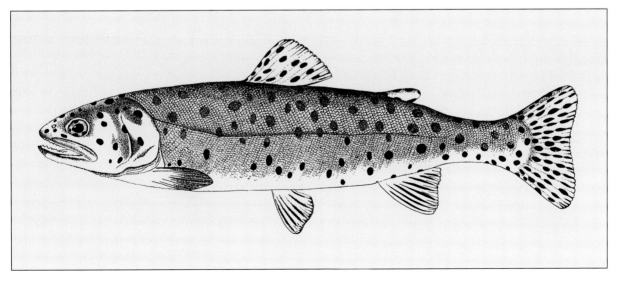

Pyramid Lake – and even then the average weight of a sample of 195 spawners was 9 kg (20 lb).

Cutthroat from Summit Lake, which have fortunately remained uncontaminated by any alien genes, provide a source of Lahontan cutthroat for restocking Pyramid and other lakes. There are no other fish in Summit Lake and its cutthroat's particular lack of piscivorous inclinations may be inherited, because when introduced into the much more fertile waters of Pyramid Lake they still do not reach anything approaching the size the indigenous fish once did.

In Tahoe the story of the vanishing cutthroat is less straightforward, and along with the usual gamut of environmental ruination and competition from introduced brown and rainbow trout, another usurper played a critical part. This was the exotic lake charr which still finds the cold deep water and plentiful crayfish much to its liking. In the spring, just as the ice thawed, the charr would desert the depths to ambush cutthroat which gathered at the stream mouths before swimming up to spawn. Isolating the lake charr's contribution to the demise of Tahoe's cutthroat from the detrimental effects of some of mankind's other activities is impossible. However, this will not be so in Yellowstone Lake if its cutthroat are devastated by the lake charr which have recently been illegally released there.

The subspecies *O. c. bouvieri* evolved in Yellowstone Lake, where, as much by luck as good management, there are still no rainbows and the indigenous population remains largely unadulterated by exotic cutthroat genes. The lake is over 2,000 m (6,500 ft) up, surrounded by thick forests of spruce and Ponderosa and lodgepole pines, as well as swamps and alpine meadowland. It is protected from commercial exploitation or even subsistence fishing by harsh winters and the borders of Yellowstone National Park which surround it. Until redside shiners and long-nose suckers arrived in the lake, cutthroat shared it with only one other species of fish, the long-nose dace, which was never common enough to be a reliable source of food for the trout. Despite the introduction of potential competition, the cutthroat appear well enough adapted to their habitat to have remained unaffected by it. Living off shrimps and snails in the shallows, or filtering out floating *Daphnia* plankton in more open water, Yellowstone cutthroat seldom weigh more than 1 kg (2 lb), although if transplanted to more fertile environments they are quite able to switch to a piscivorous diet and grow much larger. The number of cutthroat in Yellowstone Lake is variously estimated at between one and four million, which is more than enough to sustain a thriving sport fishery, especially when most fish have to be returned to the water so that they can be caught again – and again.

From 1905 to 1955 there was a huge hatchery at Yellowstone Lake, which, by 1940, was producing over forty million eggs a year for propagating all over the western USA. Having evolved in the absence of any competition, *bouvieri* was not always suited to its new still-water homes if these were already occupied by other species of fish, but the genetic legacy of these transplants is still apparent all over the southern Rocky Mountains.

Cutthroat persist in Yellowstone River down as far as the falls in the park. As the river glides out of the lake, huge fronds of weed wave gently in the current, and for many miles downstream cutthroat on the flats can indulge in an almost unending invertebrate feast. This is perhaps the richest stretch of cutthroat habitat in the world, and a telling contrast to the river below the falls, where the indigenous fish are joined by an assortment of introduced brown and brook trout, as well as the inescapable rainbows with which the cutthroat sometimes hybridise. An idea of the staggering abundance of fish that the lake could support, comes from the 1881 diary of Edward Hewitt, whose task it was to feed a party of forty soldiers from a small stream running into it:

> The stream was just alive with trout, which seemed to run from three to four pounds apiece. I was not sorry to quit as I was really tired out. For once I had caught all the fish I could take out in one day. There must have been between four hundred and fifty and five hundred pounds of cleaned trout, but the soldiers polished them off in two meals . . .

The Yellowstone fish are yellowy-brown, sometimes with a touch of olive, and their largish round spots are clustered round their tails and the tops of their backs. In keeping with their lake-living history, they still tend to have more gill-rakers than any other subspecies in their group, except those which evolved in Lake Bonneville (*O. c. utah*). Now confined to mountain streams in Utah, these Bonneville fish look very like Yellowstone cutthroat, from which they are recently derived, and it is only over the watersheds into the Colorado River or the Rio Grande that the true diversity of cutthroat marks and colours really shows itself.

Colorado River cutthroat (*O. c. pleuriticus*) are almost indistinguishable from their greenback (*O. c. stomias*) relations. Both have suffered alarmingly from introduced competition, which they have proved unable to counter, slowly retreating into their last headwater strongholds above impassable waterfalls. They have more scales than any other cutthroat, and are brilliantly coloured with orange and gold, the males turning pinky-crimson on their bellies and cheeks as spawning time approaches.

The greenback has the biggest spots of the species, sometimes nearly the size of its eye and giving its 'wrist' and tail an almost leopard-skin look. Besides its other homes, it once shared Twin Lakes near Leadville in central Colorado with the now extinct yellowfin, *O. c. macdonaldi*. Yellowfin are known only from seven specimens fished out of Twin Lakes in 1889, and by repute from the boasts of earlier fishermen. Whether or not they were ever a distinct subspecies, they are now recorded as extinct, hastened on their way by the damming of the lakes, the diversion of inflows and then the inevitable introduction of alien species. Somehow the two forms must have remained reproductively isolated from each other, because while greenbacks seldom weighed more than 500 g (1 lb), yellowfins grew ten times as large. Now the greenbacks have gone from Twin Lakes too, driven out by the arrival of rainbows, as well as brook and lake charr and even landlocked Atlantic salmon. Hungry Leadville miners also contributed to their decline and were equally prepared to use dynamite to kill fish and to blast rocks.

At one time only five unadulterated populations of greenbacks remained in the mountain tributaries of the Arkansas and South Platte Rivers, a desperate enough predicament to qualify them for 'endangered' listing under the ESA. Now, from these isolated stocks, several new self-sustaining populations have been established, usually in lakes first rendered fishless by poisoning any unlucky exotic fish already there. This has at least proved successful enough to have the greenbacks moved to the 'threatened' list, and in some places they are even doing well enough to be caught – and released.

There are a lot more Colorado than greenback cutthroat, but most stocks still struggle to retain their identities. Isolated populations of Colorado cutthroat, of varying degrees of purity, hang on in the tributaries of the Colorado River above the Grand Canyon, as well as in sections of the Green River up in Wyoming. For long, much the largest purebred population held out in Trappers Lake, but with the recent and unplanned arrival of rainbow trout their genetic integrity is also fast disappearing. By good fortune, some of these Trappers Lake fish had been taken to Williamson Lakes in California long before the rainbows arrived. Now, like the Lahontan cutthroat of Summit Lake, they provide a pool of fish with which to stock or restock streams and lakes within their original territory.

The cutthroat that reached the Rio Grande are also descended from the Colorado fish, which they closely resemble. These fish are living on the very frontiers of their range, supremely vulnerable to the slightest environmental upsets. The journals of early fishermen testify to the much wider distribution that *O. c. virginalis* enjoyed just a hundred years ago, although it is sometimes difficult to be sure what rivers or what fish these writers are describing. Today the Rio Grande subspecies is confined to small highland streams where cattle trample the banks, and the much harder-to-catch imported brown trout tend to dominate wherever the waters are open for fishing. Whether cutthroat were ever found in Texas or Mexico is uncertain. Accounts of the Civil and Spanish Wars sometimes recorded fishing expeditions, but neither their maps nor the memories of their authors are necessarily reliable, and with the innumerable transplants in later years the historical range of Rio Grande cutthroat may never be known for sure.

In the face of the rainbow trout's near-global invasion of the cooler fresh waters of the world, it is easy to forget that cutthroat were naturally more widespread in the North American interior than their cousins. Europeans came across them much earlier too, and the fish that sustained many an early explorer of the West were almost invariably cutthroat not rainbows. Spaniards probing northwards through Pueblo country in 1541 found 'a little stream which abounds in excellent trouts and otters' in the Sangre de Cristo Mountains of what is now New Mexico, but the first real description of cutthroat comes from the pen of Meriweather Lewis.

The mission of Captains Lewis and Clark was to explore the territory of the Louisiana Purchase, and in 1805 they set off up the Missouri River. The river splits near the area known as Great Falls in today's Montana, and on 13 June, up the southern fork, above a series of foaming cataracts, one of the party caught several trout, which Lewis describes as

> from 16–23 inches in length, precisely resemble our mountain or speckled trout [brook charr] in form and the position of their fins, but the specks on these are of a deep black instead of the red or goald of those common in the U' States. These are furnished with the long teeth on the pallet and tongue and have generally a small dash of red on each side behind the front ventral fins; the flesh is pale yellowish red, or when in good order, of a rose red.

These cutthroat were the first trout-like fish the captains encountered on their way up the Missouri, although they had already found new whitefish and suckers. Both were meticulous recorders of everything they saw despite a lack of any formal scientific training. Lewis's observations of the red marks below the jaw, and teeth on the vomer bone, immediately identify the fish's most distinctive features. Not until after they had come across rainbow trout and staggering numbers of Pacific salmon did their efforts at identification became understandably confused. Cutthroat were only formally christened *Salmo clarki* in London in 1836, after analysis of a pickled fish sent from Fort Vancouver on the lower Columbia River, and 'as a tribute to the memory of Captain Clarke [sic], who notices it in the narrative prepared by him of the proceedings of the Expedition to the Pacific, of which he and Captain Lewis had a joint command, as a dark variety of Salmon-trout'. The type specimen was undoubtedly a coastal cutthroat, so *clarki* designates both the species and this particular subspecies. Lewis only got to describe a subspecies, the Westslope trout, as did several other lesser luminaries of scientific exploration.

Rainbow trout received their original Latin tag *Salmo gairdneri* at the same time, although for the next hundred years there was no consensus over the taxonomy of either species, neither within each species group nor as to where to draw the dividing line between them. Perhaps the relict trout of the desert highlands in Mexico and Arizona still hover on the border. Whatever their formal classification, identifying one species or subspecies from another was seldom a problem so long as they lived where Nature intended, which usually meant rainbows and cutthroat occupied quite separate areas. That is the case no longer, and over the past hundred years most inland stocks of cutthroat have become hopelessly hybridised. Their unique sets of genes have been diluted either through the introduction of non-native races of their own kind (especially from Yellowstone) or by the continual stocking of rainbows into waters which were naturally far beyond that species' reach. Now it is a question less of identifying a particular race or subspecies than of estimating the extent of hybridisation. Dentition can provide useful clues, particularly the basibranchial teeth on the base of the tongue, which cutthroat have and most rainbows lack; otherwise gauging genetic impurity involves more detailed analysis of proteins and DNA.

The natural overlap between rainbows and cutthroat is largely confined to coastal rivers, and to the lakes from which they flow. Resident cutthroat share a few Idaho tributaries of the Snake River with both sea-going and resident rainbows. There, cutthroat minimise competition by occupying narrow headwater streams or slower-flowing stretches of river than the larger rainbows. Even where both species migrate, the smaller cutthroat are able to spawn in shallower creeks, their passage eased by seldom weighing more than 2 kg (4 lb), despite their time at sea.

Some British Columbia lakes are home to resident stocks of rainbow and cutthroat trout. Competition is less confrontational in open waters, and the cutthroat usually surrender their favoured midwater feeding grounds to the rainbows, and forage on the bottom or the surface. If cutthroat live long enough to reach a size when they can catch and swallow other fish, they become much more piscivorous than rainbows, which, as a result, the cutthroat then tend to outgrow. This is exceptional, though, and in most environments where they coexist, rainbows dominate the gentler cutthroat. Furthermore, if the two species occupy similar but separate habitats, rainbows nearly always grow larger.

Avoiding rather than countering competition seems to be the strategy which has helped cutthroat survive so long over such a wide area. Their passive natures render them particularly vulnerable to the incursions of exotic species, and also make them utterly unsuitable for stocking outside their natural habitat – unlike many of their relatives which have proved easier to establish in alien environments than to reintroduce back into their native ranges. While aggressive domineering rainbow trout are thriving in suitable waters all over the world, often to the detriment of the local fish faunas, the records of successful cutthroat transplants beyond western America are sparse indeed.

In most of their highland homeland, Lahontan Basin and Yellowstone cutthroat have never experienced much competition from other fish. Their territory is generally beyond the reach of migratory salmon, although a few chinook reach the Salmon and Clearwater Rivers in Idaho and theoretically produce some young fry with which cutthroat may one day compete. Westslope cutthroat, on the other hand, have had to interact more with other species in the course of their evolution, especially whitefish, bull charr and northern squawfish. As a result, they may be better equipped to face the challenge posed by exotic arrivals, which almost invariably drive other cutthroat into retreat. Coastal cutthroat are also adept at meshing their lives with those of the other fish – salmon, steelhead and sculpins – which share their streams.

Those cutthroat squeezed upwards as the Bonneville and Lahontan Basins slowly dried out were fashioned for life in lakes, not cactus-fringed desert streams, and they seem ill adapted to the niches they now occupy. Many other cutthroat though, still haunt the habitats they evolved in, and for which they are theoretically ideally suited. They should have an enormous advantage over introduced species that are suddenly forced to adapt to life in waters for which they are not genetically designed. Yet even these cutthroat seem to surrender whatever advantage they may have gained through the millennia in the face of introduced competition; and it is not only their pacific characters which make them so vulnerable.

Cutthroat spawn in the spring, which means their fry emerge later than those of many of their potential competitors. By then, young brown trout or brook charr have been hatched for several months, the weaker ones have died, and the survivors have all claimed their feeding territories. For the gentle young cutthroat, just out of their gravel nurseries, to find themselves surrounded by much larger fish, already feeding confidently, makes for an anxious start to their lives, and often sets them at a disadvantage from which they never recover. As well as hatching earlier, brook charr are quick to mature, and by often being ready to spawn a year earlier than cutthroat, seize a further lead over their competitors in the race to reproduce. They are more generalised feeders and this may also help them out-compete cutthroat. Similar sized brook charr are probably, if anything, less assertive than cutthroat; after all, the docile charr have surrendered much of their own territory in the Appalachian Mountains to introduced rainbows. Being naive and easily caught was also said to have contributed to the demise of brook charr in their eastern homeland, but, somewhat ironically, this is also held out as one reason why native cutthroat fare less well than introduced brook charr in the west.

Rainbow trout are spring spawners too, and if their young are to gain an early advantage over cutthroat of the same age it is unlikely to be as a result of significant differences in size. Sharing spawning seasons – and, where the species have been recently introduced to one another, redds too – makes hybridisation more likely; and the enthusiasm with which both species take to breeding with the other is, in human terms, little short of promiscuous. Hybridising with rainbows is far more likely to bring about the extinction of native cutthroat than being gradually squeezed out of their natural territories. Unfortunately for the future of both species, the hybrids are also particularly fertile. Southern cutthroat and some rainbows both have sixty-four chromosomes, although the fertility of hybrid offspring seems strangely unaffected by whether both parents have similar chromosome counts or not.

Almost all cutthroat need to spawn in running water, and those living in lakes move out when the time comes to breed. Yellowstone fish find their way up one of the sixty or so spawning tributaries that feed the lake; some of them also spawn in the outflow, their young genetically programmed to reach the lake by swimming upstream rather than down. Occasionally, fish introduced into remote upland still waters lacking any feeder streams have managed to spawn on gravel beds aerated by upwelling currents. In very high mountain lakes, stocked cutthroat may fail to breed even though conditions seem ideal. This is simply because spring comes too late and autumn too soon to give the fish enough warm days for their eggs to hatch, and for the young to emerge from their nurseries in time to start feeding for themselves.

Rising temperatures and longer days trigger the breeding urges of both cutthroat and rainbow trout – quite the opposite stimuli to those which influence charr, salmon and brown trout. About 5°C is often the critical temperature at which Pacific trout are finally induced to spawn, although further south this may be several degrees higher. Whatever the temperature, it arrives much earlier in the south and so, therefore, does the trout's spawning season. Sea-going cutthroat spawn in January in Oregon, but not until well into April in Alaska.

By the end of autumn, eggs or sperm cells are already well developed, fuelled by the rich feedings of summer, whether at sea or in fresh water. During the winter fish feed very little, just enough to keep them ticking over but not to fuel any growth or the further development of eggs or milt. As spawning time approaches, being already close to maturity, cutthroat are quick to seize the advantage of ideal conditions when these arrive. To some extent, an inclination to spawn early or late may be under genetic rather than environmental control. Hatchery fish are selected both to mature and to spawn early. In the wild they often breed a month or so before any native fish the river still supports. Emerging earlier can give these hatchery offspring both a critical size advantage and first choice of feeding territories; together these may ultimately lead to their dominating native fish to the point of extinction. On the other hand, the different breeding seasons of domestic and wild fish at least help keep domestic genes out of the wild pool.

Many sea-going cutthroat, due to spawn early the following year, return to fresh water in the autumn – a habit which gave them the name 'harvest trout'. Their choice of winter retreat is often influenced by how much the river freezes and for how long, as well as by how much further they have left to travel. They may rest up in deep holes for the winter, often many together, almost motionless, before moving up into the headwaters in the spring. Others leave their migrations until later, and lake dwellers only move out of their still-water homes when they are almost ready to spawn.

Like many other salmonids, male cutthroat may be ready to breed a year sooner than females, and both sexes are likely to mature earlier in the south. There, even females may spawn after their second winter, in contrast to those from more northerly populations which often do not start maturing until the approach of their fourth. Age at death is affected by age at maturity as well as by other hereditary and environmental factors. Yellowstone fish seldom live more than six or seven years. Tiny fish breeding in the inflows of icy mountain lakes, where warm days are so few that young hatch successfully only every second or third year, may reach an age of fifteen.

Spawning takes its inevitable toll, particularly on fish in warmer waters, which lead easier lives but often die after only breeding once. Elsewhere the proportion of repeat spawners varies between area and subspecies, from 15 to 40 per cent of breeding fish. Coastal and lake-living cutthroat are more inclined to breed again, sometimes up to four times before they die. Males appear to die sooner than females which may be because they started spawning at an earlier age. Furthermore, all male salmonids seem to find spawning more stressful than females do, probably because they use much more energy on the redds, fighting other males for mates. The fact that males die earlier may be one reason why there are often far more females on the redds, and why the females then breed with smaller males – deliberate couplings, not just furtive contributions to the production of the next generations by satellite males.

Not all cutthroat which can reach the sea do so, although specific stocks from particular lakes or rivers tend to behave fairly consistently – unlike brown trout in the short coastal streams of northern Europe, where some migrate, leaving others behind. Many populations of cutthroat find enough food in fresh-water lakes to detain them all their lives, and never go to sea. Other cutthroat are isolated from their fellows by high waterfalls, which, over the generations, have acted to suppress migratory tendencies by preventing sea-going fish from returning to spawn where they hatched. Cutthroat which are destined to migrate spend two, three or four years in fresh water, occasionally even five or six, nosing around for caddis larvae and salmon and sculpin eggs, or feeding in more typical salmonid style on the invertebrates drifting down on the current. Then, sometimes as early as March but more often in the short nights of May or June, smolts emerge from quiet backwaters or from under banks, slipping into the current and moving gently down to the sea.

Smolts are, on average, between 15 and 25 cm (6–10 in) long when they arrive to start their sojourn in the sea. This usually lasts from two to six months with the odd fish occasionally overwintering in the estuary. Unlike steelhead, these densely spotted cutthroat are neither great explorers nor exploiters of the ocean, reluctant to cross open stretches of deep water and usually content to remain within the familiar influence of the stream that succoured them since birth. Some will travel along the shore as much as 70 km (45 miles) from their home estuary, and in the course of their marine explorations, cutthroat have colonised Vancouver and other inshore islands, but nowhere beyond North America.

Larger cutthroat, returning to sea for a second or subsequent time, usually reach the estuary a month or so earlier than smolts, in good time to ambush newly arrived salmon fry – often tiny pinks scarcely out of the gravel, or chum only a few weeks older. The cutthroat only head for deeper water when the salmon have left, and until they do prey and predator move in and out with the tide, schools of cutthroat foraging in the shallows and the breaking waves in search of crustaceans and small fish. There is inevitably a price for this better feeding – and one which those cutthroat that cruise around lakes all summer never have to pay – and that is much greater risk of danger, especially for smolts which have never experienced the environment of an estuary before. Once cutthroat have survived to smolt size, they have little to fear from fresh-water predators, but at sea Pacific hake, spiny dogfish, mergansers and divers are all ready to take advantage of the new arrivals. Larger cutthroat on their second or third visit to the sea also make easy meals for harbour seals.

Not being great oceanic travellers – perhaps about as adventurous as any Arctic charr or Dolly Varden which reach the sea – cutthroat seldom swim back into rivers other than their own. Like Arctic charr, not all returning cutthroat are ready to breed, and anywhere between 5 and 50 per cent will not mature until they have spent a second season at sea. Then, having spawned once, they usually do so every year until they die. Cutthroat spawning in shorter rivers, with easy journeys up to the redds, are more likely to live to breed again; they can also afford to reach the estuary much later than fish like those travelling to the headwaters of the Skeena River in British Columbia.

The silvery sheen of fresh-run cutthroat mutes the orange slashes below their chin, leaving their more tightly packed spots as the most obvious distinction between them and rainbow trout. Sea-going cutthroat may live nine years or more, and it is odd they do not

Coastal cutthroat.
(Richard Grost)

grow larger than they do, not least because they often continue feeding in fresh water right up until they spawn – albeit somewhat sporadically and in a fairly impoverished environment. When some individuals of a species migrate to the sea and others do not, it is very rare to find sea-going fish not outgrowing their kin which stayed behind. However, sea-going cutthroat seldom grow to weigh more than 2 kg (4 lb) and are dwarfed by the monsters from the record books of Pyramid Lake.

Time as well as space may separate spawning rainbow and cutthroat trout. Both spawn in the spring, but rainbows often do so a month later than cutthroat. This, as well as the fact that they often occupy different stretches of water, has helped the two species retain their respective genetic integrities throughout the 10,000 years or more they have shared rivers along the west coast of America. Hybridisation has therefore never been the problem for coastal cutthroat it has for those inland. There is always a risk that if stocked fish spawn in the gap between the two native species doing so, this may create a continuous spawning season which would eventually merge the genes of the otherwise reproductively isolated species. Wild hybrids are not uncommon in Puget Sound streams, but often appear when unnatural circumstances, like reduced water flow or silted redds, squeeze too many fish onto too small a breeding area. Hybrids also show up much more as young fish, perhaps suggesting that their survival rate is poor. A far greater threat to the success of native coastal trout may be stocking their rivers with millions of Pacific salmon smolts, which, at least in estuaries, may chase the same food as the cutthroat.

Cutthroat cannot look after themselves in environments which now so little resemble those in which they evolved; they need committed human assistance to help them survive. However, those stocks in most danger of disappearing lack the size and glamour which attract the attentions and efforts of the sport or commercial fishermen, who often emerge as the most effective guardians of the fish they want to catch. If they were simply a prodigious source of good food, cutthroat would receive the protection usually accorded to such a resource, but they are not, and some of them are so rare they cannot even be fished for for fun. Rather, they need looking after for more abstract, abstruse and less definable reasons. These may be parcelled up under the notion of 'conservation for conservation's sake' – simply protecting them because they are there or to preserve their genes for posterity. This is a hard concept to promote, especially when the creature concerned is a cold-blooded fish, not a cuddly panda. All the same, there is now at least an appreciation of what has already been lost to mankind's greed and stupidity – as well as of what still remains to be lost if concerted attempts are not made to preserve it.

All of which leads to one further thought. Many of these tiny upland populations of cutthroat trout are simply relics of a long-lost landscape, forced by a changing climate to struggle for survival in waters for which they are not yet well suited. Are they not a hair's breadth away from extinction anyway, without any nudge from mankind? Of course give them every chance to survive in their native environment, but are many of the efforts to conserve them not actually running counter to the natural currents of our time?

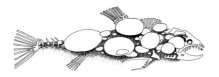

10
Six Pacific salmon

Pacific salmon are spread in a vast north-stretching arc, from Japan and Korea in the east, round to California in the west, as well as far along the Arctic shores of Russia and Alaska. After grazing the ocean for months – or years – nearly every survivor eventually heads back to the stream, lake or river where it was born, like thousands of generations before it. Several different species may use the same waterways to take them to their breeding grounds, where they even spawn in the same gravel. Physically, for most of its life, one salmon looks much like another. Many of the newly hatched fry are marked with dark stripes on their flanks, and once at sea the silvered fish may surge around on the same oceanic circuits, distinguished by little more than scale size or spots on backs or tails. Only on returning to fresh water do they begin to proclaim their identities to the world, with the startling changes of colour that precede spawning and death.

   Yet, for all these superficial similarities of appearance, range and habit, each of the six salmon is a species unto itself, with a life history setting it clearly apart from all the others. Indeed, the various species lead such diverse lives that they seem caught up in some vast great game of evolutionary trial and error, in which they must try to work out the *modus*

The North Pacific Rim.

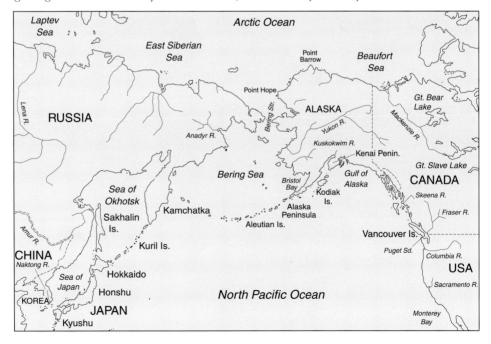

vivendi that will best assure their future. Within each species too, fish act so differently from their fellows that the rules and conclusions which seek to define the behaviour of that species are hardly ever without exceptions and qualifications.

Sockeye

Sockeye (*Oncorhynchus nerka*) are the standard bearers for the whole community of Pacific salmon. Their crimson-turning migrations, mass deaths and fine flesh have given them a higher public profile than any other fresh-water-hatched fish in the world. Beneath this spectacle is a species which has evolved almost as many alternative ways of successfully completing its life as all the other members of its genus put together. Whatever environmental catastrophe may befall the Pacific rim, sockeye somewhere should be able to survive it.

After emerging from the gravel, young sockeye generally spend the first year of their lives in a nursery lake. There never were many sockeye in California or Oregon, largely because very few rivers in that part of America drain out of lakes. Now there are none south of the Columbia River which demarcates their southern limits in America. Moving northwards, numbers increase, culminating with the huge runs which invade Alaska's Bristol Bay in early summer. These contribute millions of tonnes to the salmon-processing industry and still escape the nets in sufficient numbers to keep populations probably just as high as they were before commercial fishing began. A few fish spawn in the Yukon River and even further north, but any found beyond Point Hope have probably lost their

Sockeye smolts.
(Natalie Fobes)

way. Over in the western Pacific, the Kamchatka peninsula is the sockeye's stronghold – *nerka* is a Russian word and 'sockeye' derives from *sukkai* which is an Indian name for the fish – and if any turn up as far south as Japan they are stragglers too.

Their limited range gives the impression of sockeye being less tolerant of extreme temperatures than other Pacific salmon. This may be true once they reach the sea, yet the most critical influence on the sockeye's fresh-water distribution is not temperature but the species' dependence on lakes as fresh-water nurseries for its young. Many tributaries of the Fraser River fulfil this need; so do the river systems draining into Bristol Bay. The Fraser is a huge, sometimes turbulent river, often clouded with silt which provides good cover for migrating fish. It drains a wonderfully diverse landscape – pine forests, aspen woods, open semi-desert and bare mountain slopes – at varying elevations and distances from the sea. Sockeye headed for Stuart Lake will have travelled 1,000 km (600 miles) to an elevation of 680 m (2,200 ft), at a speed of 50 km (30 miles) per day by the time they get to their spawning grounds, whereas those bound for Weaver Creek are scarcely out of salt water before they reach theirs. This makes sockeye spread their entry into the main Fraser River over several months, and they may be in the estuary waiting to begin their final journeys at any time from late June to early September. In contrast, the lakes round Bristol Bay are all close to the sea, almost equally so, and in early July there is a massive, almost simultaneous, influx of fish headed for the various river systems draining into the bay.

Sockeye usually spawn in the inflows of what are to be the nursery lakes for their young, which drift down on the current into the lake immediately after they emerge. Sometimes the mature fish return to lay their eggs in an outflow, where the lake above naturally regulates the flow and there is very little risk of a sudden spate washing eggs out of the gravel or sweeping alevins away from the security of the nest too soon. Brown trout may spawn in outflows too, as do cutthroat from Yellowstone Lake, and the instincts of any fry born there typically lead them upstream rather than down. On the Kamchatka peninsula and up the Russian coast of the Bering Sea, lakes are few. There, true to the adaptive flexibility of their family in general and species in particular, sockeye have adopted alternative lifestyles, and the young spend their first year in river backwaters or spring-fed streams that do not freeze solid in the winter.

Occasionally their environment forces sockeye fry to behave more like pink or chum salmon and to head immediately to sea. Above the sockeye's spawning grounds in British Columbia's Harrison River is a succession of rapids, and fry swim straight down into the Fraser estuary, substituting its creeks and tidal pools for the fresh-water lake they are not strong enough to reach. In different areas of the Sitkine River drainage, in northern British Columbia, sockeye have adopted all three different life strategies; some river-spawned young head straight to sea after emerging, others spend almost a year in the river, while those with access to a lake use that as their nursery

For many sockeye, lakes have an importance extending far beyond their use as a rearing area for the young, and, uniquely among their genus, some populations breed in still waters. Measuring 2,600 sq. km (1,000 sq. miles), Lake Iliamna is the largest lake in Alaska, emptying into Bristol Bay through the Kvichak River. In some years over twenty million mature fish escape the nets and swim up into the lake. There they spread around its edges, holding up in conspicuous shoals, often at river mouths, for as long as a month, and then making their final surge up one of the huge networks of inflows into Iliamna. Yet some will go no further, finding areas of shoreline round the lake or its scattered islands, where water wells up from underground or is moved through the gravel by wave-driven currents, and conditions are as conducive to successful spawning as they are in feeder streams.

These lake spawners may find ideal redds down as deep as 30 m (100 ft), but sockeye more often spawn in much shallower water, typically only 2 or 3 m (7–10 ft) deep. The females usually excavate their nests in coarse gravel, just as if they were spawning in a stream, but occasionally, if the stones are too large to shift, fish scatter their eggs and milt over cracks and crevices in the lake bed, more in the way of lake charr than Pacific salmon. Lakes tend to stay warmer through the winter than the streams that feed them, and which, even if they do not freeze up, flow full of melting snow and ice. Eggs will therefore hatch sooner in still waters, especially if warm water is welling up between the stones throughout the year, and sockeye spawning there do so later than they would if they were breeding in streams. Evidence suggests that lake spawners are distinct stocks rather than simply surplus fish which, in peak years, have opted to stay away from the overcrowded redds in running waters. In Lake Kuril, near the desolate, once volcanic tip of the Kamchatka peninsula, and in Cultus Lake off the lower Fraser River, shoreline spawning is the rule rather than the exception. There underground turbulence continues aerating sockeye eggs long after the fish that laid them are dead.

Whether hatched in still or running waters, most of a young sockeye's first year is spent in its home lake. Further north, where days are shorter and fish grow more slowly, their lake life may last two, and occasionally even three, years. How long they spend at sea varies just as much. Some sockeye – a few females (jills) but mostly males (jacks) – return to fresh water having matured after only a year away. Far more typical is for sockeye to spend two or three years cruising the oceans before coming back to breed.

Their staggered downstream and upstream migrations combine to cushion each generation against an environmental catastrophe in one year that might wipe out entire populations of fish with less flexible life cycles. Although this strategy has clear advantages over the more rigid schedules that, for instance, a pink salmon's genes impose upon it, the runs of some stocks of sockeye still follow distinct patterns. Numbers running up the Lower Adams River peak every four years, when up to ten times as many fish return to spawn as in the intervening ones. Nearly all will have spent one winter unhatched in the river's gravel, one in Shuswap Lake and two at sea, making them 1.2 fish. The runs of sockeye up the Kvichak River are much less cyclical, but fish typically spend one winter in fresh water and three at sea (1.3) sometimes creating five-year highs.

Some *Oncorhynchus nerka* never go to sea. These are not only the odd residual males that mature in fresh water, as Atlantic salmon, coho, chinook and masu may do, but quite distinct populations which never leave their nursery lakes. Usually known as 'kokanee', they complete their life cycles without ever tasting salt water. They are naturally spread throughout most of the sockeye's range, and probably owe their original existence to a combination of the lake-living habits of the juveniles and occasional fish maturing in fresh water. Kokanee mature at different ages, most often three or four, but this can vary both within and between lakes. Like landlocked Atlantic salmon (sebago) on the east coast of America, or the non-migratory masu (yamame), kokanee are much smaller than their sea-going counterparts, averaging around 1 kg (2 lb). Often kokanee and sea-going sockeye begin life in the same nurseries, but there are also many lakes where the only *O. nerka* are kokanee. Fish would now find many of these lakes inaccessible from the sea, so non-migratory tendencies have been selectively promoted from one generation to another.

Sockeye waiting in Lake Iliamna before moving up one of the inflowing rivers to spawn.
(Greg Ruggerone)

Only occasionally do the two forms interbreed, and where they coexist, different spawning times, areas or habits usually contribute to their reproductive isolation. The smaller kokanee can spawn in shallower streams than larger sea-fattened fish, but what really seems to maintain the genetic distinction between the two forms is simply that even when they share the gravel, fish prefer to mate with others of their own kind.

Stocks of kokanee are genetically closer to those of sea-going sockeye in the same lake system than they are to kokanee in other lake systems. This suggests that the tendency not to migrate has emerged independently, and repeatedly, since the salmon began to spread throughout their existing range some 12,000 years ago. Whatever the ecological forces which combined to encourage the emergence of stay-at-home behaviour, they seem to have acted in parallel with similar results all round the rim of the Pacific. Despite thousands of generations of landlocked lives, kokanee still retain the ability to adapt to a marine existence and to find their way home to spawn in their natal stream. Like brown trout, in particular, when kokanee are released in strange lakes, they do not necessarily remain true to their inherited instincts, and are quite capable of responding to pressures from their environment and heading off to sea.

Usually kokanee are stocked into lakes and reservoirs towards the southern limits of their range where the outflow, if there is one, is too warm in its lower reaches, or else the sea is. Introductions into the south-western states of the USA, and also Hokkaido, have proved particularly successful in establishing these landlocked fish. The habit of feeding away from the shoreline in more open waters, which they are often the only fish to exploit, has endeared kokanee to fishery managers; so has their ability to breed in still waters in the absence of a good inflowing stream. Kokanee from Colorado (where they are introduced) were the first Pacific salmon to be deliberately stocked into the Great Lakes,

in 1964. They still breed there naturally, but in the public eye have been eclipsed by the much more successful introductions of pinks (which arrived earlier, but accidentally), coho and chinook.

The consignment of eyed sockeye ova shipped to New Zealand in 1901 almost certainly derived from sea-going fish hatched in the Adams River. Today, the sockeye in the Waitaki River system on the South Island comprise the only self-sustaining population in the southern hemisphere. These are now literally landlocked by the Waitaki Dam, although they appear to have taken up their fresh-water life voluntarily, before the dam was built. This is most probably because, like almost all other salmon transplanted or hatched south of the equator, none of those sockeye which originally went to sea ever found its way home, and so natural selection has repeatedly favoured fish which do not migrate.

Runs of sea-going sockeye have proved slightly easier to establish in the streams around their native ocean. Each year, hundreds of thousands of salmon now swim up to Frazer Lake, on Kodiak Island off the south coast of Alaska, their colonisation eased by the construction of fish ladders and an initial stocking programme involving the introduction of both mature and immature fish, as well as eggs. Similarly, many of the sockeye now swimming into Seattle's Lake Washington are descended from fish which originally arrived there through human endeavour rather than the forces of Nature.

Sockeye are called 'red salmon' in Alaska, because of the colour of their flesh rather than their spawning skin, and also sometimes 'bluebacks' from their salt-water livery. At sea they are typically salmon-silver and most easily identified by the lack of spots on dorsal fins and tails – which sets kokanee apart from rainbow trout in the lakes they share. Sockeye's larger scales are also very distinctive and their pale gums help distinguish them from chinook. There is no difference in the colouration of the sexes out at sea, and only when their hormones begin to suppress the impulse to feed, and sockeye head for home, does it become possible to distinguish between them – and then more by shape than colour. Males start to narrow across the back, becoming more hump-backed and eventually even brighter coloured and with more contrasting green heads than their mates. From a distance shoals of sockeye look first blue, then purple, as they hang in the edge of the river's current or round the lake shore, before finally announcing their readiness to spawn with a final surge upstream in their crimson brilliance.

Two male and one female sockeye on the gravel of the Tazimina River which flows into Lake Iliamna.
(Andrew Hendry)

Pink Salmon

If, as seems generally agreed, the Salmonidae family had its origins in fresh water, then pink salmon (*Oncorhynchus gorbuscha*) are now further down the evolutionary trail than any other. In many rivers they actually spawn below the high water mark, and the eggs and alevins are only washed with pure fresh water at low tide. Even fry hatched further up river head downstream as soon as they emerge from their gravel sanctuaries, showing an affinity for the sea that not even chum can rival. There are no natural stocks of landlocked pink salmon, although as a species they still retain the ability to make long journeys upstream to spawn, and in the Great Lakes a flourishing population of introduced fish defies all its natural instincts and thrives without ever sensing the sea. Pinks may not attract the attentions of naturalists or fishermen to the extent that other salmon do, yet their drab spawning dress and supposedly inferior taste mask an intriguing life cycle, quite unlike that of any other Pacific salmon.

There are most likely more pinks than any other salmon in the world, not least because scattered spawning stocks are spread far along the Arctic Ocean coastlines, giving them a range only matched by chum. The pinks which occasionally edge as far as the Canadian waters of the Beaufort Sea are almost certainly strays, and cannot yet be said to mark an expansion of their species' range, but fish breed between Point Hope and Point Barrow and have been reported as far west as the Lena River along Russia's northern shores. All down the Bering Sea coastline there are spawning stocks of pink salmon, on either side of the Kamchatka peninsula and round the Sea of Okhotsk, down to Hokkaido and Korea. Over on the east coast the realistic limit of their contiguous range is the Puget Sound, although from time to time stragglers appear still further south.

Male and female pink salmon on the redds.
(Richard Grost)

Pink fry are quite different from other young salmon in lacking any dark parr marks on their flanks. Once at sea a pink salmon of either sex is best identified by the large 'soft' spots – almost blotches – on its back, dorsal fin and all over its tail, as well as by much smaller scales. When spawning time approaches, fish start to darken to slaty grey, dark green or rusty brown above their lateral line, remaining paler below with occasional tinges of pink, although hardly enough to merit their name, which may be a better reflection of the colour of their flesh. 'Humpback' is a more common, and perhaps more appropriate, appellation, reflecting the males' grotesque change in shape as the breeding urge takes hold. Other salmon, particularly sockeye, grow less pronounced humps, but the males of all species develop the ferocious looking teeth and the hooked snout which so characterise their genus.

Pink salmon have often stopped feeding and started to mature long before they reach the influence of fresh water. The timing depends partly on how far upstream they will spawn. It is under genetic control, each stock of pink salmon having evolved its own specific schedule to fit the length of its river journey. Then cues from the environment, like day length or water temperature, trigger off the hormonal changes which bring on maturity.

Fish breeding below the high-water mark, as many of them do, mill around in the estuary, often announcing their arrival by swimming along just under the surface and leaping right out of the water. Perhaps they do this to shake off lice and other parasites or to take air into their swimbladders to compensate for the lower density of fresh water. Their migratory journeys are already almost over and the tide will carry them easily up to the redds where, like all other Pacific salmon, they too will die after spawning. The inevitable deaths of pink salmon, spawning so close to the estuary, provide convincing evidence, if such is needed, that it is the general disintegration of their body and internal organs which kills salmon, and not just the long arduous and foodless fresh-water journeys that most of them have to endure.

Pink salmon from small coastal rivers, breeding well upstream of the estuary, prefer the impetus of a spate of fresh water to start them on their journeys. Sometimes this never comes. Then salmon which have waited in vain, and whose systems have brought them close to spawning, will try to reach the redds no matter how little water there is to help them, shoals of desperate fish rattling the gravel continuously as they struggle through the shallows between pools. Dependence on a spate can work both ways, and a flash flood surging suddenly down the river may dangerously delay fish or even prevent them from reaching their spawning areas altogether.

Salmon with long journeys ahead of them are still fresh and silvery when they reach the river mouth, only turning colour and changing shape on their way upstream. Some migrate far up the Fraser, beyond the narrows of the canyon at Hell's Gate, and on into the Thompson River, at least 250 km (150 miles) from the sea. In the Skeena River, which emerges from the heart of northern British Columbia at Prince Rupert, pink salmon are known to defy the normal migratory patterns of their species and travel nearly 500 km (300 miles) to spawn.

The first pink salmon to arrive in an estuary are often strangers, merely sensing the water, making both the trial and the error before moving on in search of the stream where they were born. Spending so little time under the river's influence as fry might imply that the pink salmon's imprinting mechanisms are less effective, and that many of these strays are actually lost. Of all the Pacific salmon, pinks are by far the most common along the shores of the Arctic Ocean. This may be because they have missed the sensory stimuli from the fresh water of their home streams, and so spread into new rivers beyond their established boundaries. However, it seems more likely that conditions in the far north favour fish which are able to escape their fresh-water rearing grounds quickly and to move south, down into the Bering Sea, before the polar winter brings sub-zero sea temperatures no salmon can survive. Much of the evidence that pinks have spread far and fast because they are the salmon least faithful to the streams of their birth derives from studies of stocks transplanted into foreign waters, although genetic studies on natural stocks also show pinks often straying into adjacent rivers.

Pinks lay fewer eggs than any other salmon – seldom more than 2,000. This is partly because they are the smallest species, averaging just over 2 kg (4 lb) at the warmer end of their range, and slightly less further north. To maintain a population of salmon, or any other creature, at its current level basically requires each female to produce two offspring which themselves survive to breed. Laying fewer eggs than any other salmon, and still being the most numerous species, implies that pink salmon have evolved a particularly successful lifestyle. This combines the creation of a protective gravel nest for their eggs with a short life, nearly all of which is spent at sea. It may be no coincidence that chum salmon are also an abundant species, and that they too often spawn equally close to the estuary, and always head straight down to sea as soon as they emerge from the gravel.

Pink fry are programmed to start downstream once their yolk sacs are absorbed, immediately after they have finally emerged from their nests. For some of them, reaching the estuary entails no more than waiting for darkness and the turn of the tide. Others face a journey of more dangerous dimensions, which forces them to feed in fresh water if they are to complete it, snapping up insect larvae and other tiny invertebrates borne down with them on the river's current. Yet no matter where they are hatched, the sea calls pink salmon so loudly that every surviving fry hatched from natural populations leaves fresh water the summer it is born.

The overriding urge of pink salmon fry to abandon their birthplace contributes to an extraordinarily rigid life cycle. Almost all pink salmon spend around eighteen months at sea – one winter – before returning to spawn as 0.1 fish and so to complete a precise two-year life. Because it is so rare for fish to stay an extra year at sea, there is virtually no overlap between generations. This inflexibility would seem to be a huge disadvantage to the species as a whole, and to render specific stocks frighteningly vulnerable to droughts, floods or other catastrophes. Environmental disasters of the scale of the 1964 Alaskan earthquake or the eruption of Mt St Helens in 1980 could bar whole runs of fish from their spawning grounds or kill off all the eggs or alevins in a particular stream, thus driving a river's entire population to extinction.

The variety in the life cycles within each generation of sockeye and chinook is held out as good reason for the continued success of these species. So, by extension, the inflexibility of pink salmon's lives should militate against them; yet it does not seem to. To some extent they may compensate for their biorhythmic rigidity with a stronger inclination to probe new frontiers and a lesser insistence on breeding where they themselves were born. What probably contributes to their success even more is simply the brevity of their lives. Short lives mean less likelihood of dying before breeding, and shorter generations imply faster responses to environmental changes and better chances for depleted populations to rebound quickly from disasters.

Their undeviating two-year life span has meant that, in many rivers, pink salmon have never established runs in the intervening 'off years', and there are repeated cycles with almost no fish one year and huge runs the next. Millions of pink salmon run up the Fraser River in odd years and scarcely a fish in even ones. Further up the British Columbia coast, numbers vary little from one year to the next, while in Bristol Bay and much of the rest of Alaska the rivers have dominant even-year cycles. Sometimes fish seem to be squeezed far up into a river's headwaters because so many others are trying to breed close to the sea, even though this may require them to suppress their instincts to stop and spawn where they themselves were hatched. A hundred years ago, so many pink salmon swam up the Amur River on the Russia/China border that in years of super-abundance the last arrivals had to probe as far as 700 km (430 miles) upstream to find unoccupied patches of gravel; now, with numbers severely depleted, they need go no more than 200 km (125 miles) at the most.

Where the cycle is particularly pronounced, fish tend to be smaller in dominant years than in off years, showing again that even in the great vastness of the ocean, growth is surely affected by intraspecific competition for the available food. In rivers where chum and pink cohabit, chum tend to do better in the pinks' off years. This may be a consequence of competition too – this time interspecific – either as juveniles in estuaries or during their first months at sea. Environmental catastrophes can shift the dominant-year cycle from odd to even or vice versa. Sustained fishing can also affect the extent to which one cycle dominates another by taking a much larger proportion of the fish from off years than from dominant ones, thus accentuating the degree of dominance still further.

Odd-year fish are more genetically akin to other odd-year fish from nearby rivers than they are to even-year ones from the same river. This supports the idea that pinks stray away from home streams, and by doing so help to reinforce populations suddenly threatened by disaster. Translocated pink salmon have shown themselves to be enthusiastic colonisers of new streams, and there seems no reason why indigenous fish should not also be continually probing unfamiliar estuaries for more favourable areas to spawn. Very occasionally, fish have been found swimming in the face of their normal two-year cycle and spending a further year at sea. If this was usual behaviour it might start more sustained off-year runs and create a tendency to level out the difference between dominant and off years. Yet the genetic profiles of odd- and even-year runs are usually quite distinct. This tends to deny the influence of three-year-old fish in the foundation of off-year stocks, except in the Great Lakes where pink salmon have defied practically all the rules ever written for them.

In 1955, the Ontario government tried to introduce pink salmon to Hudson Bay. There are no Atlantic salmon in the bay and it was hoped this exotic species could form the basis of both sport and subsistence fisheries. The transplant project, which was destined to be yet another in the long list of total failures, involved planting eggs from the Skeena River into artificial nests, and also releasing young fry derived from the same stock into inflowing streams. Rather than bringing the fry directly from British Columbia, they were held at hatcheries on the shores of Lake Superior, before being flown up to Hudson Bay. By the end of June the stocking programme was completed, but 21,000 fry were still left in the hatchery and these were casually tipped into a drain emptying out into the Current River. In 1959, two mature pink salmon were caught by sport fishermen on the Minnesota shore of Lake Superior, and from then on, with no further artificial assistance, pink salmon began to spread all over the lake. Ten years later, the fish appeared in Lake Huron, and within the next decade in Michigan, Erie and Ontario. Now, subsisting largely on a diet of rainbow smelts, pink salmon are established throughout the entire Great Lakes system.

From an idle release of surplus fish into a supposedly wholly unsuitable environment began the most spectacularly successful salmon translocation ever, and the foundation of the only self-sustaining fresh-water population of pink salmon in the world – within or without the fish's native range. Indigenous fish usually pay the price for the success of an exotic species, and there may now be fewer rainbow smelts – themselves also introduced – for the lake charr and other predators. Yet charr have been found with juvenile salmon in their stomachs, and the fish fauna of the Great Lakes is now such a mishmash of introduced and indigenous species that the specific impact of one species on another is almost impossible to assess.

Superior is the second largest lake in the world, trailing only the Caspian Sea, and so if any North American stretch of water approximates to a sea, then it is this. None the less, one of the most astonishing consequences of letting three tankfuls of fry out into a drain was to prove that pink salmon can easily survive without access to salt water. These fish have also spread throughout the Great Lakes so far, so fast, that they seem to have responded to much more than the localised pressures of their own overpopulation. They are suspected of spawning in lake shallows as well as more conventionally in the inflows. The main runs are of odd-year fish, but over the past thirty-five years, enough pink salmon have delayed maturing until their third year to found a substantial even-year run as well. That maturity is primed more by reaching a given size than the striking of some internal clock seems also to be borne out by the occasional occurrence of ripe male yearlings, and in the laboratory, even of fish that only matured aged four.

While the offspring of 21,000 pink salmon fry were settling into Lake Superior, Russian biologists began to release the first of what was to be a total of forty-eight million juveniles along their country's north-west coast. These mostly derived from Sakhalin Island, just north of Hokkaido in the Sea of Okhotsk. The Russians hoped to spread both pink and chum salmon around the White Sea by capitalising on their tolerance of low water temperatures, and can generally be said to have succeeded with pinks. The population now seems well enough established to be exploited by a thriving commercial fishery, and in their continual search for new horizons pink salmon appear to have colonised rivers in northern Norway too. Strays sometimes turn up in Iceland, and the first of several British records appeared in nets set off the Scottish coast, below Aberdeen, as early as the summer of 1960.

Within their natural range, the main purpose of transplanting pinks is to establish runs in river systems where few, if any, fish return in off years. With one or two unspectacular exceptions in southern Alaska and around the Puget Sound, they have all failed, despite efforts to produce genetically suitable fish by using frozen sperm from the river's dominant-year stocks. Quite often some of the released fry have returned to spawn, and sometimes a few of their offspring as well, but all too often the runs have dwindled down to nothing, leaving no living reminder of the effort and expense. Attempted transplants to Atlantic rivers in Maine and Newfoundland also first flattered to deceive, and populations of introduced pink salmon in Chile and the Black and Baltic Seas also seem to have faded away – leaving those in the White Sea as the only self-sustaining sea-going stocks beyond the Pacific rim and its adjacent Arctic Ocean coastline.

Chum Salmon

Chum salmon (*Oncorhynchus keta*) stretch the frontiers of their range even further than pinks, although, as wild fish, they are probably now outnumbered by their smaller relatives. Johann Walbaum first described chum, and the four other common species of Pacific salmon – sockeye, pink, chinook and coho – in 1792. His *Artedius Piscium* was based largely on the observations of George Wilhelm Steller, the naturalist on Vitus Bering's fateful, scurvy-ridden explorations of the north Russian coast fifty years earlier. In Kamchatka, where Steller took his first specimen, *keta* just meant fish, so as *Salmo keta* they began their scientific existence and as *Oncorhynchus keta* they now continue it. Colloquially they are often get called 'dog salmon', probably because they were, and sometimes still are, used as dog food, rather than in recognition of the particularly ferocious looking teeth males develop before spawning.

Like the other Pacific salmon, chum are flexible in their lifestyles, but not so flexible that any naturally live out their whole lives in fresh water. They can, but the only ones to have proved this so far have done so in laboratory tanks. Somewhere, a fresh-water lake may be waiting to welcome chum fry, which have escaped from a hatchery, and to provide the ideal environment for them and their offspring, but so far transplants of chum have been less successful than those of any other salmon. There may be small runs in the White Sea and perhaps also in southern Chile, whose coast is a complete aquacultural free-for-all, and where almost every species of salmon, trout and charr has at one time or another turned up in Andean rivers after escaping from estuary cages.

The six species of Pacific salmon divide easily into two groups according largely to the social habits of the fry – shoalers and non-shoalers. This grouping actually has wider implications in that living in shoals is generally incompatible with staying long in rivers, where the limited resources are best apportioned by fish which make their own individual spaces. The time that chinook, coho and masu spend in fresh running water represents a distinct and vital stage in their growth, when their more competitive territorial instincts give them the best chances of survival.

Pinks, chum and sockeye are more social fish in early life. Most sockeye combine their shoaling instincts with at least a year in fresh water by exploiting the open areas of nursery lakes, where food is easily gathered as part of a shoal and predators are much better avoided. Chum are almost as anxious as pink salmon to turn downstream. For both species a day in fresh water seems a day wasted and individuals all rely on the safety of numbers to help more of them survive the hazards of their seaward journey. Like pink salmon, some chum spawn below the limits of the high tide, and the downstream migration of their young is timed in minutes and measured in metres; for other newly emerged fry though, their journey may take months and be better gauged in thousands of kilometres.

The migrations of mature salmon up to their spawning grounds are both conspicuous and dramatic, made all the more so by the death that inevitably follows. The downstream journeys of young fry may be less conspicuous, but are actually far more dramatic, and for many of the tiny fish will also end in death. Some striped chum fry travel huge distances to the sea, but, unlike coho, sockeye and stream-type chinook, they set off at an age when life is motivated entirely by instinct and experience is nil.

With no conception of the sea, and only the current to guide them through its often opaque and silted waters, chum hatched in the Canadian headwaters of the Yukon River

Chum spawning.
(Kazutoshi Hiyeda)

start straight out on a journey of 3,200 km (1,990 miles) as soon as they emerge from the safety of their gravel. This is usually just after the ice has begun to break up. The nights are too short and the journey too long for them to migrate only under cover of darkness, and the turbid meltwater gives the young fish some protection all the way down to the Bering Sea. Travelling shoals of chum fry pack less tightly together than young pinks do, and are also less inclined to huddle close to their fellows in time of danger. All the same, their instincts tell individuals of both species that their chances of surviving attacks by predacious Dolly Varden, or the stealthy attentions of a great blue heron, are better if they bunch together than if they all fan out in different directions.

Pink and chum salmon share far more than the behaviour of their young, although much of what they have in common follows on from this. Their minimal dependence on fresh water may be what enables both species to breed in Arctic rivers, and chum have found their way even further along the northern coastlines of America and Russia than pinks, although in much smaller numbers. Many of these wanderers are probably lost, but a small stock almost certainly sustains itself in the drainage of the Mackenzie River, far to the east of the Alaska/Canada border. There chum have been found in both the Great Bear and the Slave Rivers as well as the Mackenzie, some having travelled as far as 2,000 km (1240 miles) upstream to spawn. To the west, along the Russian coast, chum have also been caught in the Lena River, which empties into the Laptev Sea. Chum tolerate warmer waters than any other salmon and spawn as far south as Kyushu in southern Japan, as well as in the Naktong River which empties into the sea on the south coast of

South Korea. In America, water extraction, hydroelectric dams and other river-ruining schemes have perhaps taken less of a toll on chum salmon and although there is now only a single self-sustaining population in California, stocks in Oregon and Washington are still relatively healthy.

The chum's tolerance of a wide range of temperature is one of the reasons for the spectacular growth in Japanese salmon ranching, which involves releasing hatchery-raised fry in the estuary and then simply harvesting them on their return from the sea. The country has long recognised the importance of nurturing breeding populations, and legislated to protect the chum's natural spawning grounds well before the creation of the first artificial spawning channel by a local samurai in 1763. The channel was an instant success: far more salmon returned to breed, allowing a much greater surplus to be harvested. So began the system of *tanegawa-no-seido*, which remained alive in parts of Honshu (Japan's largest island) until well into the 1950s. Only then did Nature finally succumb to numbers, and since then eggs and milt have been mixed in hatchery bowls rather than on spawning channel gravel.

Japan's first hatchery was built at Chikkote on Hokkaido in 1888 using American technology and design. The potential for producing chum fry astounded local aquaculturists, who quickly responded by setting up more hatcheries all over Hokkaido and on northern Honshu. Yet for all the millions of young fish sent off to sea, the numbers that returned, either to breed or be eaten, remained disappointingly low. After peaking sharply at the end of the nineteenth century, the graph flattened out at levels not much above those of the pre-hatchery era; and there, until about 1970, it remained. Stagnant technology, overfishing and the inevitable destruction of marine and fresh-water habitat combined to suppress any possible benefits from increasing fry output, until one simple change was made to the rearing programme – feeding the fry for two months before releasing them.

Almost at once, the ratio of returning to released fish tripled from 1 to 3 per cent and catches rose from three million to over thirty million in hardly ten years. The graph has since stopped rising so steeply and some hatcheries now concentrate on pink and masu salmon, and are even trying to ranch sea-going sockeye. Never the less, chum ranching from over 300 hatcheries, both privately and nationally owned, continues to satisfy much of Japan's enormous hunger for fresh fish. It may also take some of the pressure off stocks of wild salmon elsewhere, but in those rivers with hatcheries on their banks, wild salmon cannot avoid ending up as the accidental by-catch in the nets set for ranched fish, and most stocks have disappeared.

The striking success following the introduction of fry-feeding only served to stress how vulnerable young fish are, whether naturally or domestically hatched, between finishing their own in-built food supplies and starting to feed for themselves. Helping them through this most delicate stage in their lives, and giving them food and protection before release, increased their chances of survival dramatically. This is the time that most wild chum salmon spend in the estuary preparing for the open sea. Only for chinook is the stay in the halfway waters of the estuary more crucial, but chinook are often older, larger and more water-wise by the time they get there, and sculpins, coho yearlings and Dolly Varden find no easier feeding than on naive, newly arrived shoals of chum fry.

Once out in the ocean, Japanese chum head generally northwards, where they mix freely with others from the rivers of Kamchatka and round the Sea of Okhotsk. Their marine migrations may take them as far east as 140°, well beyond a line drawn south from

Anchorage, and further than any other Asian-hatched Pacific salmon travel. Otherwise, they might move up into the Bering Sea, where chum from western Alaska are also feeding alongside fish hatched close to the shores of the Arctic Ocean, which have moved quickly south to escape the polar winter. Chum from Canadian and Washington rivers seldom wander further west than the International Date Line. This could imply that they feel no need to because feeding is better in the American half of the northern Pacific Ocean than the Asian, whether or not competition there is less. The implication is further endorsed by the fact that both chum and pink salmon taken from similar latitudes tend to be larger in the east than the west.

Chum spend from two to five years at sea, usually three or four in the north of their range and two or three further south. Staying so long there, they grow larger than any other Pacific salmon except chinook. Commercial fishing boats have reported fish caught off river mouths as heavy as 20 kg (44 lb), but these are as far beyond the average weights as a 50 kg (110 lb) chinook. Despite maturing later and spending longer at sea, northern fish are still smaller than those born in more southerly rivers when they return to breed. Yukon fish average just over 3 kg (7 lb) compared to those from the Fraser and Columbia Rivers, which usually weigh well over 5 kg (11 lb). The average size of chum salmon homing back to the hatcheries on Honshu and Hokkaido has tended to decrease as numbers increase – another message from the ocean's depths that its bounty is not limitless. Not surprisingly, the Japanese fish ranching industry is now caught in the dilemma of whether to aim at producing many smaller fish or fewer larger ones.

The size chum reach before returning to spawn is not only constrained by numbers of their own kind; it may also be limited by competition from other salmon, particularly pinks. This may affect chum at any stage of their lives, from the gravel to the Gulf of Alaska, especially in the dominant years of the pink's cycle in areas where the pink's on-off rhythm is particularly pronounced. Fraser River pink salmon have a very distinctive cycle, and it is hardly surprising that chum fry grow larger, and that more survive, in the odd years when hardly any pinks hatch and competition is almost non-existent. More than this, chum also return to spawn in larger numbers when there are fewer pinks. This suggests that evolution has selectively favoured chum which are likely to mature and return to breed in those years when spawning space is at less of a premium, and there will be an easier start to life for their young. If both species arrive together, they may spawn on the same stretches of gravel, although chum often spawn earlier. Any hybrids (chumpies) are remarkably fertile and may grow better than either of their parents, but fertility quickly falls away in future generations.

As it does all Pacific salmon, the urge to return home strikes chum when they are still far out in the open ocean. Shining silver and without any spots on backs, fins or tails, their marine diet has not given them the same rich red flesh as sockeye. Instead their muscle is less fatty and much lighter coloured, with even a yellowish tinge, becoming paler still as the fish cease feeding and begin to draw their bodies' own reserves out of the muscle mass. Spawning times are earlier further north, but there are often distinct summer and autumn or autumn and winter runs in the same areas, and even the same river. Occasionally chum manage to defy the usual influences of the climate by returning as late as November or December to spawn in rivers like the Chilkat in the Alaskan panhandle, where spring water wells up to keep the ice at bay all year (see Chapter 11). If, like the Yukon fish, chum have a long fresh-water journey ahead of them, they maintain their silvery freshness until well up the river. More often, though, they start to turn an uneven browny-olive in the estuary, the male finally becoming blotched with maroon, while a distinct dark stripe appears along the female's lateral line, and then they will soon be ready to spawn.

Coho

Coho (silver) salmon (*Oncorhynchus kisutch*) demonstrate one of the traits which most distinguish them from other Pacific salmon the moment they emerge from the gravel: they start feeding near where they hatched. Most salmon turn their heads downstream before they have even thought of feeding for themselves, but coho's instincts tell them otherwise, and in the struggle for survival their first task is to establish a tiny fresh-water territory.

Emerging from the stones of a river bed is a confusing time for any salmonid. The self-contained food store is nearly empty and the dark security of the stream bed must be exchanged for open water and brilliant daylight. At the same time, young coho have to take on the swirling current, and instead of just abandoning themselves to its forces and drifting downstream to a lake or estuary, they must start looking for food and space. Young fry mill around, disorientated and unsure of their next moves, before slowly easing off the redds into riffle edges or under banks. Gradually spacing themselves out in quieter water, aggressive defence of their little domains, rather than easy absorption into shoals of siblings, is their immediate strategy for survival – survival which is only assured by continually increasing the size of their territories at the expense of their fellows.

During the first year of their lives, young coho act very like their *Salmo* cousins. They choose the same sort of territories as brown trout do, opting for slower water along the edge of the stream or for pools created by logs and rocks, where they wait for whatever current-carried food might reach them. In slacker water they tend to be less territorial, spacing themselves out in a hierarchy of descending size and strength, according to the quality of the habitat. At the head of the pool are the largest fish, getting first pick at the most nutritious mouthfuls, while the smaller ones are lined up further downstream or on the bottom. When they start feeding coho fry make many mistakes, nipping at any little passing morsel which conforms to their inherited image of a good meal, until experience tempers instinct and flecks of bark and aquatic vegetation are shunned in favour of a carnivorous intake. Staying close to the banks gives many young coho the chance to snap up terrestrial insects dropping off branches into the water, but these are an unreliable source of food and during most of the summer fry continue to depend on midge larvae and tiny crustaceans.

Coho often have to share their nurseries with the young of other species of fish, particularly in short coastal streams where steelhead and cutthroat have also spawned. Some competition between the struggling juveniles is inevitable, but in the presence of deeper-bodied coho, the streamlined trout fry tend to occupy open faster sections of water. (The trout may actually be driven into this swifter water by the more aggressive and earlier hatching young coho, because in the absence of coho, trout often prefer the lies that the salmon otherwise secure.) If they do find themselves in the same pool, trout and salmon still manage to keep their distance, and coho tend to take floating food near the surface while the trout grub around below them.

This uneasy truce continues throughout the summer, but as the earth tilts northwards, bringing shorter days, cooler water and dwindling food supplies, the whole fish population begins a general shake-up in preparation for winter. If young coho stay in the main river

Coho fry.
(Richard Grost)

they risk being swept away by the floods that follow autumn rainstorms, or later by melting ice and snow, so they often seek shelter in side streams, beaver ponds and backwaters. Sometimes there is no alternative to a river refuge, and juveniles fall back into large still pools where they can better hold against the floods. The cold water and dearth of food slow up their metabolisms and so suppress their aggression, and young salmon and trout see out the winter together in relative harmony.

Fish that reach a quiet backwater, perhaps even warmed by springs and never clouded by sudden floods, may carry on feeding. Others in less favoured lies find very little to sustain them in the winter and must wait until spring before they start growing again. Slow growers may have to spend a second year in fresh water or even a third, much depending on the latitude of their natal stream. True to the salmon's general pattern of being ready for the sea sooner where it is warmer, none of the few remaining Californian coho, and less than 10 per cent of those from British Columbia, spend a second year in fresh water; yet in many rivers in Alaska and Kamchatka, at least half of them do.

Unlike pink salmon, which only proved they could live out their lives in fresh water when tipped into the Great Lakes, a few coho mature naturally without ever going to sea. These are not occasional residuals lingering on in nursery streams, but instead entire populations, or at least large proportions of populations, which have adopted fresh-water lives, rather like stocks of kokanee. They are all lake-living fish, reaching weights of up to 2 kg (4 lb) before maturing, spawning and dying – just like their kin which have lead more conventional sea-going lives.

Some internal clock sets migratory coho off downstream to exploit their long-evolved ability to survive in both fresh and salt water, and simultaneously begins to prepare them for the shock of the sea. Latitude also affects the timing of their journey, and the late spring of the far north often stops them leaving until after midsummer. Then, when they are about 10 cm (4 in) long, the oval parr marks on their golden-brown flanks begin to fade, their once orange fins become transparent and dark-edged, and by the time they reach the estuary they are cryptically coloured for the open water – there to spend the next one, two, or even three years. The smolts' journeys down the Yukon, Skeena or Fraser systems may be several hundred kilometres long, but these are exceptional; so are their 500 km (300 miles) migrations from the headwaters of the Kamchatka River. Instead, for most young coho, life begins up short coastal streams or tributaries, further up than it does for pink or chum, but still leaving the loose schools of smolts a fairly safe and simple journey to the sea.

Coho smolts are viciously piscivorous, both on their way to the estuary and when they get there. They relish the opportunity to plunder tightly packed shoals of pink or chum fry only just out of the gravel. If these tiny fish have not yet arrived, the young coho will have to content themselves with a diet of amphipods and the larvae of herring and smelt before moving out to sea. Coho seem to spend very little time at the river mouth, unlike pinks, chum or chinook, yet for all their haste to leave fresh water behind, they wander less around the open ocean than any other salmon except ocean-type chinook. Many of them spend their marine years without ever straying further than the thin coastal strip inside the continental shelf.

Young coho swim out into the sea from Point Hope down to northern California. They run in smaller numbers than sockeye, which throng down bigger rivers in their millions. However, they are more versatile in exploiting smaller streams which empty straight into the sea, or insignificant tributaries that other salmon often eschew. At the southern end of their range, the warmth of the sea pushes smolts northwards on the start of what for some is a great counterclockwise circuit of the Gulf of Alaska. Others from more temperate rivers of British Columbia and the Puget Sound just travel up and down the coast, some going no further than the Strait of Georgia between Vancouver Island and the mainland. Over in the west, there is a strangely isolated population in the Anadyr River, almost across the Bering Sea from the Yukon delta. Otherwise Asian coho are concentrated further south, down the Kamchatka peninsula, round the Sea of Okhotsk and on Sakhalin and the northern tip of Hokkaido. Their migrations take them out into the more open ocean, but, like all coho, they are reluctant to linger where the temperature is below 7°C, and this only allows the northern wanderers a very short feeding season in the Bering Sea.

Some male coho only spend five or six months at sea. Like early maturing sockeye, these are jacks ready to breed a year earlier than most of their fellows. When the time comes for spawning, they do not compete directly on the redds with older hook-jawed males for their moments of ecstasy. Instead they sneak in and fertilise eggs just after the female has begun mating with a larger fish. Whether a male coho is to mature early or late seems to depend on reaching a given size by a certain age – it is usually the larger fry that are set for the life of a jack – as well as on inherited tendencies. The sea is a dangerous place, and by cutting down their time there jacks are less likely to fall victim to predator or parasite attacks. They therefore have more chance of getting back to the spawning grounds than older fish which spend an extra year or more at sea. The trade-off for shortening the odds on surviving to spawn would seem to be doing so less well, yet much of the evidence points to jacks breeding just as successfully as older males. If this is really so, will the jack's life one day become the norm for coho, and longer-lived males the exception?

At this stage in the coho's evolution, there is probably a critical balance between numbers of sneaking jacks and of aggressive older males, which is naturally maintained when sufficient fish of both sizes spawn successfully. Sometimes natural or unnatural causes inadvertently tilt the balance in favour of one life strategy or another. Most fishing nets favour jacks, allowing them to slip through mesh designed to ensnare larger fish; so do regulations requiring that smaller fish are returned to the water. Lower water levels also discriminate against larger fish, which often have trouble struggling through the trickles to reach the redds, and even then may be grounded in their efforts to chase away the intruding jacks that wriggle much more easily through the shallows. Although hatcheries tend to ignore jacks in selecting returning males for breeding stock, doing so has not resulted in fewer jacks in areas where most coho are artificially bred. This may be because hatchery fish grow faster, reach maturity sooner and therefore may still be inclined to return to breed after five or six months at sea.

Never the less, in the natural environment, so far as such a state still exists, jacks remain in the minority, although the proportion of jacks varies wildly between rivers and years. Sometimes jacks account for less than one in a hundred returning fish. At the other extreme they may very occasionally even outnumber older males – and then usually in rivers where smolts are larger than average, or in years preceding peaks. Of the older fish,

Coho male returning to
spawn.
(Richard Grost)

most only spend one winter at sea, and it is rare to find any staying there for two before returning to spawn. One-winter fish may weigh anything between 3 kg and 5 kg (7–11lb) and older fish half as much again.

Out at sea, their metallic blue backs and dark spots on the back, dorsal fin and upper half of the tail help distinguish coho from other salmon. As spawning time approaches, males begin to turn almost sockeye-red below their lateral lines, while the rest of their bodies darken to brown or olive-green. Females are pinker below, and the spots on both sexes stay with them in their breeding dress. They arrive on the redds much later than other species, and it is not unusual to find them spawning well into the new year, sometimes in the process excavating the eggs of salmon which bred earlier and are now long dead.

Coho have also reached the Great Lakes. Their introduction was deliberate, unlike the pink salmon's, and they have adapted well to life in fresh water. As early as 1873, ten years before brown trout reached America, and when almost nothing was known about propagating salmon artificially, coho fry were tipped into Lake Erie. This effort, like many others, failed to found a population that sustained itself for more than a generation or two. Nearly a century later, in 1966, when pinks were already well established round the shores of Lake Superior, juvenile coho were again released into Lakes Superior and Michigan. These were smolts, deliberately kept long enough in running water to absorb its chemical make-up. That autumn steelhead fishermen caught lots of precocious young males, and 'coho fever' began to infect fishermen and biologists alike. More smolts were released the following year, with exceptionally high survival rates. In the next two years this 'superfish' took on a further role in the public eye – that of biological controller of alewives. These had followed sea lampreys up the Welland Ship Canal, although they did not appear in any numbers until the 1940s. Finding life in the Great Lakes to their liking they multiplied to plague proportions before the population collapsed in 1967, leaving billions of dead fish littered over long lengths of beach and their rotting stench hanging over lakeside townships all summer. Local opinion has given coho the credit for keeping alewives under control ever since.

Today, the coho spawn naturally in several Great Lake inflows, but both commercial and sport fisheries are largely sustained by hatchery output. This is much less objectionable than it would be if coho were naturally found there. All the same, the continual stocking contributes to the massive imbalance of the whole fish community in the Great Lakes, from which so many indigenous species have disappeared and into which a whole host of other exotic imports have been introduced.

Other runs of alien coho may persist in foreign waters. So far, repeated efforts to convince them of the attractions of New England's rivers have been unsuccessful – as have most attempts to re-establish the native Atlantic salmon there. Coho are popular in fish farms, from which there is always the chance of their escaping or being deliberately released, but it takes several generations to say that a run of escapees has become self-sustaining, and if any has it is likely to be in Chile. Europe has dabbled with farmed coho from time to time, and biologists express occasional concern about the possibility of unwanted fish establishing feral populations to the detriment of local Atlantic salmon and brown trout. Never the less, it must be long odds against accidental escapees succeeding where all intentional introductions of sea-going stocks have failed. Round the shores of their native Pacific, coho are also being reared for the table, but the output of hatchery fish to satisfy the demands of fishermen is already so huge that the impact of a few farmed escapees on the wild gene pool is hardly likely to be discernible.

Chinook

There are less chinook (*Oncorhynchus tschawytscha*) than any other Pacific salmon except the localised masu, but then the natural order is of pyramids of abundance and size in which larger animals nearer the top are usually less common than smaller ones lower down. Commercially caught chinook weighing over 50 kg (110 lb) have found their way into the record books, and in some of the rivers on Alaska's Kenai Peninsula (there called 'kings'), fish of 20 kg (44 lb) pass unremarked. Compare these to the little two-year-old pinks of 2 kg (4 lb) and it is no surprise to find them at either end of the salmon's population scale.

Chinook are most closely related to coho: both often rear in rivers and the young of neither species move in shoals. They can be confused at sea too, if size does not distinguish them, and the colour of their gums may provide the only certain means of identification; chinook's are black while the coho's are much paler. The breeding range of the two species is almost identical. There are chinook from the Anadyr River to Hokkaido in the western Pacific and from Point Hope to northern California in the east. Any fish turning up far outside their established range, like the chinook caught at Fort Liard, which had travelled 1,500 km (950 m) from the Beaufort Sea up the Mackenzie River with a shoal of spawning chum, are strays – and evince the fallibility of their navigational systems.

Chinook have also added to the ichthyological chaos in the Great Lakes, where they now spawn naturally, but as transplants they are most renowned for comprising the only certainly self-sustaining population of sea-going salmon in the southern hemisphere. These are the quinnat on the South Island of New Zealand (see Chapter 2). It is the total failure of so many other efforts to transplant salmon (including many others involving the same species in the same New Zealand rivers in which it now thrives) that makes this success so remarkable. Why, of all the billions of salmon eggs, fry and smolts introduced into foreign waters, should these chinook eggs, arriving in New Zealand from California's Sacramento River at the turn of the century, provide the foundations for this unique stock of fish? There is no answer yet, but the success is self-evident in several different rivers emptying out along a stretch of over 200 km (125 miles) of eastern coastline, and in a few west coast streams as well. No one has yet explained the reasons for all the transplant failures, which makes trying to account for this sole success doubly difficult.

Wherever they are, chinook are creatures of deeper fresh waters than any other salmon. They are big powerful fish, and their largest runs are up big powerful rivers. There are still good stocks of fish in the Sacramento/San Joaquin river system despite mankind's frightening rearrangement of the Californian environment, and some of the 500,000 chinook which swim up the Yukon make the longest spawning journeys of their species – as do the chum and coho which also breed in that river. The Nushagak empties into Bristol Bay and receives about the same number. The Fraser never had many chinook, and the runs up most of the other rivers of British Columbia and the Alaskan panhandle are often only a few thousand strong. The Columbia was once the greatest of all chinook rivers. However, it will take nothing less than the destruction of most of its dams to bring chinook back in anything approaching the numbers that swam there before the Europeans arrived, hatcheries and fish passes having almost totally failed to mitigate the dams' effects.

A river's chinook stocks are made up of either stream- or ocean-type fish, or more often a combination of the two. Despite sharing a river, the radically different behaviour of the two types keeps them reproductively isolated from each other, epitomising the versatility of the species and helping to ensure its success against environmental disasters. Stream-type chinook spend at least a year in fresh water before setting off to sea. Ocean-type fish are often hatched only a pink-salmon distance upstream, giving the newly emerged fry no more than a night's journey to the estuary, where they then tend to linger for several months before moving into open water.

Out at sea, ocean-type chinook may travel some distance up or down the coast, but seldom far from the shore, in contrast to the stream-type fish which join all those other salmon surging round on circuits of the northern Pacific. Spawning so far upstream, stream-type adults usually return to the estuary earlier in the year than their ocean-type fellows, but clear-cut classification is very difficult. Not all chinook arriving later in the year are necessarily ocean-type fish, and some still have long migrations ahead of them. To add even more to the potential for confusion, some rivers have two distinct runs, but both produce stream-type juveniles. As adults, rather than continuing to be split into ocean- and stream-type fish, the species tends to be divided into spring and fall chinook, according to the timing of their return to fresh water.

Genetic analysis has revealed, perhaps surprisingly, that stream-type and ocean-type chinook from the same river are more akin to each other than to fish of the same type from other rivers. This would seem to indicate that the two types have evolved independently, and repeatedly, in each of the river systems where both coexist. One type probably colonised the rivers where they are today as the glaciers began retreating 15,000 years ago. Then the other evolved separately within each river system in response to selective, and probably similar, pressures from the fresh-water environment. There are parallels with the evolution of *O. nerka* too, and non-migratory kokanee appear more closely related to sea-going sockeye from the same river system than to other kokanee from different systems.

Nearly all Asian chinook are stream-type, as are most Alaskan fish. They arrive back at the estuary in small shoals of silver, barrel-like salmon with dark spots on their backs, dorsal fins and all over their tails, bearing little resemblance to the browny-pink, soft-gutted fish they will soon become. With long upstream journeys ahead of them, they begin swimming towards their spawning grounds in June or July, slowly darkening as they do. Their flesh colour ranges from deep orange to near-white. This variation is under direct genetic control and white-fleshed chinook are the only Pacific salmon which are unable to fix carotene in their muscle.

Moving from north to south, a continuum of gradually changing behaviour emerges. In the Fraser, nearly 65 per cent of the chinook are ocean-type as, today, are 75 per cent of the Columbia's fish. (This may actually be a misleading figure and a reflection of no more than the appalling obstacle course that confronts the stream-type fish still trying to reach the river's upper reaches. One hundred and fifty years ago, before the river's dams and water extraction schemes began to impede their magnificent migrations, stream-type fish may have predominated.) In California, 90 per cent of mature chinook are ocean-type fish. Only in British Columbia are there a few rivers with no stream-type fish at all.

Chinook with distant spawning grounds reach the estuary earlier in the year than those spawning lower down the river, although in spite of, or perhaps because of, their staggered arrivals, spring and fall fish both often end up spawning at almost the same time of year. Those chinook which have battled their way up falls and rapids to the headwaters of the Skeena River spawn between mid-August and mid-September, only just ahead of the later-arriving fall fish which breed close to the estuary.

A female chinook close to spawning.
(Richard Grost)

Chinook often spawn in deeper faster water than other salmon, not least because they are stronger fish, able to hold against more powerful currents and shift much larger stones as they excavate their nests. Sometimes they breed in shallow, more typical salmon spawning areas, and the homing instincts that urge them over 3,000 km (1900 miles) to reach the headwaters of the Yukon override any chance of their stopping to spawn in the great open river much nearer the sea. The flow of water through the gravel, rather than above it, is more important to the successful hatching of the eggs of chinook than to those of any other salmon. Chinook eggs are large, with much less surface area in relation to their volume, making the percolation of the water-borne oxygen supply especially vital.

Whether they first swim freely in the great open waters of the Columbia below Priest Rapids or in a tiny trickle at the head of the Skeena River, newly emerged chinook fry all begin life by letting the current carry them off downstream. How far down depends on their type and where they were spawned. Their first reactions can only be instinctive, and while ocean-type chinook do not inherit the impulse to head for the sea as quickly as chum or pink fry do, they will all have left the river by the end of their first summer.

Chinook moving upstream – their pink colouring has yet to show and they will not be spawning for several weeks.
(Natalie Fobes)

Stream-type young appear to inherit more aggressive, territorial natures appropriate for their longer sojourn in fresh water. Occasionally, chinook opt neither to head down to the estuary with the ocean-type young nor to stay as long as a year in the river. Instead, they spend several weeks in fresh water before some trigger – probably environmental – stimulates their seaward move. Variable stream flow, early competition from coho, steelhead or other chinook, as well as their own rate of growth, may all affect the downstream drifts of these maverick fish, classed as ocean-type chinook but conforming to the normal behaviour of neither type.

Alaskan and other stream-type chinook spend at least a year in their natal rivers. After a summer's feeding in open territories, they seek out quieter places for the winter, where being able to rest up and conserve their energies is more important than the chance to intercept occasional morsels of food. Then, with the warming water and longer days of spring, most of the yearlings leave their sheltered retreats and turn downstream. A few may remain unmoved by the urge to migrate, and spend a further year in the river. Probably at some time during their first year these fish fell short of some physiological benchmark and so failed to qualify for the next year's smolt stage, their systems demanding a second year in fresh water. This extra year can alter the biological rhythms of some males, prompting them to mature towards the end of their second summer in fresh water without ever going to sea. It seems likely that they are then able to spawn effectively, but not that they will ever reach the sea having done so. Coho residuals only mature in still waters, and in this occasional deviation from their normal life cycles chinook are more like Atlantic salmon.

True ocean-type chinook are much more consistent in their habits than those hatched further upstream. Estuaries are particularly important to these fry, and their time there represents a much more distinct stage in their lives than it does for pink or chum fry. Nearly all the big rivers on the eastern Pacific coast fan out into marshy deltas, which create ideal refuges for chinook to gather size and strength for life in the sea. As with all species able to survive in both fresh and salt water, the estuary plays its part in helping the systems of young fish adapt to one environment from another, but for ocean-type chinook fry its function as a nursery and feeding ground is equally important. They spend up to two months there, and yearling stream-type smolts may be arriving just as the current year's ocean-type hatching are heading out to sea. The larger stronger stream-type yearlings are much better prepared for a marine life than the newborn ocean-type fry, and they move through the estuary almost as fast as their systems will let them.

The Pacific peregrinations of stream- and ocean-type chinook have been pieced together from fishery returns and research samples. Naturally fishery returns reflect fishing techniques and the distribution of fishing effort, and can therefore be misleading. Drift nets do not catch fish swimming below them, and sea-bed trawlers miss fish near the surface. The chinook's piscivorous nature is exploited by an extensive troll fishery, but its catches say little about the distribution of chinook beyond the inshore waters where most of the trolling boats fish. The data gathered by research vessels gives a more balanced picture, but their recoveries are minimal compared to the fishing industry's. Tagging projects often focus on the stock from a particular river or hatchery, and so the information derived from recaptures tends to be clouded by that stock's own inherited behaviour. Never the less, even though it takes more to recreate distinct patterns of behaviour than pulling the odd Sacramento River chinook out of the Gulf of Alaska, or catching one hatched in the gravel of an Oregon stream in the Bering Sea, a few general

trends have become apparent.

Stream-type chinook migrate much further out into the open water than ocean-type, and account for most of the fish caught in the middle of the northern Pacific, as well as in the Bering Sea – although this latter seems generally beyond the migratory reach of fish from British Columbia and the coastal states of America. Ocean-type fish feed and fatten along the continental shelf, or even further inshore. Nearly all the fish caught by troll boats are ocean-type, feeding their way up and down the coast. The fact that stream-type fish are seldom taken by troll fisheries, but are instead netted in river mouths, suggests that these chinook are far out at sea when hormones send the first signals of impending maturity. This causes them to put aside their inclinations to feed and turn their heads straight for the estuary, only resting when they reach it.

Because they go to sea at least a year earlier, ocean-type fish are always larger than stream-type ones of the same age, and if stream-type fish eventually weigh more it is for no other reason than that they have lived longer. Ocean-type chinook, which never overwinter in a river, are often 0.3 fish on their return. Stream-type chinook from the Yukon may be 1.5 or 2.5 fish, having spent one or two winters in the river and then up to five at sea before returning to spawn. Some stream-type residual males spawn as 2.0 fish, having never reached the sea; and males of either type may return to spawn after only one winter there, often maturing a year earlier then females.

Columbia River below Priest Rapids Dam – one of the few stretches of the river which still flows as Nature intended, and a spawning area for wild chinook.
(Author)

Masu

Masu (*Oncorhynchus masou*) push the behavioural borders of their genus further than any other species of Pacific salmon, as well as stretching the map of *Oncorhynchus* as far south as Taiwan. They are unknown around the rim of the eastern Pacific, both in its rivers and to most of its people – even those familiar with their own salmon. If an affinity for fresh water implies having changed little since they first evolved, then masu are the most primitive of all Pacific salmon. As a species, they spend less time at sea than any other salmon, which may be why they have spread no further than the rivers of eastern Asia. By extension, if they left the ancestral line before any of the other salmon, they are the species most closely related to the Pacific trout, and much about them suggests this is so.

Asian salmon are sometimes divided into two distinct species – masu (*Oncorhynchus masou*) and amago (*O. rhodurus* and 'sweet child' in Japanese). Amago have a very limited distribution in southern Japan. There they often overlap with masu, from which they are distinguished by the crimson spots which masu lack; otherwise, the form, physiology, habits and habitat of both are almost identical. Throughout the amago's range the sea, and often the lower reaches of the rivers, are too warm for comfort, therefore effectively forcing these fish to live out their lives in cooler, upland streams. Masu are far more widespread, but in the south they too are primarily fresh-water fish. Non migratory masu are known as 'yamame' ('mountain girl'), and it seems more realistic to treat both them and amago as races of a single species, which is in any event broken into many other taxonomic fragments.

The most intriguing fragment is in Taiwan. There, a tiny relict population of masu has been squeezed up into the cool of the mountains by the slowly warming climate.

Japan and its surrounding seas.

Overfishing forced the Japanese colonial government to designate the fish a natural monument, but with Taiwan's independence in 1945 intangible conservation ideals had to make way for the human population's economic welfare. Orchards of fruit trees replaced indigenous forests, pesticides and fertilisers leached into the rivers, and within forty years *O. m. formosanus* was down to a three figure population. Now, after belated protection in 1984 as a cultural asset, it hangs precariously onto its existence, landlocked in small tributaries of the Ta-chia River, whose topography combines an altitude of around 1,750 m (5,750 ft) with a gentle gradient and a stable pebbly bed – and by so doing, extends the range of *Oncorhynchus* below the twenty-fifth parallel, and level with the tip of Mexico's Baja Peninsula.

There are both masu and amago on Kyushu and Shikoku, the two most southerly of Japan's four main islands. Their shores are washed by the warm waters of the Japan Current, which effectively means that all their salmon are also non-migratory, other than a few amago which occasionally get as far as the estuary. The two races are never naturally found in the same streams, but have been artificially redistributed to such an extent that hybrids are now common, and the genetic integrity of many individual populations has disappeared in years of uncontrolled interbreeding. The hills are steep and the streams flow fast over flat rock, down small waterfalls and into short stony pools. There are no charr on the islands and the only other fish in such fast water are Chinese minnows and a fresh-water goby. Young salmon use up much of their energy in countering the current and there is very little aquatic insect life to nourish them. Bamboos and evergreen trees crowd along the banks, keeping water cool in summer and also compensating for the dearth of water-hatched insects by providing a seasonal supply of terrestrial food from the overhanging branches.

Masu water in Taiwan – the Chi Chia Wan river.
(Wang Ching Hwa)

Neither fresh-water masu nor amago grow much more than 30 cm (12 in) long. The amago continues to be recognisable by its crimson spots and both races keep their parr marks all their lives. The only exception are the peculiar iwame, which live in a few Honshu rivers, as well as on Kyushu and Shikoku, and are distinguished from other landlocked salmon by never developing any parr marks at all. Some researchers go so far as to give them their own species – *O. iwame* - but most consider them forms of either of the other two races.

There is very little difference in colouration between the sexes of any of the non-migratory forms of salmon, even when they are close to spawning; nor do males develop the aggressive-looking hooked snout and prominent teeth of their sea-going counterparts. Counts of fin rays, scales, and gill rakers usually show little distinction between migratory and non-migratory populations of masu. Very often the two will interbreed unless separated by impassable falls. Then there may be discernible meristic differences between populations, as there are between fish above and below the Akadaki Fall on the Ohata River in northern Honshu. By interbreeding so freely, the different forms would seem to demonstrate closer kinship than, for example, kokanee and sea-going sockeye which rarely mate with each other.

Some of these non-migrants subvert one of the fundamental tenets of Pacific salmon life history by not dying after they have spawned – as strong a physiological link as any with rainbow and cutthroat trout. Even before spawning, the digestive tracts and other internal organs of most salmon have disintegrated to the point of uselessness, but spent masu have been seen feeding, and some scale analysis also supports the contention that non-migratory masu may spawn more than once.

Further north on Honshu, and on Hokkaido, there are no amago, only masu, most of which have more conventional salmonid habits, and head to sea after a single winter in fresh water. Where amago stop, charr start, and Dolly Varden and white-spotted charr share many of the streams with masu, all these fish tending to migrate more in the north of Japan. There are also migratory masu in most of the rivers of the island of Sakhalin, the south-west corner of Kamchatka and up the mainland coast from the Korean peninsula to well beyond Russia's Amur River.

Adult masu arrive back in the river mouth much earlier than other salmon – as early as April in the south and slightly later further north. Their springtime appearance usually coincides with the melting snow and flowering cherry trees, and their Japanese name, *sakura-masu*, means 'cherry trout'. Despite arriving so early, masu are several months away from spawning and still sea-silver with no spots on their bodies or fins. Most of them have only spent a year away at sea and may not weigh more than 1500 g (1 lb), although 2 kg (4 lb) is usual and 5 kg (11 lb) exceptional. Time at sea appears to blur the growth of their scales and it is difficult to decipher how long they have been there. Hokkaido fish only seem to spend a year in the ocean, but Russian masu may be away for two, or even three.

During their first weeks back in fresh water masu rest up in deep pools low down the river. There, a few of them seem to defy the other universal truism of salmon behaviour by continuing to feed – albeit sporadically and not for much longer – and thereby provide further evidence of their close relationship with Pacific trout. The evidence for fresh-water feeding is poorly documented and their food unidentified, but fish in more than one Hokkaido river have shown that they have not abandoned their appetites out at sea.

As the summer progresses, both sexes start to darken, becoming marked red on black or black on red, as if streaked with running paint. Even though they reach the river later,

*Masu salmon in Taiwan –
no Taiwanese salmon reach
the sea.*
(Wang Ching Hwa)

northern populations spawn earlier, perhaps at the end of July, while in Hokkaido they wait until September. On Sakhalin and in other northerly streams, nearly all the spawning fish have spent time at sea, only a few males remaining behind in fresh water. Further south, the proportion of males that shun their seaward migration increases quite strikingly, and down on the northern tip of Honshu nearly 90 per cent of migrating smolts are female. When they return, these survivors of the ocean's dangers are far outnumbered by the stay-at-home males, and on the spawning grounds each large sea-grown female may be attended by several little male acolytes, all scrabbling to fertilise her eggs.

The instincts of newly emerged masu first encourage them into shoals, grouping together over the gravel beds from which they have just emerged. There they begin to feed for themselves, until their shoaling bonds gradually loosen as they grow in size and confidence. Masu never develop into the aggressive, territorial little fish that coho or stream-type chinook become, but they do gradually spread themselves out in faster flowing water, where the food supply is more consistent. The larger stronger fish tend to take up stations at the head of a run, where they have first nip at passing midge larvae and other tiny insects, leaving the weaker fry further back to take whatever is left. Later in the summer, the young masu move downstream, searching for winter refuges beneath the banks of the main rivers or in tributaries which are often warmed by spring water. On sunny winter afternoons they may emerge from their hideaways to take advantage of occasional hatches of insects, and like coho, no masu go to sea until they have spent at least one winter in fresh water, sometimes even two.

In early spring, those yearlings that have reached a length of about 12 cm (5 in) are called to sea, just as the older fish are coming back into fresh water. The smolts pass quickly through the estuary, which is not an important staging post, and once out beyond the river's influence, most of them seem to head north for the comfort of cooler waters in the Sea of Okhotsk. There they concentrate close to the shores of Kamchatka and Sakhalin before moving out into the middle of the sea in September, and south again as it starts to freeze over. Soon afterwards, they begin turning up in nets off the shores of Hokkaido and the Korean peninsula, as they exploit the rich feeding in the Sea of Japan. Sandlance, Japanese pearlsides, anchovies and Atka mackerel are all perfect sized prey for growing masu, as are squid, large shrimps and other floating crustaceans.

Some of the returning masu will be hatchery products, although very few compared to the numbers of chum salmon. Masu are much less abundant than chum, and broodstock is often in short supply, but the main difficulty with rearing masu is that they are only ready for the sea after a year, unlike chum which can be introduced into an estuary after three months or even less. Tipping young masu fry straight into the river once they have begun feeding, or even after a three months' start on an artificial diet, produces very poor rates of returning adults. Much better results come from rearing fish right through to the smolt stage the following year and then stocking them. This is very expensive for the hatchery, especially if it is also rearing chum, and the best compromise is to let the masu go in November and then use the same rearing facilities to prepare chum fry for release in May.

Most hatcheries are involved in ranching operations to some extent, but masu are also produced for repopulating depleted streams, and the comparative successes of different restocking attempts continually emphasise the importance of using broodstock from the same river. Where fish have been brought in from distant rivers to supplement existing wild stocks, the proportion of introduced fry returning as adults has always been very disappointing – showing yet again that a salmon is not just a salmon, a masu is not just a masu, but a fish now fitted specifically for its own river after thousands of generations of natural selection.

11
Pacific salmon ecology

Once ensnared in the monofilament strands of a drift net, salmon become carcasses and figures – slabs of flesh for sale and entries on tables of commercial catches. The lives they lived as members of their species and as strands in a great and intricate web linking mountain trickles to the midst of the Pacific Ocean are ended – prematurely and ingloriously. Their genes are lost to that species for ever, and its future is left in the guts of a statistic of living fish – the spawning escapement – which indicates how many salmon are to be 'allowed' back upstream to breed. These are the fish which human management decides should be spared to die the death that Nature, not man, intends, in order to maximise the number of salmon that can be caught in years to come. This is a death that follows breeding by weeks, even days, and ensures that every salmon is orphaned by the time it hatches. Yet after millions of years of evolutionary refinement, this death has now emerged as giving the next generation the greatest chances of survival.

The most widespread exponents of semelparity – death after only breeding once, and sometimes referred to with splendid scientific irreverence as 'big bang reproduction' – are the insects. Some other fish, as well as salmon, only breed once, like fresh-water eels and most smelts. A few, such as the brook lamprey, never even feed as adults and are as certain to die after they first spawn as any salmon. Most Atlantic salmon are also killed by their efforts to reproduce and only about 5 per cent of Britain's Atlantic salmon live to breed again. However, they die discrete, drawn-out deaths throughout the winter, unlike their Pacific relations which litter the river banks with their stinking carcasses and thicken the water with rotting flesh. Has Nature ever seemed more wasteful to mankind than in raising Pacific salmon to their spawning splendour, and then never allowing them to breed again? Perhaps not, but their very numbers proclaim that somehow the waste is worth it.

All Pacific salmon stop feeding when they leave the sea, except for some early-returning masu whose appetites are only finally suppressed after several weeks in fresh water. Rivers are no more than waterways to breeding grounds. If salmon still had to feed their way upstream very few would ever survive to spawn, either because feeding would use precious time and energy or simply because there is not enough food in the river to sustain them. By shunning the very limited resources of the river and drawing on ocean-gathered energy to fuel their upstream journey, vast numbers of fish find their way far inland, 'The multitudes of this fish are almost inconceivable' wrote William Clark in 1805, after his first encounter with migrating Pacific salmon.

When Lewis and Clark were crossing the Great Divide, only Indian nets dipped into the rivers, salmon swam as far south as Monterey Bay and sockeye runs into the Fraser River were reckoned in tens of millions. Throughout the 20,000 km (12,400 miles) of streams and rivers that drained the Columbia basin, up to sixteen million salmon of all five eastern Pacific species were estimated to spawn. Many of today's salmon runs are sorry shadows of their former selves and some populations have disappeared forever, especially in the south, but amidst the inevitable environmental gloom, there is still much brightness. A combination of the fish's resilience, thoughtful management and perhaps more favourable long-term conditions in the northern Pacific, continues to sustain catches of sockeye from Alaska's Bristol Bay at record levels, and in 1993 twenty-four million sockeye and seventeen million pinks returned to the Fraser, very few of which were artificially bred.

From the moment fish stop eating, they begin to draw on their bodies' reserves. Many pink salmon snap up their last squid while they are still far out at sea, but fish are usually close inshore by the time they finally lose the urge to feed. The upstream migrations of pink and chum salmon can sometimes be measured in metres, pushing them no further than the intertidal waters at the river mouth. More often, though, it is a punishing journey to the redds, and fish are little more than skinfuls of spawn or milt by the time they approach the gravel from which they emerged. Chinook may travel over 3,000 km (1,900 miles) up the Yukon River, right through Alaska and far into Yukon Territory, before reaching their spawning grounds, and the ancestral homes of some stocks of Fraser River sockeye are at least 1,000 km (600 miles) from the sea. Only powerful fish can make long journeys, and salmon travelling far up river have very different genetic constitutions from those that spawn near the estuary. Yet no matter whether they spawn within scent of the sea or far up in highland headwaters, all Pacific salmon are living, rotting corpses by the time they have finished doing so.

Like charr, all salmon show that they are preparing to spawn by changing colour dramatically. The scarlet bodies of thousands of sea-fattened sockeye are one of the most spectacular sights in the natural world. Coho turn a less vivid red and the skins of other species of salmon are usually tinged with pink, but darken so much that they might be different fish from the silver creatures of the ocean they once were. The colour changes in breeding adults, particularly sockeye, result from the movement of carotinid pigments out of the flesh and into the skin and eggs. Once perceived as enhancing the fish's ability to absorb extra oxygen, the adoption of brilliant redness is now thought to increase the chances of successful mating, just as birds take on their finest plumage at breeding time.

Unusually for the fish world, the sex of spawning salmon becomes easily identifiable, often by colour and also by the male's physical changes. Not for nothing is *Oncorhynchus* (hooked jaw) so called, and males of all species also grow prominent teeth. Pinks and sockeye look as though they have been squeezed in a vice, developing humped backs which often protrude far above the surface, the fish seemingly quite oblivious of the fact that almost half their bodies are out of the water. The humps may grow from the production of albyminoids, by-products from the conversion of body reserves into energy, which in females are diverted to the development of their eggs.

At the beginning of their migrations upstream, salmon start absorbing their scales; their skins also thicken and secrete a protective layer of mucus which helps prevent invasions of fungus and bacteria. As they struggle into the current, being pounded against rocks and each other, wriggling up through shallows often scarcely deep enough to swim in, and throwing themselves at waterfalls time after time, their bodies begin to show the strains of migration. Cuts become infected, warming water allows in fungal infections, and as they approach the end of their journey, the fish seem driven by an even greater desperation that will only allow them to stop when they reach their home stream, or die

trying. Frayed fins, or simply stubs where fins once were, and pale patches of bare flesh or fungus start to testify to the trials of their journeys. Stocks of fat and protein which fired their struggles have also had to fuel the development of eggs and milt, and even internal organs begin to break down and make their own contribution to the fast dwindling pool of energy that salmon still need for breeding. By the time a salmon starts to spawn, over 70 per cent of its body is water.

On their way up the river, each fish is driven by its own private urges, brought together with its fellows by the parallel workings of a million internal clocks, all similarly primed to respond to changes in day length, water flow or temperature. Together they edge their way upstream, seeking out the slower flowing channels of the river, and pausing to rest between frantic bursts through stronger currents. Held in shoals by the common traits of their species they seem impelled by a single mind as they thread upstream towards their destination. Gradually shoals may fragment as one group after another scents its home tributary and leaves the main stream, and by the time the salmon reach their spawning grounds, each one is its own fish, no longer one of a school of others but a salmon with only its destiny left to fulfil. Other fish have ceased to be fellow travellers, and now males

Male (top) and female sockeye, before being returned to the water.
(Andrew Hendry)

see males as potential rivals and females as potential mates. From the peaceful coexistence of massed individuals, united by a common compulsion, emerges a river full of snapping, lunging creatures whose urge to reproduce has suppressed even the urge to survive.

Crowded salmon spawning grounds are a cauldron of continual aggression interspersed with those occasional moments of passion that secure the species' future. Where the water is scarcely deep enough to cover their backs, and their dorsal fins protrude like the tips of aquatic plants, the sense of frenzy is heightened by the continual sound of splashing fish chasing one another round the shallows. No fish, it seems, can rest easily. Females must compete with one another for nest sites, and their attacks on intruding females are sometimes lethally vicious. Once a male has secured a mate he must continue repelling the challenges of other, unattached males, sometimes seizing them in his jaws just in front of their tails where their bodies are narrowest. Other males, which cannot find females, roam the spawning grounds in the hope of promoting their roles from subordinate (satellite) to dominant (alpha) males by edging established males away from the sides of their mates. And to add further to the confusion, jacks may be hanging around, having spent less time than other males at sea and swum easily back through the mesh of nets designed for bigger fish. A few salmon, particularly sockeye and masu, spawn without ever leaving the river, and these smaller residuals also lurk on the fringes of the redds, aggravating older males and ready to sneak in and add their genes to the pool. At the same time, trout or charr may be gently finning in the current, awaiting the chance to gobble up salmon eggs before the female has time to bury them.

There is no rest for any fish on the redds, and even after they have spawned males may head off in search of other mates. Any female still carrying unshed eggs will feel urged to dig out a further nest, usually about 30 cm (12 in) in front of the previous one. And when all her eggs are laid and death may be only days away, the female still guards her nests against the later diggings of other salmon in search of spawning space, until finally drained of the strength to do so any longer.

Spawning arenas appear astonishingly chaotic when masses of fish are jostling one another on small patches of pebbles. If space is really scarce, smaller fish may be squeezed downstream onto less perfect breeding grounds, where the gravel is too fine or the water too shallow. Otherwise they may have to override the precision of their homing instincts and force their way far upstream of their own birthplace in search of somewhere new to breed. However great the confusion seems, strong fish still secure prime territories and manage to space out their redds to make the most of the crowded gravel beds. Even in peak years, when spawning seems particularly haphazard, fertilisation on good redds is still astonishingly successful and seldom far off 100 per cent. The real dangers from overcrowding come when salmon rush in after the first wave has spawned, or a second run arrives once all the earlier spawners are dead, and the late arrivals then dig up existing nests.

Ignoring for a moment the destructive influences of humankind on salmon populations, if the success of a species is counted in numbers, then Pacific salmon are now spectacularly successful. Most species are continually adapting to changes in the environment and every step on their evolutionary path serves to enhance their chances of survival. The Pacific salmon, which all die after spawning, are more recently evolved than their trout relatives, for which death is less inevitable. This in itself suggests that, defying all rational thought, the strategy of spawning only once is an improvement on being able to do so more often. Many sea-going brown and rainbow trout breed several times, and on the numbers scale of success, are not doing nearly as well as Pacific salmon; nor are their Atlantic cousins. The very key to the success of their lives seems to lie in death.

A million large sockeye may weigh 3 million kg (3,000 tonnes) on returning to the estuary. When they left as smolts, they only weighed about 10 g each and so nearly all their collective 3,000 tonnes has been gathered up in the ocean. A salmon may use up over a third of its body energy in reaching its birthplace, but by the time it dies a quarter of this energy is still left in the carcass. As this decays, nutrients are gradually released into the river, collectively effecting a vast transfer of the sea's resources to the fresh-water environment. Step by step, nitrates and phosphates work their way back up the food pyramid, somewhere in the middle of which, the next year, will be the growing salmon fry. So by giving their bodies back to the river that raised them, the parents help more of their young to survive.

The nourishment of the next generation is half a year and several steps on the food pyramid away from the rotting corpse of an ocean-grown salmon. Many other creatures benefit more directly from the flesh, but only a few actually take live fish out of fresh water. Ospreys and bald eagles may just be able to flap off with a fully grown pink salmon in their talons, but other mature salmon are usually too heavy for even the magnificent Stellers sea eagles to lift – and these are twice the size of the bald eagles whose place they take over on the shores of the western Pacific. Human fishing pressure also eases off in fresh water and there is no danger from drift nets or trolling boats, only from Indian subsistence fisheries and sportsmen. River otters take a few fish, so do seals in the fresh waters of Lake Iliamna, but bears, especially brown (grizzly) bears, can play havoc with running salmon which are forced to hold up below waterfalls or to flap their way through the shallows. Although salmon may be much harder to capture when they are still strong and not long out of the sea, they repay bears the extra effort it takes to catch them with much more goodness in their flesh; and best of all, half the salmon are then full of eggs. Once salmon have reached their spawning grounds they are easily scooped out of the

Dead sockeye left in a tangle of branches by falling water levels.
(Natalie Fobes)

Grizzly bear feasting on a fresh-run sockeye at Brooks Falls.
(Greg Syverson)

shallows, and even more so when they are spent – although by then they are scarcely worth the energy it takes to swipe them out of the water.

The best-known bears in the world catch sockeye salmon at the Brooks Falls in southwestern Alaska. The most spectacular concentration is not far away on the McNeil River where over fifty brown bears can be seen together, gathered round a staggered series of shallow falls, fishing for chum. Bears arriving at the McNeil River in midsummer are often gaunt and ragged, not long out of their dens, and may add a quarter to their body weight after feasting incessantly on fish for over a month. They are usually solitary creatures, but the fishing is so good and the fish so nutritious that they are prepared to tolerate the stresses of direct and sometimes confrontational competition. The best fishing stations, where most salmon can be caught with least effort, are occupied by the strongest, most dominant bears at the top of the ursine hierarchy. Others have to settle for less favourable positions and adapt their fishing techniques to suit the water.

Salmon are often attracted by the less powerful current in the shallows at the river's edges, where they are easily pinned by a bear's great paws. The waterfall pools are far too turbulent for a bear to see below the surface; there it stands motionless in the foam, feeling for salmon with its feet to trap them on the river bed, before dipping down and emerging with a fish in its mouth like a retriever with a duck. In deeper pools bears sometimes behave almost like seals, completely disappearing to pursue fish under water, while down at the tail younger ones are trampling around, clumsily chasing fish up and down the shallows. On the Brooks River, salmon trying to leap falls rather than swim them may be snapped straight out of the air.

Once it has a salmon in its mouth, a bear usually carries its catch protectively ashore, or onto a sand bar, there to be eaten in whatever peace the other bears allow. Older stronger bears sometimes reach a stage when they never bother to fish for themselves at all and instead simply pinch salmon off others. Hungry bears gnaw most of the flesh off the first fish they catch, but as summer moves on they become more choosy, often deftly slitting open the salmon with tooth or claw and just removing the eggs. When salmon are close to spawning their eggs become detached from the membranous sac, and then bears may simply be able to squeeze the loose eggs out of a fish without even opening it up. Allowing instinct to dominate appetite, one bear at McNeil Falls caught ninety-one fish in a day, most of which it left uneaten.

Not much fat or protein is left in a spawned-out salmon, and still less once it is dead, but there is enough goodness to turn the heads of true terrestrial predators towards this annual bounty. In the autumn, even if they are not preparing to hibernate, mammals face a bare winter landscape thickly covered in snow, and for several months food of any kind is hard to find. Black and brown bears both eat dead fish, although with less enthusiasm than they show for live ones, perhaps just nipping out the fat-rich brain, and by the time the last spawners are dead, most bears have retreated into their dens. Racoons and river otters are also avid eaters of fish flesh, even when it has begun to rot. Like bears, they are able to retrieve salmon bodies from the water, leaving the remains on the bank for skunks, coyotes, weasels, wolves and mink. The pecking order also gives mice, shrews and Douglas squirrels their share. Blacktail deer may occasionally shelve their vegetarian instincts to nibble at the stranded remains, and in New Zealand even cattle are said to pick at the decaying carcasses of chinook (quinnat).

Like the other members of their genus, bald eagles are actually much more dependent on carrion than on live fish. They are also local migrants and can move from the scene of one salmon spawning frenzy to another, exploiting the different timing of the fish's runs. The most spectacular concentration of eagles in the world collects together in midwinter in the Chilkat Valley of south-eastern Alaska, where a late run of up to 500,000 chum salmon breed in the river's upper reaches. Warm springs well up and keep the water flowing all through the winter, attracting up to 3,500 birds which gather there to feast off the spawned-out remains of dead and dying fish. From the middle of October, when the first eagles flap onto the bare branches of the large black cottonwoods of the Bald Eagle Council Grounds, as the Indians call them, they are served with a continuous supply of salmon right up until January. And even then, when all the salmon have died and left the next generation safely buried in the gravel of the Chilkat River, enough frozen carcasses are slowly thawing on the banks for resident breeding birds to peck away at all through the winter.

With a 2 m (7 ft) wingspan, Stellers sea eagles dwarf their American relatives, and groups of these majestic black and white birds often congregate round salmon spawning grounds in Japan and on the Kamchatka peninsula. In northern Kamchatka, rivers freeze solid and lakes ice over, locking in their piscine food supplies and pushing a thousand sea eagles down south to Kuril Lake, where up to eight million sockeye return to breed each year. Warm springs well up all over this volcanic wasteland, keeping the streams and lake ice-free all year, and stretching the salmon's breeding season right through from July to March. Shoal after shoal surges onto the choicest redds, and both white-tailed and golden

Bald eagle on a chum carcass.
(Natalie Fobes)

eagles, as well as many other species of birds, also join in the orgy of overindulgence.

Spawning salmon provide a nutritional windfall for many other birds, and when rotting carcasses are scattered over gravel bars and mud banks, and caught up in the roots and branches of fallen trees, it often seems surprising that more of them are not joining in the feast. Some glaucous-winged gulls nest far inland and peck away at the corpses, often joined by others which have made their way up from the coast. Otherwise it is the resident birds which seem to make the most of the dead fish, particularly the scavenging corvids; crows, ravens, magpies and Stellers and grey jays may all be lured down from their coniferous perches by the stinking remains of salmon. Red-tailed hawks are common all through North America and have their share of fish flesh, as do dippers, winter wrens, woodpeckers and even tits.

Falling water levels only strand some of the dead fish, and many of the spawned-out corpses never leave their element. The attendant rainbow trout, Arctic charr or Dolly Varden that followed the breeding salmon up to the redds lunge at pieces of rotting flesh, but these morsels are so devoid of goodness that they may be eaten as much for the maggots in them as for the remaining shreds of protein. Meanwhile, worms, fungi and bacteria invade the decaying fish, slowly breaking them down into basic nutrients to be recycled back into the base of the food pyramid.

Single, unburied eggs are the main attraction for the hosts of smaller fish which move up with salmon to their breeding grounds. Most sockeye spawn in lake inflows, and may spend two or three weeks at the inflow mouth until they are finally drawn towards the redds, attracting legions of camp followers while they wait. Once the sockeye begin their move, behind them, almost snapping at their tails, come loose groups of trout and charr, waiting to suck up eggs that female salmon fail to bury properly or which later spawners expose by their own excavations. As salmon start to dig their nests, they displace insect larvae and other invertebrates, giving these smaller fish an appetiser before the eggs appear. Arctic charr, bull charr and Dolly Varden are enthusiastic eaters of both salmon eggs and fry. At one time Dolly Varden's tails earned a bounty, so predacious were they thought to be, but now it seems they confine their egg eating to loose or partly buried eggs which would never have hatched anyway. The eggs that gulls bob down below the surface to retrieve, or goldeneye and other diving ducks manage to harvest off the bottom, or dippers find in their ungainly walk along the river bed, are also unburied ones, part of the huge expendable surplus that ensures the survival of the few. Only sculpins can really get at well covered eggs which might otherwise have hatched, and may cause serious damage by doing so. Prickly sculpins and torrent sculpins are often common on salmon redds, and can wriggle their way in among larger gravel to gorge on deeply buried eggs without even emerging from the stones between mouthfuls.

Viewed from out of the water, the efforts of spawning salmon look haphazard in the extreme, but fertilisation is deceptively efficient. Eggs and milt are almost always discharged simultaneously – as they have to be for successful fertilisation – and the huge numbers of sperm ejected by each male usually ensure that at least one reaches almost every egg before it closes up, even if these are not all then safely buried. Thereafter, the activities of sculpins or subsequent spawners, sand and silt in the nest, extremes of temperature and floods or droughts may all take their toll, gradually eroding away at the number which eventually hatch – but by then the fish that laid and fertilised the eggs are all dead.

As with all their close relatives, water temperature controls how long the eggs of Pacific salmon take to hatch, as well as the time between hatching and the tiny alevin emerging from the gravel. Eggs take longer to hatch in colder water, and each maturing salmon's inherited biological clock is set to take this into account. Spawning is usually earlier in more northerly latitudes and the timing can be particularly delicate. If eggs hatch too soon, then fry may emerge before the ice has melted and spring has brought on that burst of minute aquatic life which is so crucial to early survival once their in-built food supplies are exhausted. The fry also risk being washed away by spring thaws, but against that those that do survive will grow bigger than later hatching fish, and this may critically tilt the scales in favour of the early emergers surviving through the summer. Salmon spawning in warmer stretches of water, either close to springs or lower downstream, do so later than those in colder reaches. Yet, while spawning may be staggered over several months, depending on the thermal regimes in specific streams, the influence of temperature on egg development ensures that the next generation's emergence from the gravel is compressed into a much shorter period.

By the end of the year, almost all adult salmon are dead. Their bodies are being recycled back into the rivers and lakes that succoured them in the early days of their lives.

The young lie buried in the stream bed, perhaps in the very same stretch of water from which their parents themselves emerged, and thousands of generations before them. The egg-eating predators that moved up behind the salmon have retreated from the streams back to the dark ice-covered security of their lakes, where most of the previous year's sockeye hatch are also spending the winter. In larger rivers chinook fry have moved away from their summer territories into backwaters on the edge of the current. Coho have sought out ponds and tributaries where they rest quietly until the spring before answering the call of the ocean. Of young pink or chum salmon there is no trace – they have all gone to sea. There fish are generally much less affected by dropping temperatures and shorter days, and can continue feeding all through the winter, but rarely so successfully that the season leaves no sign of its passing on their scales.

The different species of Pacific salmon are perhaps most distinguished from one another by their behaviour between emerging from the gravel and reaching the sea. Even within a single species, the pattern of downstream migrations can be very different. The natural inclinations of some chinook send them down to sea almost as fast as chum fry; those of others, even from the same river, urge them to stay behind for a year or more. Each spring, the water prepares to receive the next generation and no suitable corner of river, lake or estuary remains unexploited in the search for food and space to live. There is little room near the redds for all the millions of new-born fish, and many of them have scarcely absorbed their yolk sacs before setting out to chase their instincts down the current.

In the spring of 1991, 380 million sockeye fry are estimated to have emerged from the 12 km (7 miles) of gravel between Adams and Shuswap Lakes, in that most famous of the Fraser's tributaries, the Lower Adams River. The previous autumn, 2.6 million sockeye had returned there to spawn - not unusual numbers for the peaks which mark their four-year cycles. In early September, chinook salmon had also arrived to breed in the deeper runs, and their hollow carcasses already littered the river banks by the time the main run of sockeye appeared. Rainbow trout were excavating their own nests among the smaller stones, and bull charr represented *Salvelinus* on the redds. To complete the cast of salmonids on this great gravel stage, a few coho finally arrived in early November when the leaves had all fallen off the trees and the water was then almost deserted. During the winter, hundreds of millions of young fish were developing in the spaces between the stones. As it is every fourth year, the potential for chaotic and lethal overcrowding the following spring was immense, and could only be avoided by the sockeye fry heading straight down to Shuswap Lake after emerging.

Both emergence from the gravel and the first tentative downstream drifts are usually shrouded by the dark of a moonless night. In sub-Arctic latitudes where fish have to wait for the ice to break up before they begin to move away, twilight may be the best cover they can expect. For pink and chum salmon the next stop is the estuary, and while the dense shoals of fry may have to feed on the way, they do not linger long enough to affect the fresh-water food supplies other fish depend on for survival. Newly emerged sockeye head quickly down to the lake that for most of them is to be their nursery for at least the next twelve months, although for those born in lake outflows, their first journey must be an upstream one. Young chinook nearly all start off downstream too, but thereafter their behaviour varies widely, some populations pressing on down to the estuary, while others gradually slow their seaward journey and then linger in the river for weeks, months or even a year or more. Quite what influences their choice of option is unclear, but competition from coho may do so. Coho behave much more like trout or even Atlantic

Chinook carcasses on the Lower Adams River, British Columbia. (Author)

salmon, spacing themselves out both upstream and downstream of their birthplace and quickly establishing territories.

Salmon and their relatives owe much of their success to the catholic feeding habits, which let them live with equal ease in sea, lake or river at different stages in their lives. They are all carnivores, but beyond that, what young fish eat depends on little more than what there is and what they are big enough to swallow. Sockeye begin feeding round the lake edges where insect life is rich, and newly arrived fry snap up the larvae or pupae of chironomids and other midges, as well as immature stoneflies, mayflies and caddis. In streams and rivers, coho and chinook start to claim territories or line up along the edge of the current that serves them up with similar fare as well as a supply of adult insects. Shoals of downstream-drifting pink and chum fry search out morsels of food as they journey towards the sea. Later in the summer, young sockeye tend to move away from the lake edge, out to where insect life is less plentiful but feeding is safer, and zooplankton, particularly water fleas *(Daphnia)* and copepod crustaceans (Cyclops), hang suspended in the open water. In energy terms, it makes most sense for a predator to choose the biggest prey it can swallow; large fry take adult insects and by the following year young coho should be able to seize small fishes.

Eat or be eaten is the law by which all animals live, except the ultimate predators in their environments, and the surplus of young salmon is so huge that many must die for the few to survive. But their deaths are seldom truly wasted, and the ocean-gathered nutrients reaching fresh water from the bodies of their parents filter still further up the food pyramid to the assortment of creatures which prey on young fish. All round the rim of the northern Pacific, salmon fry play a central role as converters of invertebrate life into the fish flesh that then sustains piscivorous predators. Many such predators depend for their own survival on the salmon's successful spawning and may be closely related to their prey – often only a species away from being cannibals. Hungry trout, salmon or charr will seldom spurn the chance to feast off smaller fish, and by doing so grow far larger, far faster than they ever would have done on a diet of fresh-water invertebrates. Catching a sockeye fry is a lot less effort for a cutthroat trout than snapping up the thousand midge larvae which weigh about the same.

Because pink and chum fry rush to the sea as fast as the current will carry them, they are much less exposed to fresh-water predators than other salmon, but are still likely to meet charr somewhere along their downstream way. Dolly Varden and Arctic charr are voracious consumers of young fish. They are also very alike, and if Dolly Varden are still branded as the most predatory charr, it is only because they are very often found in the lower reaches of salmon rivers as well as in more southerly latitudes where the river life is better researched. Bull charr have only recently been recognised as their own species and are probably the most destructive predators of all, but they are generally distributed further inland than most salmon spawn.

Cutthroat and rainbow trout seem less partial to young pink or chum fry, although some lake-living rainbows depend on young sockeye to see them through the summer. In the Adams River, with its four-year cycles, the trout population is held in check by the lean years between the peaks. When there are fewer salmon fry, predators may have a much greater proportionate impact on their prey than they do in peak years, but even in these comparatively lean years the fry surplus may still be so large that in fact predator numbers vary very little. Predators can only afford to rely on young pink salmon for their survival in rivers without distinctive dominant-/off-year cycles, and when the Pacific fish was introduced into the Kola Peninsula in northern Russia, both sea trout and Atlantic salmon quickly developed a taste for the new-found fry.

Lingering much longer in fresh water than pink and chum salmon puts coho and chinook at much greater risk of being eaten by other salmonids, but equally this means they grow large enough to make meals of smaller fish. Coho are perhaps the most serious of all pink and chum fry predators, and are also known to eat young chinook and sockeye, and even their own kind. Masu spend at least a year in fresh water as well – sometimes a lifetime – and they too can make destructive forays into shoals of newly hatched fish in the few Japanese rivers where there are still wild populations of other species of salmon.

Young salmon which stay on in still waters face attacks from many other predatory fish besides their immediate relatives. Most such salmon are sockeye, but juveniles of other species often have to pass through lakes or reservoirs on their way downstream, past the massed ranks of larger fish waiting at inflows and outflows for the naive young migrants. Lake charr grow huge, very slowly, without ever going to sea, on a largely piscivorous diet, and will certainly not ignore the bonanza of juvenile sockeye in the Alaskan lakes where the two cohabit. Sheefish (inconnu) are whitefish and so more distantly related to salmon than lake charr are (see Chapter 1). They grow faster than any other Arctic fresh-water fish, and in the Yukon River, near their southern limits, lie in wait to ambush young chum and chinook. Mountain whitefish have also sometimes been found with fry in their stomachs, even though they are largely bottom feeders.

Also along the Pacific slope of western Canada and America, from the Columbia basin to the north of British Columbia, live northern squawfish (bigmouth minnows), probably the most destructive of all the young salmon's fresh-water predators. They are still-water fish and in the sockeye's nursery lakes tend to move out into the open water and live off young salmon throughout the winter. Their numbers have exploded in the chain of dam-

Sockeye smolts heading
downstream.
(Greg Ruggerone)

created reservoirs that is now the lower Columbia River, adding yet another hazard to the smolts' migrations (see Chapter 12). White sturgeon also lurk on the bottom of the Columbia River, sometimes living as long as humans and weighing up to 500 kg (1,100 lb); salmon smolts are often found in their stomachs, although hydroelectric turbines might well have killed many of these young fish first.

Having hundreds of siblings makes life fiercely competitive for young salmonids from the moment they emerge. The absence of interspecific competition is a luxury naturally granted only to fish which exploit environments so inhospitable or inaccessible that others either cannot survive in them or have never reached them. Pacific salmon move easily from fresh to salt water and back again, and must be able to feed off whatever the lake, river or sea has to offer. They are generalists not specialists in their exploitation of the world's waters, and as long as these are cool and clean enough they can usually survive.

Somewhat peversely, however, the salmon pay a high price for the flexibility, which itself is so critical to their success. This is to meet continual competition from other species of fish, as well as from their own kind. Almost everywhere a salmon swims, other members of the Salmonidae family are living lives that coincide in some way with its own, as are many other different fish with more specialised environmental requirements. At every stage in its growth, a salmon will find other fish chasing after the same morsels of food as itself. Yet so tangled is the web of aquatic interrelationships that the roles of competitor, predator or prey are continually shifting. And one inevitable consequence of competition is that a fish's closest competitors are nearly always also its own predators' alternative prey.

Pygmy whitefish, pond smelts and three- and ninc-spined sticklebacks all chase the same invertebrates as young salmon. Three-spined sticklebacks may even outnumber sockeye fry in nursery lakes, and are often the only other small fish feeding on open-water plankton. Yet at the same time as they are competing with young salmon, all these species also take the pressure off the sockeye by providing trout and charr with an alternative source of food. Sockeye fry may even join shoals of sticklebacks to try and evade attack by young coho. Masu grow large enough in fresh water to catch and swallow the pond smelts with which they competed as juveniles, and by the time many coho leave fresh water they are eating sticklebacks. Sculpins feast on salmon eggs and fry, but the planktonic larvae of coast range sculpins make nutritious feeding for young sockeye. Only their leaving fresh water just as they are becoming effective predators of other fish prevents salmon from balancing the scales and pursuing the young of those fish that once pursued them.

Birds and mammals invade the aquatic world too, and take their share of young salmon, but they make far less impact on the huge surplus than fish do. Coho can be especially vulnerable to the falling water levels of summer; these shrink the gentle riffles that were perfect for their first territories to ever smaller pools where they can be easily caught by dippers, crows and even American robins. To see them into the spring, river otters depend on larger coho juveniles which they chase under the ice of beaver ponds and small streams. They are the only serious fresh-water predator to take salmon fry migrating down the river and mature fish coming up. Belted kingfishers are more natural avian fishers; like most kingfishers they usually fish from a perch and this confines them to feeding close to the bank, although not as close as great blue herons, which can only stalk the shallows on foot.

Much more effective fish catchers are common and hooded mergansers. These can chase and swallow fish under water, and with their serrated beaks are quite able to catch salmon smolts as well as tiny newly emerged fry. They have large broods, and if most of the young survive the summer, a family can easily clear its home pools of young salmon. Glaucous-winged gulls are often found far inland and will take small fry, as well as loose eggs and bits of rotting flesh. Nearer the sea they may be joined by Bonaparte's and short-billed gulls and Arctic terns, and a shoal of smolts caught out in daylight close to the estuary may be attacked by birds from above and fish from below.

If the water flows quietly, young migrating salmon turn and swim downstream, noses to the sea, but in faster, more turbulent stretches of river they often face back into the current for better control and let it carry them away at its own speed. Not only do chum and pink fry reach the estuary far sooner than other salmon, they also ease into life at sea with much less stress, perhaps because they are less well adapted to fresh water in the first place. The young of both species are similarly programmed to set off downstream as soon as they emerge, and only the date when they do so and the length of their river journey affect the time of their arrival. Within the same species larger individuals, whose lower surface area to body volume ratio buffers them better against water loss, are able to adapt to salt water much more efficiently than smaller ones. Larger fish are also less likely to end up in a predator's jaws.

For other species of salmon, preparation for life at sea involves more dramatic, hormone-induced changes. These begin when the young fish are still far away from the influence of salt water, slowly streamlining their bodies and silvering over the finger marks on their flanks. Such changes may prompt every fry in a river to head to sea after a year, while in other rivers no fish prepares to leave fresh water until after its second winter. Even more confusingly, salmon from the same population may start becoming smolts at

different ages. Like all those other salmonids whose migratory behaviour is so variable, Pacific salmon appear to be urged to turn seawards by a combination of both environmental and genetic influences (see Chapter 2). The genetic constitutions of stream- and ocean-type chinook are quite distinct, indicating that their inclination to migrate at a specific age may be passed on from one generation to the next. Yet before their bodies will answer the call of the genes, it seems that young salmon must reach a minimum size by a particular time of year – perhaps related to day length, water temperature, decreased water flow or a combination of these – and if they miss the break that year, they must then wait until the next. In the shorter, more northerly summers the window of opportunity to head to sea seems to open only briefly each year. Coho or chinook smolts in Alaska are therefore invariably older than those from California, where the window stays open for longer and fish grow much faster in the extended feeding season and warmer water.

Occasionally, even Pacific salmon, despite their ancestral affinity with the sea, stay on in lakes or rivers for so long that maturity overtakes them before smolting does. Maturity and seaward migration are in some ways mutually exclusive in that approaching maturity suppresses the migratory inclinations of any salmon still left behind in fresh water. Most pink salmon breed so close to the sea, and migrate so soon after emerging, that there is no

Gulls feeding on sockeye smolts in Alaska.
(Greg Syverson)

possibility of their ignoring its call. Newly hatched chum are also so powerfully programmed to head downstream that residuals are unknown, but sockeye, especially towards their southern limits, quite often mature in their nursery lakes. Not to be confused with the non-migratory kokanee, these residuals are usually males, larger as juveniles than the rest of their year class and providing yet another example of the species' flexibility. They are most likely the founders of the stocks of fresh-water kokanee, which slowly evolved their distinctive behaviour in one lake after another, and remain reproductively isolated from sea-going sockeye by continuing to breed with fish of their own size. If, one day, landslides block their waterways to the estuary, or the earth gets so much warmer that some sockeye stocks can no longer reach the sea, then only by maturing in fresh water will they be able to survive.

Estuaries are complex environments where the mixing of fresh and salt water is affected by varying combinations of tide, wind, current and temperature. The river tends to form an upper fresh layer, separated to varying extents from the sea water below by a brackish zone in between. As they leave pure fresh water salmon smolts may congregate near the surface, clinging to its freshness in schools of similarly-sized fish – pinks, chum and even ocean-type chinook often mixing together. Early arrivals tend to spend longer in the shallows, treating the estuary more as a home than simply a staging post on their seaward journey. The ocean-type chinook, which head quickly downstream after emerging, may spend several months there, moving up on the high tide to feed over the grass and marshland, and then being drawn back into the muddy creeks.

As well as introducing river-reared fish to the chemistry of salt water, estuaries serve as rich feeding grounds where smolts can gain strength and size before taking on the dangers of the open sea. Both hatching and downstream migration are timed quite independently of conditions in the estuary, and the smolts' arrival has evolved to coincide with the usual springtime burst of marine life which warming water and longer days bring. Shoals of tiny fish are swept around by tides and currents that also carry countless flecks of marine plankton – crab larvae, shrimps and masses of other crustacea. These are the smolts' first taste of the rich diet of the open ocean that is to sustain coho jacks for the next six months of their lives, and big female chinook from the Yukon River for the next six years.

There may be chinook smolts in an estuary at almost any time of year, so staggered are their migrations and the length of their fresh-water stay. The young of other species behave more consistently, and by midsummer – even earlier further south – most of them have headed out to sea. How long smolts remain in the estuary often depends on how large they are. Bigger fish can better escape predators and are in less danger out at sea than smaller ones, so coho and sockeye, which are at least a year old when they reach the estuary, spend very little time there. Coho yearlings are already large enough to feed off fish and can devastate shoals of pink and chum fry, darting in among the smaller fish, whose instincts are to bunch still tighter together in the face of danger. Sea-going cutthroat may be even more destructive, usually arriving at the estuary just before the salmon, and making up for their winter's starvation with a vengeance.

Despite the danger of attacks by larger predatory fish, the estuary is a generally comfortable environment for young salmon. It provides rich supplies of seafood, as well as familiar fresh-water insects which the river still carries down to the smolts. Salmon shoals are not an irresistible temptation to sea-going Dolly Varden, whose predatory attentions are often diverted by sandlances and capelin. Birds – different kinds of terns, gulls, ducks and divers – may take their share of small fish, but are seldom condemned for making serious inroads into salmon numbers. The beluga (white) whales that move into the river mouths of Bristol Bay are attracted far more by the chance to feast on mature sockeye returning to spawn than on little smolts heading out to sea. This estuarine limbo is perfect for huge numbers of small fish, but if salmon are to grow they need to forsake its security and search out larger prey, and this means moving out into open water away from the shore.

Most Pacific salmon spend about two thirds of their lives in the ocean – coho nearer half. This is a time which, when reduced to its bare evolutionary bones, seems designed to maximise the number of eggs produced by each female at the end of her life, and perhaps also to give males and females the strength and size to mate successfully. Just as the length of the fresh-water phase in salmon's lives varies between and within species, so does time spent at sea, although it can be relatively constant for particular stocks of salmon such as the Adams River sockeye which nearly all spend one winter in fresh water and two at sea (a 1.2 cycle).

As species, only pink salmon live really predictable lives, the young bolting down to the estuary straight after emerging, and returning there eighteen months later, ready to complete their two-year spans. Coho seldom spend more than a year and a half (one winter) at sea either, nor do Japanese masu. The marine sojourns of sockeye, chum and particularly chinook are much less consistent, but all salmon go to sea to grow as fast as they can. The strategy of their species largely measures success in size, and so they set out to gather goodness from the sea, joining great circular currents created by the outlines of the Pacific rim, or swimming up and down the coastline in continual search of less pelagic prey.

The ocean itself can be unreliable. Long regarded as a stable boundless source of food for sea-going salmonids and all the other creatures living there, it is now seen to be susceptible to the pressures of great climatic events, hatchery overproduction and overexploitation. Climate changes bring variations in currents, temperature and atmospheric pressure which touch the lives of the very smallest marine organisms at the bottom of the food pyramid, and so, ultimately, affect every other animal further up it. Particularly at their southerly limits, young coho and chinook are critically dependent on great upwellings of cool food-rich water brought on by complex combinations of winds and currents.

In most years, cold, sub-Arctic water is pushed far down into the warm California Current, infusing it with oxygen and bringing up a nutritious and distinctive mix of northern zooplankton from the ocean depths that gives young salmon precious nourishment at a critical time of their lives. Occasionally, these cool fronts press straight into the great warm curtain of El Niño, and the rich convergence zone is pushed far to the north. Sweeping up the coast of South America, El Niño lays a mantle of tepid impoverished water all up the west coast of America, which can have a devastating affect on salmon numbers and catches. Upwellings are suppressed, the salmon's thermal limits are shifted northwards and newly arrived smolts, as well as older fish, may struggle to find enough food to survive. While salmon are becoming stressed in water warmer than they prefer, Pacific mackerel are granted a temporary extension of their range and probe their way up the coast from California to gorge on smolts or to compete with older salmon for other small prey fish.

Global warming – if it exists as a true long-term phenomenon, not just a temporary aberration – could be pushing isotherms imperceptibly northwards. Successive generations of salmon may find the 12°C thermal contour, which generally marks their southern oceanic limits, and in winter runs along a line of about 40°N, gradually

An Arctic tern brings a salmon smolt to its young.
(Andrew Hendry)

retreating towards the Arctic. Salmon are not only opportunistic, they are also wonderfully adaptable, and if they must adapt their behaviour, and even their form or physiology, then eventually they will. For now, though, there are still distinct patterns to their marine migrations, shaped and altered throughout their evolutionary histories in response to seasonal changes in the water's temperature and the outline of the ocean. The distinctive behaviour of its own species most influences the course of a salmon's ocean odyssey, although hardly more than the location of the river from which it enters the sea.

Charr hardly ever overwinter at sea – their metabolisms seem ill suited to spending more than a few months in salt water. This restricts them to feeding close inshore, sometimes fattening almost unnaturally fast in their first weeks down from the river. Cutthroat trout seem reluctant to travel much beyond the influence of the estuary, and despite their appellation, ocean-type chinook seldom stray far from the shore either. Some coho are also unwilling to join the great oceanic merry-go-round that the true wanderers follow, and confine themselves to moving up and down the coast. How far both coho and pink salmon travel at sea must be influenced by their spending less time there than other salmon, although pinks seem to fill their eighteen months with one great oceanic circuit. The sockeye's marine migrations once made them frighteningly vulnerable to deep-water drift nets, but thankfully these are currently no longer a threat, and whether for this or other reasons, sockeye have responded with spectacular increases in their numbers.

Steam-type chinook and steelhead are the greatest seafarers, the trout demonstrating how distinct they are from true salmon by occasionally reaching the sea again after spawning once, twice and very rarely even three times.

A fish's basic migratory inclinations are inherited, but are often tempered by environmental variables like water temperature and abundance of prey. Evidence of the temperatures salmon prefer is confusing and even contradictory. What is certain is that no salmon can tolerate temperatures below 0.8°C because their blood then freezes, although sockeye and chum both seem to be able to survive when the water is down at 1°C, and pinks at 3°C. Pinks and chum from along the Alaskan and Russian Arctic coastline must move quickly southwards through the Bering Straits, away from the mouth of their natal rivers, where the sea is much too cold for them to live through the winter.

Of all the Pacific salmon, coho and chinook probably prefer warmer water than any others, between 5°C and 9°C. Chum seem to tolerate much the widest thermal range. Chum from Hokkaido or chinook from the Sacramento River system, where conditions are already marginal, move northwards as soon as they reach the open water towards the comfort and better feeding in cooler seas. Fish are not always able to follow their inclinations, though. Oregon coho, which turn north on reaching the sea, often end up being pushed south of their river mouths by the spring currents that flow faster than the fish can swim. Later in the summer the current slackens, and having grown stronger, the young salmon can then head where their instincts urge them.

The right turn that most southern smolts make when they leave American rivers starts many of them on the huge counterclockwise roundabouts created by the currents in the Gulf of Alaska and the Bering Sea. Eventually, any salmon unwilling to feed and fatten off the continental coasts set off on a lap of the ocean that takes about a year before bringing them back where they began. Bristol Bay sockeye follow more complex routes, first turning left and south through gaps between the Aleutian Islands, and then making a series of much less distinct circuits. Kamchatka sockeye and chum also set off southwards, and then mostly head north to summer in the Bering Sea before heading back south again in the winter. The migrations of Asian pink salmon are much more distinct counterclockwise circles which also start southwards.

Salmon most often follow currents, but they are more than mere passengers, and their wanderings use up much of the energy they gather from almost continuously grazing the ocean. They are just as opportunistic feeders in salt water as in fresh, even though they have a far wider choice of food at sea, as well as the strength and size to indulge it. Some closely related groups of fish, like the cichlids in the lakes of Africa, parcel out an area's available food supplies by each becoming a specialist feeder. Salmon, on the other hand, remain true generalists all their lives, and their wide-ranging appetites stay with them to such an extent that different species feeding in the same area of ocean are often eating the same range of food. Some apparent preferences can be put down to the distinctive dentition or habits of the species. Sockeye have smaller teeth than other salmon which tends to make them less piscivorous. Chum are probably the most specialised feeders of all, concentrating on zooplankton and by doing so keeping direct competition with other species to a minimum.

Once they reach open water, chinook are the greatest fish eaters of their genus, although if there are no herrings or pilchards around, they easily settle for pelagic shrimps. Available prey varies from one area to another. Rockfish and anchovies dominate the diets of southerly stocks, while those further north are more likely to live off herrings and sandlances. The diets of coho are little different and equally opportunistic, although they eat more Dungeness crab larvae (*Cancer magister*) and other invertebrates. If one source of food was to be singled out above all others for its importance to salmon, it would be squid. These are molluscs with internal shells, of the order Cephalopoda, floating plankton-like in the open sea, and able to propel themselves backwards by squirting out jets of water. Some can even leave the water and flying squid (e.g. *Ommastrephes bartrami*) nourish both Pacific and Atlantic salmon in the ocean.

Salmon may be forced to alter their diets because of seasonal variations in the abundance of particular prey, or when their migrations take them out of an area dominated by one source of food to where another is more plentiful. For masu, which are also largely piscivorous, Japanese pearlsides may be their most important food in the winter, even though these are small creatures, seldom more than 3 or 4 cm (1–2 in) long. In spring, sailfin sandfish and sandlances take their place, but this is largely because the salmon move further north as the temperature rises. Interspecific competition may also affect salmon diets, and chum have been found to eat squid and other soft animal plankton in years of pink salmon abundance, and to shift to a regime of crustaceans when pinks are less plentiful. As well as sweeping predators northwards, El Niño brings prey for older salmon, and shoals of Pacific anchovies are encouraged far further north than usual by the warmer water.

Plankton are not masters of their own destinations. They are scattered around at the whim of the current and their abundance is a true sign of the ocean's fertility. Sometimes plankton are very locally distributed – much more so than fish – making them a reliable indicator of where salmon have been feeding. Chum, pinks and sockeye are all very dependent on large plankton, which float freely in the same currents as the salmon swim in. Small squid, larval crabs and suspended clouds of shrimps and other crustacea are crucially important food, especially in the winter. They are all much easier to catch in the underwater gloom than fish, particularly the euphasid shrimps, many of which are fatally endowed with their own source of light. The distribution of plankton can also vary vertically with the ocean's temperature. Smaller animal plankton prey on plant plankton which, being dependent on light for its energy, floats closer to the surface. Summer feeding is much richer in the top 10 m (33 ft) of water, although salmon swim down as deep as 100 m (330 ft) after layers of plankton with their own circadian rhythms – like the photophobic species which rise up to the surface at night and then retreat away from the light to the depths when day comes.

Salmon feed as individuals, but often travel in loose schools pursuing similar prey and reacting in the same way to given conditions, thereby giving the mistaken impression of acting in a more co-ordinated manner than they really are. They are constantly competing, but like so much about their ocean life, the extent to which their growth and survival is affected by available food supplies or by their own numbers is still unclear.

The average size of salmon returning to the Japanese chum ranches has definitely declined, in step with the huge increase in numbers of fry released. At the same time average age at maturity has increased. There is also evidence that both Fraser River pinks and Bristol Bay sockeye are smaller in years when there are more of them. Numbers of one species or stock may affect those of another. In some years when Bristol Bay catches of sockeye are high, fewer tend to return to the rivers of British Columbia. Competition from pink salmon affects not only the feeding behaviour of chum, but also their abundance. In rivers with distinct dominant-/off-year runs of pinks, chum show up in greater strength when pinks are scarcer.

Against this are arrayed statistics purporting to show that numbers and sizes of particular stocks of salmon actually vary in parallel. This may indicate that salmon are fundamentally affected much less by competition between themselves than by further reaching environmental influences. Maybe no more can be concluded than that if hatcheries have now overpopulated the Pacific Ocean with salmon, there is no evidence of competition proving lethal, only of it perhaps affecting growth. This may not seem dramatic, but it could trigger a chain of unusual consequences. If pink salmon grow slower, and so mature later, will more of them live three- rather than two-year lives?

Eventually, all salmon head for home. Water is usually warmer on the surface and salmon can make their migrations easier by swimming through the cooler layers below. Off northern Japan, autumn surface temperatures may be as high as 20°C, and to ease the stress to their systems even chum, with their tolerance of the warmth, have been found travelling at depths of up to 450 m (1,500 ft) on their way back to spawn.

The timing of a salmon's return seems connected to the development of its eggs or milt, and as the urge to breed increases, so the desire to feed declines. Like horses reined to face their stable, salmon seem to swim fast and straight towards the shore, at speeds and for distances that may seem to speak loudly for the strength of their desires, but that in fact are the most energy-efficient. One body length per second is about optimum speed, and if the average length of a maturing sockeye, which has spent two winters at sea, is about 50 cm (20 in), this translates out at a speed of just over 43 km (27 miles) a day. Fish have often covered distances of over 1,000 km (620 miles) back to the mouth of their natal river in times that meant minimum average speeds of over 45 km (28 miles) a day. Sometimes salmon swim at speeds seemingly born of desperation, and Russian chum are known to have covered 1,200 km (750 miles) in fifteen days. Pinks are smaller than most other salmon, which makes the 70 km (43 miles) they have been timed to swim in a day all the more remarkable.

Spawning close to the sea, as most chum and pinks do, means they have often stopped feeding, and are usually more mature than other Pacific salmon, by the time they reach the estuary. One reason why chum are not popular with the food industry is that when caught off the coast they are often close to spawning, and therefore taste less good than those other salmon which have not yet begun to draw on their bodies' reserves. At the other end of the scale, masu returning to Hokkaido often spend up to three months on a very short upstream fresh-water migration, and may continue feeding into the estuary and even the river.

Salmon from the same stock all reach the river mouth with an extraordinary collective precision – most of them within a week of each other. If, as is most likely, they were scattered round a wide arc of ocean when their biological clocks struck the signal to return, each would need to set a different course for home and require the most sophisticated navigational skills to follow it (see Chapter 2). The striking of these clocks must be genetically controlled; there seems no other way to summon all members of each population, almost simultaneously, back to the estuary. Sometimes runs peak a few days earlier or later, perhaps as a result of variations in ocean temperature. When the water is particularly warm, salmon may start home from further north than usual, giving some longer and others shorter return journeys, depending on their eventual destinations. Their arrival is often timed to reflect the length of the river journey facing them – the first sockeye to return to the Fraser River at the end of June are the early Stuart run, with over

1,000 fresh-water kilometres (600 miles) to travel. There are few more fundamental differences between stocks of salmon than the timing and length of their spawning migrations and the physiological adaptations required to complete them.

More than any other fish, except perhaps brown trout, Pacific salmon have created an awareness that biodiversity does not come to a sudden shuddering halt at the species level. It is convenient to discuss the ecology of salmon by reference to the species, not least because a species can be described by its simple binomial Latin tag, yet this can tend to obscure the huge variety resting within each one. This is especially apparent in fresh-water-breeding fish, separated by watersheds that effectively keep different stocks apart from one another. Even though the Pacific Ocean is a great mixing ground for salmon born in thousands of different rivers of several countries and two continents, the instincts driving them back to their streams of birth still ensure that stocks remain distinct. Sometimes, disorientated fish may infuse one stock with genes from another. Had it not been for odd errors in their navigational systems, or a questing urge to exploit new waters, salmon could never have spread so completely up almost every suitable stream within their range, nor been able to recolonise waters depleted by earthquakes or volcanic eruptions. Yet for all this occasional mixing, salmon stocks remain quite distinct. Over 10,000 years or more, each stock has evolved the unique genetic constitution to give it the best chances of living the life of its stock, race and species in its own particular environment.

The Fraser River, fifty kilometres up from Vancouver.
(Author)

12
Pacific salmon – Yesterday, Today and Tomorrow

All is not well with Pacific salmon. In the face of the exploding human population all is not well with almost every other wild creature on the planet. More *lebensraum* for mankind means less for the world's other inhabitants. Salmon lead particularly complex lives which take them from fresh water to the sea and back, across political and environmental boundaries. They demand cool clean rivers and healthy food-filled oceans, and also carry one colossal burden with them wherever they go – man loves to eat them. Some of the chapters in their history over the last 150 years make depressing reading, and their status in parts of their original range is woeful. But overall, it is surprising that the six species of Pacific salmon are not in a worse state than they are.

The relative health of salmon stocks gives no cause for complacency or self-congratulation. Mankind's care and concern for the salmon has usually manifested itself in no more than a series of belated and half-hearted reactions to one perceived crisis after another. Yet there is still reason to wonder at, even celebrate, the resilience and adaptability that has sustained these magnificent fish in the face of so much adversity. Is even a degree of guarded optimism justified? The complexities of the salmon's biology are now much better understood; there is far greater public reluctance to tolerate wholesale desecration of their habitat, and for many people, the salmon's destiny is increasingly seen to mirror mankind's. As Roderick Haig-Brown wrote: 'If there is ever a time when the salmon no longer return, man will know he has failed again and moved one stage nearer his own final disappearance.'

Salmon – and bison and passenger pigeons – lived in relative harmony with their human North American neighbours until Europeans arrived, the prey-predator balance maintained by a combination of social restraint and primitive technology. The first human invaders, whether they crossed over the Bering land bridge or edged their way round the ice line in boats, and whether they arrived 14,000 or 20,000 years ago or even much earlier, could scarcely have survived their journey without fish, and must have brought over the basic skills to catch them. They are unlikely to have had nets, but probably knew how to dry or cure fish for winter and long journeys.

Once into Alaska, these wandering explorers may have found ice-free corridors far up into the tundra, providing them with natural routes southwards, down beyond the land of permanent frost to where trees grew in the valleys, salmon swam the rivers, and the hillsides were covered in bushes that burst out in a summer's farewell of different berries. Every year the salmon came, more some years than others, but always enough to feed the settlements which grew up by shallows, waterfalls or estuaries, wherever fish were easiest

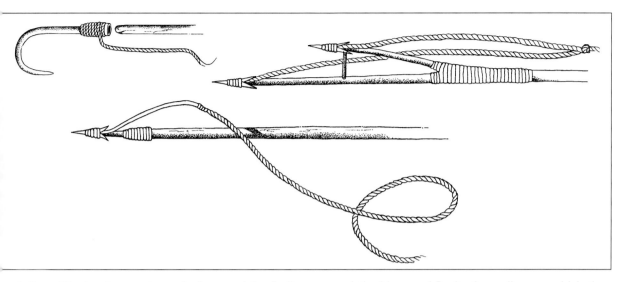

*Indian gaff hook and
fishing spears.*

to catch. Just as plains Indians revered the bison and Inuits the caribou on which they each relied for their survival, so salmon also took on a cultural and spiritual significance; this elevated them far above a mere source of food, and acknowledged that life depended on them as much as on the warmth of the sun.

For all their spiritual status, however, fish still had to be caught. Using the materials with which Nature had endowed their adopted homeland, the coastal Indian tribes of the Pacific North-west found ways of fishing which were as varied as they were ingenious. Salmon were easiest to catch as they ran up to spawn, when huge numbers of fish squeezed themselves through narrows and over shallows in their frenetic urge to return to their birthplace. They also crowded below waterfalls or rapids, gathering up their strength before taking on the force of the water, or waiting for it to rise or fall to the critical level that would allow them to carry on upstream. There, in these resting places, they could be speared, either with simple spears or with harpoons whose detachable heads were loosely tied to the shafts with long lengths of twine. Gaffs worked in the same way, their shafts' only use being to set the large hooks of wood or bone in a salmon's flank before the wriggling fish was hauled ashore by the twine to which the hook was bound.

Where the stream was very narrow, salmon could be gaffed or speared from the bank, and often fishermen constructed precarious-looking platforms, which jutted out over the water and brought them closer to their fish. Until Celilo Falls, on the Columbia River, was submerged by The Dalles Dam in 1957, hundreds of Indians gathered there each autumn when the river fell and chinook massed in the foam below. Balanced on rocks and scaffolding, using nets and spears, they fished every hour the salmon lingered, slitting open their catch to dry in the warm wind that parches the valley.

Traps and weirs could be devastatingly effective in the shallows, but rarely so effective as to threaten the next generation of salmon. In temperate latitudes, where river levels rise and fall with floods and droughts, salmon may wait weeks in an estuary before they are either able or inclined to move upstream. Here they could be cut off by a strategically built weir, low enough to allow fish up and over it on the rising tide, but high enough to strand them behind it as the water retreated, then to be speared, gaffed or netted. Around the Arctic ocean shores, Inuits caught migrating Arctic charr in the same way, but the

Fishing at Celilo Falls on the Columbia River before they were submerged by The Dalles Dam.
(Oregon Historical Society – ORHI 92427)

streams run steadier there, charr spend less time in the estuary, and it usually required a second weir higher up to stop the fish from leaving the turning tide behind and actually continuing on upstream (see Chapter 5).

Inuit weirs were built of stone – there is none but the most stunted vegetation in their tundra homeland and for long they thought driftwood grew on the ocean floor – but Coastal Indians had extensive supplies of wood and often blocked the paths of migrating fish with fences of poles joined by sections of lattice stretching right across the river. Salmon searching for a way past the fence were either netted out by waiting fishermen perched above the water on tripods, or else led by the current into basket traps as they swam along looking for an opening. Traps were made from strips of cedar or hemlock and came in a great range of sizes and designs. They mostly worked on the funnel principle, encouraging fish in without letting them out, and could be used in conjunction with fences and weirs.

Nets were also made from cedar, using the fibre from the inner bark, which was spun into a twine. The stalks of stinging nettles made the strongest twine, first being split and softened, and then dried out ready for spinning. Mesh size varied, depending on the type of fish the net was designed to catch and the method of fishing. Gill nets had to have large enough mesh to let the fish's head in, but not the rest of its body. Seine mesh was much smaller, but not so small as to make the net impossibly unwieldy in the water. Dip nets on the ends of long shafts were useful for river fishing, but the greatest advantage that nets brought the Indians was to enable them to fish in the estuary and off the shore. This extended their fishing season, and made them less dependent for their whole year's food supply on those few frenzied days when the salmon began their run upstream.

As well as eating salmon, Indian villagers bartered them for other goods that would lessen the labour of their daily lives. Salmon were a natural currency – as potentially valuable to an Indian as a dollar to a miner. Every extra fish above the subsistence catch meant a new cooking pot or buffalo hide, and yet overexploitation was almost unknown, and waste was severely punished. Salmon were a gift from the gods, giving the tribe its life. The fish's death was necessary for the tribe to survive, and their arrival was celebrated at the Ceremony of the First Salmon, which melded prayers for a heavy harvest with apology and appeasement, reverence and respect. This was no contradiction; in the minds of Indians, the gods had given them salmon – and ducks and fir trees – so they could survive. Taking more than they needed was an inconceivable abuse – as well as a waste of time – which left less, not only for others further up the river, but also for spawning the next generation.

And so man and salmon remained in balance – and through the Indians' self-sustaining credo, so did man and man. The Pacific coast Indians grew no crops nor raised any animals. They lived entirely off the bounty of Nature, and by the standards of the time Nature supported many of them. Nature largely meant salmon, and for the Indians fishing was an art born of necessity. It represented thousands of years of experiment and inventiveness with methods and materials – combining skins and seaweed, bones and antlers, bark and branches to create fishing equipment which lacked for nothing in its effectiveness, even if today it may be described as 'primitive'.

But this is in the past now, and steel, nylon and plastic have consigned these traditional fishing artefacts to the museums of anthropology – their development suspended with the arrival of the European. He appeared on the Indians' marine horizon at the end of the eighteenth century and began to blight their landscape twenty years later. Spaniards had been up and around the coast long before Robert Gray anchored the *Columbia Rediviva* at the mouth of the river that was to take his ship's name, but had made no serious efforts to set up a permanent presence. Gray was there in 1790 and two years later George Vancouver was exploring the maze of straits and islands further north. Fur financed many of the expeditions that followed later; however, it was an arduous and dangerous journey round Cape Horn and up the coast of South America and there was never any likelihood of serious settlement until a trail west could be opened up over land.

The first to probe their way across the tangled mountains of the American west were Captains Meriweather Lewis and William Clark. They were unlikely explorers, but no less diligent for being servants of the government; nor were they blind to the natural riches of the land that, following the Louisiana Purchase, Thomas Jefferson dispatched them to survey in 1804. Clark now lends his name to the cutthroat trout, *Oncorhynchus clarki* (see Chapter 9), and his diaries show him to have been continually overwhelmed by the numbers of salmon in the rivers and the extent of the Indians' dependence upon them. All down the Columbia there were 'great quants. of Salmon on scaffolds drying'; it was

October and in every village were 'many squars engaged Splitting and drying Salmon', which must have made it particularly galling to find one day 'the Indians not very fond of Selling their good fish, compels us to make use of dogs for food'.

Behind Lewis and Clark came others whose names are also remembered by posterity on the maps of today – Simon Fraser, David Thompson and Alexander Mackenzie – charting the way for those first true settlers who came to live rather than explore. Some sought adventure or escape, others their fortune, but whatever the motives driving them westwards, very few had abandoned the European's ethic of exploitation and personal enrichment. Quite simply, natural wealth only existed to be turned into personal gain. Inspired by the usual nineteenth century assumption of the bottomlessness of Nature's pit, first fur, then forests and finally salmon were converted into fortunes, which, however great they seemed at the time, now appear pathetically insignificant beside the social and environmental costs of making them.

The Hudson Bay Company had learned to preserve and package salmon on the Atlantic coast. It was forever pushing back the frontiers of commerce, and began exporting salted salmon from the mouth of the Columbia River in 1823, until the Oregon Treaty confined its operations to Canada. Other commercial fisheries focused on feeding the trickle of early settlers, which fast became a flood when gold was found in California, on the American River in 1848. Salmon may seem ill suited to the Californian climate, but 150 years ago there was enough cold water in the rivers draining the Sierra Nevadas and the Coastal Range to sustain runs of chinook as far south as the Ventura River, just north of what is now the great sprawl of Los Angeles. Chum once bred in the San Lorenzo River, which empties into Monterey Bay, and millions of salmon swam up the Sacramento and San Joaquin River systems – as a few still pass under the Golden Gate today.

Salmon probably made more money for fishermen than gold ever did for miners, until the inevitable overfishing set catches into decline. Up until 1864, most fish were still being netted out and sold on the local market, but that year a chunk of salmon was sealed into a can – and with it the future of *Oncorhynchus* over the next fifty years.

The world's first tin of salmon came off a barge moored in Sacramento and owned by the Hume brothers, who had left New England after dams and pollution killed off most of the Atlantic salmon. Much of their early output was inedible, but the simple technology did not take long to refine, and they were only stopped short of their first fortunes by the rapid decline of the salmon's. The same miners whose hunger had inspired the emergence of the fishing industry were quick to set in train its destruction. Hydraulic mining techniques relied upon diverting currents to power high pressure jets that scoured the hillsides, silting up breeding grounds and nursery streams, and clogging waterways with logjams. Many rivers became impassable to migrating fish, salmon runs fell away, and in 1867 the Hume brothers moved their barge's operations to Astoria, where, at the mouth of the Columbia River, salmon still swam by in their God-given numbers. Soon, tins of the fish began adorning the shelves of stores in England, Australia and South America. Demand led supply by the nose, canneries sprang up on river bank sites all along the Pacific coast, and before long at least fifty factories were busy tinning Columbia River fish alone.

Canada's European immigrants have never squeezed their environment to the same extent as their southerly neighbours – nor have there ever been as many of them – but the miners who chased the rainbow's end northwards needed feeding and usually ate salmon for every meal. The first cannery appeared on the banks of the Fraser River in 1870, and

Fraser River fishing fleet.
(Vancouver Public Library
– photo 22437)

by 1913 there were forty to process its record run of thirty-one million sockeye, and forty more to deal with the rest of British Columbia's fish. Alaska was only eight years behind Canada with its first cannery, despite the difficulties of shipping personnel and machinery up there, and by the start of the Second World War 156 factories were stuffing the territory's dwindling runs of sockeye into tins.

The fishing industry's greed was boundless. Many of the first netsmen were Scots and Scandinavians who brought their skills with them from the east coast. Others were Russians who had moved round the Pacific rim, first to hunt sea mammals to near-extinction, before turning their energies to the exploitation of salmon. Armadas of small craft crowded the mouths of the great west coast rivers, hanging out gill nets in almost end-to-end curtains of mesh – especially deadly in rivers like the Fraser, whose cloudy waters hid nets from the fish, even in daylight. Any salmon that managed to reach fresh water were met by fences and traps across the shallows, as well as by the lethal fishwheels. Constantly turning in the current, these looked like millwheels and scooped migrating salmon out of the river as fast as they swam into the rotating dipnets.

Huge profits in the early years of the industry attracted more and more fishermen, with ever more killing means of fishing until, inevitably, what had started as the exploitation of Nature descended into its abuse, and catches began to plummet. In desperation the canners then turned to other species of salmon to make up for dwindling runs of sockeye and chinook, still reassured by the reluctance of state legislatures to interfere with the operation of free enterprise. Out came millions of coho, chum and steelhead, and by the time fishwheels were eventually banned (they are still used by subsistence fishermen on the Yukon River) and strict close seasons introduced, it was too late to save the salmon in many of America's more southerly streams.

Mining may have seemed the quickest road to riches, but this, along with almost every other human activity, demanded timber. Logging promised surer, if less spectacular,

Fish wheel on the Columbia River.
(Oregon Historical Society – photo GI - 7492)

profits for anyone prepared to cut and extract it than gold ever would. Conifers stretched far up every hillside, and the river below provided fast and effortless transport for logs down to the sawmills. If the river was too narrow or shallow to carry the huge old-growth trunks of Douglas fir and Sitka spruce, loggers would simply build a 'splash dam'. Once the water had built up behind it, the dam was broken, sweeping the great trunks down on the ensuing flood, and most of the river bed and bankside vegetation with them. Such a dam effectively destroyed the sockeye runs in the Upper Adams River above Adams Lake, reducing the river to a pathetic trickle when it was not in roaring flood.

Now, within a hundred years, old-growth trees have become so scarce that tourists flock along marked trails to marvel at them. Yet then, this vast primeval rain forest seemed limitless, stretching on over one mountain slope after another. As the most easily removed redwoods and hemlocks crashed to the ground, lumber moguls extended their horizons to more distant and difficult sweeps of forest. First railways, then roads, opened up once unreachable valleys, while at the same time timber felling and removal equipment became rapidly more mechanised and efficient. No longer could its remoteness save a tree from the saw. Whole hillsides were bared to the earth, which washed down into the rivers, while filthy water poured off access roads covering spawning gravel in mud. Some streams were blocked to migrating salmon by woven tangles of logs and branches, while removing every stick of salvageable wood reduced others to straightened, featureless channels where no fish could ever hope to breed.

As well as transporting timber and tinned salmon, railways carried young fish to stock empty waters. If a train was delayed, or for any other reason fish became stressed before reaching their destinations, they might be tipped into the nearest river. It is unlikely that many of these survived to adulterate the genes of local stocks or found new populations. What is undeniable, though, is the responsibility of the railways for the greatest catastrophe in the twin stories of Canada's salmon and the people who depended upon them.

Hell's Gate, in the Fraser Canyon, sapped much of a salmon's dwindling reserves of energy on its final journey up to spawn. The canyon is impressively narrow, and as he made his way down it in 1808, Simon Fraser had to edge precariously along log shelves suspended from the cliff. Wherever possible, railways followed river valleys, and if engineers had to dig into, or tunnel through, the mountainsides, then they would. Laying the Canadian National Railway from Vancouver to Kamloops was made doubly difficult by the Canadian Pacific Railway having already set its track on the less difficult bank opposite, and clearing a way called for particularly drastic blasting and excavations. These

The silty waters of the Fraser River above Hell's Gate.
(Author)

culminated, in 1914, in a huge slice of mountainside slipping into the canyon, so narrowing the river that only the most powerful salmon, in the lowest water, were able to fight their way any further.

The 1913 catch of thirty-one million sockeye had been the biggest on record, but with the rockslides the sockeye runs collapsed and entire Indian communities were forced to abandon their homelands. To conserve the few fish that still managed to return, the Government was forced to impose restrictions limiting Indian fishing still further. Chief James Stager's village, where 'three-quarters of my people are away for their living because they cannot get sufficient Salmon . . . Last winter four people had to live on seventy Salmon', was typical of hundreds of others up and down the river, each of whose inhabitants had once been able to depend on 500 g (1 lb) of fish a day.

Pink salmon suffered too, as well as the great Adams River runs of sockeye (see Chapter 11), and although railway engineers sweated to try and ease the fish's passage upstream by clearing some of the rockslides, only the construction of simple fishways thirty years later began to bring the salmon back in strength. Salmon are attracted into the fishways by the less powerful current, and as 33 m (108 ft) separate the historic high and low water levels in the canyon, they are built at four separates levels to allow fish through at any height of river. The United States eventually agreed to contribute half the cost of the fishways on

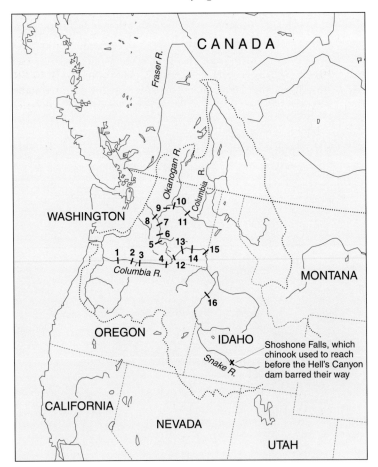

The Columbia and Snake River basin (dotted line) and the main hydroelectric dams on the rivers:

1 Bonneville
2 The Dalles
3 John Day
4 McNary
5 Priest Rapids
6 Wanapum
7 Rock Island
8 Rocky Reach
9 Wells
10 Chief Joseph
11 Grand Coulee
12 Ice Harbor
13 Lower Monumental
14 Little Goose
15 Lower Granite
16 Hell's Canyon

the grounds that, then at least, its fishermen caught many of the Fraser salmon in the Juan de Fuca Strait, but bickering over the two countries' respective contributions set the sockeye's return back many crucial years.

On the Columbia, salmon were to face even greater and more permanent barriers to their spawning journeys – the sheer walls of hydroelectric dams. When only Indians fished the river, peak runs of all species together are variously estimated at between seven and sixteen million. By the time the first mainstream dam, Rock Island, was opened in 1933 the demands of the canners had already set salmon numbers tumbling. Logging and mining had also taken their toll in the upper forested stretches, while down on the Columbia plateau vast quantities of water were being siphoned out to turn the sage-brush semi-desert into green oases of orchards and vegetable farms. Still, it was the dams that finally destroyed the Columbia River's wild salmon; that much is unarguable. So is the fact that the same dams supplied cheap electricity to the whole of the north-western United States – and continue to do so.

The Columbia is far from being the only river whose flow is now staggered by dams and reservoirs, nor was it the first. There were dams up and down the Sacramento valley before the end of the nineteenth century, and any chinook that negotiated the Red Bluff Diversion Dam on the Sacramento River were blocked by the Shasta Dam and forced to spawn below it. Many of the smaller tributaries in the Columbia basin were dammed long before anyone thought of taking on the mainstream current of the whole vast river, and there were dams up Fraser tributaries, like the splash dam on the Upper Adams River, which blocked off much ideal spawning gravel. Yet in the Columbia valley, from the head of the reservoir above the 100 m (330 ft) drop of the Grand Coulee Dam down to the great concrete complex of the Bonneville Dam, there are now a string of man-made lakes, showing for 900 km (550 miles) scarcely a sign of the drowned river which struggles to flow beneath their placid surfaces, nor of the fish battling through this lethal obstacle course to and from the sea. All the hardships dams create for migratory fish have beset the Columbia's salmon, and the river has become a testing ground for every possible means to mitigate the impact of these barriers.

One aspect of the damage dams do can only be countered by their removal; that is the flooding of spawning grounds. Chinook will not breed in the lake that used to be their river, nor will coho or steelhead. Underneath each dam lies a drowned network of running waters that hatched thousands of generations of trout and salmon until, one fateful year, it was glassed over by a vast expanse of still water. Having once bred throughout the length of the mainstream of the Columbia, chinook can now only do so in the 80 km (50 miles) of Hanford Reach between Priest Rapids and McNary Dams.

Grand Coulee Dam is impassable to fish. Finished in 1942, it barred salmon from 1,750 km (1,100 miles) of the upper Columbia River and tributaries, but its place as the end of all salmon's journeys was taken ten years later by Chief Joseph Dam just below. Now about a third of the Columbia basin, including almost all the catchment area in Canada, is barred to salmon, and those chinook urged to spawn in the Okanogan River have to negotiate nine dams before reaching their birthplace. The Snake River starts life in Wyoming, but its salmon can get no further than dams in Hell's Canyon in Idaho. And every dam a salmon surmounts going upstream, it also had to pass through, over or round on its way down.

The original design for Bonneville Dam, which is still the first to confront a returning salmon, made no provision for a fish pass. 'We don't intend to play nursemaid to the fish,' said the head of the Army Corps of Engineers before construction began in 1933, while fishermen and conservationists were still fighting for the fish to be given some way round the dam. Given the lack of precedents for its designers to follow, the laddered pass proved remarkably successful, and now all the dams up as far as Chief Joseph have fish passes, although this is no guarantee that fish either find or use them.

The maelstrom below each dam wall is a chaos of confusing currents and varying temperatures, as water gushes out of the turbines, down the fish passes or over the spillway. Seeking out the gentler flow that guides them to the pass is harder for some salmon than navigating their way around the ocean for three years. Many simply die of exhaustion on their way up the river while others may eventually make it past all the dams, but too late to spawn. From above, the water in fish ladders looks to flow in gentle steps, but in reality each step asks the salmon for an effort. Whether or not the total energy a salmon uses in negotiating first the dam and then the reservoir is much more than it would have expended if the river was undammed, is debatable. However, once in fresh water, salmon are living off their own reserves of non-renewable energy, and if climbing up ladders uses extra, irreplaceable calories these might be the ones which would otherwise have fuelled their breeding.

Perhaps between 5 and 10 per cent of mature salmon die at, or because of, each successive dam on the Columbia, gradually eroding the numbers of those precious fish that have struggled and survived to reach the river again. A chinook only 200 km (125 miles) away from spawning is of far more value to its race than it was as one of the huge excess of year-old smolts with several danger-ridden years in front of it. Yet proportionately, dams are far more dangerous to young fish on their way downstream than to adults coming home. There is not much flow in a large reservoir. This can confuse fish whose internal clocks have turned their heads towards the sea. Under natural conditions, fry or smolts ride easily down on the current. Stretches of open water take much longer to pass through, even if young fish know which way to travel and are not tempted down irrigation ditches or other unscreened extraction channels.

Still waters may not suit juvenile salmon, but other species of fish flourish in them and find the disoriented young migrants especially easy prey. Northern squawfish in Columbia River reservoirs eat so many smolts that fishermen were paid a bounty for them under the slogan 'Catch a squawfish and save a salmon' – the latest in a list of supposedly damaging predators, including bald eagles, common mergansers and Dolly Varden charr to attract a price on their heads. While the squawfish are natives, walleye are not. Members of the perch family, these have spread rapidly, largely at the expense of salmon and steelhead smolts – although defenders of their introduction argue that they also prey enthusiastically on young squawfish.

The dangers of losing their way or becoming a meal for larger fish in the open water are minimal compared to those awaiting small salmon at the dams. Here at last they sense a guiding current which all their instincts urge them to join; yet it is a current that leads, not smoothly to the sea, but instead towards spinning turbines, gas-saturated water and massed ranks of predators lurking in the tailrace. Nearly all dams incorporate devices to keep young fish away from turbines, although their effectiveness varies enormously and is always hard to assess. Most such devices try to deflect fish away from the turbine intakes into bypass channels, which eventually deliver them safely down below the dam. How well these work depends largely on how many fish they succeed in steering away from the intakes, but even fish that avoid the turbine blades may be injured by knocking into the

The futuristic fish pass to help smolts round the McNary Dam.
(Author)

deflection screens or the walls of the bypass.

At the height of the smolt migrations, ring-billed gulls gather below dam walls, despite the wires strung across the river to keep them away, and pick stunned or dead fish off the water's surface. Even ospreys settle for smaller prey than they prefer when it is so easy to catch. Smolts taking the roller-coaster ride through the bypass channels may be less stressed and disoriented when they reach the bottom than the survivors of the whirling blades of the turbines. Even so, the fish spurt out in such huge numbers that shoals of waiting squawfish and walleye, often joined in the spring by exotic channel catfish, are fed conveyor-belt meals of naïve little salmon, almost straight into their mouths.

Locks let ships up past the Columbia's lower dams, and when the run of smolts is at its peak they can be collected up and barged or trucked down for release below. Transporting small salmon avoids another of the dangers besetting both young and old fish at the bottom of a dam – gas-bubble disease. Water plunging steeply down into the pool below becomes super-saturated with gas, particularly nitrogen, and fish are affected in the same way as divers who come up to the surface too fast and get the bends. Theoretically, one of the safest ways to help small salmon down a dam is to open the spillways, and now, to prevent the plunging water becoming overladen with gas, most spillways are built with a lip which deflects water outwards, away from the dam, into the pool below.

Salmon can be hastened through the reservoirs between dams by increasing the current. Adding water to the usual flow or lowering reservoir levels – theoretically even down to the natural level of the river – are both simple sounding and superficially attractive ideas, but the advantages to migrating fish of cutting a few days off their downstream journey are debatable. Against that are arrayed the problems and cost of losing the capacity to generate power while reservoirs are down, and of juggling water levels between dams. Transportation avoids these difficulties, as well as the hazards of negotiating the dams, and short of returning stretches of river to their original state and removing dams altogether, seems the preferred option. It is aesthetically unappealing, and may also interfere with the salmon's homing abilities, but then the whole of the lower Columbia River presents a totally unnatural environment anyway. Most of its salmon are hatched in trays, not gravel beds, and their production panders to the requirements of sport or commercial fishermen rather than trying to fulfil more complex and less quantifiable, symbolic, cultural or spiritual needs.

There are hatcheries all round the Pacific rim, most of which exist to mitigate the effects of environmental degradation by supplementing depleted stocks of wild fish. The first one appeared in 1872 where it was most needed – on the McCloud River, which is a tributary of the, even then, polluted and silted Sacramento. In those days, a salmon was just a number and by the time it was a number it was dead. Chinook were simply chinook and if the original fish had gone from a river, others could always be found to replace them – with hindsight, as naïve an idea as expecting primitive Africans to have been able to settle in Alaska or taking Inuits to live on the equator. Today chinook are known to be spring or fall, stream-type or ocean-type fish, fitted to struggle over 3,000 km (1,900 miles) up to the headwaters of the Yukon, or to ease just a few kilometres up the short swift rivers on the east coast of Vancouver Island. Now man sees a salmon as belonging to its population, its stock, its race as well as its species, to each of which it passes on its own unique combination of genes, once, before it dies.

Their homing habits keep most salmon from one stream quite apart from those of another. Birds, mammals or insects may be loosely confined by their own environmental preferences, or by no more than the limits of dry land. They may range far, mixing genes into one large pool, their specific stock perhaps island- or even continent-sized. But the chinook swimming up to spawn in the Okanogan River are the direct descendants of the fish that first nestled into its gravel beds perhaps 12,000 years ago – those momentous summers when the ice had begun to melt and salmon could edge their way a little further upstream each year. Since then, while occasional strays have contributed their genes to subsequent generations, the stocks in the different Okanogan tributaries have been long enough apart to evolve their own identities.

When spring floods wash away the banks where common sandpipers or sand martins breed, the birds can simply fly off to another stream and pick new nest sites. But if salmon find the gravel silted over, or their way barred by dams, they are unable to breed, and their contribution to the genetic diversity of their species may be lost for ever. A species of salmon is the sum of its stocks, and each stock destroyed is a chip off the block of the whole.

Ironically, it has taken the massive failure of so many restoration projects to drive home to their conceivers just how different is a sockeye spawning in the Harrison River near the Fraser estuary from one passing the creek outlet at the start of its 500 km (300 mile) journey up to the Lower Adams River. The American public eye has also become much

Priest Rapids dam on the Columbia River.
(Author)

more focused on the concept of a species comprising a multitude of different stocks through the terms of the Endangered Species Act (ESA) of 1973, which provides for the listing, not only of species, but also of 'any subspecies of fish . . . and any distinct population . . . of any species of fish'. In 1990, the winter chinook of the Sacramento River became the first such population to receive the Act's protection, closely followed by both the spring/summer and fall chinook of the Snake River and the sockeye of Redfish Lake in Idaho.

The plight of Snake River fall chinook was never quite so dire as the Redfish Lake sockeye's, hence their listing as 'threatened' rather than 'endangered', but the chinook have become something of a symbol of both the damage man can do to fish and the effort and money deemed worth spending to right it. Chinook are big and powerful, their migrations are long and spectacular, and they once swam as far as the Shoshone Falls in Idaho, nearly 1,000 km (600 miles) on from the Snake's conjunction with the Columbia. Now those that reach Hell's Canyon, which bars their further progress up the Snake, have had to negotiate eight dams on their way up – the same eight they did as fry on their way down. The few hundred that still make it now fly the flag for their genus in the continual confrontation between the environment and the economy. One of the objects of the listing process was to test the effectiveness of the ESA to compel power authorities to regulate water flows for the benefit of fish as well as of the consumers of electricity. In this it may not have fully succeeded, but at least the salmon's welfare has now been elevated by statute to a matter of national concern.

Meanwhile, chinook are helped at every turn. They are artificially spawned and then implanted with coded wire tags in their noses, which furnish details of their size and place of release, and with passive integrated transponders in their abdomen to help researchers gather information about the timing and speed of their migrations. They are tested through turbines and down spillways, and barged and trucked to the sea – all at colossal cost, which raises the question whether, even given that all this money should be spent on conserving salmon, is this the best way to spend it?

Now that the distinctions between different stocks of each species of salmon are so much better appreciated, the possible shortcomings of the hatchery panacea become more apparent. The fundamental objections revolve around the impact hatchery-bred fish have upon the wild populations with which they have to coexist, either in the river or the sea. They are a loud echo of the concerns shouted around Atlantic shores over the consequences of fish farm escapees interbreeding with wild salmon (see Chapter 3). Whether or not these concerns are justified will take much longer to prove, but there is at least a realisation that hatcheries are not the sovereign remedy for disappearing salmon they were once perceived to be.

Although they may claim very different reasons for doing so, all hatcheries exist to produce salmon. Early immigrants felt little moral obligation to preserve the environment for posterity, nor much guilt at its destruction – they were too busy making their fortunes or simply trying to stay alive. Nothing more than the profit motive inspired the building of the early hatcheries, and their object was to give commercial fishermen more fish to catch. Some hatcheries still exist simply to send salmon out to graze the ocean, then to be caught as they home back where they came from. The huge Hokkaido chum ranches pour two-month-old fry into the river, which head straight out to sea and are harvested three or four years later, on their return. The main objective of hatcheries near the Columbia and Fraser estuaries is to provide both sport and commercial fishermen with salmon to catch in the sea. Other hatcheries are more concerned with maintaining or restoring endangered populations, but even these may actually prejudice the wellbeing of any wild salmon in the same river.

The lower river hatcheries are probably the least damaging to wild stocks. Some fisheries are supported entirely by hatchery-bred salmon – perhaps because there is nowhere for wild fish to spawn in the river – and netting these close to home will not damage any other stocks of fish. However, by catching them further out at sea, the very fishing the hatcheries are there to sustain may be taking endangered wild fish from other streams at the same time. The more fish the hatchery produces and the more fishing effort it encourages, the greater may be the accidental by-catch of wild salmon.

Like any other salmon, hatchery-bred fish home back to the scene of their birth, where those required for breeding are killed and stripped. It takes very few adults to supply the milt and roe to produce the next generation – the hatching rate of eggs kept on serried trays in continual darkness and aerated by a constant trickle of cool water is far higher than under natural conditions – and all the rest are there to be caught. Southern British Columbia hatcheries release millions of coho upon which the fishery in the Strait of Georgia, between the mainland and Vancouver Island, is totally dependent. Catches of hatchery salmon have risen steadily, but the price for the fishermen's success has been a continual decline in numbers of wild salmon, which still get entangled in the same nets as the hatchery fish – a policy of managing fish for fishermen and not for the fish.

It may have taken the extinction of the passenger pigeon and the obliteration of most of America's bison to convince its immigrants that Nature's bounty is not, after all, inexhaustible; yet it has taken far longer to dispel the notion that the ocean's resources, if not infinite, can at least continue to nourish ever-rising numbers of salmon. Hatcheries around the whole of the Pacific rim are estimated to release five and a half billion fish annually, and at last it is dawning on fishery policy makers that salmon must surely continue competing for food at sea just as they did in the river or the estuary. Out in the ocean they are larger, and competition is less lethal, but to climb the dam bypasses as far as Hell's Canyon, a wild salmon still needs all the size it can gather, while its domestically bred kin require little strength to reach a hatchery near the mouth of the Columbia. That chum salmon returning to Hokkaido's hatcheries are demonstrably smaller than they used to be is more likely to be a response to the huge increase in their numbers than to any other imbalance in the ocean's ecology.

The interaction of wild and hatchery fish in fresh water is easier to observe, and thus speculation is better supported by science. Salmon have evolved, reproductively isolated in their own ancestral streams, into the fish with the best chances of answering the demands of their environment. Having battled their way through life, and seen nearly all their siblings die along the way, there is one final battle to fight, and that is on the spawning grounds. With the males' struggles to mate, evolution plays its last card – the final chance for the fittest of the fit to pass on their strengths to the next generation. Charles Darwin even used the salmon as an example of sexual selection in *The Origin of Species by Means of Natural Selection* (1859): 'How long in the scale of nature this law of battle descends, I know not; . . . male salmon have been seen fighting all day long.'

In the hatchery, man mixes the milt and the roe and his selection processes are very different from Nature's. Never knowing how many salmon may come back to the hatchery, it is tempting to use the first fish back as broodstock, in case no more return. Early hatching smolts are likely to be larger on their release and therefore theoretically better equipped to survive. After repeated selection of early arrivals there will be progressively fewer latecomers, the gene pool of the hatchery fish will be depleted, and the population's ability to adapt to natural conditions reduced.

Size can give hatchery smolts an early advantage in life. This may soon be lost in the face of the hazards in the wild, where moving earthbound shadows bring danger not food and fish need immune systems rather than chemicals to fight diseases, but not before this superior size has been used to the detriment of native fish. The crowded rearing quarters of the hatchery troughs and frenzied feeding on showers of pellets both reward aggression, which may be carried into the natural environment. There, coho or stream-type chinook, which have been living off current-borne invertebrates, are sometimes all too easily displaced by the larger, more forceful hatchery fish, and may then starve to death.

If all these artificially selected fish either found their way back to the hatchery or were caught at sea, there would be no chance of their interbreeding with wild salmon, but they do not and are not, and there is – in theory at least – and this above all else may be driving hatcheries into disrepute. The escape of farmed fish from their cages and their possible impact on wild populations raise similar concerns. Whether these are fully justified is still being debated, but at least when hatchery fish are used to enhance wild salmon stocks, rather than simply to satisfy the needs of fishermen, they are now bred from wild parents which have made it back to the redds where they were born – not from fish selected for life in a cage before gracing the supermarket slab.

Spawning channels offer a compromise between wild and artificial habitats – especially for sockeye, which are hard to rear past hatching. Long serpentine beds of ideal sized

gravel beds, shaded by bankside trees and irrigated by a constant flow of cool clean water contrive to create near-perfect spawning environments. Returning fish are diverted off the mainstream into the channel until it is full, the surplus then often being allowed to breed naturally further up the river. The channels are an effective means of enhancing wild stocks without introducing alien genes into the river system. Near the mouth of the Fraser River, sockeye and chum certainly spawn more easily, and successfully, in the predator-free shallows of the Weaver Creek spawning channel than in the floods or droughts of the creek from which they have been deflected. Egg to fry survival rate for spawning channel fish is well over 60 per cent, whereas 5-10 per cent is more usual in the wild. At the same time, the forces of natural selection still play their part in producing the next generation, and there is still frenetic competition between females for space on the gravel and among males for the chance to mate.

The first spawning channels were designed by a Japanese samurai, in the middle of the eighteenth century, to protect breeding chum (see Chapter 10). The principle seems simple, almost foolproof, but early Canadian channels failed in their attempts to hijack fish headed much further upstream, and to get them to spawn lower down in water far warmer then their metabolisms favoured. Now more care is taken to match spawning

Sockeye and chum on the gravel beds of the Weaver Creek spawning channel.
(Author)

conditions in the channels with those in natural spawning sites nearby. Despite the dangers of disease, and some disappointing results, spawning channels are generally an improvement on most hatcheries, although both can be condemned for increasing the unintended and unavoidable by-catches of wild fish. The 45,000 sockeye admitted into the Weaver Creek spawning channel are responsible for increasing the catch of mature fish by around 300,000. But while these are being enthusiastically harvested amidst justified claims of the channel's success, so too are the much less expendable wild sockeye from nearby Cultus Lake, which move into the Fraser estuary at about the same time. The Fulton River spawning channel in the Babine Lake of the Skeena River system is even more successful in producing sockeye, but wild steelhead, far less abundant although with enormous recreational value, are continually being taken in salmon nets. In this case the by-catch may not actually be unavoidable, because steelhead tend to swim closer to the surface than sockeye, which could be specifically targeted by deeper-fished nets.

Adult hatchery fish may seem more inclined to stray than wild ones – as if they knew that on returning to the confines of the concrete, even those selected for breeding would be denied the right to end their lives, spent and sexually satisfied. Their imprinting mechanisms may become confused under artificial conditions, or after being raised in a hatchery and released elsewhere (see Chapter 2). Perhaps some hatchery salmon simply get caught up in shoals of wild fish, but whatever the circumstances, they may end up interbreeding. With hatcheries having produced three quarters of the coho in the coastal streams of Washington and over half those returning to the rivers of California, how can it be otherwise? Does this therefore mean the integrity of wild stocks of salmon is being constantly eroded by the genetic input from domestically bred fish? Yes, for certain, but how much that matters is far less easy to answer.

Most populations of wild salmon have only been where they are for 10,000–12,000 years. Chinook in the Yukon, which would have been one of the last great rivers to unfreeze, may have lived 1,500 generations there, while pink salmon could have been in the streams round Puget Sound for 6,000 successive two-year lifespans. Those first questing salmon were presumably quite unsuited to an environment they had only just colonised, yet they managed to survive in it, and slowly became better adapted to its uniqueness with each generation. Now the fitness acquired over 10,000 years is being diluted by unnatural and perhaps unfit fish. Yet to say this spells the end of salmon in affected streams may be to ignore the adaptability and resilience which have helped them survive so long all round the rim of the Pacific. The salmon's powers of survival in the face of environmental catastrophes are immense. This is no justification for human complacency over their present plight, but it can provide grounds for optimism – as can the greater current understanding of the complexities of salmon genetics and the dangers of wantonly releasing hatchery clones.

Broodstock for artificial breeding is now selected from a far broader, more random base, not just from the first and biggest fish to arrive at the hatchery gates, leaping up and demanding entry. The importance of using wild fish from the same river, or at least from the same watershed, as foundation broodstock is theoretically well appreciated, although there is depressingly little evidence that such careful selection is actually repaid in the form of improved returns. Some projects even try and use new wild broodstock each year, thus restricting evolutionary selection for the domestic environment to a single generation. This is an extravagant use of wild fish, and is only justified if there are more than enough for the broodstock to be collected without harming the population. Initial plans to restore the dwindling runs of Snake River spring/summer chinook in Oregon's Imnaha River (listed as 'endangered' under the ESA), relied on plundering 300 of the remaining 1,000 wild fish for the hatchery. Only after intervention by Nez Pearce Indians was this reduced to 150.

Unless wild salmon can be easily identified as such, it is impossible to monitor the success of natural stocks properly, or to expect fishermen to return any they catch. This means marking hatchery fish, and is now seen as essential to the success of any enhancement scheme. Clipping the adipose fin is the easiest way to ensure the future identification of hatchery fish. Another splendidly futuristic way is to subject salmon eggs to repeated temperature changes or other shocks. This imprints a fish's otolith bones in its ear with a bar-like code, unique to the output of a given year from a particular hatchery. The code can then be read and the mature fish's origins identified, but only once the fish has been killed. This is one of the process's disadvantages; another is the expense of first having to cut open the fish's head and grind down the otolith.

Hatcheries are increasingly recognised as tools of conservation and restoration rather than of supplementation and enhancement. Fish cannot breed successfully in the wild until the environment meets the minimum requirements for their survival and successful reproduction, and attention and resources are now focused on increasing available habitat. Sometimes this entails no more than clearing logjams, protecting banks from further erosion or enforcing the treatment of poisonous effluent. Other remedies are more dramatic, and where a dam bars salmon runs from the valleys of a watershed, the only way to bring fish back may be to remove the dam. This has such huge social and financial implications that it really only bears consideration if the dam's working life is nearly over. Never the less, it is no longer a wholly academic option, and was thoroughly researched in connection with the two dams on the Elwha River in Washington's Olympic Mountains. Of all the difficulties and uncertainties which contributed to the idea being taken no further than the 1994 report, disposal of accumulated sediment was probably the greatest.

There is now a much greater understanding that a river's wild fish are its capital, whose gradual erosion may lead eventually to spiritual, cultural or ecological bankruptcy. Preserving this capital is far more important than gearing resources for the short-term gains, which have historically been the goal of most hatcheries. 'What is man without the beasts?' wrote Chief Seatlh. 'If all the beasts were gone, man would die from great loneliness of spirit, for whatever happens to the beasts happens to man.' These are fine, much quoted words, but the ears that hear their message often seem as deaf as they were 150 years ago.

There was little time for Indian wisdom then, when the only spirit was that of free enterprise, and even now, to a fishermen out in the Strait of Georgia or over on Hokkaido, a salmon is a salmon, whether it has its adipose fin clipped or not, and once in the net it is money in the bank. Along the river's edge, down at its estuary and out at sea there are fishermen whose levels of expectations have, over the past hundred years, been largely settled – and satisfied – by the output from hatcheries. Many of these fishermen live off the sale of the fish they catch or by guiding other fishermen who come to fish for fun. Continuing to satisfy these levels of expectation is presently seen as being incompatible with efforts to restore stocks of wild salmon. This is the near-unanimous conclusion of scientific thinking, but beyond the borders of science lie a whole range of social, cultural, political and economic implications which need debating in a much larger arena.

Once salmon were masters of their own destiny. Today this destiny is in the hands of mankind. Now salmon move through the fresh-water borders of countries and states, provinces and prefectures, down into fishing zones and across lines of latitude and longitude which often demarcate the right to kill them. They are the subject of international treaties and national agreements, catch quotas and hatchery statistics. The responsibility for their welfare is shared out between commissions, councils and agencies, and all of this is because it has to be, now that salmon can no longer look after themselves. The forces arrayed against them are too oppressive even for their amazing powers of survival, so man exploits with the one hand and attempts to restrain with the other.

That both Pacific and Atlantic salmon are under such pressure wherever they swim is largely because they swim so far. Salmon are often born in the fresh waters of one country and fished for in the territorial waters of another, or in the no-man's-waters of the high seas. While Atlantic salmon fed secretly at sea they needed no international protection, but ever since they were found grazing the ocean off the Greenland coast, they have been the subjects of a series of temporary treaties and agreements, cobbled together in response to their fluctuating fortunes. Trying to balance the competition to catch Pacific salmon is even harder; as well as recreational and commercial fishing interests, there are those of the Indians to consider and protect. Reconciling the hopes and expectations of all these fishermen with the interests of *Oncorhynchus* seems, by definition, almost impossible until what is good for the fish is finally also seen to be good for the fisherman.

Salmon often cross national frontiers during the course of their fresh-water journeys to and from the sea. The chum and chinook that reach the headwaters of the Yukon move from Alaska into Canada long before they spawn. A few of the chinook that make it to the Okanogan River in Washington breed in Canada, but dams prevent any other salmon reaching the Canadian section of the Columbian watershed – unthinkable today but not in 1933. Some of the tributaries of the lower Fraser have their origins in Washington state, and to compound the vagaries of country boundaries still further, almost all the major rivers flowing through south-eastern Alaska originate in British Columbia. Over on the western side of the Pacific, masu may find themselves in China after passing through the lower reaches of the Tumen and other rivers of Korea, and much of the upper Amur forms the border between Russia and China. At sea, salmon become the objects of even greater potential for discord or dispute, and so most in need of international protection. Large salmon are valuable to whoever catches them, but the closer they are to spawning, the more precious they become to the future of their species.

The potential for disagreement between the USA and Canada is enormous, and there is every good reason for the existence of the 1985 Pacific Salmon Treaty, governing relations between them where salmon are concerned. Until Canada decides to dam the Yukon just upstream of the Alaskan border, or Alaska elects to do so just downstream of its border with Canada, much the greatest problem for the two countries is the offshore interception by fishermen from one country of salmon bound for the rivers of the other. The Alaska panhandle deprives Canada of almost half its natural western coastline and therefore of much lucrative fishing. This is one reason why Canada has often asserted that a country has the right to harvest salmon born in its rivers, to the exclusion of any other country. The assertion receives little support from the USA, which points to the nourishment salmon receive at sea in its own territorial waters, in the same way as Greenland, with only a single spawning stream, countered the arguments of producer countries around the Atlantic.

Meanwhile, ocean-type chinook born in Canada are forever being caught as they feed close inshore by the nets and trolls of Alaskan fishermen, who also intercept sockeye on their way back to the Fraser. Southward migrating chinook – many of them heading for the Columbia and other American rivers – are taken by Canadian trollers off the west coast of Vancouver Island. Canada points out that Washington and Oregon fishermen rely far more on intercepted salmon than its own fishermen do; and both Canada and the Pacific North-west states of the USA argue that they lose far more of their fish to Alaskan fishermen than vice versa. On the Asian coast, Japan has been accused of catching Russian salmon for the last 200 years, although there is now much more co-operation between the two countries. The same arguments rage around the Atlantic; drift nets off north-eastern England and north-western Ireland continue, in the face of violent criticism, to intercept salmon bound for the rivers of Scotland and other parts of Europe.

The fish that take up most of the energies of the Pacific Salmon Commission (which regulates the Pacific Salmon Treaty) are sockeye returning to the Fraser River. A combination of the complex island geography of the west coast of Canada and the line taken by its border with America, as well as the unpredictability of the sockeye's migration routes, make agreement over total catches and their partition between the two countries tortuously difficult – and occasionally even unreachable. The Commission's reports are sometimes dispiritingly dotted with phrases like 'no progress was made with respect to renegotiating harvest shares' or 'negotiated recommendations were not reached'.

As if to compensate for some of the coast lost to Alaska, the southern border of Canada dips down to scoop the whole of Vancouver Island within its territory. Separating the island from Washington state's Olympic Peninsula is the Strait of Juan de Fuca. Most salmon heading for the Fraser, whose watershed is almost entirely in Canada, used to pass through this strait, where they were assailed by armadas of both Canadian and American fishing boats. At one time American boats took even more fish than Canadian ones, and not until 1946, after much prevarication on both sides, was an effective agreement finally activated. (The difficulty in reaching a consensus was an ill omen for the salmon's future to anyone who cared to look for it.)

Now, each year the Commission first attempts to forecast the total number of pink and sockeye salmon likely to head back to the river, and from that figure to derive the escapement which should be allowed up to spawn. It then allocates a percentage of the 'total allowable catch' to American fishermen and regulates fishing seasons accordingly. However, for all its good intentions, even if its forecasts are reasonably accurate, the Commission cannot make the sockeye return through the Strait of Juan de Fuca. Now far more (35 per cent in 1996) are frustrating the forecasts, and the American fishermen, by coming back down the Strait of Georgia, between the east coast of Vancouver Island and the mainland. This may be because the ocean is warming and the salmon now begin their homeward migrations from north, rather than west of the island (see Chapter 2).

The treaty is founded on the principles of equity and co-operation between the countries in the management and conservation of their salmon. Its overriding aims are to prevent overfishing, provide for the optimum (not maximum) production of salmon, and ensure that each country receives benefits equivalent to the numbers of salmon originating in its waters. Canada has always seemed more concerned to adopt a tit-for-tat attitude with regard to the whole equitable aspect of the treaty – 'a Canadian fish for an American fish'. However, the equitable principle is particularly difficult to apply to catch allocations of salmon headed for the transboundary rivers of south-eastern Alaska, most of which were bred in the Canadian headwaters. The Treaty was drafted with no regard to the historical treatment of salmon by either country. In this way it could be seen to absolve the USA of the reckless destruction of its own stocks, but ultimately it is there for the good of the fish, not to apportion blame nor reward forethought.

There are no dams on the Fraser, nor on the mainstreams of any of the other great Canadian rivers. Alaskan rivers are also largely undammed, but lower America has ended up sacrificing its Columbia River salmon for cheap electricity. Why then, argue both Canada and Alaska, should they now suffer for this wanton greed? Generally, large human populations and sustained runs of salmon are mutually exclusive in close proximity to each other, and neither British Columbia nor Alaska is nearly as densely populated as the north-western USA. Alaska is now rightly proud of the current state of its salmon stocks, and considers that efforts to restore salmon runs should be proportionate to the responsibility for their decline, and has little to gain from being a signatory to the treaty anyway. Canada has more, largely as a result of the complexities of its borders. The Pacific North-west can contribute very little to the equation; California's salmon have all but disappeared, many of the Columbia's wild runs are 'threatened' or 'endangered', and the Pacific fishery is largely sustained by hatchery outpourings.

Of the total harvest of North American salmon, Alaska catches 80 per cent and Canada 15 per cent. So on grounds of neither protection nor production can the USA expect to speak very loudly at any forum where the salmon's future is discussed. Snake River fall chinook are listed under America's ESA and about 300 are annually counted back up the river. South-eastern Alaska harvests around 300,000 chinook each year, and yet is expected to curtail its own fishery to help restore a population of fish that have to negotiate eight Columbia River hydroelectric dams both on their way down from, and back up to, their ancestral home!

The management of eastern Pacific salmon is further confused by the recognition of Indian interests as being distinct from all others. Elsewhere, fisheries are either recreational or commercial, but in North America they may also be Indian, and juggling catch allocations to satisfy all three means tempering the wisdom of Solomon with the patience of Job and then hoping for the impossible. Many present-day Indian communities in Washington are the descendants of tribes that signed treaties to formalise their relationships with the central government – Treaty Tribes. Beginning with the Treaty of Medicine Creek in 1854, these treaties were all negotiated by the territorial Governor, Isaac Stevens. Article III promised that 'The right of taking fish, at all usual and accustomed grounds and stations, is further secured to said Indians, in common with all citizens of the Territory'. The Article's repeated interpretation throughout this century has not only tested judicial sentiment towards the Indians – perhaps unavoidably tinged with the USA's collective guilt – but has also served to unite the interests of many of the scattered Indian communities, that once depended on fish, into a cohesive political end economic force.

As early as 1905 the courts created a powerful precedent, which has strongly favoured the Indian cause ever since. The Winans brothers operated fishwheels at the Celilo Falls – long the traditional fishing grounds of the Yakima Indians. The brothers contended that because they had state licences and the Indians did not, the Indians should be barred from fishing there. The Supreme Court disagreed and declared that Indians could not be deprived of their ancestral rights by the selective issue of licences or other cosmetic regulations. In dismissing the claim, it laid down precedents for treaty interpretation that have never since been overturned. Treaties reserve rights, rather than grant them, and their language is to be construed according to the understanding of the tribes at the time of signing, in whose favour any ambiguities are to be interpreted.

Subsequent cases relied heavily on the Winans judgement, one judge recognising that salmon fishing was 'not much less necessary to the existence of the Indians than the atmosphere they breathed'. Still, despite the attitude of the courts, state authorities continued finding ways to favour the commercial fishermen, who usually fished at sea or in the estuary, at the expense of the Indians, whose historic fishing grounds were nearly always further upriver. Only too often, by the time the commercial nets were finally hung up to dry for the season, there were just enough salmon left for spawning and no surplus for the traditional Indian harvest. To compound the Indians' misery, the authorities continued justifying their actions by alleging that the wording of the treaties gave all citizens, of whatever ethnic origins, an equal right to fish the traditional fishing grounds – a blatant attempt to crowd out the Indians, whose numbers were rapidly declining in proportion to the immigrants'.

If American immigrants cared little about the wellbeing of the Indians, they cared about the Indians' rights to fish for salmon even less, and it took the federal government, on behalf of seven treaty tribes, to take on the state of Washington in 1970 before these rights were legally reaffirmed. Judge Boldt's decision – subsequently upheld by the Supreme Court – centred on the phrase 'in common with'. In the absence of any direct Chinook translation, he interpreted this, with the help of Webster's 1828 dictionary, to mean 'divided equally with', and ordered that up to one half of the harvestable number of salmon in runs traditionally fished by Treaty Tribes should be reserved for their use.

Although the judgement proved far easier to deliver than to enforce, it formalised the Indians' rights and effectively demanded the recognition of these rights in all fishery policy decisions of the future. The rights it upheld were emphatically tribal not individual. This proved a strong unifying influence on particular tribes and villages, encouraged the fair allocation of the harvest share among all their members, and did much to revitalise a sadly flagging culture.

Section 35 of the Canadian constitution theoretically affirms 'the existing aboriginal and treaty rights of the aboriginal peoples'. Prior to 1990, the Department of Fisheries and Oceans (DFO) had regulated the fishing of 'first nations' with arbitrary and impromptu sets of rules. These sought to take account of fluctuations in salmon numbers and to balance a minimum spawning escapement with allocations of quotas between fishing groups. But that was before Ronald Sparrow was caught fishing with too long a net. From this humble transgression came forth a momentous decision of the Supreme Court of Canada, which forced the DFO to rethink the whole of its fishery policy. The decision was intended to provide 'a measure of control over government conduct and a strong check on legislative power'. It required that each Indian band be consulted before being subjected to any fishing restrictions, and that these should only be imposed after all possible alternatives had been explored and discarded. Unanimously, the court immortalised Mr Sparrow in legal history, gave the Indians what amounted to an enormous constitutional spanner, and turned the whole sequence of fishery management policy on its head.

Salmon returning to spawn meet offshore nets first, and quotas are revised almost daily as fish draw closer to the estuary and their numbers can be estimated with increasing accuracy. As they start moving up river, forecasts begin giving way to facts, and it become easier to allocate more precise catches to the different fresh-water fisheries, while still

A subsistence fish wheel on the Yukon River.
(Natalie Fobes)

allowing enough salmon through to breed. Such was the whole rationale behind the DFO's *modus operandi* and the logic is inescapable. Now it was suddenly forced to start working backwards, unable to allot any commercial or recreational quotas before first agreeing, by consultation not decree, catches for each individual Indian band.

And so emerged the Aboriginal Fisheries Strategy (AFS), which ushered in communal rather then individual licensing and a whole array of inducements to encourage Indian co-operation. No amount of habitat enhancement programmes, new employment opportunities and innovative local fishery projects could mask the one fundamental outcome of the Sparrow decision: the Indians' slice of the salmon pie had to get bigger. In an effort to reallocate salmon from one fishery to another, the Government began buying out commercial fishermen through a licence retirement programme. These reallocated salmon have since proved to be some of the most expensive fish in the world. This is far from being the only aspect of the AFS to have strained relations between Indian and commercial fishermen, which reached a nadir when it appeared Indians could sell their surplus fish and were no longer confined to fishing for 'food, social and ceremonial' purposes only.

The Indians are at a cultural crossroads, and there is no denying that, as well as giving them food, salmon still provide spiritual contact with the natural world and vital links to their past. In the context of the total North American harvest Indians take very few – about 5 per cent – although the fish they do catch are closer to spawning than those

caught by any other fishermen. Sport fishermen catch about the same. They may want to eat what they catch, have vague spiritual notions about being at one with Nature while they fish, and perhaps even perceive themselves as unofficial custodians of their quarry – but fundamentally they fish for fun.

The quintessential salmon angler stands on a river bank casting out into the current. Other casual fishermen answer the call of the sea and go out in small boats to troll offshore for coho and chinook, almost the only fishing which exploits the salmon's appetite. Sport fishermen may be allocated a relatively small quota each year, but there are many of them and each has a voice. The urge to feel a salmon on the end of a line sustains small businesses and feeds families from Anchorage to San Francisco, and if providing social and economic benefits was the criterion for granting fishing licences, the whole ocean would become one great recreational fishery. As it is, the world needs feeding; it consumed over 1.5 million tonnes of salmon in 1995, and the figure is still rising.

The commercial fishing industry was once comprised of fleets of small boats, managed by small-scale enterprises. In some areas this is still the case, but catching power is becoming increasingly concentrated in fewer bigger boats owned by fewer bigger companies. Where the health and success of a local community depends on the health and success of its salmon runs, there is every incentive to conserve them. Large, highly

'Combat fishermen' on Cook Inlet at the mouth of Bird Creek, Alaska, casting for returning coho.

(Author)

mobile fishing vessels, rushing to exploit one concentration of salmon after another, have scant concern for the good of particular stocks of salmon – profit today is their motive, only too often followed by someone else's poverty tomorrow. The huge sums of capital invested in these vessels demand commensurate return, expectations need to be sustained, and the only way to sustain them is by hatchery production. Towards the salmon's southern limits, at least two thirds of the commercial catch is hatchery produced. Wild fish continue to struggle against the competition from domestic output, and to be swept up in nets unable to discriminate between their origins. Moving northwards, the impact of hatcheries on catches lessens. In central Alaska ranched pink salmon make up about half the total harvest, but north of the Alaska Peninsula, almost the entire salmon catch is wild.

In 1976 the USA declared a 200-mile (320-km) exclusive fishery management zone, which effectively gathers in much of the northern Pacific down the Alaska Peninsula and the Aleutian Islands. Since 1992, Japan has withdrawn its mother-ship factory fleet, and interception of immature North American fish out on the high seas is, at least for now, a problem of the past – although the USA and Canada now seem to vent the aggression they once reserved for Japan on one another. Sockeye, pink and chum salmon make up around 90 per cent of the Pacific salmon harvest, over a third of which is ranched – hatchery-bred, before being released into the wild to fatten on the ocean's goodness. Trollers, seine netters and gill netters ply their way around the rim of the Pacific, their activities tightly controlled in an attempt to divide what is perceived to be the ecologically expendable surplus of fish among all those who want to share in it. Regulating methods of fishing, the hours and days of fishing, and numbers and size of fish all theoretically helps ensure that no more fish are hauled out of rivers and oceans than the waters can afford to surrender.

If nets only caught what they were allowed to catch, the task of fishery management would be unimaginably simpler. However, since natural fibres gave way to nylon, gill nets in particular have become deadly by day or by night, and quite unselective. Nets set for autumn chum in the lower Fraser River also ensnare rare steelhead, while coho are always getting tangled up in those set to catch the far more numerous pinks and sockeye. Just as boys worming for trout cannot put back small fish that have swallowed the hook too far down their throats, so trollers for chinook may not be able to release undersized fish unharmed, and any fish which has nylon tight around its bleeding gills may be dead by the time the net is winched in. Fish are often far more at risk of incidental than deliberate death in a fisherman's net, and never more so than in the maws of a trawler which gulps up every living creature on or near the sea bed.

Off the coast of British Columbia, chinook are continually caught up in trawls dragged for hake, as are green sturgeon, which are now dangerously rare. Some fishing methods allow fish to be returned relatively unharmed. Indians never needed to take surplus salmon from weirs and traps, game fish can be unhooked from barbless hooks without even being touched, and unwanted fish can often be released from seine nets with a good chance of surviving to swim another day. But a trawl gulps up every living creature in its way, and most of what is thrown back into the sea is already dead – first pressed into the back of the net by its drag and then crushed under the weight of tonnes of other fish as the trawl is winched aboard. Often these are fine edible fish, but because the boat is only licensed for one species the rest must go to waste. In the end, whether regulators accept the waste of the incidental catch or allow the sale of everything the trawl drags up is academic; it is the very act of trawling that is so devastating, no matter what the boats are allowed to do with what they catch.

Successful fishing is often about getting to the fish before anyone else does. Seine netters usually work close inshore, searching straits and channels for the surface ripples that betray schools of salmon moving towards the river mouth. The net is stretched out and round the fish with the help of a small skiff, and then drawn tight below, enclosing the fish in a purse of mesh that is then lifted out of the water. Seines catch the close-shoaling salmon – chum, pink and sockeye – while trollers, fishing much further offshore, hook mainly coho and the particularly piscivorous chinook, which are often far away from their home river. Commercial trolling is much like overdeveloped sport fishing, the boat dragging behind it several weighted lines attached to outriggers, from each of which, like droppers, dangles a series of hooks baited with strips of herring.

Perhaps the most prolific and successful salmon fishery in the world is in Alaska's Bristol Bay, to which an average of 35 million sockeye return each year – successful at least in ecological terms, even if the actual fishing is chaotic. Every year the Alaskan Department of Fish and Game estimates the harvestable surplus of fish in each of the six main river systems. To do this it makes use of three principal indicators; the numbers of spawners three, four or five years ago whose offspring should be returning in the current year, counts of smolts from earlier years which should now be spawning, and figures from the previous year's catch that might indicate numbers of siblings appearing in the current year. The estimates are continually revised right through the fishing season as catches start to prove the accuracy or otherwise of the predictions. The sockeye arrive in the middle of June. and within a month they have nearly all swum up the Kvichak River to Lake Iliamna, up the Egegik to Becharof Lake, or up to any of the twenty-five other lakes

A sockeye ensnared in the nylon mesh of a gill net.
(Andrew Hendry)

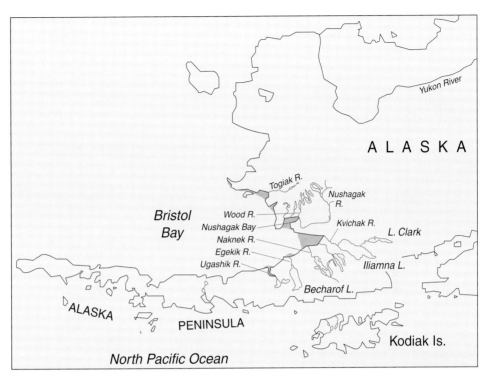

Bristol Bay, Alaska, showing the main lake systems and commercial fishing areas (shaded).

which were once their nurseries. There they wait to redden and ripen before making their final upstream run to spawn.

Fishing is restricted to gill netting in the bay of each river, usually within a line 5 km (3 miles) out from the shore. Despite Alaska having chosen to limit fishing effort by restricting numbers of boats, there are still nearly 1,900 chasing anywhere between one (1973) and forty (1983) million harvestable fish for little over two weeks in an atmosphere of frenzied and sometimes violent competition. Pole position is right on the line demarcating the outer fishing limit. The nets set furthest out will be first to ensnare incoming salmon, but space there is so tight that it may be worth fishing over the boundary and risking the consequences. Aeroplanes and helicopters buzz around above the armadas, checking for illegal fishing, but no longer, since two collided in mid-air, spotting salmon. Boats cannot be more than 32 ft (9.75 metres) long, and most have power rollers that pay out and pull in the net which, in times of plenty, may be weighed down with up to 3,000 fish trapped around their gills. Fishing never stops at the height of the sockeye run, except to transfer the catch to tenders which carry it to processing vessels or canneries.

The bay is divided into four districts. When forecasts for one district are particularly low it may be closed to fishing, allowing all the salmon up to spawn, and then possibly opened later if predictions have proved too pessimistic. Boats are only allowed to fish the district in which they have registered; they can move to a new district in mid-season, but must wait forty-eight agonising hours before starting to fish there. The pressures on captains to choose the best district at the start of the season are huge – fortunes are there to be made or missed by putting the cross in the right or the wrong box on pre-season application forms.

Restricting fishing to bays ensures that nets only take fish destined for the particular inflowing river, but beyond that it is very difficult to target, or spare, salmon from distinct populations within that river system. Fraser River sockeye arrive at the estuary all through the summer, timing their arrival according to how far upstream they have to travel before reaching the redds. This helps fishery managers identify the fish's destination even before they reach fresh water, and to adjust fishing quotas accordingly. Bristol Bay spawning streams are all relatively close to the sea, and to be stock-selective over the course of two weeks is much harder. However, there is still some correlation between arrival time and destination, and all the fish bound for a particular stream may appear within the space of a few days. When catch targets are set low, it is still better to fish for fewer hours each day over a longer period, so that the impact of fishing effort is not concentrated on one individual stock of salmon.

Alaska's salmon catches are higher now than ever before, and not a single Bristol Bay sockeye has seen the carefully cleaned gravel of a spawning channel or the concrete walls of a hatchery tank. There are enhancement programmes further south, but most of the state's salmon are still wild, and the peak 1994 catch of 194 million fish is all the more remarkable for the troughs which came before it. The fishery once described as having 'a pathetic history of ruinous exploitation' and in such a mess that President Eisenhower declared Alaska a federal disaster area, now controls commerce with science at a cost of less than 10 per cent of the value of the catch, in contrast to the Pacific North-west states which spend far more on the management of salmon than their marketable worth. Alaska is not shamed by the massive commercial exploitation of its natural bounty, only anxious that through careful management it remains sustainable.

One way of countering the dangers of over-exploitation is through a system of limited entry. This restricts the issue of new licences but allows the transfer of existing ones on the open market, thus effectively creating a means for a fisherman to own the right to fish and

Bristol Bay fishing fleet at the height of the sockeye season.
(Greg Syverson)

an incentive to enhance the value of that right. Bristol Bay licences have changed hands for over $300,000 and those that confer the opportunity to fish for longer than a frenzied fortnight, like the intercept fisheries down the Alaska Peninsula, are worth far more. The risk of the ownership of fishing rights gradually drifting out of the hands of local communities is partly mitigated by the requirement that the licence holder must always be on his boat when it is fishing. One further step down the road to privatisation is the conversion of licences into individually transferable quotas (ITQs) giving their owners the right to a specific share of the total allowable catch rather than just the right to fish. This can make the actual fishing less competitive, but increases the danger of quotas becoming concentrated in the hands of the few.

About 90 per cent of Alaska's catch goes to Japan, which still needs to import at least half the salmon its population consumes and owns over three-quarters of the USA's fish processing industry. Its highly successful chum-ranching operations make a considerable contribution to local production, and help satisfy the demands of a population which eats ten times as much fish as the average American. Salmon are graded into seven categories headed by *mejika* which is 'ocean-bright' with firm meat and healthy silver skin. Lightly salted fillets (*teien*), raw fish (*sashimi*), fresh salmon, smoked salmon, and roe, either as whole skeins of eggs (*sujiko*) or single caviar-like eggs (*ikura*), are all sold on the 25 hectare (62 acre) Tsukiji fish market. There Tokyo's residents satisfy their cravings for fish, fish and more fish, as well as for more bizarre products like *hizu* which is salmon nose cartilage marinated in herbs and vinegar.

Human overpopulation has forced most wild salmon out of the snow-fed streams of the feudal lotus land that was once Japan, and its fishing fleet has long been forced to plunder Russian waters. Over the past 200 years salmon have much influenced Japan's relations with Russia, which have swung between the extremes of open warfare and concerted co-operation. A succession of bilateral agreements with different countries have squeezed Japan's fishing activities like a balloon, forcing them to contract in one area and then expand in another. The most dramatic expansion came with the development of the devastating mother-ship fleets, which, beginning in 1927, netted immature salmon out in their oceanic feeding grounds and canned them at sea. The Second World War put a stop to this and also destroyed most of the Japanese fishing fleet; but within ten years of the war ending fourteen mother-ships and over 400 catchers had resumed their deadly harvest and it took nearly twenty years of concerted international pressure before Japan finally agreed to stop raping the open ocean.

Japan has always been far ahead of Russia in fishing and processing technology, and Russia now continues licensing Japanese mother-ships to operate in its territorial waters. The fleets catch and process intercepted pinks and sockeye, and Japan pays for its privileges by managing joint-venture hatcheries in Russia, which also ranch chum. Russia's potential for increasing its salmon production is huge, and regulating its harvest is made much simpler by not having to take account of any sporting interests or claims for traditional native rights.

The salmon's future is ultimately tied up with the demand for its flesh. If a few idlers wanted to catch occasional salmon in moments of leisure, then the only real threat to the fish's existence would be the continuous assaults on the environment from other directions. Starting and ending their lives, as many of them do, in cold northern rivers, beyond the limits of most present-day human habitation, would guarantee them a place on the planet much longer than many other fish. But the world needs feeding, its

*Japanese fisherman
catching ranched chum
salmon on their return to
the river.*
(Natalie Fobes)

population is forever rising, salmon taste delicious and, recently at least, their price has been tumbling.

The rising demand for salmon is increasingly satisfied by farmed and ranched fish; together these now account for over 40 per cent of the total production and will probably overtake the wild catch by the end of the century. Ranching is an intriguing idea, simple in theory but much less so in practice, which involves releasing hatchery fish to go and graze the ocean and then exploiting their breeding urges by harvesting them on their return. Frank Buckland first suggested ranching Atlantic salmon in *Fish Hatching* (1863):

> If to the cost of an animal reared and fattened on a farm, we add the risks that are run in maintaining him in health and condition until he is fit for human food, the profit . . . is not very great; but in the case of salmon, we can send a fish down to the sea . . . and he there grows and fattens, without cost or trouble of any kind, and when he returns to us in the highest condition, he returns to us worth about as much as a prime fed sheep, which has required to be watched and cared for till it reached that condition.

The impetus to Sweden's success in ranching Atlantic salmon was the devastating effect of so many hydroelectric dams on the spawning efforts of its wild fish. But *Salmo salar* fry need nurturing in fresh water for at least a year before they silver up ready for the Baltic, while chum fry are fed for only two months before being released into the estuary to fend for themselves. Japan has emphatically demonstrated how effective ranching chum can be, and other Pacific ranching schemes have imitated its success, particularly in southern Alaska where they are managed by the local commercial salmon fishermen.

Coho are the easiest Pacific species to farm, and are raised, as also are some chinook, in the inlets of Washington and British Columbia. Alaska has never allowed any salmon farming, on the original grounds that it did not want farmed fish to compete with the wild catch and so reduce the incomes of fishermen. Generally, there is much less salmon farming round the Pacific rim than in the Atlantic. Wild Pacific salmon are far more prolific; they sell for less than their Atlantic cousins, and ranching, rather than farming, satisfies much of the total demand. After many generations of artificial selection for hatchery conditions, Atlantic salmon are now fully domesticated, convert their food better, and use less energy milling around their cages. They are now even being farmed on the Pacific coast of North America, amidst probably unwarranted anxiety over the consequences for local species of accidental escapes. Farmed Atlantic salmon from Norway, Scotland and even Australia are also taking the pressure off wild stocks of the Pacific species by helping satisfy the demand for salmon flesh; so are imports from Chile. There, no species of salmon, trout or charr has been spared from the rearing experiments, which have now left coho and Atlantic salmon the preferred species.

Fish farms will always have their detractors, and some of the worries about the way they operate are well warranted. However, it is all too easy to forget what might happen to wild stocks without competition in the market place from the sale of cage-reared salmon. International agreement on the harvest of the oceans has proved almost impossible to achieve, and would become harder still if the salmon's price was much higher and there were far fewer of them around. Presently, there is some profit to be made both from catching a wild sockeye in Bristol Bay and from raising a coho in a cage. Supplies of wild salmon are limited, catches are now carefully controlled by most producer countries, and there is probably very little scope for wild fish to be safely exploited any further. Ranching and farming operations, especially in eastern Russia, have certainly not reached their maximum potential and their output is generally reliable. Wild fish numbers are far more erratic and although a dearth of wild salmon in one country is often balanced by a bonanza in another – 1995 was disastrous for fishermen in Canada but exceptional for those in Alaska – this is far from always so.

Mankind is perpetually nibbling away at the edges of the salmon's range, and for as long as the human population continues growing or nations become more affluent and demand more space, this is inevitable. At the same time, North Americans, motivated by an uneasy blend of guilt and genuine concern, are no longer prepared to sit back and watch the desecration of their continent through thoughtless industrial or agricultural development, and much tighter environmental controls reinforce their disquiet. In some parts of the USA, however, particularly in the Columbia River, the amount of money and resources being thrown at micropopulation of near extinct salmon could seem excessive to even the most committed conservationists.

There may be as many salmon grazing the Pacific ocean now as there ever were, and no species is remotely endangered, only odd fragments of some of them. Each species consists of a multitude of stocks and populations, one genetically distinct from the other, which together make up the whole. As one stock after another disappears, this whole is chipped away at, becoming gradually more genetically impoverished in the process. So the conservation of a salmon species implies the conservation of all its parts, while other more mobile and genetically homogenous creatures – many birds, mammals and pelagic fish – may be far more easily protected. The ESA accepts this implication, but is such all-embracing protection a luxury that, approaching the twenty-first century, it is unrealistic to offer any animal? Elevating Snake River fall chinook to the status of an endangered species, while chinook from other stocks are still streaming up the rivers of Alaska and British Columbia in their tens of thousands may seem illogical and unreasonable, and thus only serve to diminish the impact of protection when and where its need is less questionable.

It is certainly a fine idea to try and close down hatcheries in the hope of helping wild fish regain some of their lost territory, but it is only viable once the fishermen, who have been led to depend on hatchery output for their livelihoods, are persuaded by financial inducements, or appeals to their higher senses, to reduce first their expectations and then their catches. This may help stocks recover, but what happens when they have? Even if every salmon in the world is wild, one river's fish are always going to be in a less healthy state than another's, and thus perceived to be in greater need of protection, and equally susceptible to being netted out with the more prolific fish. Science and sociology together must fight for the salmon. Meanwhile, the Canadian and American governments continue subsidising both the sport and the industry of fishing by churning out millions upon millions of salmon fry, eventually to seize the baits and fill the nets of fishermen whose only contribution to the production of their fish is the cost of a licence.

Common and scientific names of the principal species of salmon, trout and charr

Unless the context requires otherwise, fish species are referred to by their common names in this book. Their scientific names are set out below.

bull charr	*Salvelinus confluentus*
Arctic charr	*Salvelinus alpinus*
Dolly Varden	*Salvelinus malma*
white-spotted charr	*Salvelinus leucomaenis*
lake charr	*Salvelinus namaycush*
brook charr	*Salvelinus fontinalis*
Atlantic salmon	*Salmo salar*
brown trout	*Salmo trutta*
Mexican golden trout	*Oncorhynchus chrysogaster*
Gila/Apache trout	*Oncorhynchus gilae*
cutthroat trout	*Oncorhynchus clarki*
rainbow trout	*Oncorhynchus mykiss*
masu salmon	*Oncorhynchus masou*
coho salmon	*Oncorhynchus kisutch*
chinook salmon	*Oncorhynchus tschawytscha*
chum salmon	*Oncorhynchus keta*
pink salmon	*Oncorhynchus gorbuscha*
sockeye salmon	*Oncorhynchus nerka*

Common and scientific names of other fish species

alewife	*Alosa pseudoharengus*
Allis shad	*Alosa alosa*
American eel	*Anguilla postrata*
anchovy	*Engraulis mordax*
Arctic grayling	*Thymallus arcticus*
Arctic lamprey	*Lampetra japonica*
Atka mackerel	*Pleurogrammus monopterygius*
ayu	*Plecoglossus altivelis*
Baltic/common sturgeon	*Acipenser sturio*

barramundi (Australian sea bass)	*Lates calcarifer*
beluga sturgeon	*Huso huso*
bitterling	*Rhodeus amarus*
bream	*Abramis brama*
brook lamprey	*Lampetra planeri*
bullhead	*Cottus gobio*
burbot	*Lota lota*
capelin	*Mallotus villosus*
channel catfish	*Ictalurus punctatus*
Chinese minnow	*Moroco steindachneri*
chub	*Leuciscus cephalus*
coast range sculpin	*Cottus aleuticus*
cod	*Gadus morhua*
coelacanth	*Latimeria chalumnae*
crucian carp	*Carassius carassius*
dace	*Leuciscus leuciscus*
desert pupfish	*Cyprindon* spp.
European eel	*Anguilla anguilla*
European grayling	*Thymallus thymallus*
fifteen-spined stickleback	*Spinachia spinachia*
flounder	*Paralichthys* spp. / *Platichthys flesus*
four-horn sculpin	*Myoxocephalus quadricornis*
green sturgeon	*Acipenser medtrostris*
hake	*Urophycis chuss*
herring	*Clupea harengus*
huchen	*Hucho hucho / H. perryi*
icefish	*Salangidae* spp.
Japanese goby	*Rhinogobius brunneus*
Japanese pearlside	*Maurolicus japonicus*
koaro	*Galaxias brevipinnis*
lake sturgeon	*Acipenser fulvescens*
lake whitefish	*Coregonus clupeaformis*
ling	*Molua molua*
longnose dace	*Rhinichthys cataractae*
longnose sucker	*Catostomus catostomus*
minnow	*Phoxinus phoxinus*
mountain whitefish	*Prosopium williamsoni*
New Zealand grayling	*Prototroctes oxyrynchus*
Nile perch	*Lates niloticus*
nine-spined stickleback	*Pungitus pungitus*
northern redbelly dace	*Phoxinus eos*
northern squawfish	*Ptychocheilus oregonensis*
ocean pout	*Macrozoarces americanus*
Pacific mackerel	*Scomber japonicus*
perch	*Perca fluviatilis*
pike/northern pike	*Esox lucius*
pilchard	*Sardinops caerulea*

piranha	*Serrasalmus* spp.
plaice	*Pleuronectes platessa*
polar cod	*Boreogadus saida*
pollack	*Pollachius pollachius*
pollan (Arctic cisco/omul)	*Coregonus autumnalis*
pond smelt	*Hypomesus olidus*
powan	*Coregonus lavaretus*
prickly sculpin	*Cottus asper*
pygmy whitefish	*Prosopium coulteri*
rainbow smelt	*Osmerus mordax*
redside shiner	*Richardsonius balteatus*
river lamprey	*Lampetra fluviatilis*
roach	*Rutilus rutilus*
rockfish	*Sebastes* spp.
Sacramento sucker	*Catostomus occidentalis*
sailfin sandfish	*Arctoscopus japonicus*
saithe	*Pollachius virens*
sand-eel	*Ammodytes* spp.
sandlance	*Ammodytes hexapterus*
sand perch	*Pinguipes* spp.
sea lamprey	*Petromyzon marinus*
sea salmon	*Pinguipes* spp.
skate	*Raia batis*
slimy schulpin	*Cottus cognatus*
smelt	*Osmerus eperlanus*
sheefish	*Stenodus leucichthys*
spiny dogfish	*Squalas acanthias*
sprat	*Sprattus sprattus*
suckers	*Catostomus* spp.
taimen	*Hucho hucho*
Tasmanian whitebait	*Lovettia seali*
three-spined stickleback	*Gasterosteus aculaeatus*
tigerfish	*Hydrocynus vittatus*
tomcod	*Microgadus tomcod*
torrent sculpin	*Cottus rhotheus*
tui chub	*Gila bicolor*
twaite shad	*Alosa fallax*
vendace (Siberian cisco)	*Coregonus albula*
walleye	*Stizostedion vitreum*
white sturgeon	*Acipenser transmontanus*
winter flounder	*Pseudopleuronectes americanus*
wolffish	*Anarhichas lupus*
yellow perch	*Perca flavescens*
zebra trout	*Apolochiton zebra*

Bibliography

Set out below is a list of references which may help anyone searching for more information on a particular topic covered in this book. The list is far from comprehensive, but I hope that by grouping references by subject matter, it may be easier for researchers to find what they are looking for. I must stress, however, that many of the sources I cite helped me with more than one chapter, and, for the most part, they are only quoted once. I must also emphasise that the other purpose of this list of references is to acknowledge the invaluable help from other people's efforts.

1. The Fish – What, Where and Why

The science of modern taxonomy rests on the dual foundations of Carl Linnaeus's *Systema Naturae* (10th edition – 1758) and Charles Darwin's *The origin of species by means of natural selection* (John Murray, London – 1859). The early march of salmonid taxonomy is well illustrated by comparisons of W. Yarrell's *A history of British fishes* (John Van Voorst, London – 1836), A. Gunther's *Catalogue of fishes in the British Museum* (Printed by order of the Trustees – 1866), F. Day's splendid work *British and Irish salmonidae* (Williams and Norgate, London – 1887), H.E. Maxwell's *British fresh-water fishes* (Hutchinson & Co., London – 1904) and C.T. Regan's wonderfully perceptive *The freshwater fishes of the British Isles* (Methuen, London – 1911).

Information on fish within the Salmonidae family, and on other related species, can be found in many general ichthyological texts, including R. Phillips and M. Rix's *Freshwater fish of Britain, Ireland and Europe* (Pan Books, London – 1985), P.S. Maitland and R.N. Campbell's *Freshwater fishes of the British Isles* (Harper Collins, London – 1992), N. Giles's *Freshwater fish of the British Isles* (Swan Hill, Shrewsbury – 1994), *Freshwater fishes of northwestern Canada and Alaska* by J.D. McPhail and C.C. Lindsey (Bulletin of the Fisheries Research Board of Canada 173 – 1970), the monumental *Freshwater fishes of Canada* by W.B. Scott and E.J. Crossman (Bulletin of the Fisheries Research Board of Canada 184 – 1973) and L.S. Berg's great work, *Fishes of USSR and adjacent countries* (Israel Program for Scientific Translation, Jerusalem – 1965). In *Trout* by E. Schweibert (André Deutsch, London – 1979) there is much elegantly written information and speculation on the Salmonidae's prehistory, which is also covered by L. Cacutt in *British freshwater fishes – the story of their evolution* (Croom Helm, London – 1979), and by J.R. Norman and P.M. Greenwood in their all-embracing book on fish biology and ecology, *A history of fishes* (Ernest Benn, London – 1963).

C. Lever's *Naturalized fishes of the world* (Academic Press, London – 1996) is a detailed compendium on man's dispersal of fish beyond their native ranges.

Many papers discuss the taxonomic relationships of the genera and species within the Salmonidae family; including F.M. Utter and J.F. Allendorf's *Phylogenetic relationships among species of Oncorhynchus: a consensus view* (Conservation Biology 8 – 1994), R.F. Stearley and G.R. Smith's *Phylogeny of the Pacific trouts and salmons and genera of the family Salmonidae* (Transactions of the American Fisheries Society 122 – 1993), and *Salmonid phylogeny inferred from ribosomal DNA restriction maps* by R.B. Phillips, K.A. Pleyte *et al.* (Canadian Journal of Fisheries and Aquatic Sciences 49 – 1992); see also *The origin and development of life history patterns in Pacific salmonids* by R.J. Miller and E.L. Brannon (in Proceedings of the Salmon and Trout Migratory Behavior Symposium, School of Fisheries, Washington, Seattle – 1982).

Charr genetics are discussed in *Genetic relationships among Salvelinus species inferred from allozyme data* by P.A. Crane, L.W. Seeb *et al.* (Canadian Journal of Fisheries and Aquatic Sciences 51 – 1994). *The classification and scientific names of rainbow and cutthroat trout* by G.R. Smith and R.F. Stearley (Fisheries 14 – 1989) is the first major paper to discuss the reclassification of these fish, and hybridisation as an indicator of genetic proximity is considered in *Hybridisation in salmonids* by B. Chevassus (Aquaculture 17 – 1979); reflected light on salmonids' interrelationships comes from *Variability in length of freshwater residence of salmon, trout and charr* by R.G. Randall, M.C. Healey *et al.* (in Common Strategies of Anadromous and Catadromous Fish: American Fisheries Society Symposium 1 – 1987), while R.F. Stearley's *Historical ecology of Salmoninae with special reference to Oncorhynchus* (in Systemetics, historical ecology and North American freshwater fishes – Stanford University Press 1992) is a fascinating attempt to determine evolutionary pathways through comparative behaviour.

The Eurasian huchen by J. Holcik, N. Hensel et al. (Dr. W. J. Junk Publishers, The Hague – 1988) is the classic source of information on these fish.

Many other books touch on the taxonomy of individual species, some of which are cited amongst the references in later chapters.

2. To Sea or Not To Sea

Diadromy in fishes by R.M. McDowell (Croom Helm, London – 1988) is unlikely to be surpassed as a comprehensive review of the subject, while specialised books on fish migration include *Fish migration* by F.R. Harden Jones (St Martin's Press, New York – 1968), *Mechanisms of migration in fishes* by J.D. McCleave, G.W. LaBar et al. (Plenum Press, New York – 1984) and B.A. McKeown's *Fish migration* (Croom Helm, London – 1984).

Technical papers tend to concentrate on different aspects of migratory behaviour. Many of the more recent ones are by T.P. Quinn of the University of Washington's School of Fisheries and are usually easily intelligible to the lay reader. They include *Current controversies in the study of salmon homing* (Ethology, Ecology and Evolution 2 – 1990) and *A review of homing and straying of wild and hatchery-produced salmon* (Fisheries Research 18 – 1993). *Homing in Pacific salmon: mechanisms and ecological basis* by A.H. Dittman and T.P. Quinn (Journal of Experimental Biology 199 – 1996) contains an overview of homing generally, as does *Homing and olfaction in salmonids: a critical review with special reference to the Atlantic salmon* by O.B. Stabell (Biological Reviews of the Cambridge Philosophical Society 59 – 1984). J.E. Thorpe's papers are also eminently readable and wide-ranging; e.g. *Smolting versus residency: developmental conflict in salmonids* (in American Fisheries Society Symposium 1 – 1987) and *Variation in life-history strategy in salmonids* (Polskie Archiwum Hydrobiologii 37 – 1990).

Many scientific papers focus on the migrations of particular species, but their conclusions are often more generally applicable; e.g. *Timing of imprinting to natural and artificial odors by coho salmon* by A.H. Dittman, T.P. Quinn et al. (Canadian Journal of Fisheries and Aquatic Sciences 53 – 1996), *Odor cues used by homing coho salmon* by E.L. Brannon and T.P. Quinn (in Proceedings of the Salmonid Migration and Distribution Symposium, edited by E.L. Brannon and B. Jonsson – 1989), *The use of celestial and magnetic cues by orienting sockeye salmon smolts* by T.P. Quinn and E.L. Brannon (Journal of Comparative Physiology 147 – 1982), *Evidence for a hereditary component in homing behaviour of chinook salmon* by D.O. McIsaac and T.P. Quinn (Canadian Journal of Fisheries and Aquatic Sciences 45 – 1988), *Migration of farmed adult Atlantic salmon with and without olfactory sense, released on the Norwegian coast* by L.P. Hansen, K.B. Doring et al. (Journal of Fish Biology 30 – 1987), *Homing and straying patterns of fall chinook salmon on the lower Columbia River* by T.P. Quinn and R.S. Nemeth (Transactions of the American Fisheries Society 120 – 1991), *Within-river spawning migration of Atlantic salmon* by T.G. Heggberget, L.P. Hansen et al. (Canadian Journal of Fisheries and Aquatic Sciences 45 – 1988) and *Marine migration and orientation of ocean-type chinook and sockeye salmon* by M.C. Healey and C. Groot (in American Fisheries Society Symposium 1 – 1987).

A pheromone hypothesis for homeward migration in anadromous salmonids by H. Nordeng (Oikos – 1977) and *A test of the hypothesis of pheromone attraction in salmonid migration* by G.A. Black and J.B. Dempson (Environmental Biology of Fishes 15 – 1985), both focus on this intriguing thesis. *Why no southern hemisphere salmon? The gyre theory* by L. Stewart (Salmon and Trout magazine 213 – 1990) also postulates thought-provoking ideas as does *Migration and the transequatorial establishment of salmonids* by D. Scott (Proceedings of the International Association of Theoretical and Applied Limnology 22 – 1985).

Other interesting papers include *Perspectives on the marine migrations of diadromous fishes* by T.P. Quinn and W.C. Leggett (in American Fisheries Society Symposium 1 – 1987), K.B. Doring's *What the salmon nose tells the human brain* (in Proceedings of the Salmonid Migration and Distribution Symposium – 1989) and D.J. Solomon's *A review of chemical communication in freshwater fish* (Journal of Fish Biology 11 – 1977).

The question of genetic differences between resident and migratory fish of the same species, and their selection of alternative life patterns, is well covered ground; see, for example J.G. Northcote and G.F. Hartman's *The biology and significance of stream trout populations living above and below waterfalls* (Polskie Archiwum Hydrobiologii 35 – 1988), *Life history patterns of freshwater resident and sea-run migrant brown trout in Norway* by B. Jonsson (Transactions of the American Fisheries Society 114 – 1985), *Genetic differentiation between freshwater resident and anadromous brown trout within watercourses* by O. Skaala and G. Naeudal (Journal of Fish Biology 34 – 1989), *Salmon breeding behaviour and life history evolution in changing environments* by M.R. Gross (Ecology 72 – 1991) and *Evolution of diadromy in fishes*, also by M.R. Gross (in American Fisheries Symposium 1 – 1987).

The practicalities of following fish at sea are the subject of *Surveying and Tracking Salmon in the Sea* by E.C.E. Potter and A. Moore (Atlantic Salmon Trust, Pitlochry, Scotland – 1992). Changes in natural migratory patterns are discussed in *Influence of suspended volcanic ash on homing behaviour of adult chinook salmon* by R.P. Whitman, T.P. Quinn et al. (Transactions of the American Fisheries Society 111 – 1982), *Environmental changes affecting the migratory timing of American shad and sockeye salmon* by T.P. Quinn and D.J. Adams (Ecology 77 – 1996) and *Salmonid colonisation of new streams in Glacier Bay National Park, Alaska* by A.M. Milner and R.G. Barley (Aquaculture and Fisheries Management 20 – 1989).

The biology of the stickleback by R.J. Wootton (Academic Press, London – 1976) remains the best source of information on these extraordinary fish.

3. Atlantic Salmon

There are many books devoted exclusively to the life of the Atlantic salmon, particularly J.W. Jones's *The salmon* (Collins, London – 1959), *The Atlantic salmon – a vanishing species* (Faber & Faber, London – 1968) and *Salmon – the world's most harassed fish* (Andre Deutsch, London – 1980) both by A. Netboy, D.H. Mills's excellent *Ecology and management of Atlantic salmon* (Chapman Hall, London – 1991), *The Atlantic salmon in the history of North America* by R.W. Dunfield (Canadian Special Publication of Fisheries and Aquatic Sciences 80 – 1985), *The Atlantic salmon* by W.M. Shearer (Fishing News Books, Oxford – 1992), and A. Barbour's *Salmon – An illustrated history* (Canongate Press, Edinburgh – 1992).

Changes in local abundance of Atlantic salmon are discussed in *The return of salmon to the Clyde* (Proceedings of the Institute of Fisheries Management – 1986), *Tidal Thames – The history of a river and its fishes* by A. Wheeler (Routledge & Kegan Paul, London – 1979), *The recovery of salmon stocks in the River Tyne* by A.S. Champion (Salmon Net 24 – 1992) and *Last stand of the Yankee salmon* by T. Williams (Trout – Autumn 1996), which are also the subject of K.A. Harvey's *The landlocked salmon in Maine* (Maine Department of Inland Fisheries and Wildlife – 1985) and *Landlocked salmon* by R.J. Behnke (Trout – Autumn 1988).

Changes in Atlantic salmon harvests and stock status in the north Atlantic by J.A. Ritter, *Quota purchase* by O. Vigfusson and A. Ingolfsson, and *Control of marine exploitation* by D.H. Mills are three of the fascinating essays in *Salmon in the sea and new enhancement strategies* edited by D.H. Mills (Fishing News Books, Oxford – 1993).

Salmon stocks: a genetic perspective by N.P. Wilkins is one of the many excellent publications put out by the Atlantic Salmon Trust (Moulin, Pitlochry, Perthshire PH16 5JQ). *Minimising the impacts of salmon aquaculture on the wild salmon stocks* by M.L. Windsor and P. Hutchinson (in Proceedings of the First International Symposium on Sustainable Fish Farming, Oslo – 1994) covers many of the problems created by the interaction of wild and domestic fish, as does D.H. Mills's *Wild or domesticated?* (Salmon Net 20 – 1988), *Genetics and the management of the Atlantic salmon* by T.F. Cross (Atlantic Salmon Trust, Pitlochry – 1989) and *The genetic impact of farmed Atlantic salmon on wild populations* by P.S. Maitland (Nature Conservancy Council, Edinburgh – 1989). *Principles and practice of stocking streams with salmon eggs and fry* by H.J. Egglishaw, W.R. Gardiner et al. (Scottish Fisheries Information Pamphlet 10 – 1984) is a comprehensive work on supplementing wild stock, while *Implications of the introduction of transgenic fish into natural ecosystems* by A.R. Kapuscinski and E.M. Hallerman (Canadian Journal of Fisheries and Aquatic Sciences 48 –1991) focuses on the potential dangers of this alarming practice.

History of the Hudson's Bay Company salmon fisheries in the Ungava Bay region by G. Power (Polar Record 18 – 1976) and *Commercial Atlantic salmon fisheries in Canada* by T.R. Porter (Salmon Net 26 – 1995) both review commercial fishing from the Canadian perspective.

World distribution of Atlantic salmon by H.R. MacCrimmon and B.L. Gotts (Journal of the Fisheries Research Board of Canada 36 – 1979) is a comprehensive paper on both the historic and man-changed status of the fish.

Interesting discussions on the genetic distinctions between fresh-water-resident and sea-going salmon, and their occasional interbreeding, are found in *Mating of anadromous Atlantic salmon with mature male parr* by R.A. Myers and J.A. Hutchings (Journal of Fish Biology 31 – 1987), *Mating between anadromous and nonanadromous Atlantic salmon* by J.A. Hutchings and R.A. Myers (Canadian Journal of Zoology 63 – 1985) and *Genetic divergence of anadromous and nonanadromous Atlantic salmon in the River Namsen, Norway* by J. Vuorinen and O.K. Berg (Canadian Journal of Fisheries and Aquatic Sciences 46 – 1989).

The report by E.C.E. Potter and A. Swain entitled *Effects of the English north-east coast salmon fisheries on Scottish salmon catches* (Fisheries Research Technical Report No. 67 of the Ministry of Agriculture, Fisheries and Food – 1982) shows how little England has done to restrict this fishing in the last fifteen years, as does I. Mitchell's *North east England drift net fishery* (Salmon Net 18 – 1985). *Spring salmon* by A. Youngson (Atlantic Salmon Trust, Pitlochry – 1994) surveys the decline of these fish and its possible reasons.

Perhaps the most wide-ranging collection of papers and essays on Atlantic salmon from an international perspective is contained in *Atlantic salmon: planning for the future*, edited by the indefatigable D.H. Mills and D. Piggins (Croom Helm, London – 1988). For the latest information on the status and exploitation of salmon stocks nothing surpasses the annual reports of NASCO (11 Rutland Square, Edinburgh EHI 2AS) and its other occasional publications, which have fine pan-Atlantic perspectives.

4. Brown Trout

The first scientific monograph on brown trout was W.E. Frost and M.E. Brown's *The trout* (Collins, London – 1967), which remains one of the best books on the fish. I hope you will also find much to interest you in my own *The trout – a fisherman's natural history* (Swan Hill Press, Shrewsbury – 1993). Brown trout from the American perspective are well covered by C.E. Heacox in *The complete brown trout* (Winchester Press, New York – 1974). J.M. Elliott knows more about the ecology and physiology of brown trout than most others and his *Quantitative ecology and the brown trout* (Oxford University Press – 1994) and *Wild brown trout: the scientific basis for their conservation and management* (Freshwater Biology 21 – 1989) are fine collections of scientific material.

A. Ferguson has pioneered the study of Lough Melvin's fish and two of his papers on its extraordinary diversity of trout are *Lough Melvin: a unique fish community* (Royal Dublin Society Occasional Papers in Irish Science and Technology, Dublin – 1986) and *Genetic differences among brown trout stocks and their importance for the conservation and management of the species* (Freshwater Biology 21 – 1989). *Genetic variation in Scandinavian brown trout: evidence of distinct sympatric populations* by F.W. Allendorf, N. Ryman et al. (Hereditas 83 – 1976) looks at the same phenomenon elsewhere.

That H.R. MacCrimmon is the world authority on salmonid distribution is well evidenced by his *World distribution of brown trout* with T.L. Marshall (Journal of the Fisheries Research Board of Canada 25 – 1968) and *World distribution of brown trout: further observations* (Journal of the Fisheries Research Board of Canada 27 – 1970). For information on trout outside their native range see J. Ritchie's *The Australian trout* (Victorian Fly-Fisher's Association – 1988), *Trout in South Africa* by B. Crass (Macmillan, South Africa – 1986), V.D. Van Someren's *The biology of trout in Kenya Colony* (Government Printer, Nairobi – 1952) and J.R. Luton's *The first introductions of brown trout in the United States* (Fisheries 10 – 1985).

Papers on trout diets are legion, and include M. Kelly-Quinn and J.J. Bracken's *Seasonal analysis of the diet and feeding dynamics of brown trout in a small nursery stream* (Aquaculture and Fisheries Management 21 – 1990), M. Kennedy and P. Fitzmaurice's *Growth and food of brown trout* (Proceedings of the Royal Irish Academy 71 – 1971), *The ecology of brown trout in English chalk streams* by R.H.K. Mann, J.H. Blackburn et al. (Freshwater Biology 21 – 1989) and *Selective predation by drift-feeding brown trout* by N.H. Ringler (Journal of the Fisheries Research Board of Canada 36 – 1979). J.R. Harris's *An angler's entomology* (Collins, London – 1952) and J. Goddard's *Waterside guide* (Unwin Hyman, London – 1988) are excellent works on aquatic insect life.

The phenomenon of ferox trout is explored by R.N. Campbell in *Ferox trout and charr in Scottish lochs* (Journal of Fish Biology 14 – 1979), by E. Fahy and W.P. Warren in *Long-lived sea trout, sea-run 'ferox'?* (Salmon and Trout magazine 227 – 1984) and later in detail by R. Greer in *Ferox trout and Arctic charr* (Swan Hill Press, Shrewsbury – 1995).

Sea trout are the subject of E. Fahy's *Child of the tides – a sea trout handbook* (Glendale Press, Ireland – 1985) and *The biology of the sea trout*, edited by E.D. Le Cren (Atlantic Salmon Trust, Pitlochry – 1984); H. Falkus's *Sea trout fishing* (H.F. and G. Witherby, London – 1962) also contains sound information on the fish as well as how to catch it. The sea trout's limited feeding habits are discussed by J.M. Elliott in *Stomach contents of adult sea trout caught in six English rivers* (Journal of Fish Biology 50 – 1997), and concern about declining stocks in Britain and Ireland prompted T.F. Cross and E. Rogan's *The feasibility of developing and utilising gene banks for sea trout conservation* (National Rivers Authority Fisheries Technical Report 4 – 1992) as well as the conference report, *Problems with sea trout and salmon in the western Highlands* (Atlantic Salmon Trust, Pitlochry – 1993).

There are many books on the practical aspects of trout farming, beginning with F. Buckland's *Fish hatching* (Tinsley Brothers, London – 1883). The latest editions of S.D. Sedgwick's *Trout farming handbook* and J.P. Stevenson's *Trout farming manual* (both Fishing News Books, Surrey) are sound technical works and there are many good scientific papers in The Proceedings of the First International Symposium on Sustainable Fish Farming (Oslo – 1994). For the impact of fishing on rivers see P.S. Maitland and A.K. Turner's *Angling and wildlife in fresh water* (Institute of Terrestrial Ecology – 1987), while the papers in *Tweed towards 2000* edited by D.H. Mills (The Tweed Foundation – 1989) provide an excellent overview of all aspects of a river's management and conservation.

5. Arctic Charr and Allied Species

Surprisingly for such an intriguing and widespread creature, books devoted to Arctic charr are almost non-existent. The collected papers in *Charrs – Salmonid fishes of the genus Salvelinus*, edited by E.K. Balon (Dr. W.J. Junk Publishers, The Hague, – 1980) make up by far the most comprehensive work on the fish, and especially *The Arctic charr* by L. Johnson and *The Dolly Varden charr* by R.H. Armstrong and J.E. Morrow.

Fascinating charr-related reading is also to be found in *Proceedings of the international symposium on Arctic charr* (University of Manitoba Press, Canada – 1984), *Proceedings of the international symposium on charr and masu salmon* (Physiology and Ecology Japan, Special Vol. 1 – 1989) and *Proceedings of the third international charr symposium* (Nordic Journal of Freshwater Research 71 – 1995). Equally interesting are the various publications put out by the International Society of Arctic Charr Fanatics (Institute of Freshwater Research, S – 178 93 Drottningholm, Sweden), and in particular the reports of the proceedings of their various workshops. *Life history of Arctic charr in the Forth River, Yukon Territory* by G. Glover and P. McCart is one of the excellent chapters in *Life history of anadromous and freshwater fish in the western Arctic* (Canadian Arctic Gas Study, Biological Report Series 20 – 1974).

The tortuous taxonomy of the charrs, and the varying interpretations of their genetic make-ups, is the subject of many, inevitably subjective, papers. R.J. Behnke's encyclopaedic knowledge of Salmonid taxonomy is evident in *Organising the diversity of the Arctic charr complex* (in Proceedings of the International Symposium on Arctic Charr) and *Interpreting the phylogeny of Salvelinus* (in Proceedings of the International Symposium on Charr and Masu Salmon); in this latter collection of papers see also *Why is there a charr problem* by L. Nyman and *Japanese charr and masu salmon problems: a review* by H. Kawanabe.

The co-existence of more than one form of charr in the same waters is covered in many papers, particularly by A.F. Walker, R.B. Greer et al. in *Two ecologically distinct forms of Arctic charr in Loch Rannoch, Scotland* (Biological Conservation – 1988), *Population structure, ecological segregation and reproduction in non-anadromous Arctic charr in four unexploited lakes in the Canadian high Arctic* by H.H. Parke and L. Johnson (Journal of Fish Biology 38 – 1991) and *The Windermere populations of Arctic charr* by C.A. Mills (in Proceedings of the International Symposium on Charr and Masu Salmon).

The landlocked charrs of Maine: the sunapee and the blueback by F.W. Kircheis (in Charrs: Salmonid Fishes of the Genus Salvelinus) is an interesting review of the status and ecology of these relict fish.

The interaction of Arctic charr and ferox trout is covered in detail in *Ferox trout and charr in Scottish lochs* by R.N. Campbell (Journal of Fish Biology 14 – 1979) who also contributed to *Status and biology of Arctic charr in Scotland* by P.S. Maitland, R.B. Greer et al. (in Proceedings of the International Symposium on Arctic Charr). *The ecology of Arctic charr and brown trout in Windermere (northwest England)* by J.M. Elliott and E. Baroudy (in Proceedings of the Third International Charr Symposium) also describes researches into the interaction of the two species.

The anadromous Arctic charr of Nauyuk Lake, NWT, Canada by L. Johnson (in Proceedings of the International Symposium on Charr and Masu Salmon) is an excellent study of a migratory population, as is *Life-history of anadromous Dolly Varden in northwestern Alaska* by A.L. DeCicco (Sixth ISACF Workshop – 1990).

Few papers deal with Arctic charr at sea: two that do are O.K. Berg and M. Berg's *Sea growth and time of migration of anadromous Arctic charr from the Vardnes River in northern Norway* (Canadian Journal of Fisheries and Aquatic Sciences 46 – 1989) and *Spatial and temporal aspects of the ocean migration of anadromous Arctic charr* by J.B. Dempson and A.H. Kristofferson (American Fisheries Society Symposium 1 – 1987).

The current status of bull charr is the subject of *Montana's vanishing bull trout* by B. Farling (Trout – Summer 1994), *Occurrence of bull trout in naturally fragmented habitat patches of varied size* by B.E. Rieman and J.D. McIntyre (Transactions of the American Fisheries Society 124 – 1995), *Conservation genetics of bull trout in the Columbian and Klamath River drainages* by R.F. Leary, F.W. Allendorf et al. (Conservation Biology 7 – 1993), and *Systematics and distributions of Dolly Varden and bull trout in North America* by G.R. Haas and J.D. McPhail (Canadian Journal of Fisheries and Aquatic Sciences 48 – 1991).

Two interesting papers on European charr are *The status of Salvelinus in France* by Y. Machino (in Proceedings of the Third International Charr Symposium) and *Historical evidence for the introduction of Arctic charr into high-mountain lakes of the Alps by man* by R. Pechlaner (in Proceedings of the International Symposium on Arctic Charr).

Commercial or subsistence fishing for charr is the subject of *Charr fishing among the Arviligjuarmiut* by A. Balikci, and by H.R. MacCrimmon and B.L. Gott (both in Charrs: Salmonid Fishes of the Genus Salvelinus); collected together in Proceedings of the International Symposium on Arctic Charr are *Historical development of the Arctic charr fishery in northern Labrador* by L.J. Ledrew, *Charr fisheries in Windermere, England during the past four hundred years: organization and management* by C. Kipling, *The Arctic charr sport fishery at Tree River, Northwest Territories, Canada, 1964 -1978* by R.W. Moshenko, R.F. Peet et al., *Management of the commercial fishery for anadromous Arctic charr in the Cambridge Bay area, Northwest Territories, Canada* by A.M. Kristofferson, D. K. McGowan et al. and *Charr and man: the philosophy of limited interaction* by L. Johnson; see also *Biological and social aspects of an Inuit winter fishery for Arctic charr* by T.G. Boivin, G. Power et al. (in Proceedings of the International Syposium on Charr and Masu Salmon).

The difficulties inherent in raising charr for the table are set out by M. Jobling, E. Jorgensen et al. in *Feeding, growth and environmental requirements of Arctic charr: a review of aquacultural potential* (Aquaculture International 1 – 1993).

6. Lake Charr

By far the most comprehensive introduction to lake charr is N.V. Martin and C. H. Olver's *The lake charr* (in Charrs: Salmonid fishes of the genus Salvelinus).

Inevitably lake charr are most studied in the Great Lakes, which tends to focus attention away from the many pristine populations further north. *Lake Ontario: effects of exploitation, introductions and eutrophication on the salmonid community* by W.J. Christie, *Lake Erie: effects of exploitation, environmental changes and new species on the fishery resources* by W.L. Hartman, *Lake Huron – effects of exploitation, introductions and eutrophication on the Salmonid community* by A.H. Berst and G.R. Spangler, *Lake Superior: effects of exploitation and introductions on the salmonid community* by A.H. Lawrie and J.F. Rahrer and *Lake Michigan: effects of exploitation, introductions and eutrophication on the Salmonid community* by L. Wells and A.l. McLain (all in Journal of the Fisheries Research Board of Canada 29 – 1972) provide excellent overviews of the lakes, their problems and their fish.

N.V. Martin's *A study of lake trout in the Algonquin Park, Ontario, lakes* (Transactions of the American Fisheries Society 81 – 1952), R. B. Miller and W.A. Kennedy's *Observations on the lake trout of Great Bear Lake* (Journal of the Fisheries Research Board of Canada – 1948) and *The lake trout of Lac la Ronge, Saskatchewan* by D.S. Rawson (Journal of the Fisheries Research Board of Canada 18 – 1961) are all earlier papers on lake charr beyond the Great Lakes.

Other papers on northern lake charr focus on the inter-relationships between the charr and their competitors or predators – e.g. *Influence of lake trout on lake-resident Arctic char in northern Quebec, Canada* by N.C. Fraser and G. Power (Transactions of the American Fisheries Society 118 – 1989) and the excellent *Ecology of Arctic populations of lake trout, lake whitefish, Arctic charr and associated species in unexploited lakes of the Canadian Northwest Territories* by L. Johnson (Journal of the Fisheries Research Board of Canada 33 – 1976).

The fascinating story of the sea lamprey's catastrophic invasion of the Great Lakes has been well documented. The volume of research may give the misleading impression, both that lake charr are struggling to survive throughout their range and that this is largely confined to the Great Lakes area of North America. *Native lake trout stocks in the Canadian waters of Lake Superior prior to 1955* by J.L. Goodier (Canadian Journal of Fisheries and Aquatic Sciences 38 – 1981) gives an idea of the number and stock diversity that once existed there. *The enigma of the lake trout* by S. Grooms (Trout – Spring 1992) and *Great Lakes trout: have we really lost what we are trying to restore* by J.H. Kutkuhn (in Proceedings of the Wild Trout Symposium, Yellowstone National Park – 1979) are two general papers on lake charr in the Great Lakes.

Some of the other papers on lake charr and sea lampreys are *The sea lamprey in the Great Lakes* by A.H. Lawrie (Transactions of the American Fisheries Society 99 – 1970), *Lake trout, sea lampreys and overfishing in the Upper Great Lakes: a review and reanalysis* by D.W. Coble, R.E. Bruesewitz et al. and *Effect of lake trout size on survival after a single sea lamprey attack* by W.D. Swink (both in Transactions of the American Fisheries Society 119 – 1990), *Changes in species interactions of the Lake Superior fisheries system after the control of sea lampreys as indicated by time series models* by J.N. Stone and Y. Cohen (Canadian Journal of Fisheries and Aquatic Sciences 47 – 1990), *Predation by sea lamprey on lake trout in southern Lake Ontario, 1982 – 1992* by C.P. Schneider, R.W. Owens et al. (Canadian Journal of Fisheries and Aquatic Sciences 53 – 1996), *Sea lamprey in Lakes Huron, Michigan and Superior: history of invasion and control, 1936 – 1978* by B.R. Smith and J.J. Tibbles (Canadian Journal of Fisheries and Aquatic Sciences 37 – 1980), *Evidence of natural reproduction by stocked lake trout in Lake Ontario* by J.E. Marsden, C.C. Krueger et al. (Journal of Great Lakes Research 14 – 1988), and *Lake trout rehabilitation in Lake Superior* by D.R. Schreiner and S. T. Schram (Fisheries 22 – 1997).

K.H. Loftus's *Studies on river-spawning populations of lake trout in eastern Lake Superior* (Transactions of the American Fisheries Society 87 – 1957) comments on this unusual behaviour; see also S.E. DeRoche's *Observations on the spawning habits and early life of lake trout* (Progressive Fish-culturist 31 – 1969) and J.S. Tait's *The first filling of the swim bladder in salmonids* (Canadian Journal of Zoology 38 – 1960).

7. Brook Charr

Unsurprisingly, much the best description of the brook charr is the chapter *The brook charr* by G. Power (in Charrs: Salmonid Fishes of the Genus Salvelinus). J.W. Mullen's *A compendium of life history and ecology of the eastern brook trout* (Massachussets Division of Fish and Game Fisheries Bulletin 23 – 1958) is also an excellent introduction to the fish. Its distribution, both natural and naturalised, is detailed by H.R. MacCrimmon and J.S. Campbell in *World distribution of brook trout* (Journal of the Fisheries Research Board of Canada 26 – 1969) and in *World distribution of brook trout, further observations* by H.R. MacCrimmon, B.L. Gots et al. (Journal of the Fisheries Research Board of Canada 28 – 1971). R.J. Behnke's article *Brook trout* (Trout – Summer 1987) covers unusual aspects of the fish's natural range, and there is a good chapter on brook charr in E. Schweibert's *Trout* (André Deutsch, London – 1979). General information is also to be found in *Brook trout: life history, ecology and management* by J. Brash, J. McFadden et al. (Wisconsin Department of Natural Resources, Publication 226 – 1958) and in *Some observations: age, growth, food habits and vulnerability of large brook trout from four Canadian lakes* by W.A. Flick (Nature (Canada) 104 – 1977).

Many of the papers on brook charr focus on their decline in the face of introductions of exotic species; e.g. *Habitat utilization by brook charr and rainbow trout in Newfoundland streams* by R.A. Cunjak and J.M. Green (Canadian Journal of Zoology 61 – 1983), *Ecological interaction of brown trout and brook trout in a stream* by O.L. Nyman (Canadian Field-Naturalist 84 – 1970), *Interactions between native brook trout and hatchery brown trout: effects on habitat use, feeding and growth* by L. DeWald and M.A. Wilzbach (Transactions of the American Fisheries Society 121 – 1992), *Tests of competitiveness between native and introduced salmonids: what have we learned?* by K.D. Fausch (Canadian Journal of Fisheries and Aquatic Sciences 45 – 1988), *Competition between brook trout and brown trout for positions in a Michigan stream* by K.D. Fausch and R. J. White (Canadian Journal of Fisheries and Aquatic Sciences 38 – 1981), *Replacement of brook trout by brown trout over 15 years in a Minnesota stream: production and abundance* by T.F. Waters (Transactions of the American Fisheries Society 112 – 1983) and *Encroachment of exotic rainbow trout into stream populations of native brook trout in the southern Appalachian Mountains* by G. L. Larson and S.E. Moore (Transactions of the American Fisheries Society 114 – 1985).

The consequences for brook charr of a warming world is the subject of J.D. Meisner's *Effect of climatic warming on the southern margins of the native range of brook trout* (Canadian Journal of Fisheries and Aquatic Sciences 47 – 1990), *Environmental extremes and native brook trout populations in the southeastern United States* by A.L. LaRoche and G.B. Pardue (in Proceedings of the Wild Trout Symposium, Yellowstone National Park – 1979) and *Effects of temperature on growth and survival of young brook trout* by J.H. McCormick, K.E.F. Hokansen et al. (Journal of the Fisheries Research Board of Canada 29 – 1972).

The story of the brook charr's introduction into Britain is covered in comprehensive detail by C. Lever in *Naturalised Animals of the British Isles* (Hutchinson & Co., London – 1977) and in selected papers such as A. L. Wheeler and P.S. Maitland's *The scarcer freshwater fishes of the British Isles, 1. Introduced species* (Journal of Fish Biology 5 – 1973) and A.F. Walker's *The American brook trout in Scotland* (Rod and Line 16 – 1976).

8. Rainbow Trout and Their Allies

There is no better general introduction to trout and charr than *Trout* edited by J. Stolz and J. Schnell (The Wildlife Series, Stackpole Books, Pennsylvania – 1991). *The steelhead trout* by T. Combs (Frank Amato Publications, Oregon – 1988) is primarily a fishing book, but there are good chapters on the fish's biology; see also I.L. Withler's *Variability in life history characteristics of steelhead trout along the Pacific coast of North America* (Journal of the Fisheries Research Board of Canada 23 – 1966).

The distribution of native and introduced rainbow trout is covered by H.R. MacCrimmon with his usual thoroughness in *World distribution of rainbow trout* (Journal of the Fisheries Research Board of Canada 28 – 1971) and *World distribution of rainbow trout. Further considerations* (Journal of the Fisheries Research Board of Canada 29 – 1972).

For a detailed insight into the taxonomic difficulties that beset both rainbow and cutthroat trout, R.J. Behnke's *Native trout of western North America* (American Fisheries Society Monograph 6 – 1992) is unlikely to be bettered for many years to come. *The rainbow trout* by G.A.E. Gall and P.A. Crandell (Aquaculture 100 – 1992) superimposes an historical perspective on taxonomy, and *Natural hybridisation between steelhead trout and coastal cutthroat trout in two Puget Sound streams* by D.E. Campton and F.M. Utter (Canadian Journal of Fisheries and Aquatic Sciences 42 – 1985) shows that cross-breeding in the wild can confound the best genetic theories. Many papers focus on specific populations of rainbow trout, e.g. *Rainbow trout of the Athabasca River, Alberta: a unique population* by L.M. Carl, C. Hunt et al. (Transactions of the American Fisheries Society 123 – 1994), *Splendid skeena* by T.R. Pero (Trout – Autumn 1990), L. Shapovalov and A.C. Taft's *The life histories of the steelhead rainbow trout and silver salmon with special reference to Waddell Creek, California, and recommendations regarding their management* (California Department of Fish and Game Fisheries Bulletin 98 – 1954) and D.W. Chapman's *Studies on the life history of Alsea River steelhead* (Journal of Wildlife Management 22 – 1958).

The relict rainbows of the south-west are much in demand as the subjects of research. Some interesting articles and papers include *War on the west – the non-recovery of Gila trout* by T. Williams (Trout – Winter 1995), *Status, distribution, biology and conservation of two rare southwestern (USA) salmonids, the Apache trout and the Gila trout* by J.N. Rinne (Journal of Fish Biology 37 – 1990), *California golden trout* by R.J. Behnke (Trout – Autumn 1992), *Golden trout of the High Sierras* by L. Fisk (California Department of Fish and Game – 1983), *Rainbow trout in Mexico and California, with notes on the cutthroat series* (University of California Publications in Zoology 67 – 1959) and *A new trout from central Mexico: the Mexican golden trout* (Copeia – 1964) both by P.R. Needham and R. Gard. See also *Spawning, habitat and behaviour of Gila trout, a rare salmonid of the southwestern United States* by J.N. Rinne (Transactions of the American Fisheries Society 109 – 1980), *Conservation and status of Gila trout* by D.L. Propst, J.A. Stefferud et al. (Southwestern Naturalist 37 – 1992), the *Arizona Trout Recovery Plan* and *Gila Trout Recovery Plan* (both published by the US Department of the Interior, US Fish and Wildlife Service, Albuquerque, New Mexico – 1979), *The taxonomic structure of six golden trout populations from the Sierra Nevada, California* by J.R. Gold and C.A.E. Gall (in Proceedings of the California Academy of Sciences 40 – 1975), and *Apache trout: restoration with a twist* by J.N. Hansen and R.E. David (Wild Trout IV. Trout Unlimited, Vienna, Virginia – 1989).

Several papers by V.A. Maksimov cover the life of rainbow trout in Kamchatka; e.g. *Reproductive biology of the freshwater mykiss from the Kamchatka River basin* (Journal of Ichthyology 11 -1971) and *Some data on the ecology of the Kamchatka trout from the Utkholok River* (Journal of Ichthyology 12 – 1972), as do K.A. Savvaitova's *Age and growth of the Kamchatka anadromous trout* (Journal of Ichthyology 9 – 1969) and *The population structure of Salmo mykiss in Kamchatka* (Journal of Ichthyology 15 – 1975).

Interesting works on rainbow trout in North America beyond their natural range include *Ecological and genetic effects of salmonid introductions in North America* by C.C. Krueger and B. May (Canadian Journal of Fisheries and Aquatic Sciences 48 – 1991), *Growth and production of sympatric brook and rainbow trout in an Appalachian stream* by W.E. Whitworth and R.J. Strange (Transactions of the American Fisheries Society 112 – 1983) and *Rainbow trout in the Great Lakes* by H.R. MacCrimmon and B.L. Gotts (Ontario Ministry of Natural Resources Report – 1972). Early hatcheries are the subject of E. Leitritz's *A history of California's fish hatcheries* – 1860-1970 (California Department of Fish and Game Fish Bulletin 150 – 1970).

Papers on introductions of rainbow trout beyond American shores include *Interaction of the native and alien faunas of New Zealand and the problem of fish introductions* by R.M. McDowall (Transactions of the American Fisheries Society 97 – 1968), *Threatened native freshwater fishes in Australia – some case histories* by B.A. Ingram, C.G. Barlow et al., *When galaxiid and salmonid fishes meet: a family reunion in New Zealand* by R.M. McDowall (both in Journal of Fish Biology 37, Supplement A – 1990) and *The origins of rainbow trout in New Zealand* by D. Scott, J. Henitson et al. (California Department of Fish and Game 64 – 1978).

The directional response of newly hatched rainbow fry is the subject of two interesting papers by T.G. Northcote; *Migratory behaviour of juvenile rainbow trout in outlet and inlet streams of Loon Lake, British Columbia* (Journal of the Fisheries Research Board of Canada 19 – 1962) and *Juvenile current response, growth and maturity of above and below waterfall stocks of rainbow trout* (Journal of Fish Biology 18 – 1981); see also *Genetic and environmental aspects of the response to water current by rainbow trout originating from inlet and outlet streams of two lakes* by B.W. Kelso, T.G. Northcote et al. (Canadian Journal of Zoology 59 – 1981).

Steelhead at sea are the subject of *Horizontal and vertical movements of adult steelhead trout in the Dean and Fisher channels, British Columbia* by G.T.Ruggerone, T.P. Quinn et al. (Canadian Journal of Fisheries and Aquatic Sciences 47 – 1990) and *Distribution and origins of steelhead trout in offshore water of the North Pacific Ocean* by R.L. Burgner, J.T. Light et al. (International North Pacific Fisheries Commission Bulletin 51 – 1992); see also *Increased straying by adult steelhead trout following the 1980 eruption of Mount St Helens* by S.A. Leider (Environmental Biology of Fishes 24 – 1989) and M. Fraker's *California sea-lions and steelhead trout at the Chittenden Locks, Seattle* (Marine Mammal Commission, Washington DC – 1994).

9. Cutthroat Trout

The most comprehensive book on cutthroat is P.C. Trotter's *Cutthroat, native trout of the west* (Colorado Associated University Press, Boulder – 1987), while R.J. Behnke's *Native trout of western North America* (American Fisheries Society – 1992) is indispensable for anyone trying to untangle the cutthroat's convoluted taxonomy; see also *Conservation and distribution of genetic variation in a polytypic species, the cutthroat trout* by F.W. Allendorf and R.F. Leary (Conservation Biology 2 – 1988) and *Genetic divergence and identification of seven cutthroat trout subspecies and rainbow trout* by R.F. Leary, F.W. Allendorf et al. (Transactions of the American Fisheries Society 116 – 1987).

The history of the discovery of the cutthroat trout by P.C. Trotter and P.A. Bisson is one of many excellent papers published together as *The proceedings of the symposium on status and management of interior stocks of cutthroat trout* (American Fisheries Society Symposium 4 – 1988).

The life of sea-going cutthroat is described by J.M. Johnston in *Life histories of anadromous cutthroat trout with emphasis on migratory behaviour* (in Proceedings of the Salmon and Trout Migratory Behaviour Symposium, University of Washington Press, Seattle – 1982), by P.C. Trotter in *Coastal cutthroat trout: a life history compendium* (Transactions of the American Fisheries Society 118 – 1989), by R.H. Armstrong in *Age, food and migration of sea-run cutthroat trout at Eva Lake southeastern Alaska* (Transactions of the American Fisheries Society 100 – 1971) and in *Ecology and management of coastal cutthroat trout in Oregon* by R.D. Giger (Research Reports of the Fisheries Commission of Oregon 6 – 1972).

Interspecific competition is the subject of *Comparative behaviour and habitat utilization of brook trout and cutthroat trout in smaller streams in northern Idaho* (Journal of the Fisheries Research Board of Canada 29 – 1972) and *Review of competition between cutthroat trout and other salmonids* (in American Fisheries Society Symposium 4 – 1988), both by J.S. Griffiths, as well as of *Rainbow trout and cutthroat trout interactions in coastal British Columbia lakes* by N.A. Nilsson and J.G. Northcote (Canadian Journal of Fisheries and Aquatic Sciences 38 – 1981).

The impending disaster of the lake trout's arrival in Yellowstone is covered in *More than a fish story* by P. Schullery (Trout – Spring 1996) and *Lake trout discovered in Yellowstone Lake threaten native cutthroat trout* by L.R. Kaeding, G.D. Boltz et al. (Fisheries 21 – 1996); see also *Movements and homing of cutthroat trout from open-water areas of Yellowstone Lake* by L.A. Jahn (Journal of the Fisheries Research Board of Canada 26 – 1969), *Effects of a century of human influence on the cutthroat trout of Yellowstone Lake* by R.E. Gresswell and J.D. Varley and *Ecology, status and management of the Yellowstone cutthroat trout* by J.D. Varley and R.E. Gresswell (both in American Fisheries Society Symposium 4 – 1988).

Many papers focus on the various relict subspecies of cutthroat; some of these are by R.J. Behnke; e.g. *The Paiute trout* (Audobon Wildlife Report – 1987), *Rio Grande cutthroat* (Trout – Autumn 1988) and *Pyramid Lake and its cutthroat trout* (American Fly Fishers 13 – 1986). Gathered together (all in American Fisheries Society Symposium 4 – 1988) are *Greenback cutthroat trout recovery program: management overview* by R.J. Stuber, B.D. Rosenlund et al., *Rio Grande cutthroat management in New Mexico* by J.A. Stefferund, *Westslope cutthroat trout in Montana; life history, status and management* by G.A. Liknes and P.J. Graham, *Status, life history and management of the Lahontan cutthroat trout* by E.R. Gerstung and *Bonneville cutthroat trout: current status and management* by D.A. Duff.

Some other interesting papers on specific populations of cutthroat are *The movement and distribution of Paiute cutthroat trout in Cottonwood Creek, California* by J.S. Diana and E.D. Lane (Transactions of the American Fisheries Society 107 – 1978), *Rio Grande cutthroat trout in Texas* by G.P. Garrett and G.C. Matlock (Texas Journal of Science 43 – 1991), J.W. Kiefling's *Studies on the ecology of the Snake River cutthroat trout* (Wyoming Game and Fish Commission, Fisheries Technical Bulletin 3 – 1978), *Status of the Paiute cutthroat trout in California* by J.H. Ryan and S.J. Nicola (California Department of Fish and Game, Inland Fisheries Administration Report – 1976) and *Life history of the Lahontan cutthroat trout in Pyramid Lake, Nevada* by W.F. Sigler, W.T. Helm et al. (Great Basin Naturalist 43 – 1983).

10. Six Pacific Salmon

There is a huge amount of literature on Pacific salmon and many of the sources I consulted furnished information for more than one chapter. By far the most detailed works on the fish are *Pacific salmon life histories* edited by C. Groot and L. Margolis (UBC Press, Vancouver – 1991), and

Physiological ecology of Pacific salmon edited by C. Groot, L. Margolis and W.C. Clarke (UBC Press, Vancouver – 1995). The bibliographies to each book are extensive, and anyone seeking more information on particular species should consult them.

Field guide to the Pacific salmon by R. Steelquist (Sasquatch Books, Seattle – 1992) is a concise introduction to the genus *Oncorhynchus* and *Salmon of the North Pacific Ocean* is a series of comprehensive bulletins published by International North Pacific Fisheries Commission from 1965 to 1968.

The papers mentioned below are selected from the vast body of published research on each fish, either because they are of a relatively general nature, or because they focus on aspects of the fish's lives which are covered in some detail in my text.

Sockeye

Their conspicuousness, abundance and habit of usually spawning in lake inflows has made the sockeye the most researched of all Pacific salmon. The classic work remains *The sockeye salmon* by R.E. Foerster (Bulletin of the Fisheries Research Board of Canada – 1968), but there are hundreds of other papers on the fish; many excellent ones are collected in *Sockeye salmon population biology and future management*, edited by H.D. Smith, L. Margolis et al. (Canadian Special Publication of Fisheries and Aquatic Sciences 96 – 1987).

Some general papers include *Limnology and fish ecology of sockeye salmon nursery lakes of the world* by W.L. Hartman and R.L. Burgner (Journal of the Fisheries Research Board of Canada 29 – 1972), *Behaviour and ecology of sockeye salmon fry in the Babine River* by P. McCart (Journal of the Fisheries Board of Canada 24 – 1967), *Distribution, growth and survival of sockeye fry produced in natural and artificial stream environments* by J. McDonald (Journal of the Fisheries Board of Canada 26 – 1969), *Mechanisms controlling migration of sockeye salmon fry* by E.L. Brannon (International Pacific Salmon Fisheries Commission Bulletin 21 – 1972), *Growth rate of young sockeye salmon in relation to fish size and ration level* by J.R. Brett and J.E. Shelbourn (Journal of the Fisheries Research Board of Canada 32 – 1975), and *Migratory behaviour of sockeye salmon fry and smolts* by W.L. Hartman, W.R. Heard et al. (Journal of the Fisheries Research Board of Canada 24 – 1967).

The sockeye's cyclical appearance is discussed by P.J. Larkin in *Cyclic dominance in Adams River sockeye salmon* (International Pacific Salmon Fisheries Commission Progress Report 11 – 1964), by C.J. Walters and M.J. Staley in *Evidence against the existence of cyclic dominance in Fraser River sockeye salmon* (in Canadian Special Publication of Fisheries and Aquatic Sciences 96 – 1987) and by W.E. Ricker in *Cycles of abundance among Fraser River sockeye salmon* (Canadian Journal of Fisheries and Aquatic Sciences 54 – 1997).

Many papers concentrate on the co-occurrence of migratory and non-migratory sockeye; e.g. *Genetic differences among populations of Alaskan sockeye salmon* by R.L. Wilmot and C.V. Burger (Transactions of the American Fisheries Society 114 – 1985), *The role of male choice in the assortative mating of anadromous and non-anadromous sockeye salmon* by C.J. Foote and P.A. Larkin (Behaviour 106 – 1988), *The effects of body size and sexual dimorphism on the reproductive behaviour of sockeye salmon* by T.P. Quinn and C.J. Foote (Animal Behaviour 48 – 1994), *Molecular genetic evidence for parallel life-history evolution within a Pacific salmon (sockeye salmon and kokanee)* by E.B. Taylor, C.J. Foote et al. and *Evidence for sympatric genetic divergence of anadromous and nonanadromous morphs of sockeye salmon* by C.C. Wood and C.J. Foote (both in Evolution 50 – 1996); see also *Anadromous sockeye salmon derived from nonanadromous kokanees: life history in Lake Toro* by M. Kaeriyama, S. Vrawa et al. (Scientific Reports of the Hokkaido Salmon Hatchery 46 – 1992) and *Distribution and nomenclature of North American kokanee* by J.S. Nelson (Journal of the Fisheries Research Board of Canada 25 – 1968). For a discussion on the effectiveness of jacks on the redds there is *Spawning success of jack sneaks in sockeye salmon* by C.J. Foote, G.S. Brown et al. (Canadian Journal of Fisheries and Aquatic Sciences 53 – 1996).

Interesting papers on the sockeye's later life include *Factors affecting marine growth of Bristol Bay sockeye salmon* by D.E. Rogers and G.T. Ruggerone (Fisheries Research 18 – 1993), *Ocean food of sockeye salmon* by F. Favorite (Commercial Fisheries Review 32 – 1970), *Distribution and origin of sockeye salmon in offshore waters of the north Pacific Ocean* by R.R. French, H. Bilton et al. (International North Pacific Fisheries Commission Bulletin 34 – 1976), *Brown bear predation on sockeye salmon at Karluk Lake, Alaska* by R. Gard (Alaska Journal of Wildlife Management 35 – 1971), *Migratory behaviour of adult Fraser*

River sockeye by P. Gilhousen (International Pacific Salmon Fisheries Commission Progress Report 7 – 1960), and *Behaviour and distribution of spawning sockeye salmon on island beaches in Iliamna Lake, Alaska, 1965* by O.E. Kerns and J.R. Donaldson (Journal of the Fisheries Research Board of Canada 25 – 1968).

Pink salmon

Papers on pink salmon breeding and egg development include: *Spawning behaviour of pink salmon* by N.A. Chebanov (Journal of Ichthyology 20 – 1980), *Effect of varying temperature regimes on the development of pink salmon eggs and alevins* by C.B. Murray and T.D. Beacham (Canadian Journal of Zoology 64 – 1986), *Two generations of hybrids between even- and odd-year pink salmon: a test for outbreeding depression* by A.J. Gharrett and S.M. Shirley (Canadian Journal of Fisheries and Aquatic Sciences 48 – 1991), *Influence of photoperiod on the timing of reproductive maturation in pink salmon and its application to genetic transfers between odd- and even-year spawning populations* by T.D. Beacham, C.B. Murray et al. (Canadian Journal of Zoology 72 – 1994), *Even year – odd year pink salmon* by C. H. Ellis and R.E. Noble (Washington Department of Fisheries Annual Report 69 – 1959).

Their early life at sea is the subject of *Early sea life of pink salmon* by J.W. Martin (in Proceedings of the 1966 Northeast Pacific Pink Salmon Workshop, edited by W.L. Sheridan, Alaska Department of Fish and Game Information Leaflet 87 – 1966), *Ecology of early sea life, pink and chum juveniles* by R. R. Parker and R.J. Le Brasseur (in Proceedings of the 1974 Northeast Pacific Pink and Chum Salmon Workshop, edited by D.R. Harding, Department of Environment, Fisheries, Vancouver – 1974), *Ecology of juvenile pink salmon from Sakhalin and Iturup Islands during the marine period of life* by A.P. Shershnev, V.M. Chupakhin et al. (Journal of Ichthyology 22 – 1982) and *Spatial variations in feeding and condition of juvenile pink and chum salmon off Vancouver Island, British Colombia* by R.I. Perry, N.B. Hargreaves et al. (Fisheries Oceanography 5 – 1996).

Other interesting papers include *Comparative developmental biology of pink salmon in southern British Columbia* by T.D. Beacham and C.B. Murray (Journal of Fish Biology 28 – 1986), *Vulnerability of pink salmon populations to natural and fishing mortality* by W.J. McNeil (in Salmonid Ecosystems of the North Pacific, edited by W.J. McNeil and D.C. Himsworth, Oregon State University Press, Corvallis, Oregon – 1980), *Marine survival of pink salmon fry from early and late spawners* by S.G. Taylor (Transactions of the American Fisheries Society 109 – 1980) and *History and present status of the odd-year pink salmon runs of the Fraser River* region by W.E. Ricker (Canadian Technical Report of Fisheries and Aquatic Sciences – 1989).

The extraordinary success of pink salmon in the Great Lakes has been well documented; e.g. *Genetic changes in pink salmon following their introduction into the Great Lakes* by A.J. Gharrett and M.A. Thomason (Canadian Journal of Fisheries and Aquatic Sciences 44 – 1987), many papers by W. Kwain including *Spawning behaviour and early life history of pink salmon in the Great Lakes* (Canadian Journal of Fisheries and Aquatic Sciences 39 – 1982), *Biology of pink salmon in the North American Great Lakes* (American Fisheries Society Symposium 1 – 1987), *Pink Salmon in the Great Lakes* by W. Kwain and A.H. Lawrie (Fisheries 6 – 1981), and *Three-year-old pink salmon in Lake Superior tributaries* by W.C. Wagner and T.M. Stauffer (Transactions of the American Fisheries Society 109 – 1980). For other expansions of the fish's range, read *The introduction of pink salmon into the Kola Peninsula* by E.L. Bakshtansky (in Salmon ranching, edited by J.E. Thorpe, Academic Press, New York – 1980), *Pink salmon in northern Norway* by M. Berg (Institute of Freshwater Research, Drottningholm, Report 56 – 1977) and *Further captures of Pacific salmon in Scottish waters* by R.B. Williamson (Scottish Fisheries Bulletin 41 – 1974).

Chum salmon

General papers include; *Ocean growth and mortality of pink and chum salmon* by W.E. Ricker (Journal of the Fisheries Research Board of Canada 21 – 1964), *Marine growth of chum salmon* by J.J. Lalanne (International North Pacific Fisheries Commission Bulletin 27 – 1971), *Behavioral ecology of chum salmon fry in a small estuary* by J.C. Mason (Journal of the Fisheries Research Board of Canada 31 – 1974), *Spawning behaviour of chum salmon and rainbow trout* by A.F. Tautz and C. Groot (Journal of the Fisheries Research Board of Canada 32 – 1975), *Distribution and origin of chum salmon in offshore waters of the north Pacific Ocean* by F. Neave, T. Yonemori et al. (International North Pacific Fisheries Commission Bulletin 35 – 1976), *Yukon River fall chum salmon biology and stock status* by L.S. Buklis and L.H. Barton (Alaska Department of Fish and Game Information Leaflet 239 – 1984), *Recent changes in age and size of chum salmon in the north Pacific Ocean and possible causes* by Y. Ishida, S. Ito et al. (Canadian Journal of Fisheries and Aquatic Sciences 50 – 1993) and *Biological mechanisms enabling sympatry between salmonids with special reference to sockeye and chum salmon in oceanic waters* by T. Azuma (Fisheries Research 24 – 1995).

Since they are being ranched so extensively in Japan a lot of literature on chum salmon is the product of Japanese researches; e.g. *The importance of estuarine residence for adaptation of chum salmon fry to seawater* by M. Iwata and S. Komatsu (Canadian Journal of Fisheries and Aquatic Sciences 41 – 1984), M. Kaeriyama's *Aspects of salmon ranching in Japan* (Physiology and Ecology Japan, Special Vol. 1 – 1989), *An economic review of artificial salmon propagation and management operations in Japan* by M.M. Abd-elmoneim and H. Masuda (Bulletin of Faculty of Fisheries, Hokkaido University – 1991) and *Deepwater migrations of chum salmon along the Pacific coast of northern Japan* by Y. Veno (Canadian Journal of Fisheries and Aquatic Sciences 49 – 1992).

Coho

Amongst papers on coho of particular interest are: *A review of the chinook and coho salmon of the Fraser River* by F.J. Fraser and P.J. Starr (Canadian Technical Report of Fisheries and Aquatic Sciences – 1962), *Distribution and abundance of coho salmon in offshore waters of the north Pacific Ocean* by H. Godfrey, K.A. Henry et al. (International North Pacific Fisheries Commission Bulletin 31 – 1975), *Marine mortality of Puget Sound coho salmon* by S.B. Mathews and R. Buckley (Journal of the Fisheries Research Board of Canada 33 – 1976), *Food abundance and territory size in juvenile coho salmon* by L.M. Dill, R.C. Ydenberg et al. (Canadian Journal of Zoology 59 – 1981), *Coho salmon survival from egg deposition to fry emergence* by J.V. Tagart (in Proceedings of the Olympic Wild Fish Conference, Peninsula College, Port Angeles, Washington – 1984), and *Variation in body morphology among British Columbia populations of coho salmon* by E.B. Taylor and J.B. McPhail (Canadian Journal of Fisheries and Aquatic Sciences 42 – 1985). An interesting, if somewhat dated, British publication by D.J. Solomon is *Coho Salmon in north-west Europe* (Ministry of Agriculture, Fisheries and Food, Lowestoft, Laboratory Leaflet 49 – 1979).

Chinook

Effects of river flow on the distribution of chinook salmon redds by D.W. Chapman, D.E. Weitcamp et al. (Transactions of the American Fisheries Society 115 – 1986) and *Chinook salmon spawner characteristics in relation to redd physical features* by J.D. Neilson and C.E. Banford (Canadian Journal of Zoology 61 – 1983), both focus on spawning while *Chinook salmon populations in Oregon coastal river basins: descriptions of life histories and assessments of recent trends in run strength* by J.W. Nicholas and D.G. Hankin (Oregon Department of Fish and Wildlife Information Report 1 – 1988) is a wider ranging report.

Papers on the genetic profiles of different types include *Differences in enzyme frequency and body morphology among three juvenile life history types of chinook salmon in the Nanaimo River, British Columbia* by L.M. Carl and M.C. Healey (Canadian Journal of Fisheries and Aquatic Sciences 41 – 1984), *Genetic relationships among populations of Alaskan chinook salmon* by A.J. Gharrett, S.M. Shirley et al. (Canadian Journal of Fisheries and Aquatic Sciences 44 – 1987), *Genetic population structure of chinook salmon in the Pacific Northwest* by F.M. Utter, G. Milner et al. (Fishery Bulletin (US) 87 – 1989) and *Genetic control of juvenile life history pattern in chinook salmon* by W.C. Clarke, R.E. Withler et al. (Canadian Journal of Fisheries and Aquatic Sciences 49 – 1992).

Information on chinook at sea is found in *Distribution and origin of chinook salmon in offshore waters of the north Pacific Ocean* by R.L. Major, J. Ito et al. (International North Pacific Fisheries Commission Bulletin 38 – 1978), *Life history of fall-run juvenile chinook salmon in the Sacramento – San Joaquin estuary, California* by M.A. Kjelson, P.F. Raquel et al. (in Estuarine Comparisons, edited by V.S. Kennedy, Academic Press, New York, – 1982) and *Coastwide distribution and ocean migration patterns of stream- and ocean-type chinook salmon* by M.C. Healey (Canadian Field-Naturalist 97 – 1983).

More about the unique population of migratory chinook in New Zealand can be found in G.D. Waugh's *Salmon in New Zealand* (in Salmon Ranching, edited by J.E. Thorpe, Academic Press, New

York – 1980), *Distribution of quinnat salmon off the east coast of South Island* 1925-78 by M. Flain (New Zealand Journal of Marine and Freshwater Research 15 – 1981), *Transplanting Pacific salmon* by F.C. Withler (Canadian Technical Report of Fisheries and Aquacultural Sciences – 1982), *Variation in life history patterns among New Zealand chinook salmon populations* by T.P. Quinn and M.J. Unwin (Canadian Journal of Fisheries and Aquatic Sciences 50 – 1993), and *Diet of chinook salmon in Canterbury coastal waters* by G.D. James and M.J. Unwin (New Zealand Journal of Marine and Freshwater Research 30 – 1996).

The phenomenon of white-fleshed chinook salmon is the subject of R.E. Withler's *Genetic variation in carotenid pigment deposition in the red-fleshed and white-fleshed chinook salmon of Quesnel River, British Columbia* (Canadian Journal of Genetics and Cytology 28 – 1986).

Masu

Most of the papers on masu salmon are in Japanese, but a few have either been translated into, or appeared originally in English. *Masu salmon propagation in Hokkaido, Japan* by H. Mayama (Bulletin of the Institute of Zoology, Academia Sinica 29 – 1990), *Salmonid programs and public policy in Japan* by Y. Nasaka (in Salmon production, management and allocation, edited by W.J. McNeil, Oregon State University Press, Corvallis, Oregon – 1988) and *Masu salmon management in Hokkaido; a review of smolt and fingerling release experiments* by H. Mayama (Physiology and Ecology Japan, Special Vol. 1 – 1989) all concentrate on masu rearing.

More general information is to be found in two papers by T. Kubo, *Anadromous masu salmon in Japan: biology and propagation* (Physiology and Ecology Japan, Special Vol. 1 – 1989) and *Studies on the life history of the 'masu' salmon in Hokkaido* (Hokkaido Salmon Hatchery Reprint 34 – 1980); see also *Spawning populations and marine life of masu salmon* by S. Machidori and F. Kato (International North Pacific Fisheries Commission Bulletin 43 – 1984). The Hokkaido salmon hatchery also publishes annual summaries of its activities in English and gives information freely from its Head Office at 2-2 Nakanoskima, Toyohira-ku, Sapporo 062, Japan.

The struggling Taiwanese masu are the subject of *Conservation of the Formosan landlocked salmon in Taiwan, a historical review* by Y-S Lin and K-H Chang (Physiology and Ecology Japan, Special Vol. 1 – 1989).

11. Pacific Salmon Ecology

Various papers describe the ecology of young salmon in fresh water; e.g. *Mechanisms stabilising salmonid fry emergence timing* by E.L. Brannon (Canadian Special Publication of Fisheries and Aquacultural Sciences 96 – 1987), *The behaviour of Pacific salmon fry during their downstream migration to freshwater and saltwater nursery areas* by J. McDonald (Journal of the Fisheries Research Board of Canada 17 – 1960), *Feeding of predaceous fishes on out-migrating juvenile salmonids in John Day Reservoir, Columbia River* by T.P. Poe, H.C. Hansel et al. (Transactions of the American Fisheries Society 120 – 1991), *Bird predation on juvenile salmonids in the Big Qualicum estuary, Vancouver Island* by P.M. Mace (Canadian Technical Report of Fisheries and Aquatic Sciences – 1983), *Feeding behaviour of the glaucous-winged gull on an Alaskan salmon stream* by P. Moyle (Wilson Bulletin 78 – 1966), *Comparative review of Pacific salmon survival rates* by M.J. Bradford (Canadian Journal of Fisheries and Aquatic Sciences 52 – 1995), *Juvenile Pacific salmon in estuaries; the life support system* by M.C. Healey (in Estuarine comparisons, edited by V.S. Kennedy, Academic Press, New York – 1982), *The ecology of juvenile salmon in Georgia Strait, British Columbia* by M.C. Healey (in Salmonid ecosystems of the north Pacific, edited by W.J. McNeil and D.C. Himsworth, Oregon State University Press, Corvallis, Oregon – 1980), *Food consumption of juvenile coho and chinook salmon on the continental shelf off Washington and Oregon* by R.D. Brodeur, R.C. Francis et al. (Canadian Journal of Fisheries and Aquatic Sciences 49 – 1992) and *Optimum swimming speeds in fish: the problems of currents* by C.L. Trump and W.C. Leggett (Canadian Journal of Fisheries and Aquatic Sciences 37 – 1980).

The salmon's time at sea is covered in detail by W.G. Pearcy in *Ocean ecology of North Pacific salmonids* (Washington Sea Grant Program, University of Washington Press, Seattle – 1992), which includes a very comprehensive bibliography. Two thirds or more of a salmon's life may be spent in the Pacific Ocean and the scarcity of research papers reflects the difficulties of following them at sea. However see *Type, quantity, and size of food of Pacific salmon in the Strait of Juan de Fuca, British Columbia* by T.D. Beacham (Fisheries Bulletin 84 – 1986), *Upper thermal limits on the ocean distribution of Pacific salmon in the spring* by D.W. Welch, A.I. Chigirinsky et al. (Canadian Journal of Fisheries and Aquatic Sciences 52 – 1995), *Change in chum salmon stomach contents associated with fluctuations of pink salmon abundance in the central subarctic Pacific and Bering Sea* by K. Tadokoro, Y. Ushida et al. (Fisheries Oceanography 5 – 1996), *Some features of ocean migrations and timing of Pacific salmon* by R.L. Burgner, *Juvenile salmonids in the oceanic ecosystem; the first critical summer* by A.C. Hartt and *Marine mammal – salmonid interactions; a review* by C.H. Fiscus (all in Salmonid ecosystems of the north Pacific, Oregon State University Press, Corvallis, Oregon – 1980), *Early oceanic migrations and growth of juvenile Pacific salmon and steelhead trout* by A.C. Hartt and M.B. Dell (International North Pacific Fisheries Commission Bulletin 46 – 1986), *Estimations of sea mortality rates for Pacific salmon* by R.R. Parker (Journal of the Fisheries Board of Canada 19 – 1962) and *Annual prey consumption by harbor seals in the Strait of Georgia, British Columbia* by P.F. Olesiuk (Fisheries Bulletin 91 – 1993).

Major range extensions of anadromous salmonids and first record of chinook salmon in the Mackenzie River drainage by C.L. McLeod and J.P. O'Neil (Canadian Journal of Zoology 61 – 1983) and *Pacific salmon in the North American Arctic* by P. Craig and L. Haldorson (Arctic 39 – March 1996) both discuss expansions of the salmon's northern range.

Papers on the salmon's last days include *Observations of fishes associated with spawning salmon* by R.J. Reed (Transactions of the American Fisheries Society 96 – 1967), *Bald eagles of the Chilkat Valley, Alaska – ecology, behavior and management* by A.J. Hansen, E.L. Boeker et al. (National Audubon Society and U.S. Fish and Wildlife Service – 1984) and *Fire, ice and eagles* by A. Ladigin (Natural History 103 – 1994). Even after death salmon continue to be researched; e.g. *Fate of coho salmon carcasses in spawning streams* by C.J. Cederholm, D.B. Houston et al. (Canadian Journal of Fisheries and Aquatic Sciences 46 – 1989).

12. Pacific Salmon Yesterday, Today and Tomorrow

Several books focus on the interrelationship between man and salmon, from either historic or contemporary perspectives. Some of them rely on excellent photographs for their impact; e.g. *Salmon of the Pacific* by A. Lewis (Sasquatch Books, Seattle – 1994) and *Reaching home – Pacific salmon, Pacific people* by N. Fobes (Alaska Northwest Books, Seattle – 1994). Others rely more on their written content such as *Mountains in the clouds* by B. Brown (University of Washington Press, Seattle – 1982), *Dead reckoning – confronting the crisis in Pacific fisheries* by T. Glavin (Greystone Books, Vancouver – 1996), *The Northwest salmon crisis* edited by J. Cone and S. Ridlington (Oregon State University Press, Corvallis, Oregon – 1996), and *A common fate – endangered salmon and the people of the Pacific Northwest* by J. Cone (Henry Holt & Co., New York – 1995). *Indian fishing* by H. Stewart (Douglas & McIntyre, Vancouver – 1977) and *Pacific salmon and steelhead trout* by R.J. Childerhose and M. Trim (Douglas & McIntyre, Vancouver – 1979) are two other interesting works. *Upstream-salmon and society in the Pacific Northwest* collated by the Committee on the Protection and Management of Pacific Northwest Anadromous Salmonids formed by the National Research Council (National Academy Press, Washington, DC – 1996) is a fascinating collection of writing on every aspect of human disturbance of the salmon's existence.

The Pacific Salmon Commission (600 -1155 Robson St, Vancouver, BC, Canada) produces a number of excellent reports every year which show how tortuously complex is the management of this resource, as does *Marine factors in the production of salmon: their significance to the Pacific salmon treaty* by J. Shelton and J.P. Koenings (Alaska Fishery Research Bulletin 2 – 1995) and US/Canada *Salmon wars – why the Pacific salmon treaty has not brought peace* by D.D. Huppert (School of Marine Affairs, University of Washington, Seattle, Report 1 – 1996).

The Columbia River's problems are particularly well documented in the papers in *Columbia River salmon and steelhead*, edited by E. Schweibert (American Fisheries Society Special Publication 10 – 1977) and *The Columbia River salmon and steelhead trout: their fight for survival* by A. Netboy (University of Washington Press, Seattle – 1980); see also R. Bruun's *The Boldt decision: legal victory, political defeat* (Law and Policy Quarterly 4 – 1982), F.G. Cohen's *Treaties on trial: the continuing controversy over Northwest Indian fishing rights* (University of Washington Press, Seattle – 1986) and *The role of Stevens*

Treaty tribes in the management of anadromous fish runs in the Columbia Basin by J.H. Marsh and J.H. Johnson (Fisheries 10 – 1985). *California's salmon and steelhead* edited by A. Lufkin (University of California Press Berkley, California – 1991) is a good work on the subject, and early fishing in the Fraser River is described in detail in *Salmonopolis: the stevenson story* by Stacey and Stacey (Harbour Publishing Co. Ltd, Vancouver – 1984).

The Bristol Bay fishery is an intriguing example of imaginative management; see *Pacific salmon management, the view from Alaska* by C.P. Meacham and J.H. Clark (Alaska Fishery Research Bulletin 1 – 1994), *The sockeye salmon of Bristol Bay, Alaska* by J.C. Conklin (University of Washington Daily, Seattle – 16 October – 1996), the reports by the Alaska Department of Fish and Game, Commercial Fisheries Management and Development Division, P.O.Box 25526, Juneau, Alaska 99802 – 5526 (e.g. its run forecasts and harvest projections) and *Managing Alaska's salmon fisheries for a prosperous future* by W.F. Royce (Fisheries 14 – 1989). The 'guru' of the Bristol Bay sockeye harvest is D.E. Rogers, who is the author of many papers on the subject and with P.M. Poe of *Escapement goals for the Kvichak River system* (University of Washington Fisheries Research Institute, Seattle – 1984); see also two papers by R.R. Straty: *Ecology and behaviour of juvenile sockeye salmon in Bristol Bay and the eastern Bering Sea* (University of Alaska Institute of Marine Sciences Occasional Publications 2 – 1974) and *Migratory routes of adult sockeye salmon in the eastern Bering Sea and Bristol Bay* (NOAA Technical Report – 1975).

The pros and cons of hatchery output are covered by R. Hilborn in *Hatcheries and the future of salmon in the Northwest* (Fisheries 17 – 1992), by R.S. Stickney in *Use of hatchery fish in enhancement programs* (Fisheries 19 – 1994), by R.S. Waples in *Genetic interactions between hatchery and wild salmonids: lessons from the Pacific Northwest* (Canadian Journal of Fisheries and Aquatic Sciences 48 – 1991) and in R.C. Simon's *Management techniques to minimise the loss of genetic variability in hatchery fish populations* (in American Fisheries Society Symposium 10 – 1991).

Spawning channels are discussed by R. Hilborn in *Institutional learning and spawning channels for sockeye salmon* (Canadian Journal of Fisheries and Aquatic Sciences 49 – 1992), in C.J. West and J.C. Mason's *Evaluation of sockeye salmon production from the Babine Lake Development Project* (Canadian Special Publication of Fisheries and Aquatic Sciences 96 – 1987) and in *Comparison of sockeye salmon fry produced by hatcheries, artificial channels and natural spawning areas* by R.W. Mead and W.L. Woodall (International Pacific Salmon Fisheries Commission Progress Report 20 – 1968). The various publications of the Salmonid Enhancement Program of the Fisheries and Oceans Canada (440-555 W. Hastings St, Vancouver, BC V6B 5G3) show the current state of Canadian fish-hatching and river improvement programmes.

Dams and their problems are the focus of *Dammed from here to eternity: dams and biological integrity* by T. Gup (Trout – Winter 1994) and many publications of Northwest Power Planning Council (Public Affairs Division), 851 SW Sixth Avenue, Suite 1100, Portland, Oregon 97204, USA and of the US Army Corps of Engineers North Pacific Division, P.O.Box 2870, Portland, Oregon 97208, particularly *Controversy, conflict and compromise – a history of the Lower Snake River development* by K.C. Petersen and M.E. Reed and the *Salmon passage notes of the Snake and Columbia River fish programs*.

More on otolith marking is found in several papers in American Fisheries Society Symposium 7 – 1990, particularly *Otolith marking* by E.B. Brothers; for its practical consequence see also *Thermal mark technology for inseason fisheries management: a case study* by P. Hagen, K. Munk et al. (Alaska Fishery Research Bulletin 2 – 1995).

The changing status of the salmon in the Pacific North-west is a much discussed topic; see, for example, *Pacific salmon at the crossroads: stocks at risk from California, Oregon, Idaho and Washington* by W. Nehlsen, J.E. Williams et al. (Fisheries 16 – 1991); see also *Connecting cultural and biological diversity in restoring Northwest salmon* by C.L. Smith (Fisheries 19 – 1994), *Evolutionarily significant units and the conservation of biological diversity under the Endangered Species Act* (American Fisheries Society Symposium 17 – 1995) and *Through a glass darkly: Columbia River salmon, the Endangered Species Act and adaptive management* by J.M. Volkman and W.E. McConnaha (Environmental Law 23)

Index